ORWELL'S MOUSTACHE

Addressing More Orwellian Matters

By Richard Lance Keeble

Published 2021 by Abramis academic publishing

www.abramis.co.uk

ISBN 978 1 84549 786 6

© Richard Lance Keeble 2021

All rights reserved

This book is copyright. Subject to statutory exception and to provisions of relevant collective licensing agreements, no part of this publication may be reproduced, stored in a retrieval system, or transmitted in any form or by any means, without the prior written permission of the author.

This book is sold subject to the conditions that it shall not, by way of trade or otherwise, be lent, re-sold, hired out, or otherwise circulated without the publisher's prior consent in any form of binding or cover other than that which it is published and without a similar condition including this condition being imposed on the subsequent purchaser.

Abramis is an imprint of arima publishing.

arima publishing
ASK House, Northgate Avenue
Bury St Edmunds, Suffolk IP32 6BB
t: (+44) 01284 700321

www.arimapublishing.com

About the author

Richard Lance Keeble is Professor of Journalism at the University of Lincoln and Honorary Professor at Liverpool Hope University. He has written and edited 43 books on a wide range of media-related topics. Chair of The Orwell Society (2013-2020), he edited *Orwell Today* (2012) and *George Orwell Now!* (2015). In 2020, Routledge published his *Journalism Beyond Orwell* and Abramis *George Orwell, The Secret State and the Making of* Nineteen Eighty-Four. He is emeritus editor of *Ethical Space: The International Journal of Communication Ethics* and joint editor of *George Orwell Studies*. In 2011, he gained a National Teaching Fellowship, the highest award for teachers in Higher Education in the UK, and in 2014 he was given a Lifetime Achievement Award by the Association for Journalism Education. He is a member of Louth Male Voice Choir, Louth Film Club and (through thick and thin) Nottinghamshire County Cricket Club.

Orwell's Moustache confirms Richard Keeble's reputation as one of Orwell's most acute and knowledgeable readers, reinventing for the twenty-first century a man we think we know: the always compelling, always contradictory figure of George Orwell whose passions, obsessions, strengths and secrets here assume new meanings through analysis of everything from Orwell's dress to his father, his wife, his jokes, his diet, his fishing, and of course, his writing and politics.

Kristin Bluemel, Monmouth University, NJ

A brilliant and consistently original assortment of responses to the always surprising complexity of Orwell's obsessions, familiar and unfamiliar – from his love of fishing, to his enduring concern with the politics of food, to the delights of recording small things in small ways in small diary entries, and much more besides. This is imaginative and in the best sense sympathetic criticism written by one of today's leading Orwell scholars.

Nathan Waddell, University of Birmingham

Contents

INTRODUCTION
Joie de Vivre and the Blairs: Father, Son and Grandson — 1

SECTION 1. GEORGE ORWELL: THE WRITINGS

Chapter 1. That Moustache and That Tie: On the Politics of Dress (and Undress) — 11

Chapter 2. The Heart of the Matter: The Fatherhood Factor — 29

Chapter 3. Advertisements and the Political Economy of the Media — 43

Chapter 4. In the Waugh-zone — 59

Chapter 5. Love of Lawrence — 69

Chapter 6. 'Peace That Is Not Peace': Dealing With the Atom Bomb — 89

Chapter 7. Throwing Light on the Crucial Quarrel with Comfort — 93

Chapter 8. Down But Not Out: 'The Spike' – And Orwell As (An Always Ambivalent) Radical Campaigner for Social Justice — 103

Chapter 9. The Pleasures and Politics of Food — 117

Chapter 10. 'Seeing What is In Front of One's Nose': The Importance and Delights of the Domestic Diaries — 139

Chapter 11. The Play's the Thing — 149

Chapter 12. Philip Bounds: On Marxism and Much More — 167

Chapter 13. On the 'Unreality' of Royal Coverage — 175

SECTION 2. EILEEN BLAIR: INSPIRATION, WIFE, MOTHER

Chapter 14. The Wedding – Through Her Eyes — 181

Chapter 15. How Eileen Saved His Life During 1938 Flu Epidemic — 187

Chapter 16. Eileen – And Orwell's Shifting Attitudes on Gender Issues — 191

SECTION 3. GEORGE ORWELL: THE MAN

Chapter 17. Warburg and the Making of Orwell — 197

Chapter 18. Angling for the Truth: The Enduring Passion for Fishing — 203

Chapter 19. The 'Invisible Masonic Network of Support': The Eton Factor — 207

Chapter 20. From the Beginning to the End: The Amazing Compton Mackenzie   227

Chapter 21. *Homage* and the Forgotten Memoir of the Spanish Civil War   233

APPENDIX

My Seven Lucky Years Immersed in Orwell   239

AFTERWORD

Anti-Semitism: Moving Beyond Upbringing and Preconceptions   243
Tim Crook

Introduction

Joie de Vivre and the Blairs: Father, Son and Grandson

Let's take a look at two photographs of Richard Walmesley Blair, Orwell's father, which Gordon Bowker includes in his biography (2003). The first dates probably from 1918 when Richard was on leave from the army. In 1912, he has retired from his post as Sub-Deputy Opium Agent, 1st grade after a lifetime working for the Opium Department in India on a pension of just £400 a year. But then, in 1917, aged 60, he surprises everyone by taking up a commission as a second lieutenant in the army, being posted to the 51st Indian Labour Company in Marseilles where he supervises the care and feeding of the mules. He is thought to have been the oldest man in his rank. As biographer Michael Shelden comments (1991: 73): 'What prompted him to take this action is not known. It may have been a delayed outburst of patriotic feeling.'

Eric Blair (later to be known as George Orwell) was at this time at Eton. According to Bernard Crick, none of his contemporaries there ever remember him mentioning his father was in the army. 'By now habitually reticent about his family, he may have found his father's posting ludicrous and his age embarrassing' (1980: 107). Is he obliquely referencing his father when, later in his novel *Coming Up For Air* (1919), the anti-hero George Bowling becomes a second lieutenant in a remote, forgotten military dump on the coast of Cornwall – guarding eleven tins of bully beef?

In the photograph, Richard sits stiffly on the right – with Eric, his mother Ida and sister Avril on her knee making up an intimate group somewhat separate from their father. He wears a military cap, jacket, tie and high leather boots. He looks very serious. As L. J. Hurst comments (2019), Richard Blair, in his war role, would have witnessed the terrible slaughter of both men and mules. And it may well be still preying on his mind when the photograph is taken.

But when was the photograph taken? Bernard Crick (1980) dates it 1916 but that seems too early; Bowker settles for 1918 which is possible. But there is another mystery in the picture. Why is Orwell's sister, Marjorie, who is five years older, not present? Could she be away at school? According to L. J. Hurst: 'Marjorie could have been at school and could not be brought back quickly to join the family while Mr Blair was on leave. A completely different view would be the one that Orwell makes in "Decline of the English murder": behind the quiet front of every middle-class family there was a secret. Marjorie's absence could be evidence of such a division in the Blair family, even if it was not murderous' (Hurst 2021; see also Cohen 2013). Sutherland is clearly wrong when he dates it 1914. But his comments are interesting: 'Eric [with his head bowed and resting on a limp wrist] has a pronounced unmilitary air. Ida leans away from her husband, using Avril as a barrier. Richard has the bearing of a major-general, at least' (Sutherland 2016: 71).

The other photograph shows a transformed man. Here Richard Walmesley is strolling down the promenade at Southwold, the Suffolk resort to which they have retired in 1922. Gone all the stress of war and work – how he is enjoying his retirement! As I observe in Chapter 2, he holds a walking stick elegantly before him. He is smiling and looking extremely relaxed and dapper. He's wearing a light suit, white polo-necked jumper, white shoes, a flowery buttonhole on his left lapel together with a colourfully displayed handkerchief in his top left blazer pocket and a lovely, large, white sun hat (with a fetching dark band) which bends enticingly over his forehead.

Interestingly, when Eileen O'Shaughnessy writes from Marrakech to her friend Norah Myles in December 1938, about the short time they spend with the Blairs before setting off for North Africa for a short break, she says: 'The whole family by the way is generally in a state of absolute penury. Of course, the nicest Blair is Mr Blair who's dying but the poor old man is 82 & he doesn't have any pain which is something' (Davison 2006: 78).

Now let's look at two pictures of George Orwell. The first shows him with his comrades in the POUM militia in Catalonia, on 13 March 1937. Known as 'The Machine Gun Photo', it was supplied to biographer Peter Stansky by Harry Milton, the sole American fighting in the battalion. Orwell, 6 ft 3 ins, stands out at the back – much taller than all the others. His newly-wed wife, Eileen, who has joined him on the frontline, crouches before him, Harry Milton on one side. No photographer is credited. But in an interview in 1982, on NPR, Milton reveals that the shot was 'photographed by a South African photo journalist who sent me some of the best shots … ' (Stansky Papers, cited in Tripathi 2021). In front of the group, a man crouches, his head bent low – almost reverentially – with his left hand holding a primitive-looking machine gun. At the back, sandbags are piled up against a wall. Despite the presence of Eileen, it's a macho image of men at war.

The other photograph shows Orwell transformed. It is one of series taken in London with his son, Richard – born on 14 May 1944 and adopted shortly afterwards – by the anarchist Vernon Richards early in 1946. Orwell, with cigarette inevitably dangling from his mouth, sits with Richard tight up against him on his lap – tying a shoelace. It's on the cover of *George Orwell at Home (and among the anarchists)* (London: Freedom Press, 1998) which carries other pictures of Orwell – always sporting a tie and jacket – pensive, chiselling wood in his office with Richard, in a corner of the image, looking admiringly up at him, unself-consciously pushing his son in a pram down a busy London road, at his typewriter and so on. Eileen died tragically on 29 March 1945, in the operating theatre of a Newcastle hospital while Orwell was away on the Continent reporting on the final days of World War Two for the *Observer*. The pictures capture the enormous affection between father and son. Indeed, Orwell surprised all his contemporaries by his instinctive caring gentleness with his baby son. Richard Blair, now retired and Patron of The Orwell Society, sums up: 'My father was completely devoted to me. When Eileen died, he really cared for me, which was very rare at that time. He fed me, changed my clothes and nappies, he gave me baths: most fathers at that time never did that sort of thing' (2019; see also Chapter 2).[1]

Orwell's relationship with his family – as on most things – was complex and ambivalent as I partly explore in Chapter 2. On his father's side, there was a long tradition of service to the Empire which he clearly followed when taking up the post of Imperial Policeman in Burma in 1922. Over time, he came to view with utter contempt the Empire as a 'racket' that was ruthlessly exploiting the native populations. Moreover, as Darcy Moore has revealed, Orwell's Scottish ancestors were deeply involved in the slave trade and knowledge of that must have deeply disturbed him (Moore 2020). But as Moore comments: 'It is interesting to ponder why Orwell, the scourge of imperialism, never wrote about his family's plantations in Jamaica but then again, nor did he explore his own father's controversial work as an opium agent' (ibid: 16). On the side of his mother, Ida Limouzin, there were strong roots in both France and Burma; she was a committed feminist, outgoing with a sustained interest in the arts – and her politically radical sister, Nellie, was to play a crucial, supportive role throughout Orwell's career as a writer.

Yet, given all these complexities within the family constellation, Orwell – the voracious reader, the one-time Spanish Civil War militiaman, the constantly engaged writer – still knows instinctively that the greatest source of satisfaction for a man could come from his loving, heart-felt relationship with his child.[2] Indeed, is not that *joie de vivre* Richard Walmesley Blair displays towards the end of his life strolling in Southwold captured, though in a very different way, by his son years later engaged in the simple act of pushing Richard in a pram down a busy London street?

THAT MOUSTACHE

The title of this book, drawn from my opening chapter that explores Orwell's fascinating attitude to dress (and undress), playfully follows in the wake of those celebrated texts, *Orwell's Nose*, by John Sutherland (2016), and *Orwell's Cough*, by John Ross (2013 [2012]). In my review of the first of these texts, I comment: 'Who knows: next there'll be *Orwell's Ear* followed by *Orwell's Throat* (Sutherland concedes that *Orwell's Bum* "may be an obliquity too far")' (Keeble 2020: 140). And, in the end, I've joined in the fun!

It's intriguing to ponder why Orwell stuck with that trademark, pencil-thin moustache which he acquires while serving as an Imperial Policeman in Burma from 1922-1927 – and keeps for the rest of his life. I suggest it is perhaps a way of reminding himself constantly of the impact his service in Burma has had on the formation of his character and ideas. Or conversely it may reflect his acknowledgement of the importance of imperial service in the Blair family's history. Significantly, in an early, brilliant study of Orwell, *The Crystal Spirit*, his anarchist friend George Woodcock quotes Malcolm Muggeridge saying there was 'a Kiplinesque side to his character which made him romanticize the Raj and its mystique' and that 'Orwell began to regard as a heroic generation the old sahib class which had endured incredible risks and hardships in the days when sanitation was rudimentary and prophylactic injections were unknown' (Woodcock 1984 [1966]: 215).

PUTTING – FINALLY – THE SPOTLIGHT ON EILEEN BLAIR

The major event in the world of Orwell Studies in recent months has been the long-awaited publication of Sylvia Topp's outstanding biography of Eileen Blair (2020). So – between explorations of Orwell's writings and life – a central section here is devoted to reflections sparked by that book. Indeed, the importance of Eileen in the very survival of Orwell cannot be under-estimated. After she bravely joins Orwell on the frontline of the Spanish Civil War in 1937, working as secretary to John McNair at the Independent Labour Party office in Barcelona, her quick-thinking saves both of them from being captured by the communists who are busy eliminating anyone they consider anarchists and Trotskyists. Just as Orwell, on 20 June, returns to the Hotel Continental, she bustles him away and they go into hiding. Over the next few days she secures the necessary papers and passports, they visit Orwell's commander, Georges Kopp, in prison – and finally escape by train to France. Then, in March 1938, the Blairs are living in a ramshackle cottage in Wallington, deep in rural Hertfordshire. Orwell catches a cold, then starts haemorrhaging from his mouth and nearly dies. As Topp highlights (see Chapter 14), it is only due to Eileen's resourcefulness – contacting first Jack Common and then her brother, Laurence O'Shaughnessy, who immediately decides to send him by ambulance to Preston Hall Sanatorium in Aylesford, Kent, where he is a consulting and thoracic surgeon – that Orwell pulls through.

Topp also argues that Eileen crucially influences his writing: 'Certainly he would not have been as prolific. Having Eileen typing drafts of essays and books, as well as using her editing skills from Oxford, was indispensable to Orwell's output. And Eileen's knowledge of psychology definitely helped him develop characters more deeply and convincing. Also, Eileen constantly stressed how important it was for Orwell to resist taking on so many reviews. She knew his health was deteriorating and she insisted he concentrate on writing novels in the years he had left' (2020: xix).

Not surprisingly then, Topp titles her biography *The Making of George Orwell*. Yet Eileen is not alone in *making* Orwell. Friendships throughout his life were crucial: as a child his conversations and shared delight in reading with Jacintha Buddicom can be seen as forming the basis for all his later literary adventures; as I highlight in Chapter 18, the network of old-Etonians – such as Sir Richard Rees, Andrew Gow, L. H. Myers, Christopher Hollis, Cyril Connolly, Roger Senhouse, Anthony Powell and David Astor – plays another vital role; there are the leftist writers, intellectuals and activists grouped around *Adelphi*; while Mabel Fierz encourages him as an unpublished writer and promotes his *Down and Out in Paris and London* with the agent, Leonard Moore, a member of her local tennis club. She is one of a number of women friends and (often secret) lovers – Eleanor Jaques, Brenda Salkend, Ruth Graves, in Paris, Lydia Jackson, Inez Holden – along with his second wife Sonia Brownell, who provide support. I even title my Chapter 16 on the crucial publisher of *Animal Farm* and *Nineteen Eighty-Four* 'Fred Warburg and the Making of George Orwell'. And then there's his family – perhaps the most important 'network': his mother, aunt Nellie and sister Avril. As Richard Blair comments, without Avril's support at Barnhill, on the remote Scottish island of Jura, *Nineteen Eighty-Four* would never have appeared (Blair 2021). Interestingly, Orwell's great friend, Richard Rees, recounts in his memoir/critique, *Fugitive from the Camp of Victory* (1961: 138):

> … a friend in Sheffield who had introduced him to a militant communist propagandist told me the following story. The communist started in on his routine vilification of the bourgeoisie, but was interrupted by Orwell who said: 'Look here, I'm a bourgeois and my family are bourgeois. If you talk about them like that I'll punch your head.'

THE IMPORTANCE OF FAMILY, FRIENDSHIP AND COLLEGIALITY

Like Orwell, I have been very lucky in having throughout my life and career amazingly supportive friends, colleagues and family members. While a journalist on *The Teacher*, the weekly newspaper of the National Union of Teachers from 1977 to 1984, there was Peter Singer; at the journalism department at City University, London, there has been, for instance, the late Henry Clother, the late Bob Jones,

Paul Anderson (now a distinguished Orwell scholar and production editor of *George Orwell Studies*), Rod Allen, Rukhsana Aslam, Spencer Ball, the late Colin Bickler, Patrick Brindle, Nick Caistor, Linda Christmas, Kristine Lowe, Jenny McKay, Colleen Murrell, Photini Papatheodorou, Richard Pendry, Hugh Stephenson, Howard Tumber, Marc Wadsworth and Julie Wheelwright. At the University of Lincoln, there has been the polymathic Brian Winston, Gail Vanstone, the late John Tulloch (another polymathic genius I celebrate in an essay republished in *Journalism Beyond Orwell,* Routledge 2020: 106-117*),* Roger de Bank, Sofia Bak, John Cafferkey, Jane Chapman, David Chiddick, Barnie Choudhury, Susan Emfinger, Jon Grubb, Sylvia Harvey, Todd Hogue, Anna Hoyle, Huseyin Kishi, Alex Lewczuk, Tessa Mayes, Mike Neary, Sue North, Nick Nuttall, Mary O'Neill, Ola Ogunyemi, Richard Orange, Sam Pidoux, Sanem Sahin, Mike Saks, Niro Siriwardena, Tony Smith, Gary Stevens, Lioba Suchenwirth, Barry Turner, James Waller-Davies, Rod Whiting, Florian Zollmann – and many others. I have long been involved in the International Association of Literary Journalism Studies and, with supportive colleagues there (David Abrahamson, Robert Alexander, Pablo Calvi, Roberto Herrsher, Willa McDonald, Monica Martinez, Bill Reynolds, David Swick) produced a number of texts over the years. I have also built up friendships with many academics internationally through my jointly editing *Ethical Space: The International Journal of Communication Ethics* (Chris Atton, David Baines, Robert Beckett, Raphael Cohen-Almagor, T. J. Coles, Tom Bradshaw, Antonio Castillo, Clifford Christians, Tom Cooper, Sallyanne Duncan, Jo Fawkes, Chris Frost, Susan Greenberg, Nick Jones, Sue Joseph, Paul Lashmar, Tim Luckhurst, Antony Loewenstein, Jake Lynch, Donald Matheson, Annabel McGoldrick, the late Peter McGregor, Denis Muller, Jackie Newton, Oliver Boyd-Barrett, Julian Petley, Adrian Quinn, Simon Rogerson, Matthew Ricketson, Pratap Rughani, Karen Sanders, Fiona Thompson, Judith Townend, Stephen J. A. Ward) and *George Orwell Studies* (Norman Bissell, Kristin Bluemel, Carol Biederstadt, the late Philip Bounds, Megan Faragher, Darcy Moore, John Newsinger, John Rodden, Luke Seaber, D. J. Taylor) – and produced many texts, bringing together the work of journalists, academics and media campaigners, with my friend John Mair. Stuart Allan, Peter Cole, Martin Conboy, David Edwards and David Cromwell, James Curran, Stephen Dorril, Alistair Duff, Andrew Fowler, Bob Franklin, John Gilliver, colleagues at Routledge, Roy Greenslade, Tony Harcup, Sarah Maltby, Milan Rai, Eleanor Rees, Piers Robinson, Jane Taylor, John Turner – and the late Phillip Knightley and John Pilger have provided me with important support.

For seven years (2013-2020), I was chair of The Orwell Society and through that made many friends. I also had a great deal of fun with the other members of the OS committee: Ron Bateman, Neil Carr, Benedict Cooper, Christopher Edwards, Dennis Frost, Masha Karp, Quentin Kopp, Ann Kronbergs, Neil Smith, Dione Venables. I am honoured that Orwell's son, Richard Blair, Patron of The OS, has written an endorsement for this book (and thanks to all the colleagues who have so warmly endorsed *Moustache*). L. J. Hurst runs the society's Facebook pages with awesome efficiency – and gave me some important angles for this Introduction. My reflections on those seven years of immersion in the world of George Orwell are included here as an Appendix as a way of saying 'thank you' to all my OS friends.

Tim Crook has been a friend and colleague – always there with useful critical comments – for many years. Recently, he has followed John Newsinger in jointly editing with me *George Orwell Studies*. To symbolise the importance of the collaborative spirit behind this book and all of my teaching and literary endeavours, Tim here provides a suitably provocative and original Appendix.

And throughout it all, I've benefited from the love, support and constructive criticisms of my partner Maryline Gagnère and our son, Gabriel. How have they managed to bear with this Orwellian obsessive for so long?

The outstanding cartoonist, Dave Miller, has drawn the wonderful artwork for the front cover.

Thanks to The Orwell Society for allowing me to republish articles from their *Journal* and website and to Abramis, of Bury St Edmunds, publishers of *George Orwell Studies* where a number of these essays originally appeared.

Over many years I have also had the privilege and pleasure to work on many publishing projects with brothers Richard and Pete Franklin who run Abramis Publishing with such calm efficiency. So it is to them that I dedicate this book.

NOTES

[1] Born in 1948, I certainly never experienced such affection from my father, Lancelot. Moreover, I never saw him saunter down a road with his head held high. He never knew his own father and was constantly preoccupied with worries – so he tended to shuffle with his head buried lost in thought. But just as Richard Blair escaped into golf, my father connected with the life force through sport. He met my mother at a tennis club, they played badminton together too; when we went on holidays – to Skegness, Llandudno, that sort of resort – we would play endless cricket on the beach or pitch and putt on the Great Orme. And he was an obsessive fan of Nottingham Forest – he had a season ticket and would go to every home match at the City Ground. He would take me to see Notts County on alternate Saturdays – so I grew up supporting two teams

[2] I speak here from personal experience with our wonderful son, Gabriel, now himself father to Rafael Emile far away in Melbourne, Australia

REFERENCES

Blair, Richard (2019) George Orwell today, *franceculture.fr*, 4 October. Available online at https://www.franceculture.fr/emissions/linvite-des-matins/george-orwell-au-present. Translation from the French by the author

Blair, Richard (2021) Memories of Jura, George Talks, 21 February. Available online at https://orwellsociety.com/about-the-society/george-talks/

Bowker, Gordon (2003) *George Orwell*, London: Little, Brown

Cohen, Deborah (2013) *Family Secrets: Living with Shame from the Victorians to the Present Day*, London: Viking

Crick, Bernard (1980) *George Orwell: A Life*, Harmondsworth, Middlesex: Penguin

Davison, Peter (2006) *The Lost Orwell*, London: Timewell Press

Hurst, L. J. (2019) Neither lions nor donkeys: Richard Walmesley Blair and the mules, Orwell Society *Journal*, No. 14, Spring pp 20-23

Hurst, L. J. (2021) The mystery of Marjorie, missing on that photograph, in email to author, 21 March

Moore, Darcy (2020) Orwell's Scottish ancestry and slavery, *George Orwell Studies*, Vol. 5, No. 1 pp 6-19

Keeble, Richard Lance (2020) *George Orwell, the Secret State and the Making of* Nineteen Eighty-Four, Bury St Edmunds: Abramis

Rees, Richard (1961) G*eorge Orwell: Fugitive from the Camp of Victory*, Carbondale: Southern Illinois University Press

Ross, John (2012) *Orwell's Cough: Diagnosing the Medical Maladies & Last Gasps of the Great Writers*, London: Oneworld

Shelden, Michael (1991) *Orwell: The Authorised Biography*, London: Heinemann

Sutherland, John (2016) *Orwell's Nose: A Pathological Biography*, London: Reaktion Books

Topp, Sylvia (2020) *Eileen: The Making of George Orwell*, London: Unbound

Tripathi, Ameya (2021) Orwell's stolen camera: Photographic authority and *Homage to Catalonia*, *George Orwell Studies*, Vol, 5, No. 2 pp 41-61

SECTION 1

George Orwell:
The Writings

Chapter One

That Moustache and That Tie: On the Politics of Dress (and Undress)

Dress is important to Orwell. Clothes feature prominently in his writings – and while at times he enjoys adopting a shabby look he can also look quite a dandy. Significantly, it is this aspect of his personality that a section of British intelligence find somewhat baffling when they follow him as he works for the BBC in 1942 and which sculptor Martin Jennings highlights in his statue of Orwell unveiled at the BBC in 2017 (Kennedy 2017). This essay takes a look at Orwell's appearance (as revealed in photographs) and examines some of his many representations of dress in his journalism, essays, novels and poetry. It also explores his depictions of people undressed and his awareness of both the symbolic and sexual power of the naked truth.

THE TIE'S THE THING
The tie is the one feature of his dress that Orwell seems attached to throughout his life. The cravat, the thicker neck scarf or bow tie (as, say, cultivated by the Russian spy, Donald Maclean, and Winston Churchill) never appealed and only rarely (such as on the frontline during the Spanish Civil War in 1937) does he go open-necked. Working class, middle class, upper class and down-and-outs all wore the tie during Orwell's time – so there is no particularly bourgeois element to his liking it. Rather, it reflects, perhaps, a liking for routine, consistency and maybe even tradition in Orwell who, though a radical and one-time revolutionary, held (like all of us) contradictory attitudes in many areas.

In all but four of the 17 photographs of Orwell in Gordon Bowker's biography (2003) he wears a tie: thus, with his father, mother and sister Avril in 1918;

standing, proudly with an erect back, his hands gripping the top of a mallet, with friends Prosper and Guinever Buddicom when 14; on an Eton field day (with Cyril Connolly amongst others) in 1920; at the Mandalay Police Training School in 1923; even, surprisingly in his tramp's uniform and on the beach with the family dog, Hector; with his lover Mabel Fierz; when feeding the goat Muriel in the garden at his Wallington home; on the ILP summer school in 1937, working at the BBC and (looking rather relaxed and jovial), holding his son, Richard, in a London street. Significantly, one of the rare times he sports an open neck is when he is shown as a young lad smoking on his way back from swimming at 'Athens' on the Thames near Eton: and Bowker dubs him 'Orwell the delinquent' (ibid). This is also one of the very few times in which Orwell is shown wearing a hat.

His father, Richard Walmseley, on the other hand, it seems, loved wearing hats: Gordon Bowker (2003), in his biography, carries a picture of young Blair with his father on leave from his military duties with his mother and sister, Avril. Here, father Blair looks rather stiff and strict, in an official looking suit and cap. Shelden (1991) shows Mr Blair, in contrast, strolling down a road in Southwold during his retirement – a walking stick held elegantly before him. He is smiling and looking extremely relaxed and dapper, wearing a light suit, white polo-necked jumper, white shoes and a lovely, large, white sun hat (with a fetching dark band) which bends enticingly over his forehead. D. J. Taylor examines the films of Southwold in the 1920s and 1930s shot by Barrett Jenkins and in one, dated 6 August 1928, he spots 'an elderly man wearing a Panama hat and a summer suit' taking a constitutional down the High Street. He writes: 'I have a hunch that this is Richard Walmesley Blair' (Taylor 2003: 236).

THE MOUSTACHE AND DOUBLETHINK

Another constant feature of Orwell's appearance is the moustache which he first acquires while serving as an Imperial Policeman in Burma from 1922-1927 – and keeps for the rest of his life (Larkin 2004: 48-49). As Richard Blair, his son, comments: 'It seems that when he started growing his moustache, he was younger and it was more vertical, but without width under his nose; as he grows older (and thinner) it becomes more horizontal and wider under his nose' (Blair 2021). Maybe it is a way of reminding himself constantly of the impact his service in Burma (where he grew to hate the imperial system of oppression) had on the formation of his character and ideas. Or conversely it may reflect his acknowledgement of the importance of imperial service in the Blair family's history (Crick 1980: 45-47): a case, then, of Orwellian doublethink over his moustache. Bowker, on the other hand, records Orwell's friend, the novelist Anthony Powell, being reminded of Gustave Doré's Don Quixote. 'The moustache he thought perhaps a gesture towards dandyism, a Wodehousean affectation from his youth, or a vestigial sign of his part-French ancestry' (Bowker 2003: 280). John Ross stresses Orwell's meticulous attention to his moustache, even keeping up appearances on the Spanish Civil War frontline in 1937 by shaving with wine which was more available than water (Ross 2012: 206).

And is it not without some element of self-irony that Orwell describes the repulsive Miss Mayfill, in *A Clergyman's Daughter* (1976 [1935]: 260), as having yellow false teeth and a 'fringe of dark, dewy moustache' while the all-powerful Party leader, Big Brother, in his dystopian masterpiece, *Nineteen Eighty-Four*, is 'a man of about forty-five, with a heavy black moustache and ruggedly handsome features' (2000 [1949]: 3)?

Orwell is sufficiently concerned about his appearance to purchase expensive, made-to-measure clothes throughout his life from Denny & Sons tailors in Southwold, the Suffolk coastal town where he lived with his parents for a while after his return, in 1927, from Burma. As Jack Wilkinson Denny, looking at his order book for September 1927, tells researcher Stephen Wadhams: '… he had a three-piece suit. October: flannel trousers. January: an overcoat. The overcoat was six pounds, and the suit was nine pounds ten shillings. An overcoat like that today would be one hundred and eighty to two hundred pounds, depending on the cloth, and his three-piece suit would be about three hundred and fifty pounds today.' He adds that he was 'a thirty seven chest man and thirty four inside leg' (Wadhams 1984: 28).

ORWELL'S DRESS SENSE: 'CLOTHES ARE POWERFUL THINGS'

John Sutherland focuses originally and entertainingly (with occasional lapses in bad taste and factual inaccuracies) on the importance of smell in Orwell's writings (Sutherland 2016). In a similar way, it's possible to highlight, somewhat idiosyncratically perhaps, the importance of dress (and the opposite: nakedness) in the *oeuvre*. There are, for instance, three contrasting scenes in *Down and Out in Paris and London* (1980 [1933]) in which Blair pawns his clothes. In the first, he is desperate having neither eaten nor smoked for a day-and-a-half and so goes to a Parisian pawnshop. But then he's surprised when offered just 70 francs for what he considers £10 worth of clothes. He decides against arguing. 'I now had no clothes except what I stood up in – the coat badly out at the elbow – an overcoat, moderately pawnable, and one spare shirt' (ibid: 23). Next, he goes to the pawnshop with two shabby overcoats and is surprised this time to receive as much as 50 francs. He reflects: 'It was almost as great a shock as the seventy francs had been the time before. I believe now that the clerk had mixed my number up with someone else's…' (ibid: 34).

When later Orwell moves from Paris to London, the crucial ritual involves the shedding of his clothes at a pawn shop and acquiring the gear of a tramp. Having handed over what he considers 'a quite good suit' he is given in exchange 'some dirty-looking rags' and a shilling (ibid: 70):

> The clothes were a coat, once dark brown, a pair of black dungaree trousers, a scarf and a cloth cap; I had kept my own shirt, socks and boots, and I had a comb and razor in my pocket. It gives me a very strange feeling to be wearing such clothes. I had worn bad enough things before but nothing at all like these; a gracelessness, a patina of antique filth, quite different from mere shabbiness. They were the sort of clothes you see on a bootlace seller, or a tramp. An hour later, in Lambeth, I saw a hang-dog man, obviously a tramp, coming towards me, and when I looked again it was myself, reflected in a shop window. The dirt was plastering my face already. Dirt is a great respecter of persons; it lets you alone when you are well dressed, but as soon as your collar is gone it flies towards you from all directions.

Orwell is fully aware of the power of clothes: he continues (ibid):

> My new clothes had put me instantly into a new world. Everyone's demeanour seemed to have changed abruptly. I helped a hawker pick up a barrow that he had upset. 'Thanks mate,' he said with a grin. No-one had called me mate before in my life – it was the clothes that had done it. For the first time I noticed, too, how the attitude of women varies with a man's clothes. When a badly dressed man passes them they shudder away from him with a quite frank movement of disgust, as though he were a dead cat. Clothes are powerful things. Dressed in a tramp's clothes it is very difficult, at any rate for the first day, not to feel that you are genuinely degraded.

JOHN BERGER ON HOW CLOTHES CAN NEVER DISGUISE CLASS

In his essay, 'The suit and the photograph', John Berger (1980) compares three photographs by the German, August Sander (1876-1964). The first (dating from 1913) shows a group of peasants on the road heading for a dance. The second shows a group of peasant musicians displaying their instruments. In the third, a group of upper-class missionaries in 1931 are staring at the camera. Berger argues that the photographs demonstrate that there is no way in which any of the groups can disguise their class. Orwell, likewise, realises that the shabby clothes cannot help him disguise his class (further emphasised by his old-Etonian accent). So while a tramp, he simply presents himself as a gentleman down on his luck – and the tramps accept him. As he writes in his short essay 'Clink' (Orwell 1980 [1932]): 'The story I always tell [is] that my name is Edward Burton, and my parents kept a cake shop in Blythburgh, where I had been employed as a clerk in a draper's shop; that I had had the sack for drunkenness and my parents, finally getting sick of my drunken habits, had turned me adrift' (ibid: 381). Bowker suggests the character Orwell invents 'sounds more Kipps than down-at-heel Bertie Wooster' (2003: 103).

In many ways, Orwell's London pawnshop ritual echoes that of Jack London in his searing exposé of East End poverty, *The People of the Abyss* (2004 [1903]), one of the books that helps inspire Orwell on his tramping exploits. London describes removing his shoes and grey travelling suit and putting on the rags of a tramp. He continues:

> No sooner was I out on the streets than I was impressed by the difference in status effected by my clothes. All servility vanished from the demeanour of the common people with whom I came in contact. Presto! In the twinkling of an eye, so to say, I had become one of them. My frayed and out-at-elbows jacket was the badge and advertisement of my class, which was their class. It made me of like kind, and in place of the fawning and too respectful attention I had hitherto received, I now shared with them a comradeship (ibid).

In contrast, Orwell speaks eloquently, not of comradeship, but of the inability to disguise class in the second, biographical and idiosyncratic part of *The Road to Wigan Pier* (1980 [1937]), the account of his journeys in the north of England investigating poverty and the plight of the miners. 'For some months I lived entirely in coal-miners' houses. I ate my meals with the family, I washed at the kitchen sink. I shared bedrooms with miners, drank beer with them, played darts with them, talked to them by the hour together. But though I was among them, and I hope and trust they did not find me a nuisance, I was not one of them, and they knew it even better than I did. However much you like them, however interesting you find their conversation, there is always that accursed itch of class-difference, like the pea under the princess's mattress' (ibid: 195).

DOWN-AND-OUTS: KEEPING UP APPEARANCES

Orwell's attention is often drawn to the down-and-outs' clothes. Of his Parisian friend Boris, he writes (Orwell 1980 [1933]: 27):

> All the clothes he now had left were one suit, with one shirt, collar and tie, a pair of shoes almost worn out and a pair of socks all holes. He also had an overcoat which he pawned in the last extremity. ... In spite of this Boris managed to keep a fairly smart appearance. He shaved without soap with a razor blade two months old, tied his tie so that the holes did not show and carefully stuffed the soles of his shoes with newspaper. Finally, when he was dressed, he produced an ink-bottle and inked the skin of his ankles where it showed through his socks. You would never have thought, when it was finished, that he had recently been sleeping under the Seine bridges.

And Boris is fully aware of the power of clothes. He comments: 'Appearance – appearance is everything, *mon ami*. Give me a new suit and I will borrow a thousand francs by dinner time. What a pity I did not buy a collar when we had money' (ibid: 38).

While later tramping in London's East End, Orwell befriends Paddy: 'He was dressed, rather better than most tramps, in a tweed shooting jacket and a pair of old evening trousers with the braid still on them. Evidently, the braid figured in his mind as a lingering scrap of respectability, and he took care to sew it on again when it came loose. … Nevertheless, one would have known him for a tramp a hundred yards away' (ibid: 88).

DRESSED FOR REVOLUTION

In December 1936, Orwell arrives in Barcelona and is so overwhelmed by the revolutionary fervour he witnesses that he immediately decides to fight alongside the Republicans against the fascist forces of General Franco. Indeed, he is lucky to escape with his life after he is shot by a sniper in the neck on 20 May 1937. At the start of *Homage to Catalonia* (1962 [1938]: 7), his first-hand frontline account, he describes meeting an Italian militiaman at the Lenin Barracks. There are distinct homoerotic undertones to the writing (see Keeble 2015) as Orwell dwells on his appearance: 'He was a tough-looking youth of twenty-five or -six, with reddish-yellow hair and powerful shoulders. … Something in his face deeply moved me' (op cit: 7). The two exchange a few words. Orwell continues: 'As he went out he stepped across the room and gripped my hand very hard. Queer the affection you can feel for a stranger!' (ibid). The battlefield has, then, become the traditional site for male bonding. Significantly, Orwell now highlights a feature of his clothes, his peaked cap 'pulled fiercely over one eye' (ibid), that seems to add to the Italian's allure.

Later on Orwell describes the overall situation in Barcelona – and he is keen to point out how the clothes he sees reflect the revolutionary spirit which so excites him:

> In outward appearance it was a town in which the wealthy classes had practically ceased to exist. Except for a small number of women and foreigners there were no 'well-dressed' people at all. Practically everyone wore rough working-class clothes or blue overalls or some variant of the militia uniform. All this was queer and moving. There was much in it that I did not understand, in some ways I did not even like it but I recognized it immediately as a state of affairs worth fighting for (ibid: 9).

At the end of the book, as Orwell and his new wife, Eileen, who has joined him at the frontline, prepare to escape from Spain as the communists ruthlessly suppress the Trotskyists and anarchists, the accompanying dampening of the revolutionary spirit is reflected in clothes. Now the safest thing is to look as 'bourgeois as possible' (ibid: 215). Orwell comments: 'By night we were criminals, but by day we were prosperous English visitors – that was our pose anyway. Even after a night in the open, a shave, a bath and a shoe-shine do wonders with your appearance' (ibid). On the train to France, Orwell reflects further on the significance of clothes:

It was queer how everything had changed. Only six months ago, when the Anarchists still reigned, it was looking like a proletarian that made you respectable. On the way down from Perpignan to Cerbères, a French commercial traveller in my carriage had said to me in all solemnity: 'You mustn't go into Spain looking like that. Take off that collar and tie. They'll tear them off you in Barcelona.' He was exaggerating but it showed how Catalonia was regarded. And at the frontier the Anarchist guards had turned back a smartly dressed Frenchman and his wife, solely – I think – because they looked too bourgeois. Now it was the other way about: to look bourgeois was the one salvation (ibid: 217).

And interestingly, when Orwell reflects on his trip by train to Spain in one of his 'As I Please' columns in *Tribune*, on 15 September 1944, he remarks on the dress of some of the men he met there: 'My third-class carriage was full of very young, fair-haired, underfed Germans in suits of incredible shoddiness – the first *ersatz* cloth I had seen' (1998 [1944]: 403).

HOW ORWELL'S BOHEMIAN DRESS FLUMMOXES THE SPOOKS

In August 1941, Orwell joins the Empire Department of the BBC as head of cultural programmes for India and south-east Asia. During his two-year, largely unhappy stint there, Orwell is closely watched by Special Branch (the source clearly being an employee of the BBC). This became clear after Orwell's Special Branch file (MEPO 38/69) and MI5 file (KV 2/2699) were released in 2005 and 2007 respectively (Smith 2013: 112). Intriguingly, Orwell's dress sense is highlighted in one report and may well have contributed to the spies' uncertainty over his political allegiances. For instance, a letter dated 20 January 1942 (file number 301/NWC/683), reports in detail on the office politics at the BBC and adds:

> Blair was at one time in the Burma Police … He was practically penniless when he found work with the BBC. This man has advanced communist views and several of his Indian friends say they have often seen him at communist meetings. He dresses in a bohemian fashion both at his office and in his leisure hours.

A later note, dated 11 February 1942 (KV/2/2699) records Orwell's broadcasts to India and continues:

> ERIC BLAIR is better known as George ORWELL, author and journalist, he has been a bit of an anarchist in his day and in touch with extremist elements. But he has lately thrown in his lot with Victor Gollancz who as you probably know has severed all connection with the Communist Party. BLAIR has undoubtedly strong Left Wing views but he is a long way from orthodox Communism.

The spooks are clearly flummoxed by Orwell's idiosyncratic brand of socialism – and even his mode of dress helps make it difficult for them to place him amongst any one particular faction of the left. James Smith comments: 'If his bohemian dress sense was not suspicious enough, Orwell was also suggested to be part of a deeper conspiracy to place politically suspect individuals within the BBC' (Smith 2013: 122).

But Orwell could also dress quite shabbily. As Meyers comments: 'He kept up with old-Etonians and upper class friends but, as if to maintain his connection with the miners and workers, developed a working-class persona. He wore his habitual battered tweed jacket with leather patches at the elbows, dark shirt, hairy tie and baggy flannel trousers. ... Orwell offered his dress and manner, his hand-rolled cigarettes and proletarian appearance as an alternative, not only to the nudists and homosexuals on the Socialist fringe, but also to bourgeois clothing and comfortable surroundings' (2000: 167). His friend, the anarchist George Woodcock, also remembers his shabby dress sense: 'with a thick, dark-coloured Viyella shirt, a shaggy tie, and shoes that were never well polished. He liked trench coats, bulky knitted scarves and leather gauntlets. I never saw him wearing a suit or, in any weather, a hat' (1984 [1966]: 26).

THE POLITICS OF DRESS AND CLOTHES RATIONING

In one of the 'London Letters' Orwell writes for the left-wing American journal, *Partisan Review*, during the war, Orwell tackles the politics of clothes rationing (see Newsinger 1999). On the surface, he says, the rationing appears to be an undemocratic measure since it hardly affects the rich who have large stocks of clothes already. 'Also the rationing only regulates the number of garments you can buy and has nothing to do with the price, so that you give up the same number of coupons for a hundred-guinea mink coat and a thirty-shilling waterproof' (Orwell 1970 [1942]: 269). However, it now seems rather 'the thing' for people not in uniform to look shabby. Orwell continues:

> Evening dress has practically disappeared so far as men are concerned. Corduroy trousers and, in women, bare legs are on the increase. There hasn't yet been what one could call a revolutionary change in clothing but there may be one owing to the sheer necessity of cutting down wastage of cloth. The Board of Trade tinkers with the problem by, for example, suppressing the turn-ups of trouser ends but is already contemplating putting everyone into battledress (ibid).

THE PLEASURE OF DRESS IN 'AS I PLEASE'

Between 1943 and 1947 Orwell contributes 80 'As I Please' columns to the leftist journal, *Tribune*, where he becomes literary editor after two unhappy years at the BBC. The subject matter is vast: writers and writing, critiques of the mainstream press, the war effort, language, personal reminiscence and experiences, media censorship and the promotion of free speech, the BBC, post-war reconstruction, racism/anti-racism/anti-Semitism, the love of nature, socialism, the ruling classes, the handling of collaborators and so on. Orwell is, in effect, through his column defining a new kind of radical politics. It involves reducing the power of the press barons, facing up to racial intolerance, defending civil liberties. Yet it also incorporates an awareness of the power of language and propaganda, a celebration of the joys of nature and an acknowledgement of the cultural power of Christianity. Above all, in the face of the vast political, cultural, economic factors driving history, it recognises the extraordinary richness of the individual's experience – summed up in his idiosyncratic columns (Keeble 2007). And dress features in a number of intriguing ways in the columns.

For instance, in his 4 February 1944 column, Orwell – ever sensitive to the politics of dress and with both a droll wit and polemical vigour – returns to the Board of Trade ban on turned-up trouser ends (now lifted) with a socialistic point about the overall war effort. A tailor's advertisement hails the lifting of the ban as 'a first instalment of the freedom for which we are fighting'. Orwell comments: 'If we were really fighting for turn-up trouser-ends, I should be inclined to be pro-Axis. Turn-ups have no function except to collect dust, and no virtue except that when you clean them out you occasionally find a sixpence there' (Anderson 2006: 94). He continues:

> I would like to see clothes rationing continue till the moths have devoured the last dinner jacket and even the undertakers have shed their top hats. I would not mind seeing the whole nation in dyed battledress for five years if by that means one of the main breeding points of snobbery and envy could be eliminated. Clothes rationing was not conceived in a democratic spirit, but all the same it has had a democratising effect. If the poor are not much better dressed at least the rich are shabbier. And since no real structural change is occurring in our society, the mechanical levelling process that results from sheer scarcity is better than nothing (ibid).

THE SYMBOLIC POWER OF NAKEDNESS

Just as clothes clearly fascinate Orwell, so does the absence of clothes – nakedness in its many manifestations. For instance, when he travels down a coal mine while researching poverty in northern England in 1936 – the results published in *The Road to Wigan Pier*, of 1937 – he celebrates, with a 'pang of envy' the 'splendid' nakedness and raw strength of the men which he observes closely. He writes: 'It is impossible to watch the "fillers" at work without feeling a pang of envy for their toughness. It is a dreadful job that they do, an almost superhuman job by the standards of an ordinary person. ... It is only when you see miners down the mine and naked that you realize what splendid men they are. Most of them are small (big men are at a disadvantage in that job) but nearly all of them have the most noble bodies; wide shoulders tapering to slender supple waists, and the small pronounced buttocks and sinewy thighs, with not an ounce of waste flesh anywhere' (Orwell 1980 [1937]: 133).

He continues: 'You can never forget that spectacle once you have seen it – the line of bowed, kneeling figures, sooty black all over, driving their huge shovels under the coal with stupendous force and speed' (ibid).[1] According to Robert Colls, Orwell is representing the miners as 'heroes stripped as heroes' (2013: 60). But Beatrix Campbell highlights critically the way in which Orwell uses an 'Etonian accolade' in describing the naked miners as having figures 'fit for a guardsman' and she suggests it's a manifestation of his homoeroticism (1984: 99). The point is picked up by Christopher Hitchens who argues there could well be a hint of homoeroticism here:

> We know that Orwell was teased heartlessly by Cyril Connolly while at Eton for being 'gone' on another boy and, while that might have been commonplace enough, we also have the claim by his friend and colleague Rayner Heppenstall that he was himself the object of an adult homosexual 'crush' on Orwell's part (1984: 103).

WHEN NAKEDNESS SYMBOLISES HUMILIATION AND VULNERABILITY

In contrast, while reporting his trips to the London underworld of tramps and beggars, he dwells on their nakedness as symbolising their complete desexualised humiliation, subservience to the whims of the Tramp Major (who runs the doss-house with an iron hand), degradation and vulnerability. In the essay, 'The spike' which (as Eric Blair) he contributes to the left-wing *Adelphi* magazine, in April 1931, his depiction of the plight of the down-and-outs mixes both compassion and squeamishness (perhaps also reflecting the assumed response of his imaginary middle class audience) (Orwell 1970 [1931], see also Chapter 8). For instance, on the 'disgusting sight' in the bathroom, he writes:

> All the indecent secrets of our underwear were exposed: the grime, the rents and patches, the bits of string doing duty for buttons, the layers upon layers of fragmentary garments, some of them mere collections of holes, held together by dirt. The room became a press of steaming nudity, the sweaty odours of the tramps competing with the sickly, sub-faecal stench native to the spike (ibid: 59-60).

As the men line up for the medical inspection, the narrator mixes cool observation with disgust (the adjectives piling on one after another):

> It was an instructive sight. We stood shivering naked to the waist in two long ranks in the passage. … No one can imagine, unless he has seen such a thing, what pot-bellied, degenerate curs we looked. Shock heads, hairy,

crumpled faces, hollow chests, flat feet, sagging muscles – every kind of malformation and physical rottenness were there (ibid: 61).

Indeed, as Beci Dobbin stresses (2012: 68), Blair's tendency towards squeamishness betrays a distinct 'class specific sensibility'.

A similar scene is depicted in *Down and Out in Paris and London* after the tramps at the spike are told to strip and wait for their medical inspection:

> Naked and shivering, we lined up in the passage. You cannot conceive what ruinous, degenerate curs we looked, standing there in the merciless morning light. A tramp's clothes are bad, but they conceal far worse things; to see him as he really is, unmitigated, you must see him naked. Flat feet, pot bellies, hollow chests, sagging muscles – every kind of physical rottenness was there. Nearly everyone was under-nourished, and some clearly diseased; two men were wearing trusses, and as for the old mummy-like creature of seventy-five, one wondered how he could possibly make his daily march (Orwell 1980 [1933]: 87).

The experience of witnessing such sights of nudity clearly impacts considerably on Orwell and so he uses it as the basis for his 40-line, ten-stanza, rhyming poem 'A dressed man and a naked man' which is published by *Adelphi* in October 1933. Typically, Orwell is using a poem to reflect on a particularly important moment or feeling – and to play with language, tone and genre (here a witty narrative built around dialogue bursting with the vernacular). Outside a spike, one man is naked (how come?) and haggling with another over the price of his clothes. After the deal is sorted, the poem ends:

> A minute and they had changed about,
> And each had his desire;
> A dressed man and a naked man
> Stood by the kip-house fire.[2]

Intriguingly, there are echoes of the tramps' naked ugliness in Orwell's depiction of Winston Smith towards the end of his horrific torture ordeal in *Nineteen Eighty-Four*. Here, Winston's enforced nakedness symbolises his total humiliation and subservience to the power of the Party and the brutal O'Brien – and more generally the destruction of the human spirit by Big Brother totalitarianism. At this key moment in the narrative, Winston comes to represent nothing less than the 'last man' in his nakedness. Orwell writes:

> 'You are the last man,' said O'Brien. 'You are the guardian of the human spirit. You shall see yourself as you are. Take off your clothes' (Orwell 2000 [1949]: 310).[3]

So Winston proceeds to his remove his 'filthy yellowish rags, just recognisable as remnants of underclothes' (ibid). And in a mirror a 'bowed, grey-coloured, skeleton thing' coming towards him is terrifying. The disgust Orwell felt towards the naked, disfigured tramps in the spike all those years ago is now captured in his portrayal of Winston:

> A forlorn, jailbird's face with a nobby forehead running back into a bald scalp, a crooked nose and battered looking cheekbones above which the eyes were fierce and watchful. The cheeks were seamed, the mouth had a drawn-in look. … Except for his hands and a circle of his face, his body was grey all over with ancient, ingrained dirt. Here and there under the dirt there were the red scars of wounds and near the ankle the varicose ulcer was an inflamed mass of flakes of skin peeling off it. But the truly frightening thing was the emaciation of his body. The barrel of his ribs was as narrow as that of a skeleton: the legs had shrunk so that the knees were thicker than the thighs. The curvature of the spine was astonishing. … he was aware of his ugliness, his gracelessness (ibid: 311).

Some commentators have suggested that there is an element of merciless self-portraiture in this writing. Richard Rees suggests the whole account of Winston's interrogation and torture 'is a reflection of Orwell's sense of the ruthless ravages of consumption upon his own body' (Rees 1961: 96). And as Jeffrey Meyers comments: 'Orwell's description of himself after the terrible effects of streptomycin [the drug brought specially over from the US to treat his TB] are close to his portrayal of Winston after his torture in the novel' (Meyers 2000: 286). For biographer Robert Colls, Orwell is evoking the image of Jews heading towards the Nazi gas chambers: 'We are all Jews now,' Colls writes (2013: 214; see also Tim Crook's Afterword). But for Dorian Lynskey, Winston is not really 'the last man'. 'He's just the latest symbolic victim to be broken down and rebuilt. … There were Winstons before and there will be Winstons to come. Like Stalin's regime during the Great Terror, the Party doesn't fear heretics, it *needs* them, because its power is renewed by crushing them' (2019: 179-180, italics in the original).

O'Brien, secret friend turned torturer, next mocks him: 'I do not think there can be much pride left in you. You have been kicked and flogged and insulted, you have screamed with pain, you have rolled on the floor in your own blood and vomit. You have whimpered for mercy, you have betrayed everybody and everything. Can you think of single degradation that has not happened to you?' (op cit: 313). To which Winston replies: 'I have not betrayed Julia.' But then, later, as the rats move closer to his face in the Ministry of Love's Room 101, he screams out the ultimate betrayal: 'Do it to Julia! Do it to Julia! Not me! Julia! I don't care what you do to her. Tear her face off, strip her to the bones. Not me! Julia! Not me!' (ibid: 328).

NUDITY AND SEXUALITY

Nudity is also associated by Orwell, not surprisingly, with sexuality. In a letter from 1932 to Eleanor Jaques, one of the loves of his life during his time in Southwold after he returns from his stint as an Imperial Policeman in Burma (1922-1927), he talks of their walks along the River Blyth: '… that day in the wood along past Blythburgh Lodge – you remember that, & your nice white body in the dark green moss' (Taylor 2003: 125). This experience of sex *en plein air* seems to impact hugely on Orwell's imagination. As Gordon Bowker comments perceptively on Orwell's character and writings: 'With women there was, for him, the prospect of a Laurentian adventure. Like Lady Chatterley's gamekeeper, he saw the countryside as his sexual stamping ground – a place to take women in both senses of the word; indeed, pastoral seduction became a feature of his fiction' (2003: 137).

In *Keep the Aspidistra Flying*, for instance, Gordon Comstock and Rosemary take the train and bus out to Farnham Common, have a meal and then head out into the open countryside with one clear intention – to make love. In a natural alcove by some bushes, he asks her to take her clothes off (Orwell 1976 [1936]: 666). And Orwell dwells on her nakedness:

> She had no shame before him. … They spread her clothes out and made a sort of bed for her to lie on. Naked, she lay back, her hands behind her head, her eyes shut, smiling slightly, as though she had considered everything and were at peace in her mind. For a long time he knelt and gazed at her body (ibid).

But alas, Gordon has not brought any contraceptives (his lack of money – which obsesses him – even interfering with his dreams of love-making) and so Rosemary rejects his advances.

And in *Nineteen Eighty-Four*, Winston Smith and Julia conduct a secret passionate affair. At the start of the novel, he sets his eyes on her at the Two Minutes Hate session, and her clothes seem to sum up her public persona (while, in fact, she is secretly promiscuous): 'She was a bold-looking girl of about twenty-seven with thick dark hair, a freckled face and swift, athletic movements. A narrow scarlet sash, emblem of the Junior Anti-Sex League, was wound several times round the waist of her overall, just tightly enough to bring out the shapeliness of her hips' (Orwell 2000 [1949]: 12).

Winston and Julia first make love *en plein air* (ibid: 142-145) but are only naked together when they have sex in the room above Charrington's junk shop. Intriguingly, here the focus is more on Winston's nakedness than Julia's:

> They flung their clothes off and climbed into the huge mahogany bed. It was the first time that he had stripped himself naked in her presence. Until now he had been too much ashamed of his pale and meagre body, with the varicose veins standing out on his calves and the discoloured patch over his ankle (ibid: 165).

Charrington, however, turns out to be a member of the Thought Police – and Winston is hauled off to the Ministry of Love to be tortured. The question of whether Julia suffers a similar fate or is, instead, a Party member luring Winston into a trap is one of the many conundrums in the text (Keeble 2019).

CONCLUSION: 'IT WAS THE CLOTHES THAT HAD DONE IT'

A close examination of Orwell's writings suggests that throughout his life the clothes he wore and he saw others wearing (whether on the streets of London while tramping, in revolutionary Barcelona or displayed in the pages of *Vogue*, a flashy American women's magazine: see Chapter 16.) are important to him and worth describing and commenting upon. Orwell is a complex man, contradictory in many aspects and certainly in his clothes sense – at one time shabby, at another time quite a dandy. Clothes, he also realises, are essentially markers of personality – and yet they can never disguise a person's class.

Conversely, states of undress also intrigue him: female nakedness always being associated with sexuality. Male nakedness, on the other hand, both fascinates and disgusts him – as his observations in the London spikes show. The system has rendered the down-and-outs nameless, 'inhumane' degenerates – reduced to animals by the Tramp Major 'who gave the tramps no more ceremony than sheep at the dipping pond, shoving them this way and that and shouting oaths in their faces' (1970 [1941]: 59). Blair/Orwell, in contrast, treats them with some measure of compassion, giving them names and distinct, contrasting personalities. In this context, their nakedness, which he describes in relentless detail, symbolises their humiliation, degradation and vulnerability.

After Orwell's first wife, Eileen O'Shaughnessy, dies suddenly in 1945, aged just 39, his great friend David Astor, the *Observer* journalist and fellow old-Etonian, becomes probably the most important person in his life. I was lucky to interview Astor (one of the wealthiest men in Britain with a long history of ties to the intelligence services) just a year before he died in 2001. In the course of our two-hour conversation I ask him: 'Did you ever talk about your times at Eton with Orwell?' And Astor replies:

> Towards the end of his life, I had a son and had to decide which school to send him to. I asked George: 'What do you think of Eton as a school?' And he said: 'I've got nothing against the education. I think it's very good. But they will have to change the school dress. I wouldn't let my son have to wear a tailcoat and make a fool of him' (Keeble 2014).

So right until near the very end, Orwell is a man acutely aware of the messages given out by clothes.

NOTES

[1] Orwell's modern languages teacher at Eton was Aldous Huxley who goes on to publish his celebrated dystopian novel, *Brave New World*, in 1932. In 1931, as part of his eye-witness account of workers' lives, written for *Nash's Pall Mall Magazine*, Huxley also celebrates the naked body of the miner as 'movingly beautiful': 'In that terrifying unnatural goblin-world of the mine, to be confronted suddenly – after what seems, to the stranger from the upper sunlight, an age of wandering through stifling labyrinths – by a pale glimmer of the naked human body ... The impression is overwhelming. How movingly beautiful it is, the body of a man. How white and smooth and, in the monstrous twilight at the coal-face, under the menace of the low ceilings of sagging rock, how delicate-looking, how defenceless and frail!' (Huxley 1994 [1931]: 70). See also Murray (2003 [2002]: 240)

[2] https://www.orwellfoundation.com/the-orwell-foundation/orwell/poetry/a-dressed-man-and-a-naked-man/. Dione Venables, in her edited collection, *George Orwell: The Complete Poetry*, Finlay Publisher, describes the poem as 'upbeat' (p. 31)

[3] Significantly, when Orwell first conceived of his dystopian novel 'some time between 1940 and the end of 1943' when Britain was seriously in danger of losing the war, his original title was *The Last Man in Europe* (Sutherland 2016: 226)

REFERENCES

Anderson, Paul (2006) *Orwell in* Tribune, London: Politico's

Berger, John (1980) The suit and the photograph, in *About Looking*, London: Writers and Readers Publishing Cooperative pp 27-36

Blair, Richard (2021) On that moustache, email to author, 18 March

Bowker, Gordon (2003) *George Orwell*, London: Little, Brown

Campbell, Beatrix (1984) *Wigan Pier Revisited*, London: Virago

Colls, Robert (2013) *George Orwell: English Rebel*, Oxford: Oxford University Press

Dobbin, Beci (2012) Orwell's squeamishness, Keeble, Richard Lance (ed.) *Orwell Today*, Bury St Edmunds: Abramis pp 62-76

Hitchens, Christopher (2002) *Orwell's Victory*, London: Allen Lane/Penguin

Huxley, Aldous (1994 [1931]) Sight-seeing in alien England, Bradshaw, David (ed.) *The Hidden Huxley*, London: Faber and Faber pp 65-76; *Nash's Pall Mall Magazine*, No lxxxvii pp 16-19

Keeble, Richard Lance (2007) The lasting in the ephemeral: Assessing George Orwell's As I Please columns, Keeble, Richard and Wheeler, Sharon (eds) *The Journalistic Imagination: Literary Journalists from Defoe to Capote and Carter*, Abingdon, Oxon: Routledge pp 100-115

Keeble, Richard Lance (2014) Exclusive: Orwell by his great friend David Astor, Orwell Society *Journal*, June, No. 4 pp 8-10

Keeble, Richard Lance (2015) Orwell and the war reporter's imagination, Keeble, Richard Lance (ed.) *George Orwell Now!*, New York: Peter Lang pp 209-228

Keeble, Richard Lance (2019) *Nineteen Eighty-Four*, the secret state and the Julia conundrum, *George Orwell Studies*, Vol. 4, No. 1 pp 43-56

Kennedy, Maev (2017) George Orwell returns to loom over the BBC, *Guardian*, 7 November. Available online at https://www.theguardian.com/books/2017/nov/07/george-orwell-returns-to-loom-over-bbc, accessed on 5 September 2019

Larkin, Emma (2004) *Finding George Orwell in Burma*, London: Penguin

London, Jack (2004 [1903]) *The People of the Abyss*, Fairfield, IA: 1st World Library: Literary Society

Lynskey, Dorian (2019) *The Ministry of Truth: A Biography of George Orwell's* 1984, London: Picador

Meyers, Jeffrey (2000) *Orwell: Wintry Conscience of a Generation*, New York and London: W. W. Norton & Co.

Murray, Nicholas (2003 [2002]) *Aldous Huxley: An English Intellectual*, London: Abacus

Newsinger, John (1999) The American connection: George Orwell, 'Literary Trotskyism' and the New York intellectuals, *Labour History Review*, Vol. 64, No. 1 pp 23-43

Orwell, George (1970 [1931]) The spike, Orwell, Sonia and Angus, Ian (eds) *The Collected Essays, Journalism and Letters of George Orwell, Vol. 1: An Age Like This 1920-1940*, Harmondsworth, Middlesex: Penguin Books pp 58-66; originally published in the *Adelphi*, April

Orwell, George (1970 [1932]) Clink, Orwell, Sonia and Angus, Ian (eds) *The Collected Essays, Journalism and Letters of George Orwell, Vol. 1: An Age Like This 1920-1940*, Harmondsworth, Middlesex: Penguin Books pp 380-386

Orwell, George (1980 [1933]) *Down and Out in Paris and London*, in the *Collected Non-Fiction*, London: Secker and Warburg/Octopus pp 15-120

Orwell, George (1976 [1935]) *A Clergyman's Daughter*, in the *Collected Fiction*, London: Secker & Warburg/Octopus pp 255-425

Orwell, George (1976 [1936]) *Keep the Aspidistra Flying*, in the *Collected Fiction*, London: Secker & Warburg/Octopus pp 573-737

Orwell, George (1980 [1937]) *The Road to Wigan Pier*, in the *Collected Non-Fiction*, London: Secker & Warburg/Octopus pp 123-232

Orwell, George (1962 [1938]) *Homage to Catalonia*, Harmondsworth, Middlesex: Penguin

Orwell, George (1970 [1942]) London Letter to *Partisan Review*, 29 August, Orwell, Sonia and Angus, Ian (eds) *The Collected Essays, Journalism and Letters of George Orwell, Vol. 2: My Country Right or Left 1940-1943*, Harmondsworth, Middlesex: Penguin pp 265-272; originally published in November-December edition

Orwell, George (1998 [1944]) As I Please, Davison, Peter (ed.) *Complete Works of George Orwell, Vol. XVI: I Have Tried to Tell the Truth, 1944*, London: Secker & Warburg pp 402-405; originally published in *Tribune*, 15 September

Orwell, George (2000 [1949]) *Nineteen Eighty-Four*, London: Penguin

Rees, Richard (1961) *George Orwell: Fugitive from the Camp of Victory*, Carbondale, Southern Illinois University Press

Ross, John (2012) *Orwell's Cough: Diagnosing the Medical Maladies and Last Gasps of the Great Writers*, London: Oneworld

Shelden, Michael (1991) *Orwell: The Authorised Biography*, London: William Heinemann

Smith, James (2012) *British Writers and MI5 Surveillance 1930-1960*, Cambridge: Cambridge University Press

Sutherland, John (2016) *Orwell's Nose: A Pathological Biography*, London: Reaktion Books

Taylor, D. J. (2003) *Orwell: The Life*, London: Chatto & Windus

Wadhams, Stephen (1984) *Remembering Orwell*, Harmondsworth, Middlesex: Penguin

Woloch, Alex (2016) *Or Orwell: Writing and Democratic Socialism*, Massachusetts, London: Harvard University Press

Woodcock, George (1984 [1966]) *The Crystal Spirit: A Study of George Orwell*, London: Fourth Estate

- **This essay is based on 'Orwell and Dress: The Naked Truth?',** *George Orwell Studies*, **Vol. 4, No. 2 pp 78-94**

Chapter Two

The Heart of the Matter: The Fatherhood Factor

One of the most important influences on George Orwell is his father. This essay, then, explores the crucial theme of fatherhood in a number of contrasting ways. It first examines the responses of both Orwell and his contemporaries to his father. It moves on to look at the many fascinating representations of fathers in his novels. Orwell's own strikingly progressive attitudes as a dad are highlighted as are, finally, the responses of his son, Richard Blair, to having the celebrated author of *Nineteen Eighty-Four* as a father.

RICHARD WALMESLEY BLAIR – LONG DUE A RE-ASSESSMENT
The conventional view of Orwell's father as a rather drab and dull figure is set by Jacintha Buddicom, his childhood friend, in her wonderfully engaging memoir of their times together, *Eric & Us* (2006 [1974]). With Orwell known to her at the time as Eric Blair, she writes:

> Eric's father Richard Walmesley Blair (called Dick) was born on 7 January 1857 so belonged to the previous generation. … He certainly seemed to us children to be very ancient and not sympathetic. He was not unkind – he never beat Eric – but he did not understand nor, I think, much care for children – after all, he hardly saw his own till he was fifty. He always seemed to expect us all to keep rather out of his way which we were reciprocatively glad to do (ibid: 13-14).

Richard Blair, a lowly Sub-Deputy Opium Agent in Upper Bengal, married Ida Mabel Limouzin, a high-spirited, vivacious woman, in Naina Tal, on 15 June 1897. He was 39, she was 22. Their first child, Marjorie, was born on 21

April 1898; after they moved to Motihari, Eric was born on 25 June 1903. In the following year, Ida with her two children moved to Henley-on-Thames leaving father in India. And though Richard spent a short time on leave at Henley in 1907 – during which time Eric's sister, Avril, was conceived, being born on 6 April the following year – he was mostly absent until he joined the family – now living in Shiplake – in 1912. As Gordon Bowker comments: 'Aged 55, after 37 years of service, Richard Blair retired from the Bengali Opium Service on a pension of just over £400 a year probably with additions from contributions set aside and a family supplement' (2003: 38). Robert Colls comments: 'The British had grossly overvalued the Indian rupee against the pound at a fixed rate of 1s. 6d and Mr Blair's pension did well out of this. Orwell always said that the British lived off the backs of Indian peasants' (Colls 2013: 11). Ida determined not to fall pregnant again so banishes Dick to his own room (Bowker 2003: 38). He occupies himself becoming secretary of the local golf club.

In his essay, 'Why I write' (1970 [1946]: 23), Orwell says: 'I was the middle child of three, but there was a gap of five years on either side, and I barely saw my father before I was eight.' Now Orwell finds himself confronted by 'a gruff elderly man forever saying "Don't"' (Bowker 2003: 38). And Buddicom comments: 'The Blairs, though certainly not demonstrative, were nevertheless a united family, and their home seemed to us a happy one. I do not think Eric was fond of his father, although he respected and obeyed him but without doubt he was genuinely fond of his mother and sisters, especially Avril' (op cit: 19).

Then in 1917, aged 60, Richard Blair surprises everyone by becoming the oldest second lieutenant in the British Army, being put in charge of the mules in a camp and depot near Marseilles. How remarkable! Orwell is noted for his extraordinary pluck – living with the down-and-outs in London and Paris (1928-1931), going down coal mines while investigating poverty in the north of England (1936), fighting alongside Republican militiamen during the Spanish Civil War and only narrowly escaping being fatally wounded (1937), reporting from the frontlines on the Continent during the final days of the Second World War (1945) and going to live the 'simple life' on a remote Scottish island with his newly adopted son (1946-1949). Perhaps this is a trait he inherits from his father. L. J. Hurst is right to stress the crucial role played by mules and horses in the First World War (Hurst 2019). 'The British Army discovered they needed to buy about 15,000 horses a month. It has been calculated that almost half a million horses owned by the British Army were killed during the First World War' (ibid: 20). Moreover, while old enough to be father to some of his colleagues, Richard Blair 'would not stand out in the crowd' since in November 1918 the Remount Department numbered 18,766 officers and men (ibid: 21).

Yet Orwell appeared strangely embarrassed by his father's 'heroics'. As Bernard Crick reports (1980: 107): 'None of Eric's contemporaries at Eton can remember him mentioning that he had a father in the Army. By now habitually reticent about his family, he may have found his father's posting ludicrous and his age embarrassing. When George Bowling in *Coming Up For Air* [1939] becomes a second lieutenant, he was given eleven tins of bully beef to guard in a forgotten military dump on the north coast of remote Cornwall.'

In 1922, soon after Orwell leaves Eton, the Blairs move to Southwold on the Suffolk coast and there is evidence that Richard, away from all the stresses of full-time employment, relaxes into happy retirement and becomes a 'new man'. Conventional biographies of Orwell have been too slow to acknowledge this. Let's consider two photographs. In Bowker's biography, on the second, un-numbered page of illustrations, Richard is shown sitting with Eric, Ida and Avril, while on leave from the Army in 1918. He appears stiff and formal in his military gear – and separate from the tender intimacy of the other group. Compare this with the later photograph of Richard strolling down a Southwold road – a walking stick held elegantly before him. He is smiling and looking extremely relaxed and dapper. Intriguingly, Orwell (perhaps echoing his father's fancy) regularly displays – in a rather dapper style – a handkerchief in his top jacket pocket: for instance, as Bernard Crick (1980) shows him with BBC colleagues, taking a cup of tea or typing in his Islington flat in 1945 and even while chiselling some wood in an office (books piled up in the background) (see Keeble 2020a).

There are conflicting accounts of Richard Blair's influence over Orwell's decision to become an Imperial Policeman in Burma in 1922 after Eton. According to Buddicom, Orwell wanted to apply for Oxford University but his father was determined on him following his career and serve the Empire in some capacity: 'Our mother and Mrs Blair united in deploring old Mr Blair's obstinate attitude regarding Eric's future. Indian Civil he had been himself and Indian Civil was the only career he would tolerate for his son. It was the last thing Eric wanted, but the tramlines were laid down' (op cit: 118). John Sutherland suggests that Andrew Gow, Orwell's Classics tutor at Eton, plays a major role – telling Richard that his son has disgraced the college by coming so low in the academic lists (137th out of 168) and so should be removed entirely from higher education. 'Richard, a man used to obeying orders, got the message and cut off any further family monetary sacrifice for Eric: no longer the hope of the Blairs' (Sutherland 2016: 75). On the other hand, Orwell's first biographers, Peter Stansky and William Abrahams, suggest that Orwell himself decided against Oxford and Cambridge. They report: 'Orwell in the 1940s told a good friend of that phase that one of his reasons for not going to university was that he felt he had been too long associating mainly with boys who were much richer than he' (Stansky and Abrahams 1972: 125n).

However, all commentators are agreed that Orwell's sudden decision to resign his position in the Imperial Police in 1927 while on leave from his duties in Burma and devote his time to becoming a writer shocks his family and is denounced by his father. According to Stansky and Abrahams: 'His presence [at the family home in Southwold] was a source of daily concern and irritation. Eric and his father had never been close: now a kind of estrangement grew up between them, the coldness more pronounced, the differences of opinion more abrasive. While his mother quite soon came round to Eric's point of view … his father did not and would not virtually until the end of his life' (ibid: 181).

To what extent then does Orwell's obsessive work routine – and his constant feelings of failure – all stem from his determination to prove himself to his father? In his last literary notebook of 1949, he writes:

> It is now 16 years since my first book was published & abt 21 years since I started publishing articles in the magazines. Throughout that time there has literally been not one day in which I did not feel that I was idling, that I was behind on the current job & that my total output was miserably small. Even at the periods when I was working 10 hours a day on a book, or turning out 4 or 5 articles a week, I have never been able to get away from this neurotic feeling that I was wasting time. … as soon as a book is finished I begin, actually from the next day, worrying because the next one is not begun & am haunted with the fear that there never will be a next one – that my impulse is exhausted for good & all (*Complete Works of George Orwell* XX: 204).

Was all that extraordinary effort all an attempt to prove to his critical father that his decision to become a writer is the right one? As Sylvia Topp comments: 'Orwell had struggled throughout his life with the worry that he hadn't lived up to his father's expectations and his greatest wish had been to convince his father that he had made a life choice worthy of his respect' (2020: 268).

All commentators tend to agree that Orwell's relationship with his father, never close, sours even further on his return from Burma and does not improve until the late 1930s – just before Richard dies in 1939, aged 82. Yet there is evidence that the reconciliation begins much earlier. In the early 1930s, joining his family in Southwold, Orwell accompanies his father in one of the old man's favourite pastimes: watching films in the tiny local cinema in Duke of York's Road near the common (Taylor 2003: 137). In 1934, Orwell writes to his friend, Brenda Salkend: 'I went to the pictures last week and saw Jack Hulbert in *Jack Ahoy* which I thought very amusing & a week or two before that there was quite a good crook film which, however, my father ruined for me by insisting on telling me the plot beforehand' (*CWGO* X: 346).

Michael Shelden writes: 'Of course, [Orwell] had never been as close to his father as he might have hoped to be, but they got on reasonably well in the latter half of the 1930s and Orwell had certainly put to rest any notion that he might be a dilettante as a writer. No doubt his father would still have preferred to see him serve out his ordinary term in the Imperial Police, but any lingering resentment over that issue had faded by 1939' (1991: 340). But here he is – like most of the other biographers – dating the reconciliation between father and son far too late.

In June 1939, just as Orwell is visiting his father in Southwold on his deathbed, *Coming Up For Air* has just been given a rave review in *The Sunday Times*. Sylvia Topp records how Avril takes the review to Richard's bedroom and reads it to him. 'A little later he lost consciousness for the last time' (op cit: 268). Orwell closes his father's eyes in the traditional way by placing pennies on the eyelids – and later walks down to the sea and throws them in (ibid).

FATHERS – AS PORTRAYED IN ORWELL'S NOVELS
The next section of the essay examines the many contrasting – and usually highly symbolic – ways in which Orwell portrays fathers in his novels.

A CLERGYMAN'S DAUGHTER (1935): FATHER LOOMS OVER ALL THE ACTION
Significantly, Dorothy Hare, the leading protagonist in this novel, is defined throughout entirely in relation to her father. As Daphne Patai notes (1984: 96):

> The very title of Orwell's second novel at once induces the reader to take a particular perspective on his protagonist. She is to be viewed not as an individual in her own right but rather in terms of her relationship to a man, a clergyman, her father. This is the only one of Orwell's novels to have such a title, one that refers to the main character and at the same time identifies this character through a relationship to someone else. Dorothy Hare is not even *the* clergyman's daughter, which would give her a more specific identity, but merely a clergyman's daughter, a generic, or rather paradigmatic, being (italics in the original).

Not surprisingly then, her father looms over all the action in the novel. We are first introduced to Dorothy as 'the only child of the Reverend Charles Hare, Rector of St Athelstan's, Knype Hill, Suffolk' (1976 [1935]: 255). And she is constantly overwhelmed by his grumbling and excessive demands. All that, together with a sexual assault by her neighbour Mr Warburton (Orwell originally described this as an 'attempted rape' but that had to be cut: see Davison 1996: 55), leads to Dorothy having a complete mental breakdown – and she awakens in the New Kent Road in central London not knowing who she is. As Christopher Hitchens comments, Orwell's feminist critics are right about one thing: 'Every one of his female characters is practically devoid of the least trace of intellectual or reflective capacity. ... Dorothy in *A Clergyman's Daughter* operates on blind and simple faith, can't keep her end up in an elementary argument with the village atheist, and collapses at the same time as her beliefs' (Hitchens 2002: 105).

But Dorothy lost in London is still haunted by her father. As the headlines in the gossip sheet *Pippin's Weekly* proclaim: 'PARSON'S DAUGHTER AND ELDERLY SEDUCER' and 'WHITE-HAIRED FATHER PROSTRATE WITH GRIEF' (ibid: 329). Underneath, the copy reads:

'I would sooner have seen her in her grave!' was the heartbroken cry of the Rev. Charles Hare, Rector of Knype Hill, Suffolk, on learning of his twenty-eight-year-old daughter's elopement with an elderly bachelor named Warburton, described as an artist. Miss Hare, who left the town on the night of the twenty-first of August, is still missing, and all attempts to trace her have failed. [In leaded type] Rumour, as yet unconfirmed, states that she was recently seen with a male companion in a hotel of evil repute in Vienna (ibid: 329-330).

Orwell here is highlighting the ways in which the mass media sensationalise and ludicrously invent facts ('fake news' is certainly nothing new) in a ruthless, profit-oriented strategy to boost sales. But he is also cleverly illustrating how Dorothy's self-perception primarily as a *daughter* reflects dominant societal attitudes as shown in the newspaper headlines. At the end of the novel, Warburton 'rescues' Dorothy and spells out her options – all of them tied to her position as a clergyman's daughter:

'After ten years your father will die and he will leave you with not a penny, only debts. You will be nearly forty, with no money, no profession, no chance of marrying, just a derelict parson's daughter like the ten thousand others in England. And after that, what do you suppose will become of you? You will have to find yourself a job – the sort of job that parsons' daughters get. A nursery governess, for instance, or companion to some diseased hag who will occupy herself in thinking of ways to humiliate you' (ibid: 417).

Not surprisingly after that psychological battering, Dorothy decides to resume her onerous duties – looking after her father at the rectory and keeping the church going.

Given the centrality of the theme of fatherhood in the novel, Orwell is careful to represent the rakish Warburton as an irresponsible parent. His three illegitimate children (he calls them bastards) 'were one of the chief scandals of Knype Hill'. 'He lived, or rather stayed periodically, in open concubinage with a woman whom he called his housekeeper. Four months ago this woman – she was a foreigner, a Spaniard it was said – had created a fresh and worse scandal by abruptly deserting him, and his three children were now parked with some long-suffering relative in London' (ibid: 277).

COMING UP FOR AIR (1939): A NOVEL ABOUT FATHERHOOD

Coming Up For Air is perhaps best seen as essentially a novel about fatherhood. Indeed, the memories George Bowling has of his father loom over the whole of the narrative just as Bowling's own experiences of being a father are the crucial drivers of the storyline

The first we hear of his father – Samuel Bowling, corn and seed merchant, of 57 High Street – comes when George ponders his current lifestyle as a travelling salesman for the Flying Salamander Life insurance company: 'It may seem queer, but my father would probably be rather proud of me if he could see me now. He'd think it a wonderful thing that a son of his should own a motor-car and live in a house with bathroom' (1976 [1939]: 449). So it is clear that, for George, it's absolutely crucial that his father be proud of him and his achievements. And as he recalls his youth, his father is ever present:

> Half-way through the morning some of the farmers would come into the shop and run samples of seed through their fingers. Actually Father did very little business with the farmers because he had no delivery van and couldn't afford to give long credits. Mostly he did a rather petty class of business, poultry food and fodder for the tradesmen's horses and so forth (ibid: 453).

He remembers an argument his father had with Uncle Ezekiel and his 'quiet, worried, conscientious kind of voice' (ibid: 455). But it's the detail of the recollections that is so striking:

> Father had been educated at Walton Grammar School where the farmers and the better-off tradesmen sent their sons, whereas Uncle Ezekiel liked to boast that he'd never been to school in his life and had taught himself to read by a tallow candle after working hours. But he was much quicker-witted man than Father, he could argue with anybody, and he used to quote Carlyle and Spencer by the year. Father had a slow sort of mind, he'd never taken to 'book-learning', as he called it, and his English wasn't good. On Sunday afternoons, the only time when he took things easy, he'd settle down by the parlour fireplace to have what he called a 'good read' at the Sunday paper (ibid).

Most of the time, he says, his father was overwhelmed by business. 'There wasn't really such a lot to do but he seemed to be always busy, either in the loft behind the yard, struggling about with sacks and bales or in the kind of dusty little cubby-hole behind the counter in the shop, adding figures up with a stump of pencil' (ibid: 456). Yet Orwell, through his narrator Bowling, is keen to show the gender dynamics in the workplace: the shop was Father's business, Mother's job, 'the woman's work', on the other hand, 'was to look after the house and the meals and the laundry and the children. She'd have a fit if she'd seen Father or anyone else of the male sex trying to sew on a button for himself' (ibid: 458). Again, Mother never said grace at mealtimes – it 'had to be someone of the male sex' (ibid: 460).

On the question of discipline, Mother was the firmer. 'Father was always "going to" give Joe [Bowling's brother who, in the end, leaves home – never to be seen again] a good hiding, and he used to tell us stories, which I now believe were lies, about the frightful thrashings his own father used to give him with a leather strap, but nothing ever came of it. By the time Joe was twelve he was too strong for Mother to get him across her knee, and after that there was no doing anything with him' (ibid: 458).

Fishing plays a highly symbolic role in the novel. Bowling dwells at length on his teenage obsession with the sport, his love of the solitude it requires, and his joy at catching enormous carp in the pond at Binfield House. He reflects: 'I *am* sentimental about my childhood – not my particular childhood but the civilization which I grew up in and which is now, I suppose, just about at its last kick. And fishing is somehow typical of that civilization. As soon as you think of fishing you think of things that don't belong to the modern world' (ibid: 473, italics in the original). Significantly, it's his father who has given him his first fishing rod – for Christmas in 1903 (ibid: 471).

After fishing, reading comes a close second obsession for Bowling. And as he tells of his own reading interests (the Left Book Club etc), his thoughts inevitably turn to Father. There were hardly any books in their house and Father had never read a book in his life 'except the Bible and Smiles's *Self Help*...' (ibid: 481).

As the narrative moves on, his father's business is hit by competition. The inexorable rise of monopoly capitalism was in the process of eliminating small firms – seemingly out of the control of 'ordinary people'. George reflects: 'None of us had any grasp of what was happening' (ibid: 485).

> Father was worried, puzzled and vaguely resentful. I can see him yet, with the meal on his bald head, and the bit of grey hair over his ears, and his spectacles and his grey moustache. He couldn't understand what was happening to him. For years his profits had gone up, slowly and steadily, ten pounds this year, twenty pounds that year, and now suddenly they'd gone down with a bump. He couldn't understand it (ibid: 484).

So George leaves school and goes to work at Grimmett's shop – and stays there for six years. After service in the war, his parents die. One day, walking down Charing Cross, in central London, a poster proclaiming 'KING ZOG'S WEDDING POSTPONED' together with the sound of traffic and smell of horse-dung bring back memories of his childhood – and he resolves to lie to his wife, take time off work and spend some time back in Lower Binfield rediscovering the Golden Age of his youth (ibid: 445). But as Gordon Bowker summarises: 'The journey is doomed – the small town had been engulfed by suburbia and his woodland paradise infested with fruit juice-drinking, sandal-wearing, nudist vegetarians and Garden City cranks. The Golden Age is done for...' (2003: 250). Significantly, the memory that dominates during his trip is that of his father. Not surprisingly, he is determined to see his shop.

> It was funny. Twenty-one years ago, the day of mother's funeral, I'd pass it in the station fly, and seen it all shut up and dusty, with the sign burnt off with a plumber's blowflame, and I hadn't cared a damn. And now, when I was so much further away from it, when there were actually details about the inside of the house that I couldn't remember, the thought of seeing it again did things to my heart and guts (op cit: 541).

The transformation of his father's workplace into a teashop symbolises the terrible decline in Lower Binfield for George. 'Father and mother,' he stresses 'have never faded out of my mind. It's as if they existed somewhere or other in a kind of eternity, Mother behind the brown teapot, Father with his bald head a little mealy, and his spectacles and his grey moustache, fixed for ever like people in a picture, and yet in some way, alive' (ibid: 543).

George Bowling's dissatisfaction with his lot as a father is also a central theme of the novel. He wins seventeen quid on a bet and secretly places the money in a bank: 'A good husband would have spent it on a dress for Hilda (that's my wife) and boots for the kids. But I'd been a good husband and father for fifteen years and I was beginning to get fed up with it' (ibid: 432)

He ponders his plight as one of the residents of Ellesmere Road – and it's horrifying: 'Just a prison with the cells all in a row. A line of semi-detached torture-chambers where the poor little five-to-ten-pound-a-weekers quake and shiver, every one of them with the boss twisting his tail and his wife riding him like a nightmare and the kids sucking his blood like leeches' (ibid: 435-436).

When he returns home and his wife, Hilda, confronts him with the evidence that he has been lying, he tries to invent excuses. In the end, George is left with three options: to tell her what he'd really been doing and somehow make her believe him; to 'pull the old gag about losing my memory', and to let Hilda go on thinking he had been with a woman and 'take his medicine'. But George ends cunningly: 'But, damn it. I knew which it would have to be' (ibid: 571). Yet significantly in this final scene, George is acting entirely as a *husband*. He has completely forgotten his role as a *father*. The trip down memory lane has shocked him so much that it has erased – at least for a time – his identity as a father. That is the hidden – and largely over-looked – tragedy in the story.

NINETEEN EIGHTY-FOUR (1949): FATHERS' BASIC ROLE – TO PRODUCE WILLING SLAVES OF THE SECRET STATE

The bleakest picture of fatherhood comes in Orwell's last novel. Orwell represents Oceania as hyper-puritanical: the aim of Party is to remove all pleasure from the sexual act; all marriages have to be approved by committee; permission is refused if the couple give the impression of being physically attracted to one another; the only recognised purpose of marriage is to beget children to serve the Party; sexual intercourse is seen as a slightly disgusting minor operation, like having an enema – and the Junior Anti-Sex league advocates complete celibacy for both sexes (Orwell 2000 [1949]: 75). In addition, all children are to be begotten by artificial insemination (artsem in Newspeak, the language of the state) and raised in public institutions. At the same time, promiscuity is permitted amongst the proles – and pornography is produced specially for them in Pornosec, a sub-section of the Fiction Department (ibid: 50). Towards the end of the novel, as O'Brien tortures Winston, he pronounces (ibid: 306):

> We have cut the links between child and parent, and between man and man, and between man and woman. No one dares trust a wife or a child or a friend any longer. But in the future there will be no wives and no friends. … The sex instinct will be eradicated. Procreation will be an annual formality like the renewal of a ration card. We shall abolish the orgasm.

Winston Smith, the anti-hero of the novel, appears as a disgruntled husband engaging in a passionate, secret – and ultimately doomed – affair with Julia, the 'girl from the Fiction Department'. Rather, his colleague at the Ministry of Truth, Tom Parsons, comes to represent Oceania's archetypal father. He lives with his wife – both of them totally dedicated to the Party – in a dingy, messy flat.

> Everything had a battered, trampled-on look, as though the place had been visited by some large violent animal. Games impedimenta – hockey sticks, boxing gloves, a burst football, a pair of sweaty shorts turned inside out – lay all over the floor, and on the table there was a litter of dirty dishes and dog-eared exercise books. On the walls were scarlet banners of the Youth League and the Spies and a full-sized poster of Big Brother (ibid: 25).

Most frightening of all, Parsons' two children, a boy of nine and a girl about two years younger, are shown as super-enthusiastic Spies for the Party and keen to see the latest public hanging of a traitor (ibid: 25-27). In this way, Orwell highlights the horror of Big Brother totalitarianism in which a father's basic role is to produce willing slaves of the secret state.[1]

ORWELL AS A FATHER: CONFOUNDING ALL EXPECTATIONS

Orwell had long expressed his wish to become a father. For instance, in April 1940, when his friends Rayner and Margaret Heppenstall celebrate the birth of a daughter, he says: 'What a wonderful thing to have a kid of one's own. I've always wanted one' (Meyers 2000: 227). But by 1944, after eight years of marriage to Eileen O'Shaughnessy, it becomes clear that they are not able to have a child of their own. 'Orwell believed he was biologically sterile, though he never actually took the test which he thought would be "disgusting". He had a similar distaste for condoms and seems not to have used them' (ibid). Eileen, exhausted by ill health and looking after Orwell, is reluctant to become a parent. But, she eventually succumbs to his persistence – and in June 1944, after Gwen O'Shaughnessy,

Eileen's sister-in-law, is told by her doctor partner that a child has become available, they adopt Richard Robertson, born to Nancy Robinson, a married woman living nearby in Greenwich, south London, whose husband is away at the front, on 14 May (Topp 2020: 377). Both parents are thrilled with their baby whom they name Richard Horatio Blair.

Yet soon afterwards, in February 1945, Orwell sets off to the Continent to report on the final days of the Second World War for his friend, David Astor's *Observer* – and *Manchester Evening News* (*MEN*). As Sylvia Topp comments perceptively on the complex emotional strands in the relationship:

> Once again, just as he had interrupted his joyful marriage after six months to fight in Spain [in December 1936], he abruptly left alone at home the son he loved and the wife who had newly dedicated herself to him, while he followed the retreating German troops, an activity he knew to be extremely dangerous. … Orwell must have realised on some level how seriously ill Eileen was. He knew she often spent days in bed and was getting weaker. But she continued to refuse to admit to herself, let alone tell him, that she needed him at home. Perhaps she was afraid he would reject her wishes even if she did ask him to stay (ibid: 393).

There is another side to the story. In September 1944, Orwell visits the Scottish island of Jura which he begins to imagine as a home for his new family far away from the demands of journalism and London. W. J. West (1992: 122-124) suggests that the main motive for Orwell taking on the assignment is to earn a 'large lump sum' to help pay for this move. Davison records (1996: 472) that Orwell earned £500 (£100 a month) from the *Observer* for his assignment. But at £35 an article, he suggests, this was not particularly large. The need for money also appears to be behind Orwell's links with the *MEN*. John Beavan, London editor of the *Manchester Guardian*, tells Fyvel that after adopting Richard, Orwell declared his need for a regular income and so Beavan has arranged a weekly book-reviewing assignment for the *MEN* (Fyvel 1982: 128-129). Moreover, Orwell could well have been on some kind of intelligence mission for Astor – which he clearly considered crucial in the country's fight against Nazi Germany (Keeble 2001). Tragically, while Orwell is away on the Continent, Eileen dies on the operating table at a Newcastle hospital, aged just 39. Orwell is left a widower – in constant search of a woman to join him and help look after little Richard.

Yet, much to the surprise of his friends, Orwell proves to be a remarkably affectionate, devoted and hands-on father. As Bernard Crick comments (1980: 464): '… he mastered the domestic arts of fatherhood with skill and pleasure.' For Christmas 1945, he spends time with Arthur and Mamaime Koestler at their farmhouse near Blaenau Ffestiniog in Merionethshire not far from Bertrand Russell's home. 'There were long walks and talks that Christmas. Orwell would carry Richard along on his hip and Celia Kirwan [then separated from her husband

and seeking a divorce] noticed how competently he coped with the little boy, bathing and changing him as if to the manner born, relaxed and unanxious about him – practical abilities very unusual in fathers of his generation' (ibid: 483). Michael Scammell comments on this same gathering in his biography of Koestler (2009: 265):

> At the Christmas gathering in Wales Celia Paget and Mamaine Koestler were both impressed by the skilful way he carried Richard on his hip and bathed and changed him with total confidence. Koestler was less enamoured of the baby who drove him to distraction by clambering over him in smelly diapers, then crawling about the house and then turning everything upside down. He felt that Orwell was too lenient with the child. But when the baby woke one morning while the exhausted Orwell was trying to sleep (he and the baby shared a room), Koestler spent an entire hour making faces through the bars of Richard's cot so Orwell could get some rest.

Biographer D. J. Taylor comments (2003: 361):

> Orwell's treatment of Richard seemed to combine lavish affection with comical cack-handedness. He asked Mary Fyvel if she would like to watch Richard have his bath. Mary suggested it would be a good idea to close the bathroom window which was admitting freezing January air. Orwell agreed enthusiastically. The bath over, he picked up Richard, draped him – undried – in a flimsy towel and carried him off along the icy passage to the sitting room. Again, advice on the correct procedure was gratefully received. ... Orwell accepted compliments on his upbringing with suitable gravity. 'Yes. You see I've always been good with animals.'

And Orwell's great friend David Astor, later editor of the *Observer*, comments, when I interview him at his London home in 2000, just a year before he dies: 'I saw him bath Richard with the greatest care but with a cigarette in his mouth' (Keeble 2020b: 41).

Orwell's relaxed intimacy with his son and clear enjoyment of being a father is captured beautifully in the photographs taken of them together in Islington, north London, by the anarchist Vernon Richards (1998: 9-14). Born Vero Ricchioni, the son of a leading Italian anarchist, he married Marie Louise Berneri, daughter of an anarchist leader murdered by the communists in Spain. In one photograph, Richard sits on Orwell's lap as his shoe laces are being done; in others, Orwell is pushing his son in a pram down a London street with a look of quiet contentment on his face.

Richard Blair, now retired and Patron of The Orwell Society, sums up: 'My father was completely devoted to me. When Eileen died, he really cared for me, which was very rare at that time. He fed me, changed my clothes and nappies, he gave me baths: most fathers at that time never did that sort of thing' (2019).

CONCLUSION

This essay has highlighted the significance of fatherhood in both Orwell's life and writings. Most commentators have placed the reconciliation between father and son to the late 1930s – yet there is considerable evidence to suggest it begins much earlier. Richard Blair tends to be considered a dull and grumpy old man. His courage in volunteering for the army in 1917 when he is 60 has not been sufficiently acknowledged – nor has his understandable change of personality once he relaxes into retirement in the Suffolk coastal resort of Southwold.

The extraordinary courage that Orwell shows throughout his life together with his constant, quirky desire to surprise and confound expectations may well have been traits he inherits from his father. The essay also shows how fatherhood remains a constant preoccupation in Orwell's novels. Finally, Orwell, in demonstrating such intimate and constant devotion to his son, Richard, particularly as they live the 'simple life' in the remote house, Barnhill, on the Scottish island of Jura, proves himself to be a 'New Man' well before the term is coined.

NOTE

[1] How shocking it is then that today in the Britain the state uses children as spies. See https://www.independent.co.uk/news/uk/home-news/child-spies-uk-mi5-police-security-services-gangs-terrorism-police-high-court-a8995606.html. Moreover, Britain is the only state in Europe where children as young as 16 can join the armed services. See https://www.channel4.com/news/exploitation-or-proud-tradition-britains-child-soldiers#:~:text=Britain%20is%20the%20only%20nation%20in%20Europe%20and,children%20can%20only%20join%20with%20their%20parents%E2%80%99%20consent. More soldiers are recruited at 16 than at any other age

REFERENCES

Blair, Richard (2019) George Orwell today, *franceculture.fr*, 4 October. Available online at https://www.franceculture.fr/emissions/linvite-des-matins/george-orwell-au-present. Translation from the French by the author

Bowker, Gordon (2003) *George Orwell*, London: Little, Brown

Buddicom, Jacintha (2006 [1974]) *Eric & Us*, Chichester: Finlay Publisher, with a postscript by Dione Venables

Colls, Robert (2013) *George Orwell: English Rebel*, Oxford: Oxford University Press

Davison, Peter (1996) *George Orwell: A Literary Life*, Basingstoke: Macmillan

Crick, Bernard (1980) *George Orwell: A Life*, Harmondsworth, Middlesex: Penguin

CWGO (1998) *The Complete Works of George Orwell*, XX Vols, Davison, Peter (ed.) London: Secker & Warburg

Fyvel, T. R. (1982) *George Orwell: A Personal Memoir*, London: Weidenfeld & Nicolson

Hitchens, Christopher (2002) *Orwell's Victory*, London: Allen Lane/Penguin Press

Hurst, L. J. (2019) Neither lions nor donkeys: Richard Walmesley Blair and the mules, Orwell Society *Journal*, No. 14, spring pp 20-23

Keeble, Richard (2001) George Orwell as a war correspondent: A reassessment, *Journalism Studies*, Vol. 2, No. 3 pp 393-406

Keeble, Richard Lance (2020a) Orwell and dress: The naked truth?, *George Orwell Studies*, Vol. 4, No. 2 pp 78-94

Keeble, Richard Lance (2020b) *George Orwell, the Secret State and the Making of Nineteen Eighty-Four*, Bury St Edmunds: Abramis

Meyers, Jeffrey (2000) *George Orwell: Wintry Conscience of a Generation*, New York and London: W. W. Norton

Orwell, George (1976 [1935]) *A Clergyman's Daughter*, in the *Collected Fiction*, London: Secker & Warburg/Octopus pp 255-425

Orwell, George (1976 [1939]) *Coming Up For Air*, in the *Collected Fiction*, London: Secker & Warburg/Octopus pp 431-471

Orwell, George (2000 [1949]) *Nineteen Eighty-Four*, London: Penguin, with an introduction by Thomas Pynchon

Orwell, George (1970 [1946]) Why I write, Orwell, Sonia and Angus, Ian (eds) *The Collected Essays, Journalism and Letters, Vol. 1: An Age Like This*, Harmondsworth, Middlesex: Penguin pp 23-30; originally published in *Gangrel*, No. 4, summer

Richards, Vernon (1998) Orwell the humanist, *George Orwell at Home (and among the anarchists)*, London: Freedom Press pp 9-14

Scammell, Michael (2009) *Koestler: The Literary and Political Odyssey of a Twentieth Century Skeptic*, New York: Random House

Stansky, Peter and Abrahams, William (1972) *The Unknown Orwell*, London: Constable

Sutherland, John (2016) *Orwell's Nose: A Pathological Biography*, London: Reaktion Books

Taylor, D. J. (2003) *Orwell: The Life*, London: Chatto & Windus

Topp, Sylvia (2020) *Eileen: The Making of George Orwell*, London: Unbound

West, W. J. (1992) *The Larger Evils*: Nineteen Eighty-Four – *The Truth Behind the Satire*, Edinburgh: Canongate Press

- **This essay originally appeared as 'The heart of the matter: Orwell and fatherhood', part 1, Orwellsociety.com, 30 April; part 2, https://orwellsociety.com/the-heart-of-the-matter-1/, https://orwellsociety.com/the-heart-of-the-matter-2/, 2 May 2020; part 3, https://orwellsociety.com/the-heart-of-the-matter-3/ 4 May 2020**

Chapter Three

Advertisements and the Political Economy of the Media

George Orwell, throughout his career as a novelist and journalist, maintains a fascination with advertisements. This focus ties in particular with the political economy approach he adopts in his analyses of the operations and content of newspapers and magazines – and with his interests in propaganda and language. Orwell is interested in the ways advertisements reflect the politics and financial status of media consumers – and he often sees the quirky and the humorous in his analyses of ads. This chapter examines critically his comments on advertisements dotted about his diaries, in his 'state of the nation' essays, in his 'As I Please' columns in the leftist journal, *Tribune*, in the 'London Letters' he composes for the American journal, *Partisan Review* – and in his novel *Keep the Aspidistra Flying* (1936) where the world of advertising features so prominently and symbolically. His fascination with the political function of advertising culminates in his depiction of the propaganda posters in the Big Brother world of his dystopian masterpiece *Nineteen Eighty-Four* (1949) – published just days before his untimely death at 46.

ADVERTISING AND THE MYTH OF MEDIA FREEDOM

Throughout all his writings on the press Orwell maintains a consistent 'political economy' approach, questioning the notion of press freedom, stressing the impact of advertisers and proprietorial control on content – and highlighting the close integration of mainstream newspapers with dominant financial, political and military interests and their essential propaganda role for the wealthy (Keeble 2020).

Significantly, his first published piece in the UK, 'A farthing newspaper' (for Chesterton's review *G. K's Weekly*) adopts a political economy approach that he is to maintain throughout his writing career (Orwell 1970 [1928]: 34-37). *Ami du Peuple*, costing just ten centimes, has recently been launched in Paris with a manifesto claiming it is 'uncontaminated by any base thoughts of gain' (ibid: 34). Eric Blair (as he then was) adds, ironically:

> The proprietors, who hide their blushes in anonymity, are emptying their pockets for the mere pleasure of doing good by stealth. Their objects, we learn, are to make war on the great trusts, to fight for a lower cost of living and above all combat the powerful newspapers which are strangling free speech in France (ibid: 34-35).

He proceeds to deconstruct, with polemical vigour, the paper's pretensions – noting that its proprietor is M. Coty 'a great industrial capitalist and also proprietor of the *Figaro* and the *Gaulois*'. In other words, it is merely putting across 'the sort of propaganda wanted by M. Coty and his associates' (see Dulley 2015: 16-17).

Underlying Orwell's comments on the press throughout his career (from that early essay on *Ami du Peuple*, of 1928, onwards) is a desire to highlight the economic factors impacting on its operations and political bias. For instance, in *The Lion and the Unicorn* (1970 [1941a]), written during some of the bleakest days of the Second World War when Britain seriously feared invasion by the Nazis, he writes bluntly: 'Is the English press honest or dishonest? At normal times it is deeply dishonest. All the papers that matter live off their advertisements and the advertisers exercise an indirect censorship over news' (ibid: 88).

Orwell now returns to his long-standing, political economy critique, highlighting the impact of advertising and proprietorial monopolies on press content:

> The unbearable silliness of English newspapers from about 1900 onwards has two main causes. One is that nearly the whole of the press is in the hands of a few big capitalists who are interested in the continuance of capitalism and therefore in preventing the public from learning to think: the other is that in peacetime newspapers live off advertisements for consumption goods, building societies, cosmetics and the like and are therefore interested in maintaining a 'sunshine mentality' which will induce people to spend money. ... Therefore, don't let people know the facts about the political and economic situation; divert their attention to giant pandas, channel swimmers, royal weddings and other soothing topics (ibid).

In one of the 'London Letters' he contributes to the American leftist journal, *Partisan Review*, in 1941, he says he has detected a change in tone of the popular press which have become 'politically serious while preserving their "stunt" make-up with screaming headlines etc' (Orwell 1970 [1941b]: 137-138).

And detailed observations on advertisements feature in his 'London Letter' for the November-December 1942. He writes:

> One periodical reminder that things *have changed* in England since the war is the arrival of American magazines, with their enormous bulk, sleek paper and riot of brilliantly coloured adverts urging you to spend your money on trash. English adverts before the war were no doubt less colourful and enterprising than the American ones, but their mental atmosphere was similar, and the sight of a full-page ad on shiny paper gives one the sensation of stepping back into 1939. ... An extraordinary feature of the time is advertisements for products which no longer exist. To give just one example: the word IRON in large letters, with underneath it an impressive picture of a tank, and underneath that a little essay on the importance of collecting scrap iron for salvage; at the bottom, in tiny print, a reminder that after the war Iron Jelloids will be on sale as before (Orwell 1970 [1942]: 270-271; italics in the original).

He moves on to consider much broader, complex issues such as workers' attitudes to the war and the future of capitalism, no less. So he highlights the 'strange fact' – recently reported by the Mass Observers and confirmed by his own limited experience – that many factory workers are actually afraid of the war ending since they foresee a return to the old conditions with three million unemployed etc. He continues:

> The idea that *whatever happens* old-style capitalism is doomed and we are in much more danger of forced labour than of unemployment, hasn't reached the masses except as a vague notion that 'things will be different' (ibid: 271; italics in the original).

He returns to the main theme observing: 'The advertisements that have been least changed by the war are those of theatres and patent medicines' (ibid).

Orwell's preoccupation with advertising often crops up in unlikely places. For instance, he begins a long review essay on *Beggar my Neighbour*, by Lionel Fielden, for *Horizon*, September 1943, reprinted in *Partisan Review*, in the Winter 1944 edition, with this somewhat idiosyncratic comment:

> If you compare commercial advertising with political propaganda, one thing that strikes you is its relative intellectual honesty. The advertiser at least knows what he is aiming at – that is, money – whereas the propagandist, when he is not a lifeless hack, is often a neurotic working off some private grudge and actually desirous of the exact opposite of the thing he advocates (Orwell 1970 [1943]: 349).

THE PLEASURE OF ANALYSING ADS

In 1943, Orwell quits as Talks Producer for the Eastern Service after two largely unhappy years at the BBC and becomes literary editor of the leftist journal *Tribune*.

As part of his role, between 1943 and 1947 he composes 80 'As I Please' columns. And his preoccupations with many aspects of advertising are regularly given full rein.

In an 'As I Please' column in 1944, he focuses yet again on the subject of advertising, suggesting that, during the war, the 'advertiser has temporarily lost his grip' and so newspapers 'are far more intelligent than they were five years ago' (Orwell 1998 [1944a]: 146). 'At the same time there has been an increase in censorship and official interference, but this is not nearly so crippling and not nearly so conducive to sheer silliness. It is better to be controlled by bureaucrats than by common swindlers' (ibid). His unrelenting critique continues:

> Most newspapers remain completely reckless about details of fact. The belief that what is 'in the papers' must be true has been gradually evaporating ever since Northcliffe set out to vulgarise journalism, and the war has not yet arrested the process. Many people frankly say that they take in such and such a paper because it is lively but that they don't believe a word of what it says (ibid).

Orwell even examines – originally and with great wit – the links between advertising, government propaganda and a short story in *Home Companion and Family Journal* (possibly purchased by his wife, Eileen Blair, and left about their flat in Mortimer Crescent, London NW6) in an 'As I Please' column of 25 February 1944. The story, he notes, tells of the adventures of a young girl named Lucy Fallows who works on the switchboard of a long-distance telephone exchange. Her job, normally boring, suddenly livens up and she finds herself in the midst of thrilling adventures involving the sinking of a U-boat, the capture of a German sabotage crew and a long motorcycle ride with a handsome naval officer (Orwell 1998 [1944b]: 103). At the end, there is this short note:

> Any of our young readers themselves interested in the work of the Long Distance Telephone Exchange … should apply to the Staff Controller, L. T. R., London, who will inform them as to the opportunities open (ibid).

This sets Orwell off on an extraordinary creative riff. First, he questions whether the advertisement will have any success: 'I should doubt whether even girls of the age aimed at would believe that capturing U-boats enters very largely into the lives of telephone operators.' But he notes, 'with interest', 'the direct correlation between a Government recruiting advertisement and a piece of commercial fiction'. Such stories are probably not written to order; rather, the departments concerned keep their eye on the weekly papers and 'push in an ad. when any story seems likely to form an attractive bait'. Orwell relishes in the absurdity of it all: he imagines 'some stripe-trousered personage in the GPO reading "Hullo, Sweetheart" as part of his official duties'. He continues with this hilarious, invented dialogue:

'Hullo, Hullo. Is that you, Tony? Oh, hullo. Look here, I've got another script for you, Tony, "A Ticket to Paradise". It's bus conductresses this time. They are not coming in. I believe the trousers don't fit, or something. Well, any way, Peter says make it sexy, but kind of clean – *you* know. Nothing extramarital. We want the stuff in by Tuesday. Fifteen thousand words. You can choose the hero. I rather favour the kind of outdoor man that dogs and kiddies all love him – you know. Or very tall with a sensitive mouth. I don't mind really. But pile on the sex, Peter says' (ibid: 103-104).

Orwell ends this opening section of the column in a reflective mood, moving from the specific and seemingly trivial to the more general and important cultural/political issue: 'Something resembling this already happens with radio features and documentary films, but hitherto there has not been any very direct connection between fiction and propaganda. That half-inch in the *Home Companion* seems to mark another small stage in the process of "co-ordination" that is gradually happening to all the arts.'

Incidentally, on 10 March, *Tribune* published a note from the editor of *Home Companion* saying the magazine received 'no payment or other consideration' from the GPO or any other government department for publishing the note. Orwell, as ever keen to engage with his readers, says he never suggested that the Amalgamated Press received payment for publishing the story, but if he seemed to imply this he apologises. He continues: 'I would still like to know, however, who was responsible for inserting the "little note" and for its precise wording, with instructions as to where to apply for a job' (ibid: 105).

In another 'As I Please' column on 9 June 1944, Orwell highlights (with almost venomous fury) the ways in which the proprietorial and advertiser control of the press impacts even on the content of literary reviews and what he describes as 'the book racket' (Orwell 1998 [1944c]):

> The literary papers of several well-known papers were practically owned by a handful of publishers who had their quislings planted in all the important jobs. These wretches churned forth their praise – 'masterpiece', 'brilliant', 'unforgettable' and so forth – like so many mechanical pianos. A book coming from the right publishers could be absolutely certain not only of favourable reviews, but of being placed on the 'recommended' list which industrious book-borrowers would cut out and take to the library the next day (ibid: 251-252).

On the power of advertisers, he writes: 'A book coming from a big publisher, who habitually spent large sums on advertisement, might get fifty or seventy-five reviews: a book from a small publisher might get only twenty' (ibid: 252).

Reading *Old Moore's Almanac* reminds him of the fun and games he had as a youth somewhat mischievously answering advertisements. In his 'As I Please' column on 24 November 1944, he lists – with evident relish – advertisements 'some of which have remained totally unchanged for at least thirty years': 'Increase your height, earn five pounds a week in your spare time, drink habit conquered in three days, electric belts, bust developers and cures for obesity, insomnia, bunions, backache, red noses, stammering, blushing, piles, bad legs, flat feet and baldness' (ibid: 472).

Many years ago, he says, he answered an advertisement from Winifred Grace Hartland who undertook to cure obesity. She replied – assuming him to be a woman – urging him to come and see her at once. 'Do come,' she writes, 'before ordering your summer frocks, as after taking my course your figure would have altered out of all recognition.' Orwell continues, revelling in the deception:

> She was particularly insistent that I should make a personal visit and gave an address somewhere in London Docks. This went on for a long time, during which the fee gradually sank from two guineas to half a crown, and then I brought the matter to an end by writing to say that I had been cured of my obesity by a rival agency (ibid).

He adds that later the magazine *Truth* revealed there was no such person as Winifred Grace Hartland; rather it was a swindle run by two American crooks, Harry Sweet and Dave Little. And Orwell ends this section, wittily, rather quirkily and with a pinch of schoolboyish 'naughtiness': 'It is curious they should have been so anxious for a personal visit, and indeed I have since wondered whether Harry Sweet and Dave Little were actually engaged in shipping consignments of fat women to the harems of Istanbul' (ibid: 473).

Orwell returns to the issue in his 17 November 1944 column. The proprietors have sent him the current issue of the *Writer* which he had wrongly stated earlier as being defunct. He is happy to correct himself, but goes on to examine the advertisements of people selling their journalism training services. One, for instance, reads: 'Plotting without tears. Learn my way. The simplest method ever. Money returned if dissatisfied. 5 shillings post free' (Orwell 1998 [1944d]: 464). Orwell comments with merciless wit: isn't it curious that the trainers are rarely well-known writers? 'If Bernard Shaw or J. B. Priestley offered to teach you how to make money out of writing, you might feel that there was something in it. But who would buy a bottle of hair restorer from a bald man?' (ibid).

Orwell constantly and deliberately subverts the expectations of his readers – moving his attention to ever-changing, surprisingly original topics. Thus, his 'As I Please' column, on 8 November 1946, begins: 'Someone has just sent me a copy of an American fashion magazine which shall be nameless' (Orwell 1998 [1946a]: 471). In fact, it was *Vogue*, which had been posted to his London address because, amongst its many photographs of glamorous women, was a profile of Orwell. So he proceeds to deconstruct the magazine, noting: 'One striking thing when one looks at these pictures is the overbred, exhausted, even decadent style of beauty that now seems to be striven after. Nearly all of these women are immensely elongated.' On the prose style of the advertisements, he says it's 'an extraordinary mixture of sheer lushness with clipped and sometimes very expressive technical jargon'. And, typically, Orwell focuses on what's missing: 'A fairly diligent search through the magazine reveals two discreet allusions to grey hair, but if there is anywhere a direct mention of fatness or middle age I have not found it. Birth and death are not mentioned either: nor is work, except that a few recipes for breakfast dishes as given' (ibid).

Another intriguing way of critiquing the press and highlighting the crucial function of advertisements appears in the 'As I Please' column on 22 November 1946. Here Orwell simply presents two lists and subjects them to 'ironic reversal', as Alex Woloch points out (2016: 246): one shows major newspapers in order of intelligence (*Manchester Guardian, Times, News Chronicle, Telegraph, Herald, Mail, Mirror, Express, Graphic*); the other in order of popularity (*Express, Herald, Mirror, News Chronicle, Mail, Graphic, Telegraph, Times, Manchester Guardian*). He comments (Orwell 1998 [1946b]: 500): 'It will be seen that the second list is very nearly – not quite, for life is never so neat as that – the first turned upside down.' For Orwell, the solution lies in the alternative press: 'In these circumstances it is difficult to foresee a radical change, even if the special kind of pressure exerted by owners and advertisers is removed. What matters is that in England we do possess juridical liberty of the Press, which makes it possible to utter one's true opinions fearlessly in papers of comparatively small circulation' (ibid).

ADVERTISING – THE 'RATTLING OF A STICK INSIDE A SWILL-BUCKET'

Advertising plays a crucial role both symbolically and in the narrative of Orwell's novel *Keep the Aspidistra Flying* (1976 [1936]: 573-737). As Gordon Bowker argues, it is a novel bursting with Rabelaisian gaiety and high spirits (2003: 171) and ads become a focus for Orwell's ironic banter and mischievous wordplay – as well as his critique of Americanised capitalism.

Gordon Comstock, the anti-hero, is a poverty-stricken aspiring poet belonging to 'the most dismal of all classes, the middle-middle class, the landed gentry' (op cit: 598). When we first meet him he is working at Mr McKechnie's bookshop. Significantly, the streets around it are completely taken over by advertisements:

> Opposite, next to the Prince of Wales, were tall hoardings covered with ads for patent foods and patent medicines. A gallery of monstrous doll-faces – pink vacuous faces, full of goofy optimism. Q. T. Sauce, Truweet Breakfast Crisps ('Kiddies clamour for their Breakfast Crisps'), Kangaroo Burgundy, Vitamalt Chocolate, Bovex. Of them all, the Bovex one oppressed Gordon the most. A spectacled rat-faced clerk, with patent-leather hair, sitting at a café table grinning over a white mug of Bovex. 'Corner Table enjoys his meal with Bovex,' the legend ran (ibid: 578).

Gordon's eyes remain fixed on the advertisements that inspire a kind of poetic flourish: 'The poster that advertised Q. T. Sauce was torn at the edge, a ribbon of paper fluttered fitfully like a tiny pennant' (ibid: 579). He struggles with the first two lines of a new poem. Orwell continues: 'His eyes refocused themselves on the posters opposite. He had his private reasons for hating them. Mechanically he re-read their slogans. "Kangaroo Burgundy – the wine for Britons." "Asthma was choking her." "Q. T. Sauce Keep Hubby Smiling" …' (ibid).

In another interval between dealing with his bookshop customers, Gordon again looks at the ads.

> He really hated them this time. That Vitamalt one, for instance. 'Hike all day on a slab of Vitamalt.' A youthful couple, boy and girl, in clean-minded hiking kit, their hair picturesquely tousled by the wind, climbing a stile against a Sussex landscape. That girl's face. The awful bright tomboy cheeriness of it. The kind of girl who goes in for Plenty of Clean Fun. Windswept. Tight khaki shorts but that doesn't mean you can pinch her backside. And next to them – Corner Table. 'Corner Table enjoys his meal with Bovex.' Gordon examined the thing with the intimacy of hatred. The idiotic grinning face, like the face of a self-satisfied rat, the slick black hair, the silly spectacles… (ibid: 584-585).

When Gordon looks at the ads he associates them with the 'sense of disintegration, of decay, that is endemic in our time' (ibid: 586). 'He looked now with more seeing eyes at those grinning yard-wide faces. After all, there was more than mere silliness, greed and vulgarity. Corner Table grins at you, seemingly optimistic, with a flash of false teeth. But what is behind the grin? Desolation, emptiness, prophesies of doom.'

Given Gordon's hatred of the world of advertising, it is somewhat ironic that he suddenly acquires a job in the accounts department of the New Albion Publicity Company – through a 'friend of a friend' of his lady friend's employer's brother, as Orwell explains, highlighting subtly and wittily the ways in which nepotism plays such a crucial role in the operations of capitalism. New Albion 'designed a certain number of large-scale posters for oatmeal stout, self-raising flour, and so forth, but its main line was millinery and cosmetic advertisements in the women's illustrated papers, besides minor ads in twopenny weeklies, such as Whiterose Pills for Female Disorders, Your Horoscope Cast by Professor Raratonga, The Seven Secrets of Venus, New Hope for the Ruptured, Earn Five Pounds a Week in your Spare Time, and Cyprolax Hair Lotion Banishes all Unpleasant Intruders' (ibid: 607-608). Lists always hold a fascination for Orwell and it is clear here how he relishes piling on the details of the silly slogans one after another.

The outraged, obsessive voices of the narrator and Gordon come together to condemn advertising as nothing less than 'the dirtiest ramp' of modern, American-style capitalism. 'Most of the employees were hard-boiled, Americanized, go-getting type to whom nothing in the world is sacred, except money. They had their cynical code worked out. The public are swine; advertising is the rattling of a stick inside a swill-bucket. And yet beneath their cynicism there was the final naïveté, the blind worship of the money-god' (ibid: 608).

In the course of the novel, Gordon quits his job at New Albion, pursues Rosemary, gets drunk, and ends up in a police cell – only for his aristocratic editor friend Ravelston (modelled on Orwell's friend, Sir Richard Rees) to pay the fine. After all that, Gordon returns to work at the bookshop. But when Rosemary becomes pregnant they reject the idea of an abortion and decide to wed and settle for a life of respectability – complete with an aspidistra in their flat off the Edgware Road. Symbolic of this retreat to bourgeois life (previously condemned in the novel for its stultifying emptiness and deadness), is Gordon's return to New Albion. In no time, he is promoted to work alongside a Mr Clew writing ads for a new deodorant produced by the Queen of Sheba Toilet Requisites Co. 'Gordon watched his own development, first with surprise, then with amusement and finally with a kind of horror. *This*, then, was what he was coming to. Writing lies to tickle the money out of fools' packets' (ibid: 609; italics in the original). He even invents a slogan: 'P. P.'

Orwell has an enormous amount of fun throughout the novel playing with the language he uses to evoke the world of advertising. The New Albion Publicity Co. is the actual name of the firm run by the father of one of his friends, Michael Sayers, and Orwell is clearly pleased to have slipped that past his publishers. When Gordon meets Rosemary for the first time, he strokes her face in the night-time darkness and quotes four lines in medieval French (attributed to Villon). When Rosemary asks him to translate he does so. In fact, it's a subtle invitation to *fellatio*. Not surprisingly Rosemary refuses – despite Gordon's persistent pleas for her to satisfy him. So again, Orwell has had fun deceiving the censor. Another Orwellian joke is the name he gives his anti-hero – for Comstock (1844-1915) was a notorious anti-vice campaigner in the States who opposed abortion, prostitution, gambling and contraception (see Bowker 2003: 171; Werbel 2018). He even enjoys playing around with the slogan 'P. P.' – exposing at the same time both the cynicism and naïveté of the advertisers and the gullibility of the public. It stands for Pedic Perspiration. 'Gordon had searched for the word pedic in the Oxford Dictionary and found it did not exist. But Mr Warner [his boss] has said Hell what did it matter anyway? It would put the wind up them just the same' (ibid: 734). But what Orwell enjoys most of all is the fact that, in French, 'peepee' is slang for piss.

Yet Daphne Patai (1984: 113) rightly identifies the appalling sexism that underlies Orwell's representation of the advertising industry. For it is women who are blamed for luring men from the path of social justice into the seductive arms of consumerism. Significantly, most of the adverts Gordon either sees or works on are directed principally at women. As Gordon rants:

Every man you can see has got some blasted woman hanging round his neck like a mermaid, dragging him down and down – down to some beastly little semi-detached villa in Putney, with hire-purchase furniture and a portable radio and an aspidistra in the window. … A woman's got a sort of mystical feeling towards money. Good and evil in a woman's mind mean simply money and no money (op cit: 649).

Patai comments: 'As ridiculous as Gordon's comments sound in their evasion of any serious consideration of women, men, and money, they are given some plausibility by the narrative focus, which allows Gordon to speak while giving Rosemary no serious argument in return. She simply laughs at him in a conciliatory and good-natured way' (1984: 114).

And Jonathan Rose argues that 'an unconscious class bias' may be at work in Orwell's representation of advertising 'as an insidious and well-financed machine for mass manipulation' (2001: 390). Linking *Keep the Aspidistra Flying* to H. G. Wells's *Tono-Bungay* (1909) in their damning critiques of advertisements, he says: 'Since advertising tells the educated classes nothing that they do not already know and competes for the attention of popular audiences, they inevitably find it banal and mind-numbingly repetitive, an endless blare that drowns out the true and the beautiful. To the uneducated classes, however, it may offer much that is new and informative' (ibid: 390-391).

THE DIARIES – AND THE CONSTANT INTEREST IN ADS

Orwell's fascination with advertisements is particularly evident in many of his diary entries. From September 1938 to March 1939, the Blairs take a break in Marrakech – paid for by an anonymous donor. Orwell has just spent six months in a sanatorium recovering from a serious health crisis, has been diagnosed with TB and is advised by his doctors to stay awhile in a hotter climate; Eileen Blair is exhausted and also needs a holiday (Topp 2020: 224-234). While in the Moroccan capital, Orwell, not in the best of health, still manages to read extensively, to complete his novel *Coming Up For Air* (1939) and the wonderfully original essay on Dickens (to be published in his essay collection, *Inside the Whale*, in 1940) – and to write many letters and diary entries.

On 22 December 1938, he takes the time to note: 'The other widely read French weekly paper is *Gringoire*. Used to be a sort of gossipy literary paper but now much as *Candide*. I notice that those papers, though evidently prosperous and having a lot of advertisements, are not above inserting pornographic advertisements' (Orwell 2010: 118).

Back in England, he maintains a regular wartime diary. For the entry on 6 June 1940, he conducts a 'rough analysis' of the advertisements in that day's edition of the *People*. So with a meticulous attention to detail, he conducts a quantitative survey: 'Paper consists of 12 pages – 84 columns. Of this just about 26 and a half columns (over one quarter) is advertisements. These are divided up as follows: *Food and drink* 5 and three quarters columns. *Patent medicines* 9 and a third. *Tobacco* 1. *Gambling* 2 and a third. *Clothes* 1 and a half. *Miscellaneous* 6 and three quarters' (ibid: 249, italics in the original). He concludes:

> Of 9 food and drink adverts, 6 are for unnecessary luxuries. Of 29 adverts for medicines, 19 are for things which are either fraudulent (baldness cured) more or less deleterious (Kruschen Salts, Bile Beans etc) or of the blackmail type ('Your child's stomach needs magnesia'). Benefit of doubt has been allowed in the case of a few medicines. Of 14 miscellaneous adverts, 4 are for soap, 1 for cosmetics, 1 for a holiday resort and 2 are government advertisements, including a large one for national savings. Only 3 adverts in all classes are cashing in on the war (ibid: 249-250).

A few days later, on 6 June, he records seeing a huge advert on the side of a bus: 'FIRST AID IN WARTIME, FOR HEALTH, STRENGTH AND FORTITUDE. WRIGLEY'S CHEWING GUM' (ibid: 250). And the following day he reflects:

> Although newspaper posters are now suppressed, one fairly frequently sees the paper-sellers displaying a poster. It appears that old ones are resuscitated and used and one with captions like 'RAF raids on Germany' or 'Enormous German losses' can be used at almost all times (ibid: 250-251).

On 13 June, he draws from his experience fighting with a Republican militia during the Spanish Civil War in 1937 to comment: 'I notice that one of the posters recruiting for the Pioneers, of a foot treading on a swastika with the legend "Step on it" is cribbed from a Government poster of the Spanish war, i.e. cribbed as to the idea. Of course, it is vulgarised and made comic but its appearance at any rate shows that the Government are beginning to be willing to learn' (ibid: 253). His preoccupation with the crucial propaganda function of advertisements within a capitalist economy of mindless consumption continues the following day with this entry which is bursting with moral outrage:

> Always as I walk through the Underground stations, sickened by the advertisements, the silly staring faces and strident colours, the general frantic struggle to induce people to waste labour and material by consuming useless luxuries or harmful drugs. How much rubbish this war will sweep away, if only we can hang on throughout the summer. War is simply the reversal of civilised life, its motto is 'Evil be thou my good' [a quotation from Milton's *Paradise Lost*], and so much of the good of modern life is actually evil that it is questionable whether on balance war does harm (ibid: 254).

Orwell returns to his long-standing political economy critique of the press and the underlying myth of media freedom in his entry for 29 June: '… the "freedom" of the press really means it depends on vested interests and largely (though its advertisements) on the luxury trades. Newspapers which would resist direct treachery can't take a strong line about cutting down luxuries when they live by advertising chocolates and silk stockings' (ibid: 265).

And just as during his youth he enjoyed responding mischievously to advertisements by assuming false identities, here he is clearly amused by an advert in a pub for pick-me-up tablets called, of all things, Blitz. So, with meticulous attention to detail and, once again, indulging his likeness for listing, he simply reproduces the ad, line by line:

> Thoroughly recommended by the
> Medical Profession
> The
> 'LIGHTNING'
> Marvellous discovery
> Millions take this remedy
> for
> Hangover
> War Nerves
> Influenza
> Headache
> Toothache
> Neuralgia
> Sleeplessness
> Rheumatism
> Depression etc etc
> Contains no Aspirin.

FROM CONSUMERISM TO BIG BROTHER PROPAGANDA IN *NINETEEN EIGHTY-FOUR*

Just as the streets in Gordon Comstock's London of *Keep the Aspidistra Flying* are dominated by advertising hoardings, so posters are everywhere in the London streets of Winston Smith's *Nineteen Eighty-Four* (2000 [1949]). At the start of the novel, Winston walks from his flat in Victory Mansions and looks around:

> Down in the street little eddies of wind were whirling dust and torn paper into spirals, and though the sun was shining and the sky a harsh blue,

there seemed to be no colour in anything, except the posters that were plastered everywhere. The black-moustachio'd face gazed down from every commanding corner. There was one on the house-front immediately opposite. BIG BROTHER IS WATCHING YOU, the caption said, while the dark eyes looked deep into Winston's eyes. Down at street level another poster, torn at one corner, flapped fitfully in the wind, alternately covering and uncovering the single word INGSOC (ibid: 4).

And the slogans on posters at the Ministry of Love and on telescreens everywhere no longer focus on tempting people to spend, spend, spend; rather they spell out the principles of the Party: 'WAR IS PEACE/FREEDOM IS SLAVERY/IGNORANCE IS STRENGTH' (ibid: 6; 19).

So the messages have changed: the consumerist capitalism of *Keep the Aspidistra Flying* has given way to the authoritarian propaganda of the surveillance, hyper-militarised state.

Moreover, the abuse of language which Orwell has detected in the advertising industry culminates in his representation of newspeak and doublespeak in the novel. Emmanuel Goldstein's *The Theory and Practice of Oligarchical Collectivism* – the dissident tract which Winston reads to his lover, Julia, in their hideaway above Charrington's junk shop – 'means the power of holding two contradictory beliefs in one's mind simultaneously and accepting both of them. ... *Doublethink* lies at the very heart of Ingsoc [the Party's ideology], since the essential act of the Party is to use conscious deception while retaining the firmness of purpose that goes with complete honesty' (ibid: 244; italics in the original). Newspeak, on the other hand, is the official language of the state, its structure and etymology outlined in an Appendix at the end of the novel. Just as advertisements use short, snappy, hyper-simplified phrases to appeal to the consumerist mind-set, so Newspeak involves the actual destruction of words. So, for instance, the Ministry of Love becomes Miniluv; the Ministry of Peace becomes Minipax, and so on (ibid: 6).

WAR IS PEACE/FREEDOM IS SLAVERY/IGNORANCE IS STRENGTH, the Party propaganda slogans displayed everywhere, are the consummate embodiments of doublethink and Newspeak. As David Runciman argues, doublethink constitutes a particularly extreme form of linguistic abuse since its language is emptied out of all meaning – and unable to hide anything. 'There is nothing hypocritical about this message because it has nothing to hide. But nor is it a metaphor. It is a lie so large and so open that it makes the terms of hypocrisy obsolete' (Runciman 2008: 186).

CONCLUSIONS

Orwell's interest in advertisements is constant throughout his career as a writer and shows up prominently in his journalism, diary entries and novels. He is extraordinarily inventive in his approach: in his diary, he conducts a laborious, meticulous, quantitative analysis of the advertising content of one issue of the *People* newspaper; in his 'As I Please' columns in *Tribune* he tackles the topic so originally and with such humour, highlighting, for instance, the subtle intrusion of government publicity in (of all places) a short story in *Home Companion and Family Journal*. That verve and wit also appear in his approach to advertisements in his novel, *Keep the Aspidistra Flying*. The abuse of language is a special concern to Orwell in many of his writings: here, in the novel, the ways in which language is distorted to form the banal, snappy, advertising slogans in the service of the 'money-god' draws particular venom. Edward Said castigates Orwell for representing Gordon Comstock, the anti-hero of the novel, for being 'indifferent to any sort of political solutions to the evils of the money world from which he is in flight' (Said 2000: 93-94). Yet, Orwell, through highlighting the crucial role of advertisements in the 'racket of capitalism', implicitly (and so all the more effectively) encourages action to counter the hyper-commercialism of society.

Moreover, while Orwell's influence on the formation of Cultural Studies as an academic disciple – with his remarkably original writings on such commonplace things as junk shops, cups of tea, sexy seaside postcards, boys' weeklies, cheap women's magazines, American crime novels and public houses – is now well-established, his crucial role in the creation of Media/Journalism/PR Studies is less well known (Crook 2020). This paper has shown that in his many writings on advertisements he maintains a consistent political economy approach. Yet this is conveyed in always accessible and often witty prose free from jargon and befuddling theoretical abstractions. Today's academics have still a lot to learn from Orwell.

- The author would like to thank Professor Tim Crook for his comments on a draft of this paper. Responsibility for the final version, of course, rests with the author alone.

REFERENCES

Bowker, Gordon (2003) *George Orwell*, London: Little, Brown

Crook, Tim (2020) Orwell and Media Studies, in email to author, 11 April

Dulley, Paul Richard (2015) *In Front of Your Nose: The Existentialism of George Orwell*. PhD thesis, University of Sussex. Available online at http://sro.sussex.ac.uk/id/eprint/56743/

Keeble, Richard Lance (2020) The myth of freedom: Orwell and the press, in *Journalism Beyond Orwell*, London: Routledge pp 15-32

Orwell, George (1970 [1928]) A farthing newspaper, Orwell, Sonia and Angus, Ian (eds) *The Collected Essays, Journalism and Letters of George Orwell, Vol. 1: An Age Like This, 1920-1940*, Harmondsworth, Middlesex: Penguin pp 34-37; *G. K.'s Weekly*, 29 December

Orwell, George (1976 [1936]) *Keep the Aspidistra Flying*, in the *Collected Fiction*, London: Secker & Warburg/Octopus pp 573-737

Orwell, George (1970 [1941a]) *The Lion and the Unicorn*, *The Collected Essays, Journalism and Letters of George Orwell, Vol. 2: My Country Right or Left 1940-1942*, Harmondsworth, Middlesex: Penguin pp 74-134; February 1941

Orwell, George (1970 [1941b]) London Letter to *Partisan Review*, Orwell, Sonia and Angus, Ian (eds) *The Collected Essays, Journalism and Letters of George Orwell, Vol. 2: My Country Right or Left, 1940-1942*, Harmondsworth, Middlesex: Penguin pp 137-149; 15 April

Orwell, George (1970 [1942]) London Letter to *Partisan Review*, Orwell, Sonia and Angus, Ian (eds) *The Collected Essays, Journalism and Letters of George Orwell, Vol. 2: My Country Right or Left, 1940-1942*, Harmondsworth, Middlesex: Penguin pp 265-272; November-December

Orwell, George (1970 [1943]) Review of *Beggar My Neighbour*, by Lionel Fielden, Orwell, Sonia and Angus, Ian (eds) *The Collected Essays, Journalism and Letters of George Orwell, Vol. 2: My Country Right or Left, 1940-1942*, Harmondsworth, Middlesex: Penguin pp 349-359; *Horizon*, September

Orwell, George (1998 [1944a]) As I Please, Davison, Peter (ed.) *Complete Works of George Orwell, Vol. XVI: I Have Tried to Tell The Truth, 1943-1944*, London: Secker & Warburg pp 145-148; *Tribune*, 7 April

Orwell, George (1998 [1944b]) As I Please, Davison, Peter (ed.) *Complete Works of George Orwell, Vol. XVI: I Have Tried to Tell The Truth, 1943-1944*, London: Secker & Warburg pp 103-104; *Tribune*, 25 February

Orwell, George (1998 [1944c]) As I Please, Davison, Peter (ed.) *Complete Works of George Orwell, Vol. XVI: I Have Tried to Tell The Truth, 1943-1944*, London: Secker & Warburg pp 251-253; *Tribune*, 9 June

Orwell, George (1998 [1944d]) As I Please, Davison, Peter (ed.) *Complete Works of George Orwell, Vol. XVI: I Have Tried to Tell The Truth, 1943-1944*, London: Secker & Warburg pp 463-465; *Tribune*, 17 November

Orwell, George (1998 [1946a]) As I Please, Davison, Peter (ed.) *Complete Works of George Orwell, Vol. XVII: Smothered Under Journalism, 1946*, London: Secker & Warburg pp 471-472; *Tribune*, 8 November

Orwell, George (1998 [1946b]) As I Please, Davison, Peter (ed.) *Complete Works of George Orwell, Vol. XVII: Smothered Under Journalism, 1946*, London: Secker & Warburg pp 497-500; *Tribune*, 22 November 1946

Orwell, George (2000 [1949]) *Nineteen Eighty-Four*, London: Penguin, with an introduction by Thomas Pynchon

Orwell, George (2010) *Diaries*, Davison, Peter (ed.) London: Penguin

Patai, Daphne (1984) *The Orwell Mystique: A Study in Male Ideology*, Amherst: University of Massachusetts Press

Rose, Jonathan (2001) *The Intellectual Life of the Working Classes*, London and New Haven: Yale University Press

Runciman, David (2008) *Political Hypocrisy: The Mask of Power from Hobbes to Orwell and Beyond*, Princeton and Oxford: Princeton University Press

Said, Edward (2000) *Reflections on Exile: And Other Literary and Cultural Essays*, London: Granta

Topp, Sylvia (2020) *Eileen: The Making of George Orwell*, London: Unbound

Werbel, Amy Beth (2018) *Lust on Trial: Censorship and the Rise of American Obscenity in the Age of Anthony Comstock*, New York: Columbia University Press

Woloch, Alex (2016) *Or Orwell: Writing and Democratic Socialism*, Cambridge, Massachusetts: Harvard University Press

- **This essay is based on 'Orwell, advertisements and the political economy of the media',** *George Orwell Studies*, Vol. 5, No. 1 pp 39-54

Chapter Four

In the Waugh-zone

Throughout his writing career, George Orwell maintains a constant critique of Roman Catholics. There is one major exception: Evelyn Waugh. This essay explores the extraordinary Orwell-Waugh relationship, the study Orwell plans on Waugh in the months immediately before he died, their meetings and correspondence – and the much-neglected witty, dystopian novella, *Love Among the Ruins* which Waugh composes in the early 1950s as a sort of tribute to the author of the recently published *Nineteen Eighty-Four*.

ORWELL AND THE CATHOLIC QUESTION

While Orwell's deeply unpleasant anti-Semitism is all too prevalent in his early writings, this attitude rapidly changes once he learns of the horrors of the Nazi persecution of the Jews (Angel 2020; Crook in the Afterword). As Michael G. Brennan comments in his excellent study of Orwell's attitudes to religion (2017: xv): 'Indeed, from 1945, Orwell offered a strident public voice in the denunciation of anti-Semitism even though during the same period – the last five years of his life – he showed no inclination to temper or adjust his apparently pathological hatred of the Catholic hierarchy.'

Orwell's biographer Gordon Bowker locates the origins of this hatred of Roman Catholics – perhaps somewhat improbably – to his being sent at the age of five to be the lone boy in a convent school which his sister, Marjorie, was attending in Henley-on-Thames. The convent is run by French Ursulines exiled from France after religious education is banned there in 1903. According to Bowker (2003: 21): 'If young Eric [Blair, as he then was] was first taught by Catholic nuns as a lone boy in a school of girls, it would explain two important and enduring aspects of his complex personality – his unremitting hostility towards Roman Catholicism and an acute sense of guilt.' In 1931, Blair certainly tells his Eton friend, Christopher Hollis, that he regularly reads the Catholic press because 'I like to see what the enemy is up to' (ibid: 27).[1] His anti-clerical polemics are particularly strident in the second part of *The Road to Wigan Pier* (1937) where he lambasts the 'sentimental democratic Catholics of the type of Chesterton' who naïvely argue that the dirtiness of the poor is 'healthy' (ibid: 54).

While fighting alongside the Republicans in the Spanish Civil War in 1937, he sees the Catholic Church put its full weight behind Franco's fascist forces – and this only serves to entrench his beliefs. He considers the hostility to the Catholics in Spain is driven largely by the economic oppression of ordinary people by landowners, industrialists and the Church. During the 1940s, in his 'As I Please' columns in *Tribune*, he accuses Catholic writers such as G. K. Chesterton and Hilaire Belloc of 'flirting with the spirit of anti-Semitism' and linked Catholic and Hindu intellectuals in a community of reactionary thought (Brennan op cit: 96). In another column, he accuses the eminent Catholics, D. B. Wyndham Lewis and J. B. Morton, of propagandising on behalf of every reactionary cause – from Mussolini, appeasement and Franco to literary censorship (ibid: 103).

Graham Greene is a Catholic who does escape his wrath. Orwell admires his idiosyncratic, sceptical, left-leaning brand of religion. And he has some good words to say about the plots and explorations of moral dilemmas in his novels *Brighton Rock* (1937) and *The Power and the Glory* (1940). Ever ready to surprise, Orwell even begins his review of *The Heart of the Matter* for the *New Yorker*, of 17 July 1948, with these words: 'A fairly large proportion of the distinguished novels of the last few decades have been written by Catholics and have even been describable as Catholic novels' (*CWGO* XIX: 404). This is because the 'conflict not only between the world and the next world but between sanctity and goodness is a fruitful theme'. But *The Heart of the Matter*, he suggests, gives the impression of having been mechanically constructed, 'the familiar conflict being set out like an algebraic equation, with no attempt at psychological probability' (ibid).

In a letter to his friend Julian Symons, dated 21 March 1948, Orwell – writing in longhand from Ward 3, at Hairmyres Hospital, East Kilbride – tells how he has just read François Mauriac's *Thérèse Desqueyroux* (1927) which started him thinking about Catholic novelists in general (ibid: 286). He is also 'trying to get hold of Léon Bloy' – the French novelist, essayist, pamphleteer and poet. Significantly, in his review of *The Heart of the Matter*, Orwell comments, approvingly, on *Thérèse* in which 'the spiritual conflict does not outrage probability, because it is not pretended that Thérèse is a normal person' (ibid: 406).

THE EXTRAORDINARY ORWELL-WAUGH FRIENDSHIP

This interest in Catholic writers continues for the rest of Orwell's life. Still being treated for TB at Hairmyres – though still reading voraciously – on 16 May 1948 he writes to Waugh, thanking him for sending copies of *Black Mischief* (1932) and *A Handful of Dust* (1934) (ibid: 406) and for his sympathetic review of his *Critical Essays* in *The Tablet*, of 6 April 1946. Under the heading 'A new humanism', Waugh describes the book as 'a work of absorbing interest'. 'The art of Donald McGill' is 'the masterpiece' while 'Raffles and Miss Blandish' – in which Orwell critiques the violence, cruelty and sexual sadism of the contemporary American crime novel – exemplifies the method in which the new school, the 'new humanism of the common man', is supreme. And on 'Benefit of clergy' – about the artist Salvador Dali and his scurrilous memoir – he comments: 'There is nothing in [Orwell's] writing that is inconsistent with high moral principles' (Davison 1996: 110).

In the 16 May letter, Orwell is keen to pick up on Waugh's comment about the 'pacifist strain' in the writings of P. G. Wodehouse. He continues: 'This started me thinking about him again, and on looking up a rare early book called "The Gold Bat" I found passages which suggested that Wodehouse had had some kind of connection with the Liberal Party, about 1908, when it was the anti-militarist party. I will add a footnote to this affect if I ever reprint the essays' (*CWGO* XIX: 339).

Orwell returns to Waugh in a review of *The Novelist as Thinker*, edited by the Cambridge academic Balachandra Rajan, in *The Times Literary Supplement*, of 7 August. In an essay, 'The innocence of Evelyn Waugh', he suggests that the author, Derek K. Savage, is wrong to concentrate on his 'immaturity'. 'He does not even mention Mr Waugh's conversion to Catholicism, which obviously cannot be left out of account in any serious study of his work. In *Brideshead Revisited* Mr Savage can see only nostalgia for adolescence and does not seem to have noticed that the essential theme of the book is the collision between ordinary decent behaviour and the concept of good and evil' (ibid: 417). Here, Orwell is clearly transferring his own current and ever-developing preoccupations about ethics, religion and writing to his understanding of the novel.

For his part, Waugh is clearly fascinated by Orwell. In his diary for 31 August 1945, he says his 'Communist cousin Claud [Cockburn] warned him against Trotskyist literature so that I read and greatly enjoyed Orwell's *Animal Farm*' which Orwell has personally sent him (*CWGO* XX: 74). And while Orwell is at Cranham sanatorium in 1949, Waugh – who lives just 18 miles away – visits him a number of times. They would clearly have had a lot to talk about. Waugh is not a fellow old-Etonian (he'd been to Lancing College and then Oxford University) but, like Orwell's great friend and *Observer* editor, David Astor, has fought in the Royal Marines during the Second World War.[2] Malcolm Muggeridge notes:

Waugh did go and see Orwell several times, and afterwards corresponded with him in a very delightful way. Despite all Waugh's efforts to appear to be an irascible, deaf old curmudgeon, a sort of innate saintliness kept breaking through. I should have loved to see them together; complementary figures, his country gentleman's outfit and Orwell's proletarian one both straight out of back numbers of *Punch* (Brennan op cit: 74).

In a letter to Orwell of 17 July 1949, Waugh says he has read *Nineteen Eighty-Four* with great admiration. But he suggests in his treatment of Winston's soul 'the metaphysics are wrong' and that the novel is spurious because it fails to acknowledge the existence of the Church. Perhaps reflecting on the scenes towards the end of the novel in which Winston is tortured in Room 101 by O'Brien, Waugh's concludes that 'men who love a crucified God need never think of torture as all-powerful' (ibid: 157).

Malcolm Muggeridge further comments on Waugh in his autobiography: 'His true charity comes out in some letters he wrote to George Orwell in his last illness which I have read; perfectly phrased in their consideration for someone in affliction, despite the fact that, ostensibly at any rate, he and Orwell were, temperamentally and in many of their opinions and aspirations as opposed as any two writers could possibly be' (Muggeridge 1975 [1973]: 223).

ORWELL'S UNCOMPLETED ESSAY ON WAUGH

The extraordinary Orwell/Waugh friendship culminates in two ways. In the first instance, Orwell dedicates some of his last hours alive to working on the draft of a short story, 'A smoking-room story' – and a serious essay about Waugh's writings. Peter Davison records how he reads during February and March 1949 Waugh's *Rossetti: His Life and Works* (1928), *Robbery Under Law* (1939) and *When the Going was Good* (1946) and even copies out at some length three passages from his writings which are of particular interest to him (*CWGO* XX: 74-79). Orwell actually lists the 144 books he reads – amazingly – during his last year (27 of them for the second time while three or four of them were pamphlets) (ibid: 219-223).

Orwell begins his essay by expressing his admiration for Waugh for daring to challenge the dominant consensus – even though he may not approve of his views: 'In our own day, the English novelist who has most conspicuously defied his contemporaries is Evelyn Waugh. Waugh's outlook on life is, I should say, false and in some extent perverse, but at least it must be said for him that he adopted it at a time when it did not pay to do so, and his literary reputation has suffered accordingly' (ibid: 75). His main offence – during the era in which leftists such as Auden and Spender held sway – is his 'reactionary political tendency'. Others such as William Empson, William Plomer and V. S. Pritchett do not fit into the pattern but they are 'lacking in political zeal' while Graham Greene is politically left 'in an ill-defined, unobtrusive way'. He argues that Waugh is the latest in a long line of English writers whose driving force is 'a romantic belief in aristocracy' 'tinged by the kind of innocent snobbishness that causes people to wait twenty-four hours on the pavement for a good view of a royal wedding'. Orwell's long-standing – and inadequately acknowledged – pre-occupation with humour (see Keeble 2015) emerges now in his appreciation of Waugh:

> The seeming immoralism of those books [*Decline and Fall* and *Vile Bodies*] (the jokes turn not merely upon adultery but upon prostitution, homosexuality, suicide, lunacy and cannibalism) is merely a reversion to the older tradition of English humour, according to which any event can be funny provided that it either didn't happen or happened a long time ago (op cit: 76).

Orwell next reveals his own quirky, somewhat gruesome sense of humour when he says the funniest event in *Decline and Fall* 'is the sawing off of a clergyman's head'. He suggests that in all Waugh's books up to *Brideshead Revisited* (1945), 'the idea of sanity and moral integrity is mixed up with the idea of country life – upper class country life – as it was lived a couple of generations ago'. A previous commentator in the American journal, *Partisan Review*, to which Orwell contributed a series of 'London Letters' during the Second World War, has already highlighted the way in which the action of Waugh's books tends to take place in an old house. 'In *A Handful of Dust* – this time a somewhat ridiculous house but beautiful in its owner's eyes – it is the pivot of the story. In *Brideshead Revisited* it appears in more magnificent form.'

But the houses in *Scoop* and *Vile Bodies* most closely resemble Waugh's private ideal: '… the middle-sized country house which required, in the days of its glory, about ten servants and which has now, if it is not merely derelict, been turned into a hotel, a boarding school or a lunatic asylum'. Orwell carefully lists the elements that make up the 'familiar scenery': the 'wet, bird-haunted lawns', the walled garden with its crucified pear trees, the large untidy porch with its litter of raincoats, waders, landing-nets and croquet mallets, the plastery smell of the flagged passage leading to the gunroom, the estate map on the library wall, the case of stuffed birds over the staircase. He continues: 'To Waugh, this is magic, or used to be magic, and it would be [a] waste of time to try to exorcise it from his mind merely by pointing out that…' (ibid: 77). And reflecting on magic and in mid-sentence, Orwell's pen ceases to flow – never to be taken up again.

In handwritten notes on Waugh that Peter Davison includes in the *Complete Works*, Orwell comments rather impishly on *Brideshead Revisited*: 'One cannot really be a Catholic & grown up.' And concludes: 'Waugh is about as good a novelist as one can be while holding untenable opinions' (ibid: 79).

WAUGH'S TRIBUTE AND CRITIQUE: *LOVE AMONG THE RUINS*

Clearly inspired by Orwell's *Nineteen Eighty-Four*, which he much admired, Waugh, in 1950, composes a much-neglected dystopian novella, *Love Among the Ruins*. It is clearly his way of paying tribute but it also serves to encapsulate some of the critical points he made of Orwell's work. Waugh originally calls his dystopian vision, *A Pilgrim's Progress*, but it is rejected by a number of publishers. One says: 'It seems to me sad that this man's talent should be wasted on such a story' while another comments: 'The theme is almost implausibly apt for satire by Waugh and yet his handling of it is, for the most part, dull-witted and tedious' (Manley 2017). Following this negative response, Waugh revises the text with a new version ready by November 1952 – with the hope that Ian Fleming's Queen Anne Press will publish a *deluxe* edition. After that idea falls through, it is finally published by Chapman and Hall in July 1953.

Love Among the Ruins (Waugh 1972 [1953]) is rarely listed amongst the notable dystopian works that follow on from *Nineteen Eighty-Four*. Yet, it's highly original, quirky, Swiftian in its bitter satire, packed with political and religious points – and certainly worth a re-evaluation. Moving away from the austere tone of his other post-war novels, it captures some of the riotous, macabre comedy of his early novels (Morère 2013). Orwell has criticised Waugh's innate conservatism and this appears with a vengeance here: it's full of jibes at socialism, notions of equality, modern avant-garde art, psycho-analysis, architectural innovations, trendy modern teaching methods and so on. Orwell has invented a language – Newspeak – in *Nineteen Eighty-Four* and here Waugh invents phrases such as 'State help me' in place of 'God help me' and so on. Just as Orwell's choice of names is usually deeply symbolic, here 'Plastic' conveys the artificiality of modern man while 'Clara' for a while brings light to his life.

We first meet the principal protagonist, Miles Plastic, being treated leniently by the state at Mountjoy prison where he is serving time for arson. In fact, conditions in the prison are far superior to those outside. Miles has grown up in an orphanage:

> Huge sums were thenceforward spent upon him; sums which, fifty years earlier, would have sent whole quiversful of boys to Winchester and New College and established them in the learned professions. In halls adorned with Picassos and Légers he yawned through long periods of Constructive Play. He never lacked the requisite cubic feet of air. His diet was balanced and on the first Friday of every month he was psycho-analysed. Every detail of his adolescence was recorded and microfilmed and filed, until at the appropriate age he was transferred to the Air Force (1972 [1953]: 183).

On release, Plastic goes to work in the 'key' Euthanasia Department. How Waugh revels in the joke:

Euthanasia had not been part of the original 1945 Health Service; it was a Tory measure designed to attract votes from the aged and mortally sick. Under the Bevan-Eden Coalition the Service came into general use and won instant popularity. The Union of Teachers was pressing for its application to difficult children. Foreigners came in such numbers to take advantage of the service that immigration authorities now turned back the bearers of single tickets (ibid: 194).

The department's director is a Mr Beamish. Here, Waugh enjoys delivering a clear jibe at the Orwell/Cyril Connolly clique: 'He had signed manifestos in his hot youth, had raised his fist in Barcelona, and had painted abstractedly for *Horizon*...' But his patients 'were kept waiting so long that often they died natural deaths before he found it convenient to poison them' (ibid: 195). Waugh also echoes Orwell's stress on the ever-presence of telescreens in *Nineteen Eighty-Four's* Oceania by having televisions constantly supplying 'entertainment' to the citizens of Satellite City.

The secret, passionate love affair between Winston Smith and Julia (who may well be a police spy engaged in a honeytrap operation) features prominently in Orwell's dystopian masterpiece. Significantly, Waugh now introduces a romantic theme – though it's macabre and completely different. Plastic falls for Clara – but, due to a hospital operation that has gone terribly wrong, she sports, of all things, a 'long, silken, corn-gold beard'. It only heightens Miles's passion for her. And while Clara has come to the Euthanasia Department she doesn't want to die. She tells Beamish: 'I told your assistant here, I've simply consented to come at all because the Director of Drama cried so, and he's rather a darling. I've not the smallest intention of letting you kill me' (ibid: 199).

Waugh next echoes the theme of sexual promiscuity of Aldous Huxley's *Brave New World* (1932) – rather than the sexual puritanism of Orwell's Big Brother society against which Winston and Julia are revolting – in describing the Miles/Clara affair: 'For Miles, child of the State, Sex had been part of the curriculum at every stage of his education; first in diagrams, then in demonstrations, then in application, he had mastered all the antics of procreation. Love was a word seldom used except by politicians and by them only in moments of pure fatuity' (ibid: 199). When Clara announces she is pregnant Miles responds immediately: 'It's hard luck on the poor little beast not being an Orphan. Not much opportunity for it. If he's a boy we must try and get him registered as a worker' (ibid: 207).

Clara suddenly disappears – but when the distraught Miles finally discovers her in a hospital operating theatre, alas, in place of the beautiful beard there's a ghastly piece of synthetic rubber. In despair, he returns to Mountjoy prison, sets it alight – and evades detection. In fact, he's promoted to a new position in the Ministry of Welfare and Rest and Culture. During the first meeting with his new bosses, Miles – like Winston – betrays his former lover. To complete his rehabilitation, he needs a wife. A Miss Flower is on hand – and together they head for the registrar's office. But the story ends ominously – with Miles fondling the cigarette lighter in his pocket intent, no doubt, on yet another act of arson (ibid: 223).

REFLECTIONS

The novella takes its title from a poem by Robert Browning (1812-1889) in which the narrator, overlooking a pasture where sheep graze, recalls that once a great ancient city, his country's capital, stood there. After describing the beauty and grandeur of the ancient city, the speaker says that 'a girl with eager eyes and yellow hair/Waits me there', and that 'she looks now, breathless, dumb/Till I come'. It ends with the beautiful line: 'Love is best.'[3] It is also the title of a painting by the Pre-Raphaelite Edward Burne-Jones (1833-1898) showing two lovers in blue robes seated amidst the ruins of buildings. There is a tragic sub-text to the painting – which blends Pre-Raphaelite, Aesthetic and Symbolist techniques and themes – since it marks the ending of Burne-Jones's four-year love affair with his model Maria Zambaco who attempted to commit suicide in 1869 after he moved to end their affair.

These aesthetic considerations are reflected in Waugh's unusual decision to carry throughout the text sketches based on the engravings that the English artist Henry Moses had made in 1822 of sculptures by Antonio Canova, a neo-classical Italian sculptor, who had died that year.[4] As Julie Morère comments (op cit): 'The novella's drawings are the perfect illustration of Waugh's artistic stance. They appear and disappear as the pages are turned, and convey a particular cadenza to the eye movement, de-centring the message and morale of the novella. Satire … appears in the gap between the classical feature of the illustrations and the futuristic temporality of the novella.'

The novella is sub-titled *A Romance of the Near Future* and there is a tension between Waugh's clear preference for looking backwards for his aesthetic models – as Orwell has critically observed – and his need here to look forward. This is Waugh's only venture into the realm of dystopian fiction, its shortness perhaps reflecting this uncertainty. But it contains a lot of 'laugh-out-loud' humour and stands as a remarkable tribute to his friendship with Orwell.

CONCLUSION

As David Lebedoff (2008) stresses, Orwell and Waugh can appear polar opposites: Orwell the dedicated socialist and anti-Catholic who was prepared to live with tramps in order to expiate his guilt of having worked for the 'racket' of the British Empire as an Imperial Policeman in Burma (1922-1927) and who always hated bullying. Waugh, in contrast, the bully, the Catholic and dedicated social climber. Yet both came to see the 20th century in a similar way – imperilled by ideologues, lies, cultural decadence and assaults on tradition. Orwell, the atheist, deplored the decline of religious faith as much as Waugh the Catholic convert.

Yet, while Waugh decided that real improvement lay only in the life to come, Orwell believed in life, here and now – as a constant challenge to understand, improve and, where appropriate, celebrate.

NOTES

[1] Hollis actually converts to Roman Catholicism in 1924. See Chapter 19

[2] In an essay, https://orwellsociety.com/spooks-and-scoops-astor-orwell-the-observer/, I stated that Evelyn Waugh worked for British intelligence during the war. This was a mistake. I have also, elsewhere, made an error in my coverage of Georges Kopp for which I also apologise

[3] https://www.poetryfoundation.org/poems/43763/love-among-the-ruins

[4] http://www.evelynwaugh.org.uk/styled-58/index.html

REFERENCES

Angel, Christopher (2020) An evolution, Orwell Society *Journal*, No. 16 pp 28-32

Brennan, Michael G. (2017) *George Orwell and Religion*, London: Bloomsbury Academic

CWGO (1998) *The Complete Works of George Orwell*, XX Vols, Davison, Peter (ed.) London: Secker & Warburg

Davison, Peter (1996) *George Orwell: A Literary Life*, London: Macmillan Press

Keeble, Richard Lance (2015) 'There is always room for one more custard pie': Orwell's humour, Keeble, Richard Lance and Swick, David (eds) *Pleasures of the Prose: Journalism and Humour*, Bury St Edmunds: Abramis pp 10-25

Lebedoff, David (2008) *The Same Man: George Orwell and Evelyn Waugh in Love and War*, New York: Random House

Manley, Jeffrey (2017) Waugh's dystopia, evelynwaughsociety.org, 1 July. Available online at https://evelynwaughsociety.org/2017/waughs-dystopia/

Morère, Julie (2013) Evelyn Waugh's artistic outcry in *Love Among the Ruins* of a godless world, *Études britanniques*, Vol. 45. Available online at http://journals.openedition.org/ebc/701

Muggeridge, Malcolm (1975 [1973]) *The Infernal Grove*, London: Fontana

Waugh, Evelyn (1972 [1953]) *Love Among the Ruins*, in *The Ordeal of Gilbert Pinfold*, Harmondsworth, Middlesex: Penguin pp 177-223

- This essay is based on 'Orwell in the Waugh-zone', Orwellsociety.com. 27 August 2020 https://orwellsociety.com/orwell-in-the-waugh-zone/

Chapter Five

Love of Lawrence

On the surface, George Orwell and D. H. Lawrence appear very different kinds of writers. Orwell – the old-Etonian, Imperial Policeman, Republican militiaman in the Spanish Civil War, BBC broadcaster, activist journalist, relatively unknown novelist until the global success of *Animal Farm* and *Nineteen Eighty-Four* at the end of his life. Lawrence – the son of a miner, ever wandering author of a series of psychologically profound, radically structured novels exploring the complexities of human relationships, spirituality and sexuality that culminate in *Lady Chatterley's Lover* – though the novel is considered obscene and banned for many years. Yet throughout his life Orwell emphasises his debt to Lawrence as a writer and constantly refers to him approvingly in his writings. Moreover, Lawrence's influence on Orwell's writing style is evident in many of his novels.

THE BIRTH OF ORWELL'S PASSION FOR LAWRENCE

In a remarkable essay in the leftist weekly journal, *Tribune*, of November 1945 (*CWGO* XVII: 385-388), Orwell reviews Lawrence's *The Prussian Officer and Other Stories*, first published by Duckworth in 1914 but now, just after the end of the war, reprinted as a Penguin. In the process, he reveals a great deal about himself, his childhood, his ideas, the birth of his passion for Lawrence – and his life-long admiration for the author of *Lady Chatterley's Lover*.

Orwell's essay, 'Such, such were the joys' (1970, 4 [1952]) composed in the late 1940s but not published until after his death because of libel problems, focuses on his largely unhappy times at St Cyprian's prep school, in Eastbourne, and is one of the very few articles in which he dwells on his childhood at any length. It could be argued that a great deal of the essay is, in any case, fiction.

But it is wrong to suggest that Orwell is strangely reticent about his childhood: in fact, he refers to it many times throughout his writings. Perhaps the most evocative representation appears in his novel *Coming Up For Air* (1939) in which he draws on his memories of his childhood in Shiplake with the Buddicom children to capture George Bowling's urge to rediscover the 'Golden Age' of his youth in Lower Binfield. As biographer Gordon Bowker comments, the scenery around Shiplake 'would haunt Orwell's consciousness and reshape his imaginary world' becoming, with Henley, the Lower Binfield, of *Coming Up For Air* 'while the countryside around inspired the visionary landscape of Winston Smith in *Nineteen Eighty-Four*' (Bowker 2003: 41).

The many references to his youth dotted about his writings and radio broadcasts – while he was a talks producer at the BBC from 1941-1943 – in the end form quite a fascinating 'autobiography'. Here, for instance, in this review of *The Prussian Officer*, Orwell begins with a personal reminiscence – telling of how he first becomes acquainted with Lawrence. 'In 1919, I went into my schoolmaster's study [at Eton] for some purpose and, not finding him there, picked up a magazine with a blue cover which was on the table. I was then sixteen and wallowing in Georgian poetry. My idea of a good poem would have been Rupert Brooke's *Grantchester*. As soon as I opened the magazine I was completely overwhelmed by a poem which describes a woman standing in the kitchen and watching her husband approaching across the fields. On the way he takes a rabbit out of a snare and kills it. Then he comes in, throws the dead rabbit on the table, and his hands still stinking of rabbit's fur, takes the woman in his arms.'

Orwell continues, saying that more than the sexual encounter, the celebration of the 'beauty of Nature' impressed him, particularly the lines, referring to a flower: 'Then her bright breast she will uncover/And yield her honeydrop to her lover.' But in the rush, he fails to notice the name of the author or even the magazine, though he presumes it's the *English Review*. Indeed, Peter Davison confirms that the poem was most likely Lawrence's 'Cruelty and love' which was first published in that journal (*CWGO* XVIII: 388).

Blair makes no move to build up his knowledge of Lawrence. Peter Stansky and William Abrahams comment (1972: 102): 'Perhaps at sixteen, in the range of his imagination and sympathies, he was not quite ready for Lawrence, for those highly-charged, seismic relationships between men and women, so different, say, from the articulate, witty and iconoclastic interchanges between the characters in Shaw that he found so much to his taste.'

Continuing his personal story in the review, Orwell tells of how four or five years later, still not having heard of Lawrence, his picks up a copy of *The Prussian Officer* (possibly at the Smart & Mookerdum bookshop in Rangoon while he is serving as an Imperial Policeman in Burma, though he does not say this) and is again impressed by Lawrence's writing – in the story that leads the collection and in 'The thorn in the flesh'. Both reflect Lawrence's horror and hatred of military discipline. But, according to Orwell, his understanding of its nature is particularly striking. So just months after the end of the Second World War, Orwell is moving away from his stance of patriotic belligerence and focusing, approvingly, on the writings of an anti-militarist and his powerful imagination. 'Something told me that he had never been a soldier, and yet he could project himself into the atmosphere of an army, and the German army at that. He had built all this up, I reflected, from watching a few German soldiers walking about some garrison town' (*CWGO* XVIII: 386).

Orwell now takes the opportunity to explain in more detail his fascination with Lawrence. 'He was in essence a lyric poet and an undisciplined enthusiasm for "Nature" i.e. the surface of the earth, was one of his principal qualities, though it has been much less noticed than his preoccupation with sex.' He continues his review: 'And on top of this he had the power of understanding, or seeming to understand, people totally different from himself such as farmers, gamekeepers, clergymen and soldiers – one might add coalminers' (ibid).

Orwell's own interest in coalminers appears most notably in *The Road to Wigan Pier* (Orwell 1980 [1937]), about his travels in the north of England examining the plight of the poor and unemployed. And his account of going down a mine and crawling through tiny, water-logged tunnels to the coalface to observe the near-naked miners at work is one of the most memorable scenes of the book. He writes: 'It is only when you see miners down the mine and naked that you realize what splendid men they are. Most of them are small (big men are at a disadvantage in that job) but nearly all of them have most noble bodies; wide shoulders tapering to slender supple waists, and the small pronounced buttocks and sinewy thighs, with no an ounce of waste flesh anywhere' (ibid: 133). Lawrence, for his part, in an essay 'Nottingham and the mining country', published the *New Adelphi* (which was to publish some of Orwell's earliest pieces of reportage): 'Under the butty system, the miners worked underground as a sort of intimate community, they knew each other practically naked, and with close intimacy, and the darkness and the remoteness of the pit "stall", and the continual presence of danger, made the physical, instinctive and intuitional contact between men very highly developed, a contact almost as close as touch, very real and very powerful' (Lawrence 1950 [1929]: 117). Orwell says that Lawrence had worked in a pit at the age of thirteen, though he was 'clearly not a typical miner'. But he is mistaken. Lawrence's father, Arthur, was a miner all his life – and Paul Morel's drunken, abusive father in *Sons and Lovers* is loosely based on him – though the writer Lawrence never worked down a pit

LAWRENCE'S 'EXTRAORDINARY POWER' OF IMAGINATION

Orwell goes on to highlight Lawrence's 'extraordinary power' of imagination. Significantly, Orwell, who wrote so powerfully of 'Shooting an elephant' (1936)

while a policeman in Burma and of being a Republican soldier during the Spanish Civil War, in his memoir *Homage to Catalonia* (1938), admires Lawrence's ability to capture in words the experience of shooting at a wild animal! '... the action is not the same as shooting at a target. You do not look along the sights: you aim by an instinctive movement of the whole body, and it is as though your will were driving the bullet forward. This is quite true, and yet I do not suppose Lawrence had ever shot at a wild animal' (ibid).

Next, Orwell praises Lawrence's account of the death scene in his short story, 'England my England', even though it is not included in *The Prussian Officer* collection, for being 'emotionally true, and therefore convincing'. Orwell clearly titles his patriotic essay 'England, your England' – composed in 1941 at a critical moment in the Second World War when invasion by Nazis appeared a distinct possibility – as a way of acknowledging Lawrence's legacy though he deliberately changes Lawrence's anti-war stance to a stirring, pro-war one. As John Worthen points out, Lawrence expresses 'his fundamental opposition to the war and to the spirit of war' in the short story (Worthen 2003: 160). But he is never a pacifist. In 1916, for instance, he condemns some pacifist pamphlets for being 'too squashy altogether' (ibid: 163).

Now, in the *Tribune* review, Orwell is much more sympathetic to Lawrence's anti-militarism. Indeed, it is interesting to wonder how much Lawrence's account of Egbert being shot in the head in a Flanders battlefield in 'England my England' reminds Orwell of his extraordinary description of being shot in *Homage to Catalonia*. For Egbert:

> A shell passed unnoticed in the rapidity of action. And then, into the silence, into the suspense where the soul brooded, finally crashed a noise and a darkness and a moment's flaming agony and horror. Ah, he had seen the dark bird flying towards him, flying home this time. In one instant life and eternity went up in a conflagration of agony, then there was a weight of darkness. When faintly something began to struggle in the darkness, a consciousness of himself, he was aware of a great load and changing sound. To have known the moment of death! And to be forced, before dying, to review it. So, fate, even in death (Lawrence 1974 [1922]: 312).

Egbert has a split second to *think about* the *experience* of being shot:

> There was a resounding of pain. It seemed to sound from the outside of his consciousness: like a loud bell clanging very near. ... After a time he seemed to wake up again, and waking, to know that he was at the front, and that he was killed. ... Bit by bit, like a doom, came the necessity to know. He was hit in the head. It was only a vague surmise at first. But the swinging of the pendulum of pain, swinging ever nearer and nearer, to touch him into an agony of consciousness and a consciousness of agony,

gradually the knowledge emerged – he must be hit in the head – hit on the left brow... (ibid).

He remembers life with his wife, Winifred, and the children but the memories bring on nausea. So inwardly he cries: 'To forget! To forget! Utterly, utterly to forget, in the great forgetting of death.' And the long account of the death agony ends with questions and exclamations, not in darkness but in a terrible light as the German cavalry arrive: 'What was that? A light! A terrible light! Was it figures? Was it legs of a horse colossal – colossal above him: huge, huge?' (ibid: 313).

In contrast to Lawrence's imaginative account, Orwell's is drawn from the actual experience of being hit by a fascist sniper on 20 May 1937 while fighting on the Huesca frontline during the Spanish Civil War. It is written from the benefit of hindsight months after the event. Egbert's instinct is to *think* about being shot – Orwell, in contrast, reflects on the 'interesting' experience as being 'worth describing in detail'. Like Egbert, Orwell is struck by the sound:

> Roughly speaking it was the sensation of being *at the centre* of an explosion. There seemed to be a loud bang and a blinding flash of light all round me and I felt a tremendous shock, such as you get from an electrical terminal; with it a sense of utter weakness, a feeling of being stricken and shrivelled up to nothing. ... I had a numb, dazed feeling, a consciousness of being very badly hurt, but no pain in the ordinary sense (Orwell 1962 [1938]: 177; italics in the original).

Egbert's memories of his family are shrouded in trauma; Orwell's thoughts of his wife, in contrast, have a light, ironic, humorous tone: 'Not being in pain, I felt a vague satisfaction. This ought to please my wife, I thought; she had always wanted me to be wounded, which would save me from being killed when the great battle came' (ibid: 177-178).

One of the many intriguing aspects of Orwell's career is that he wrote in many genres – poetry, essays, journal columns, polemical articles, social and cultural commentaries, war reports, radio broadcasts, book, drama and film reviews, novels, diaries, letters – but never short stories. A short story, 'A peep into the future' (a parody of H. G. Wells in which schoolboys revolt and end the 'reign of Science'), appears in Eton's *Election Times*, No. 4, of June 1918 and is attributed to Blair (*CWGO* X: 48-50). While in Paris in the early 1930s he composes some short stories but destroys them as worthless; at the end of his life he is drawing the outline of a 40,000-word novella he titles 'A smoking-room story'. It is interesting, then, that Orwell, in his review of *The Prussian Officer* collection, directs particular praise on Lawrence's short stories.

He writes: 'With few exceptions Lawrence's full-length novels are, it is generally admitted, difficult to get through. In the short stories his faults do not matter so much because a short story can be purely lyrical, whereas a novel has to take account of probability and has to be cold-bloodedly constructed.' He singles out for praise 'Daughters of the vicar' which is part of *The Prussian Officer* collection, concisely summarising its plot. The elder daughter, Mary, marries a comparatively well-to-do clergyman, who happens to be a dwarf and an 'utterly inhuman creature'. The younger daughter, Louisa, 'whose vitality is not to be defeated by snobbishness, throws family prestige overboard and marries a healthy young coalminer'. In Orwell's description of her as 'the underfed, downtrodden, organ-playing daughter of a clergyman wearing out her youth' does she not resemble in some way Dorothy Hare, the central character of his novel *A Clergyman's Daughter* (1935)? And while the plots of the two novels are certainly different, in the choice of title is not Orwell acknowledging once again his literary debt to Lawrence?

Orwell ends his review expressing the hope that Penguin will reprint Lawrence's collection of short stories *England My England*. One of the stories he highlights is 'Fanny and Annie' (he spells it incorrectly as 'Fannie and Annie'). In it, Fanny returns with a heavy heart to 'a little ugly town on top of the hill' to marry her first love – foundry worker Harry Goodall. A chapel service they both attend is interrupted by the loud shouts of a 'stoutish, red-faced woman' denouncing Harry for making her daughter, Annie, pregnant. Does this, then, not remind you of the end of Orwell's first novel, *Burmese Days* (1934), when the anti-hero John Flory is denounced at a church ceremony by his mistress Ma Hla May? 'Look at me you white men, and you women, too, look at me! Look how he has ruined me! Look at these rags I am wearing!' she yells (Orwell 1976 [1934]: 241). Flory never recovers from this public humiliation and ends up committing suicide.

How much 'Fanny and Annie' inspired the end of *Burmese Days* we will never know. Orwell is clearly determined to keep quiet about that in his fascinating *Tribune* tribute to Lawrence.

Orwell's long-lasting fascination with the short story 'The Prussian Officer', in particular, emerges in his novel *Coming Up For Air* (1939), where the anti-hero, George Bowling, includes it in the list of books he devours – and which start him thinking – while posted for two years in a non-job for the West Coast Defence Force during the war. Along with H. G. Wells's *The History of Mr Polly*, Conrad's *Victory*, Compton Mackenzie's *Sinister Street* (all of them, perhaps not surprisingly, amongst Orwell's favourites), Bowling remembers 'a back number of some magazine with a blue cover which had a short story of D. H. Lawrence's in it. I don't remember the name of it. It was a story about a German conscript who shoves his sergeant-major over the edge of a fortification and then does a bunk and gets caught in his girl's bedroom. It puzzled me a lot. I couldn't make out what it was all about, and yet it left me with a vague feeling that I'd like to read some others like it' (Orwell 1976 [1939]: 501). Later, he gets hold of *Sons and Lovers* 'and sort of half-enjoyed it' (ibid: 502).

LAWRENCE CONSTANTLY PRESENT

Lawrence appears in Orwell's letters and writings throughout his life – though, significantly, he never references such works as *The White Peacock* (1911), *The Trespasser* (1912), *The Rainbow* (1915), *Kangaroo* (1923) or *Mr Noon* (1934) and neither his plays nor his explorations of psychoanalysis draw his attention.

While burdened with the routine tasks of a teacher in Hayes, Middlesex, on 20 July 1933, he writes to his friend Eleanor Jaques: 'I have been reading in D. H. Lawrence's collected letters. Some of them very interesting – there is a quality about L. that I can't define, but everywhere in his work one comes on passages of an extraordinary freshness, vividness, so that tho' I would never, even given the power, have done it quite like that myself, I feel he has seized on an aspect of things that no one else would have noticed. In another way, he reminds me of someone from the Bronze Age' (*CWGO* X: 320). And in a letter to his life-long friend, Brenda Salkend, dated 15 January 1935, from Hampstead NW3, he talks of recently reading one or two of D. H. Lawrence's short stories. 'As well as Max Beerbohm's *And Even Now* and for the I don't know how many-th time, Maupassant's *Boule de Suif* and *La Maison Tellier*' (ibid: 368).

In another gossipy, newsy letter to Brenda Salkeld – ending with 'With much love and many kisses', of 7 May 1935, from 77 Parliament Hill, Hampstead, he tells of reading *Women in Love* 'which is certainly not one of his best'. He goes on: 'I remember reading it before in 1924 [so when in Burma] – the unexpurgated version that time – and how very queer it seemed to me at that age. I see now that what he was trying to do was to create characters who were at once symbolic figures and recognizable human beings which was certainly a mistake. The queer thing is when he concentrates on producing ordinary human characters, as in *Sons and Lovers* and most of the short stories, he gets his meaning across much better as well as being much more readable' (ibid: 386).

England My England even features in a list of 39 'Best Books' he recommends to Brenda in 1936 – between Joyce's *Ulysses* and Somerset Maughan's *Ashenden* (ibid: 308).

His admiration for the still officially censored *Lady Chatterley's Lover* appears in his review of *The Open Air*, a collection of pieces by Adrian Bell, for the *Listener*, 2 December 1936. He writes: 'The book contains comparatively little that is familiar. Open it anywhere and you will almost certainly go on reading. But it would be worth opening for two items alone even if there were nothing else of value in the whole book. One is Gerard Manley Hopkins' lovely poem "Felix Randal" in which the rhythm seems to eddy out of the name like smoke out of an ember; the other is a few lines from Lawrence's *Lady Chatterley's Lover* in which the hideous noise of village school-children having a singing lesson is somehow hit off for ever' (ibid: 526).

A reference to Lawrence even crops up in his review of *The Novel To-day*, by the Marxist Philip Henderson, in *New English Weekly*, of 31 December 1936. He begins: 'Few people have the guts to say outright that art and propaganda are the same thing' (ibid: 532). He continues: 'Most of the time, Mr Henderson is keeping up a pretence of strict critical impartiality, but it is strange how invariably his aesthetic judgments co-incide with his political ones. Proust, Joyce, Wyndham Lewis, Virginia Woolf, Aldous Huxley, Wells, E. M. Forster (all of them "bourgeois" novelists) are patted on the head with varying degrees of contempt; Lawrence (proletarian turned bourgeois, which is worse) is viciously attacked; Hemingway, on the other hand, is treated rather respectfully (because Hemingway, you see, is rumoured to be toying with Communism); Barbusse is bowed down to…' (ibid: 533-534).

MEETING LAWRENCE IN WIGAN

Lawrence appears a number of times in *The Road to Wigan Pier* (1937), Orwell's first-hand account of travelling in the north of England investigating the plight of the poor and the miners' lives.

Towards the end of the first chapter, he leaves Wigan by train. As he sees the hills of the industrial landscape covered with snow, he remembers, of all people, Lawrence. '… out here the snow was untrodden and lay so deep that only the tops of the stone boundary-walls were showing, winding over the hills like black paths. I remember D. H. Lawrence, writing of this same landscape or another near by, said the snow-covered hills rippled away into the distance "like muscle". It was not a simile that would have occurred to me. To my eye the snow and the black walls were more like a white dress with black piping running across it' (Orwell 1980 [1937]: 131).

In the second, somewhat idiosyncratic, iconoclastic, deliberately provocative and semi-autobiographical section of *The Road*, Orwell devotes a long section to Lawrence. He first highlights, with some contempt, the 'proletarian cant' of communist writers such as Alec Brown and Philip Henderson who constantly stress how the bourgeoisie is dead, its culture bankrupt. In contrast, Lawrence makes the same points but is much more 'sincere' (ibid: 200-201): 'It is curious how he harps upon the idea that the English bourgeoisie are all *dead* or at least gelded. Mellors, the gamekeeper in *Lady Chatterley's Lover* (really Lawrence himself), has had the opportunity to get out of his own class and does not particularly want to return to it, because English working people have various "disagreeable habits"; on the other hand the bourgeoisie, with whom he has also mixed to some extent, seem to him half dead, a race of eunuchs. Lady Chatterley's husband, symbolically, is impotent in the actual physical sense. And then there is the poem about the young man (once again Lawrence himself) who "got up to the top of the tree" but came down saying…' Here, Orwell quotes the first two-and-a-half stanzas of the poem

'Climbing up', which begin: 'Oh you've got to be like a monkey/if you climb up the tree!/You've no more use for the solid earth/and the lad you used to be.'

Orwell moves on to a more combative, if decidedly idiosyncratic, witty approach to Lawrence. 'Lawrence tells me that because I have been to public school I am a eunuch. Well, what about it? I can produce medical evidence to the contrary but what good will that do? Lawrence's condemnation remains. If you tell me I'm a scoundrel I may mend my ways, but if you tell me I am a eunuch you are tempting me to hit back in any way that seems feasible. If you want to make an enemy of a man, tell him that his ills are incurable' (ibid: 201).

Lawrence appears later in the text when Orwell is discussing *Intelligentsia of Great Britain*, by D. S. Mirsky, a former prince who converted to communism. Conrad is said to be 'no less imperialist than Kipling' while Lawrence is described as writing 'bare-bodied pornography' and as having 'succeeded in erasing all clues of his proletarian origin' (ibid: 207). Orwell mocks this view adding humorously that this is like suggesting Lawrence 'had been a pork-butcher climbing into the House of Lords!'

LAWRENCE'S IDEALISATION OF THE PAST

Just before the outbreak of war, in August 1939, Orwell's home in Wallington, Hertfordshire, is raided by the police. The authorities have intercepted one of his letters to Jack Kahane, of Obelisk Press in Paris, notorious for publishing 'dirty' books such as the novels of Henry Miller and Lawrence's *Lady Chatterley's Lover*. The police take away the offending titles and he is given a warning by the Public Prosecutor not to import such things again. But the police return *Lady Chatterley's Lover* on the grounds that Orwell, as a writer, 'might have a need for books which it was illegal to possess' (Shelden 1991: 346). As Orwell writes to his publisher, Victor Gollancz, it appears 'Miller's books have not been in print long enough to have become respectable' (see Bowker: n.d.).

In his wide-ranging survey of contemporary literature in his next major essay, 'Inside the whale', of March 1940, Orwell stresses the importance of Lawrence:

> Lawrence at first sight does not seem to be a pessimistic writer, because, like Dickens, he is a 'change-of-heart' man and constantly insisting that life here and now would be all right if only you looked at it a little differently. But what he is demanding is a movement away from our mechanised civilisation, which is not going to happen, and which he knows is not going to happen. Therefore his exasperation with the present turns once more into idealisation of the past, this time a safely mythical past, the Bronze Age. When Lawrence prefers the Etruscans (his Etruscans) to ourselves it is difficult not to agree with him, and yet, after all, it is a species of defeatism, because that is not the direction in which the world is moving. The kind of life that he is always pointing to, a life centring round

simple mysteries – sex, earth, fire, water, blood – is merely a lost cause. All he has been able to produce, therefore, is a wish that things would happen in a way in which they are manifestly not going to happen. 'A wave of generosity or a wave of death,' he says, but it is obvious that there are no waves of generosity this side of the horizon. So he flees to Mexico and then dies at forty-five, a few years before the wave of death gets going (*CWGO* XII: 97).

Later in the essay he has more praise for Lawrence. He writes: 'One only has to think of *Ulysses, Of Human Bondage*, most of Lawrence's early work, especially his short stories and virtually the whole of Eliot's poems up to about 1930, to wonder what is now being written will wear so well' (ibid: 99).

In reviewing *English Ways*, by Jack Hilton, for the *Adelphi*, July 1940, another reference to Lawrence is slipped in: 'Lytton Strachey, in his essay on Stendhal, remarked that people who have the national characteristics in an exaggerated form are not always approved of by their own countrymen. He instanced Shelley and Nelson, and if he had been writing a little later he would probably have added D. H. Lawrence' (ibid: 203).

LAWRENCE THE PROLETARIAN WRITER

Orwell is to work (with great creativity but somewhat unhappily) as a talks producer for the Eastern Service of the BBC from 1941-1943. Before then, in December 1940, Orwell takes part in a discussion on 'The proletarian writer' on the BBC (published in the *Listener*, of 19 December 1940) and, not surprisingly, Lawrence features prominently. Desmond Hawkins begins by suggesting that the crucial moment occurred when Ford Madox Ford, the editor of the *English Review*, met D. H. Lawrence and saw in him the portent of a new class finding expression in literature. 'Lawrence's *Sons and Lovers* really did break new ground. It recorded a kind of experience that simply had not got into print before. And yet it was an experience that had been shared by millions of people. The question is why it had never been recorded earlier' (ibid: 295).

Orwell answers by highlighting the role of education. 'After all, though Lawrence was the son of a coalminer he had an education that was not very different from that of the middle class. He was a university graduate, remember. Before a certain date – roughly speaking before the nineties, when the Education Act began to take effect – very few genuine proletarians could write: that is write with enough facility to produce a book or a story' (ibid). Orwell goes on to contrast Lawrence with Dickens. 'Dickens does not write about the working class; he does not know enough about them. He is *for* the working class, but he feels himself completely different from them – far more different than the average middle-class person would feel nowadays' (ibid, italics in the original).

Lawrence crops up prominently in another BBC talk for the Eastern Service by Orwell, on 10 March 1942, titled 'The re-discovery of Europe'. Lawrence is linked in a group of modern writers along with Joyce, Eliot, Pound, Huxley and Wyndham Lewis which he compares to an older group including Shaw, Wells, Kipling, Bennett and Galsworthy (*CWGO* XIII: 211-212). He moves on to compare in detail Lawrence's 'England my England' and 'The Prussian officer' with Wells' 'The country of the blind'. 'The ultimate subject matter of H. G. Wells's stories is, first of all, scientific discovery, and beyond that the petty snobberies and tragicomedies of contemporary English life, especially lower-middle-class life' (ibid: 213). He continues: 'Now, if you turn to Lawrence's stories, you don't find this belief in Science – rather a hostility towards it, if anything – and you don't find any marked interest in the future, certainly not in a rationalised hedonistic future of the kind Wells deals in. … What you find is a persistent implication that man has thrown away his birthright by becoming civilised. The ultimate subject matter of nearly all Lawrence's books is the failure of contemporary men, especially in the English-speaking countries, to live their lives intensely enough' (ibid).

Childhood, perhaps surprisingly, is to be a subject of constant fascination for Orwell. And Lawrence appears during a remarkable radio discussion on this topic, organised by Orwell on 6 October 1942. Each member of the panel, Herbert Read, Stephen Spender, William Empson, Mulk Raj Anand, along with Orwell, chooses items about childhood and discusses them. Lawrence's poem 'The piano' is read by Empson in a selection that focuses on childhood as a time of innocence. Orwell follows up with this comment: 'But childhood also has its pathetic side & also its nightmare side. A child lives a lot of its time in a very terrifying world. And even seen from the outside a child is a very pathetic thing' (*CWGO* XIV: 79-80).

LAWRENCE THE GREAT SHORT STORY WRITER

Orwell takes the opportunity while reviewing a range of texts for *The New Statesman and Nation* in January 1941 – *The Beauty of the Dead*, by H. E. Bates, *Welsh Short Stories*, selected by Glyn Jones, *The Parents Left Alone*, by T. O. Beachcroft, and *The Battlers*, by Kylie Tennant – to discuss the current state of the market for short stories and their qualities or otherwise. Lawrence receives nothing but praise. He begins with a typical sweeping generalisation: 'Everyone who has had connections with the book trade knows that books of short stories are the worst sellers' (*CWGO* XII: 371). And he goes on to argue: '… in the nearly twenty years since Lawrence published *England My England* very little has been written in this line that has even seemed worth reprinting.' The current batch he dismisses as suffering from a 'sort of flatness and greyness' in which nothing ever happens (ibid: 372).

Much better were the stories of earlier periods. And so he lists Poe, Thackeray, Twain, Kipling, Conrad, H. G. Wells, Somerset Maughan and Joyce. Of Lawrence's output, he selects 'England my England' (again) and 'The fox' for special mention.

Most of them, he says, do not despise the old-fashioned 'plot' – 'The fox', for instance, 'has a plot that could have been used by Edgar Wallace' (ibid). Orwell's comments draw a fierce response from V. S. Pritchett who, in the following week's *New Statesman*, suggests that his reading of the boys' weeklies, *The Gem* and *The Magnet*, has 'confused his mind' (ibid: 374). '… those of D. H. Lawrence and Joyce are flagrant examples of that poetic evocation of "atmosphere" and "character" which Mr Orwell declares to be the bane of the modern short story' (ibid).

Lawrence is referenced on 10 March 1944 in one of the 80 'As I Please' columns he contributes to *Tribune* between 1943 and 1947. Focusing mainly on another of his literary heroes James Joyce, Orwell considers his reputation – academic critics could not resist kicking his corpse, he suggests. 'This was in accordance with the grand old English tradition that the dead must always be flattered unless they happen to be artists. Let a politician die and his worst enemies will stand up on the floor of the House and utter pious lies in his honour but a writer or artist must be sniffed at, at least if he is any good. The entire British press united to insult D. H. Lawrence ("pornographer" was the usual description) as soon as he was dead' (*CWGO* XVI: 118).[1]

LAWRENCE AND ENGLISH IDENTITY

The English People is an essay commissioned in September 1943 by Collins in collaboration with the British Council, but not published until 1947. In it, Orwell indulges his tendencies towards both wild generalisation and acute, specific observations – on topics such as common traits, the moral outlook of citizens, the myth of press freedom given its centralised ownership structure, political attitudes, the class system, language and ending with 'The future of the English people'. He argues that there is a distinct English identity. Thus, 'Individuals are felt to conform to a national pattern. D. H. Lawrence is felt to be "very English" but so is Blake; Dr Johnson and G. K. Chesterton are somehow the same kind of person' (ibid: 203-204).

In his essay attacking Salvador Dali, 'Benefit of clergy', of 1944, Orwell takes the opportunity to defend Lawrence from his detractors. He talks of there being an impulse 'not only to crush every new talent as it appears but to castrate the past as well. Witness the renewed highbrow-baiting that is now going on in this country and America, with its outcry not only against Joyce, Proust and Lawrence but even against T. S. Eliot' (ibid: 237).

The *England My England* collection is clearly one of Orwell's enduring favourites. In discussing short stories in an 'As I Please' column on 2 June 1944, he suggests modern publications prefer them much shorter than the great ones of the past. 'D. H. Lawrence's "England my England", Joyce's "The dead", Conrad's "Youth", and many stories by Henry James would probably be considered too long for any modern periodical' (ibid: 246). He follows this issue up in an essay 'How long is a short story' for *Manchester Evening News*, on 7 September. Here he highlights Lawrence's masterpieces – 'The fox' and 'England my England'. The problem with the latter, though, is that it is too short to be printed as a separate book, but too big for any modern English periodical (ibid: 383).

LAWRENCE'S INFLUENCE ON ORWELL'S WRITING STYLE

Lawrence's impact on subsequent writers is generally seen as being vast. Anais Nin, Henry Miller, Alan Sillitoe, Doris Lessing, David Storey, Norman Mailer, Bernard Malamud, Alberto Moravia, Lawrence Durrell, poets W. H. Auden, Ted Hughes, Gary Snyder, Seamus Heaney – to name but a few (see Meyers 1987). Orwell is hardly ever mentioned in this context. And yet Orwell's reading of Lawrence – in particular his short stories – while serving as an Imperial Policeman in Burma is to have an enormous impact on his writing style.

This is most evident in his first novel, *Burmese Days* (1934). According to Peter Stansky and William Abrahams, the influences of Lawrence, Samuel Butler and Somerset Maugham are striking: 'Lawrence's Way led to the deeply felt descriptions of landscape … Maugham's Way to the sardonic observation of the Kyauktada Club in action; Orwell's Way to the anti-imperialism which is the dominant theme of the novel …' Of Lawrence's prose, they say it is written with greater intensity of vision and feeling than Butler and Maugham are capable of – 'marvellous phrases and sentences that evoked a landscape, or the physical presence of a character, or the nuances of emotional response, a whole range of possibilities that the storyteller straightforwardly telling his story had not time or inclination for' (Stansky and Abrahams 1972: 175).

According to biographer D. J. Taylor, Lawrence 'cast a substantial shadow over Orwell's literary development' (2003: 45). The hunting scenes in *Burmese Days*, in particular, when the shooting provokes a distinct sexual excitement, show 'a discernible Lawrentian trace' (ibid). Take for instance this moment when Flory hands Elizabeth Lackersteen the pigeon she has shot: 'He put it limp and warm into Elizabeth's hand. She could hardly give it up, the feel of it so ravished her. She could have kissed it, hugged it to her breast. All the men, Flory and Ko S'la and the beaters, smiled at one another to see her fondling the dead bird. Reluctantly, she gave it to Ko S'la to put it in the bag. She was conscious of an extraordinary desire to fling her arms around Flory's neck and kiss him; and in some way it was the killing of the pigeon that made her feel this' (Orwell 1976 [1935]: 174). Later, they shoot a leopard. 'She and Flory stood looking down at the leopard, close together, but not clasping hands this time. … Flory and Elizabeth walked side by side across the stubble field. … The light shone level across the field, gilding the stubble stalks, and striking into their faces with a yellow, gentle beam. Elizabeth's shoulder was almost touching Flory's as they walked. … They made no rendezvous, but it was understood between them that they would meet. Also, it was understood that Flory would ask Elizabeth to marry him, though nothing was said about this either' (ibid: 178).

Flory and Elizabeth also witness a girl dance during a *pwe* – a native Burmese play – that also has distinct Lawrentian elements as Orwell stresses its provocative animality, overt sexuality and the ways in which it draws from a civilisation 'stretching back and back'. 'Then she danced in a grotesque posture as though sitting down, knees bent, body leaned forward, with her arms extended and writhing, her head moving to the beat of the drums. The music quickened to a climax' (ibid: 135). Watching the spectacle, Flory reminds Elizabeth that while she has read books and been in civilised places 'Don't you think this is worth watching in its queer way? Just look at that girl's movements – look at that strange, bent-forward pose like a marionette, and the way her arms twist from the elbow like a cobra rising to strike. It's grotesque, it's even ugly, with a sort of willful ugliness. … And yet when you look closely, what art, what centuries of culture you can see behind it!' (ibid).

Orwell's lush descriptions of the Burmese landscape in which men strip off their clothes and luxuriate might also be considered to reflect the influence of Lawrence. For instance, Flory goes on a walk. "The jungle grew greener here, because of the water, and the trees were taller. At the edge of the stream there was a huge dead pyinkado tree festooned with spidery orchids, and there were some wild lime bushes with white waxen flowers. They had a sharp scent like bergamot. … Flory threw off his clothes and stepped into the water. It was a shade cooler than the air, and it came up to his neck when he sat down. Shoals of silvery *mahseer*, no bigger than sardines, came nosing and nibbling at his body' (ibid: 105).

Biographer Jeffrey Meyers highlights in Orwell's novel *A Clergyman's Daughter*, of 1935, the 'Lawrentian descriptions of Dorothy communing with nature or fending off the attentions of an older admirer, Mr Warburton…' (2000: 119). While a distinctive Lawrentian influence appears in Orwell's novel of 1936, *Keep the Aspidistra Flying*. 'With all its faults the novel is disarmingly honest, and Gordon's love affair is strangely moving. When Rosemary is about to surrender to him ("But in her heart she was still frightened," imitates D. H. Lawrence), he himself equating poverty with unworthiness if not impotence, draws back…' (ibid: 130). Orwell's anarchist friend George Woodcock is more critical in his early, outstanding study of his life and writings, *The Crystal Spirit* (1984 [1966]). Of the novel he writes: 'It has a verbose, repetitious style quite unlike that of any of his other books, and while there is often a genuine tone of ironic mockery, this frequently breaks down into an obsessive didacticism reminiscent of D. H. Lawrence at his worst' (ibid: 119).

'SUCH, SUCH WERE THE JOYS' (AND SORROWS) OF SEX FOR ORWELL

According to biographer John Worthen, almost all of Lawrence's writing, particularly after he meets Frieda Weekley in 1912, aims to create a language of our experience of the body and its desires. In 1929, for instance, he writes how it is 'our business to realise sex. Today, the full conscious realisation sex is even more important than the act itself' (Worthen 2005: xxii). Sexuality, indeed, also features significantly throughout Orwell's writings (Keeble 2019).

Orwell's (partly fictionalised) memoir of his time at St Cyprian's prep school, near Eastbourne, between 1911 and 1917, 'Such, such were the joys' (1970 [1952]) is remarkable for its sexual explicitness (Keeble 2018a; Keeble 2018b). The fictionalisation, in effect, serves to distance Orwell from the narrative and its emotional, hyper-personal content. Yet the influence of Lawrence is unmistakable. At the start of Section IV there is a lengthy discussion of sex and homosexuality in particular. Sex becomes linked with secrecy, betrayal, ignorance, confusion and shame. Earlier, he reported how he had 'sneaked' to his favourite teacher, Brown, 'a suspected case of homosexuality' (1970 [1952]: 401). All this leads to an account (how true, how fictional?) of his own sex life and of the sexual development of youths in general. Orwell was never much impressed by psychoanalysis, as biographer Gordon Bowker stresses (Bowker 2003: 48). Yet, if openness about feelings and sexuality (making the personal political) is another mark of today's New Man, then Orwell is ahead of his times (Keeble 2018a: 85). Here, he admits to being 'in an almost sexless state, which is normal or at any rate common in boys of that age' (1970 [1952]: 402). Carefully, he teases out the chronology of his sexual awakening. At five or six 'like many children' (so aiming to generalise from the personal), he moves through a period of sexuality.

> My friends were the plumber's children up the road and we used sometimes to play games of a vaguely erotic kind. One was called 'playing at doctors' and I remember getting a faint but definitely pleasant thrill from holding a toy trumpet, which was supposed to be a stethoscope, against a little girl's belly (ibid: 403).

Next, he falls deeply in love with a girl named Elsie (intriguingly, the name Orwell also gives to the woman with whom George Bowling, the anti-hero of *Coming Up For Air*, has an affair when he's 20 in Little Binfield and sees in the distance by chance on his nostalgic return years later). And he goes on to dwell on his boyhood sexual confusions with what appears compelling honesty (though it may well be all fiction). Most of the Facts of Life (those capital letters indicating their Importance and Severity) are learned through watching animals.

Indeed, it's interesting to see how often in his writings Orwell records his fascination with copulating animals. While researching poverty in northern England – to be published in *The Road to Wigan Pier* (1937) – he notes in his diary for 3 March 1936, while staying at 154 Wallace Road, Sheffield: 'For the first time in my life saw rooks copulating. On the ground, not in a tree. The manner of courtship was peculiar. The female stood with her beak open and the male walked round her and it appeared as though he was feeding her' (2009: 48). While on holiday convalescing with his wife, Eileen, in Marrakech, he writes in March 1939 to Jack Common who is looking after their cottage in rural Hertfordshire, the Stores, while they are away, concerned about the mating of their goat Muriel. 'I hope Muriel's mating went through. It is a most unedifying spectacle, by the way, if you happened to watch it' (Topp 2020: 243). On the way back on board *SS Yasukunimaru*, in the Bay of Biscay, in 1939, he writes in his diary, remembering: 'The father monkey copulated with the mother or began to do so when she was carrying the baby in her arms' (ibid: 133). Later, he notes: 'Pigeons making their mating flight fly steeply up into the air then volplane down' (ibid: 138). And in his celebrated *Tribune* essay 'Some thoughts on the common toad' (1946), Orwell delights in describing the copulation ritual in some detail:

> For a few days after getting into the water the toad concentrates on building up his strength by eating small insects. Presently he has swollen to his normal size again, and then he goes through a phase of intense sexiness. All he knows, at least if he is a male toad, is that he wants to get his arms round something and if you offer him a stick, or even your finger, he will cling to it with surprising strength and take a long time to discover that it is not a female toad. Frequently one comes upon shapeless masses of ten or twenty toads rolling over and over in the water, one clinging to another without distinction of sex. By degrees, however, they sort themselves out into couples, with the male duly sitting on the female's back. You can now distinguish males from females because the male is smaller, darker and sits on top, with his arms tightly clasped round the female's neck. After a day or two the spawn is laid in long strings which wind themselves in and out of the reeds and soon become invisible (Anderson 2006: 306).

The section of 'Such, such...' climaxes with him noticing his penis sometimes standing of its own accord – and his feeling of shame (op cit: 403).

SEXUALITY AMIDST THE DYSTOPIAN GLOOM

The representation of passionate sexuality lies at the heart of both the themes and narrative of *Nineteen Eighty-Four*. According to Cass R. Sunstein (2005: 241):

> Orwell suggests that totalitarian governments favour 'sexual puritanism', which induces 'hysteria', something that such governments mobilize in their own favour. This is the image of patriotic frenzy as 'sex gone sour'. On this view, sexual freedom embodies freedom and individualism, and it is the deepest enemy of a totalitarian state. A state that allows sexual freedom will be unable to repress its citizens.

Or, as Robin West stresses (2005: 248): 'Erotic sex, Winston Smith insists in *Nineteen Eighty-Four*, is a truly *political* and even revolutionary act.'

Indeed, the secret affair between Winston and Julia, the 'girl from the fiction department', is depicted in a distinctly Lawrentian way. For instance, when they meet in a wood and make love for the first time, Orwell writes: 'The next moment, it was hard to say by whose act, she was in his arms. At the beginning he had no feeling except sheer incredulity. The youthful body was strained against his own, the mass of dark hair was against his face, and yes! Actually she turned her face up and he was kissing the wide red mouth. She had clasped her arms about his neck, and she was calling him darling, precious one, loved one. He had pulled her down on to the ground, she was utterly unresisting, he could do what he liked with her' (Orwell 1976 [1949]: 814).

On a critical note, this stress on the 'utterly unresisting' Julia reflects Orwell's obsession – throughout his novels – with sexual performance as 'possession' and the affirmation of manhood (Patai 1984: 248). We are told that Julia has had many affairs, is sexually active and it is she who initiates the affair with Winston. But in the sex act itself, she conforms to the sexist stereotype of submissiveness. And according to the American feminist Kate Millett, in her seminal study of sexism in literature, *Sexual Politics* (1972 [1971]) Lawrence's representation of sexuality is similarly informed by patriarchy: 'Lawrence's knowledge of Freud was sketchy and secondhand, but he appears to be well acquainted with the theories of female passivity and male activity and doubtless found them very convenient' (ibid: 240). Neither Orwell nor Lawrence include any form of foreplay (or postplay) in their depictions of the sex act ('fucking' as the gamekeeper Mellors calls it in *Lady Chatterley*). According to Anthony Burgess: 'Somewhere back in Mellors' previous life is an estranged wife who seems to have been "demanding". Connie [Lady Chatterley] demands nothing but tenderness (*Tenderness* was one of Lawrence's proposed titles), and she seems to get this mostly from immediate penetration, the phallus entering like a deep thrust of peace' (Burgess 1985: 238-239).

Julia, who may well be a Party spy engaged in a honeytrap operation with Winston (see Keeble 2020), still articulates a clear understanding of the Party's strategy to eliminate the sex instinct – and a Lawrentian concern over this: 'There was a direct intimate connexion between chastity and political orthodoxy. For how could the fear, the hatred, and the lunatic credulity which the Party needed in its members be kept at the right pitch, except by bottling down some powerful instinct and using it as a driving force? The sex impulse was dangerous to the Party, and the Party had turned it to account' (op cit: 822). Sexuality, in other words, was a pure kind of life force that could one day destroy the Party.

Linked to this celebration of sexuality in the novel is the way in which Orwell represents the proles, the mass of the population, non-Party members, in whom 'hope' is said to rest. Indeed, there is a distinct Lawrentian feel when he writes of the proles: 'They held on to their primitive emotions.' As David Dwan comments:

'Orwell often maintained that reason could alienate us from our humanity as much as it could express it – a position that informs his mistrust of intellectuals. All too often they cut loose from their moral intuitions in the pursuit of some rational scheme' (Dwan 2020: 69). Yet while the novel exults the animal instinct, human animals are more generally represented as repulsive creatures. As Dwan continues: 'So people quack like ducks, breathe like fish, resemble rodents, or move like insects' (ibid: 71).

CONCLUSION

As this essay has highlighted, the extraordinary impact of Orwell's first serious reading of Lawrence in Burma is to last throughout his life. Lawrence crops up regularly in his writings and broadcasts – often in surprising contexts. So it is intriguing to ponder why Lawrence scholars – Orwell scholars much less so – to date have largely failed to acknowledge this.

In conclusion, it's worth quoting Jeffrey Meyers who, significantly, has written biographies of both writers, and who *does* acknowledge the links between the two writers. Orwell, he says, was influenced by Wells, admired Joyce, was taught by Huxley, befriended Eliot and Waugh, and satirised Auden.

> But the writer he most resembled was D. H. Lawrence, who died in 1930 just as Blair was beginning his literary career. … Both writers lived in restless poverty for most of their lives, were fiercely independent and had a crusading spirit. They were good at household tasks: cooking and mending clothes. They idealized working class life, believed the workers were warm-hearted and in touch with their emotions. They disliked cities, machine civilisation and the worship of money, loved the countryside and had a deep knowledge of nature. They hated the class system, attached bourgeois values and had their defiant books suppressed. In private life they had a puritanical streak, refused to use contraceptives and feared or believed they were sterile. They were given to ferocious exaggerations, violent fantasies, outbursts of rage and prophetic doom. They suffered poor health all their lives, were treated by the same doctor and died of tuberculosis in their mid-forties. Above all, they were courageous writers, faced with formidable adversaries, who spoke the truth (Meyers 2000: 96-97).

NOTE

[1] My mother, Marianne Theresa Burrows (always known as Molly) was the cousin of Louie Burrows to whom D. H. Lawrence was engaged for a while before he met Frieda Weekley. The Burrows family were, predictably, scandalised by the relationship and, as a child growing up in Nottingham in the 1950s, I remember them damning Lawrence as a 'pornographer'. Louie always kept a high regard for Lawrence and chose not to marry until he had died

REFERENCES

Anderson, Paul (2003) *Orwell in* Tribune, London: Politico's

Bowker, Gordon (2003) *George Orwell*, London: Little, Brown

Bowker, Gordon (n.d.) Orwell's library, Orwell Foundation. Available online at https://www.orwellfoundation.com/the-orwell-foundation/orwell/library/gordon-bowker-orwells-library/

Burgess, Anthony (1985) *Flame into Being: The Life and Work of D. H. Lawrence*, London: Heinemann

CWGO (1998) – *The Complete Works of George Orwell*, XX Vols, Davison, Peter (ed.) London: Secker & Warburg

Dwan, David (2020) Orwell and humanism, Waddell, Nathan (ed.) *The Cambridge Companion to* Nineteen Eighty-Four, Cambridge: Cambridge University Press pp 64-78

Keeble, Richard Lance (2018a) 'Such, such were the joys' and the journalistic imagination, *George Orwell Studies*, Vol. 2, No. 2 pp 69-90

Keeble, Richard Lance (2018b) 'The art of Donald McGill': Orwell and the pleasures of sex, *George Orwell Studies*, Vol 3, No. 1 pp 21-36

Keeble, Richard Lance (2019) Beyond the dystopian gloom: Orwell and sexuality, Joseph, Sue and Keeble, Richard Lance (eds) *Sex and Journalism: Critical Global Perspectives*, London: Bite-Sized Books pp 88-96

Keeble, Richard Lance (2020) The secret state and the Julia conundrum, Keeble, Richard Lance, *George Orwell, the Secret State and the Making of* Nineteen Eighty-Four, Bury St Edmunds: Abramis pp 12-25

Lawrence, D. H. (1976 [1914]) *The Prussian Officer and Other Stories*, Harmondsworth, Middlesex: Penguin Books

Lawrence, D. H. (1974 [1922]) England my England, in *The Collected Short Stories of D. H. Lawrence*, London: Book Club Associates pp 286-313

Lawrence, D. H. Lawrence (1950 [1929]) Nottingham and the mining country, *Selected Essays*, Harmondsworth, Middlesex: Penguin Books pp 114-122. Available online at https://www.spokesmanbooks.com/Spokesman/PDF/135Lawrence.pdf

Meyers, Jeffrey (ed.) (1987) *The Legacy of D. H. Lawrence: New Essays*, New York: St Martin's Press

Meyers, Jeffrey (2000) *Orwell: Wintry Conscience of a Generation*, New York: W. W. Norton

Millett, Kate (1972 [1971]) *Sexual Politics*, London: Abacus

Orwell, George (1976 [1935]) *Burmese Days*, in the *Collected Fiction*, London: Secker & Warburg/Octopus pp 73-249

Orwell, George (1980 [1937]) *The Road to Wigan Pier*, in the *Collected Non-Fiction*, London: Secker and Warburg/Octopus pp 125-231

Orwell, George (1962 [1938]) *Homage to Catalonia*, Harmondsworth, Middlesex: Penguin Books

Orwell, George (1976 [1939]) *Coming Up For Air*, in the *Collected Fiction*, London: Secker & Warburg/Octopus pp 431-571

Orwell, George (1976 [1949]) *Nineteen Eighty-Four*, in the *Collected Fiction*, London: Secker & Warburg/Octopus pp 743-925

Orwell, George (1970 [1952]) Such, such were the joys, Orwell, Sonia and Angus, Ian (eds) *The Collected Essays, Journalism and Letters, Vol. 4: In Front of Your Nose 1945-1950*, Harmondsworth, Middlesex: Penguin Books pp 379-422; *Partisan Review*, September-October

Orwell, George (2009) *Diaries*, Davison, Peter (ed.) London: Penguin

Patai, Daphne (1984) *The Orwell Mystique: A Study in Male Ideology*, Amherst: University of Massachusetts Press

Shelden, Michael (1991) *Orwell: The Authorised Biography*, London: William Heinemann

Stansky, Peter and Abrahams, William (1972) *The Unknown Orwell*, London: Constable

Taylor, D. J. (2003) *Orwell: The Life*, London: Chatto & Windus

Topp, Sylvia (2020) *Eileen: The Making of George Orwell*, London: Unbound

Woodcock, George (1984 [1966]) *The Crystal Spirit: A Study of George Orwell*, London: Fourth Estate

Worthen, John (2005) *D. H. Lawrence: The Life of an Outsider*, London: Allen Lane

Chapter Six

'Peace That Is Not Peace': Dealing With the Atomic Bomb

George Orwell's reflections about the atomic bombings of Hiroshima and Nagasaki on 6 and 9 August 1945 – in a wide range of writings – are among his most important and insightful.

His first major statement comes in an essay, 'You and the atom bomb', published in *Tribune* on 19 October 1945 where he concentrates on the bomb's impact on the state. '... the discovery of the atomic bomb, so far from reversing history, will simply intensify the trends which have been apparent for a dozen years at least,' he says (*CWGO* XVII: 319). The great age of democracy and of national self-determination was the age of the musket and the rifle. Most nations could get hold of rifles so that Boers, Bulgars, Abyssinians, Moroccans and Tibetans could fight for independence, sometimes with success. Thereafter, every development in military technique has favoured the state. In 1939, there were only five states capable of waging war on the grand scale – now there are only three – and perhaps only two (ibid: 320). He writes:

> So we have before us the prospect of two or three monstrous super-states, each possessed of a weapon by which millions of people can be wiped out in a few seconds dividing the world between them. ... It has been rather hastily assumed that this means bigger and bloodier wars and perhaps an actual end to the machine civilization. But suppose – and really this is the likeliest development – that the surviving great nations make a tacit agreement never to use the atomic bomb against one another? Suppose they only use it, or the threat of it, against people who are unable to retaliate? In that case, we are back to where we were before, the only difference being that power is concentrated in still fewer hands and that the outlook for subject peoples and oppressed classes is still more hopeless (ibid).

The outcome is indefinite 'peace that is no peace'. This is Orwell, then, in his bleakest mood. Is there any hope? Only if cheap and easily manufactured weapons can be developed that are 'not dependent on huge concentration of industrial plant'. He takes James Burnham's *The Managerial Revolution* (1941) to task for predicting that Germany, not Russia, would dominate the Eurasian land mass. Yet Burnham's essential world view has turned out correct. 'More and more obviously, the surface of the earth is being parcelled off into three great empires, each self-contained and cut off from contact with the wider world and each ruled, under one guise or another, by a self-elected oligarchy' (ibid). Without directly saying so, Orwell suggests that most likely some combination of Western Europe and the United States, a nuclear-armed Soviet Union and East Asia, led by China, will dominate this new, permanent state of 'cold war'. All this clearly anticipates the world of *Nineteen Eighty-Four* in which three super-states, Oceania, Eurasia and Eastasia, are at constant war. As Dorian Lynskey comments in *The Ministry of Truth: A Biography of George Orwell's* 1984 (2019): 'Having invented the phrase "cold war", he also anticipated the doctrine of mutual assured destruction.'

The *Tribune* essay significantly draws a response from Alex Comfort, the pacifist with whom Orwell has earlier engaged in a controversy in verse over the cases for and against waging war. Following the spat, the two, remarkably, become friends. In an article in *War Commentary*, just three weeks after the atomic blasts, Comfort condemns them as acts of 'criminal lunacy which must be without parallel in recorded history' (Laursen 2018: 88). Now, in his letter to *Tribune*, Comfort begins by praising Orwell for putting his finger 'as usual, on the wider analytical point' that different types of weapons tend to produce particular types of societies. Yet, he stresses, 'another conclusion is possible besides mere resignation to the omnipotence of tyrants equipped with nuclear energy. Not only are social institutions dictated by weapon-power: so are revolutionary tactics, and it seems to me that Orwell has made the case for the tactical use of disobedience, which he has tended to condemn in the past as pacifism' (ibid: 90).

Early in 1946, Orwell gives a talk to the Red Flag Fellowship and again expresses concern over the coming of the atom bomb. If war breaks out between the US and the USSR, he says, he would choose the US, since, despite all the faults of uncontrolled capitalism, they had at least liberty. The Soviet Union was so despotic there was little hope of liberty ever emerging there

His fears over the emergence of phony wars between a tiny number of super-states, first expressed in 'You and the atom bomb', appear again in his essay 'Toward European unity' for the July/August 1947 issue of the American leftist journal, *Partisan Review*. 'Within each nuclear-armed state,' he says, the 'necessary psychological atmosphere would be kept up by complete severance from the outer world and by a continuous phony war against rival states. Civilization of this type might remain static for thousands of years' (*CWGO* XIX: 163). As Bernard Crick comments in his 1980 biography: 'This is *Nineteen Eighty-Four*' (1980: 521). But this time a new mood of idealism mixes with the pessimism. There is hope – and it lies in European democratic socialism 'where people are relatively free and happy and where the main motive in life is not the pursuit of money or power'. 'Apart from Australia and New Zealand, the tradition of democratic Socialism can only be said to exist … in Scandinavia, Germany, Austria, Czechoslovakia, Switzerland, the Low Countries, France, Britain, Spain and Italy. Only in those countries are there still large numbers of people to whom the word "Socialism" has some appeal and for whom it is bound up with liberty, equality and internationalism' (op cit: 164).

Atomic warfare plays a crucial role in *Nineteen Eighty-Four*. On one occasion, Winston Smith meets Julia, the 'girl from the Fiction Department', with whom he has a passionate affair, in the ruins of a church destroyed in a nuclear attack 'thirty years' earlier – which suggests the revolution which allowed the Party to seize power occurred in 1954. And when Winston reflects on his childhood in London, one of his earliest memories is of a sudden air raid. 'Perhaps it was the time when the atomic bomb had fallen on Colchester. He did not remember the raid itself, but he did remember his father's hand clutching his own as they hurried down, down, down into some place deep in the earth…' (Orwell 1976 [1949]: 761).

To a certain degree, Orwell's retreat to the remote Scottish island of Jura in the last years of his life in order to concentrate, away from the drudgery of journalism, on writing what was to become his dystopian masterpiece, was also inspired by his fear of atomic warfare. As he confides to his friend Tosco Fyvel on 31 December 1947: 'This stupid war is coming off in abt 10-20 years, and this country will be blown off the map whatever happens. The only hope is to have a few animals in some place not worth a bomb' (*CWGO* XVII: 240-241). And to his friend, Julian Symons, in October 1948, he writes: 'If the show [of atom bombs] does start and is as bad as one fears, it would be fairly easy to be self-supporting on these islands provided one wasn't looted' (ibid: 468).

After the publication of *Nineteen Eighty-Four* on 8 June 1949, in London, and five days later in New York, Orwell discusses with his publisher, Fredric Warburg, who visits him at Cranham sanatorium, his serious concerns over the misinterpretations of his great novel's focus – in particular, on its warnings about atomic warfare. In Warburg's follow-up note on the discussion, which appears in Volume XX of the *Complete Works*, edited by Peter Davison, Orwell makes clear the Soviet Union is not the primary target. Rather, 'the danger lies in the structure imposed on Socialist and on Liberal capitalist communities by the necessity to prepare for total war with the USSR and the new weapon, of which of course the atomic bomb is the most powerful and the most publicized. But danger lies also in the acceptance of a totalitarian outlook by intellectuals of all colour' (*CWGO* XX: 134).

So right until near the very end of his life, atomic warfare is a major preoccupation of George Orwell – a fact worth remembering as people all around the country gather to mark the 75th anniversary of the attacks on Japan.

REFERENCES

Crick, Bernard (1980) *George Orwell: A Life*, Harmondsworth, Middlesex: Penguin

CWGO (1998) *The Complete Works of George Orwell*, Davison, Peter (ed.) XX Vols, London: Secker & Warburg

Laursen, Eric (2018) *The Duty to Stand Aside: Nineteen Eighty-Four and the Wartime Quarrel of George Orwell and Alex Comfort*, Chico, CA: AK Press

Orwell, George (1976 [1949]) *Nineteen Eighty-Four*, in the *Collected Fiction*, London: Secker & Warburg/Octopus pp 743-925

- **This essay originally appeared as 'Orwell and the Atom Bomb', Orwellsociety.com, 6 August 2020. https://orwellsociety.com/orwell-and-the-atomic-bomb/**

Chapter Seven

Throwing Light on the Crucial Quarrel with Comfort

One of the delights of Orwell scholarship is the way in which it constantly throws new light on events and characters marginalised or ignored in the conventional biographies. Take Alex Comfort, for instance. He tends to receive only a passing mention following his intriguing poetic skirmish with Orwell in the columns of *Tribune* during the Second World War. After Comfort (later to gain international fame following the publication of his *The Joy of Sex*) promotes his anarchist pacifist response to the war against the Nazis in a fifteen-stanza poem, 'Letter to an American visitor', Orwell responds with an equally vitriolic Byronic satire 'As one non-combatant to another (A letter to Obadiah Hornbooke)' (see Crick 1980: 438-439, 443; Bowker 2003: 291-292, 299, 304; Meyers 2000: 218, 219). He does not appear at all in Robert Colls's biography (2013) nor in Michael Shelden's (1991).

Eric Laursen's excellent text, *The Duty to Stand Aside: Nineteen Eighty-Four and the Wartime Quarrel of George Orwell and Alex Comfort* (AK Press, Chico, California and Edinburgh, 2018) examines the Comfort/Orwell relationship in forensic detail and, in the process, explores a number of crucially important issues relating to pacifism, anarchism, war-fighting, freedom of expression, the value of friendship – and the cancer of secrecy.

ORWELL – FROM ANTI-WAR TO PRO-WAR

Between returning from the Spanish Civil War in 1937 to the outbreak of the Second World War in 1939, Orwell adopts an outspoken anti-war position. Any war would, he maintains, do nothing more than extend imperialist possessions and interests. Laursen notes Orwell publishing an article in *New Statesman and Nation*, in 1937, advocating 'anti-war agitation' on these grounds:

1. That war against a foreign country only happens when the moneyed classes think they are going to profit from it.

2. That every war when it comes, or before it comes, is represented not as a war but as an act of self-defence against a homicidal maniac ('militarist' Germany in 1914, 'Fascist' Germany next year or the year after). The essential job is to get people to recognise war propaganda when they see it, especially when it is disguised as peace propaganda (Laursen 2018: 23).

In 1938, Orwell joins the anti-war Independent Labour Party (founded in 1893 as a left-wing organisation to further the interests of the working class and by the 1930s a left alternative to the Labour Party) and in September signs the ILP manifesto 'If War Comes We Shall Resist It'. Early in the following year, he contributes a book review to *Peace News*, the journal of the pacifist Peace Pledge Union, and in March, with German troops marching into Czechoslovakia, Orwell writes to his friend, the anarchist poet Herbert Read, arguing that war preparations will lead to 'some kind of Austro-Fascism' in Britain (ibid: 23-24). But then Orwell's views suddenly change. As he recounts in 'My country right or left' (1940), during the night before the announcement of the Russo-German pact in August 1939, he dreams the war has begun and it becomes clear that he is both relieved and that, as a patriot, he will support the war effort (Taylor 2003: 272).

SETTING THE BROAD POLITICAL CONTEXT

One of the many strengths of Laursen's text is the way in which it places the Orwell/Comfort spat within a broad historical and political context. Here, he indicates the strength of the anti-war movement during the lead-up to the conflict: up to 175,000 Britons were members of pacifist groups in 1940. But then many like Orwell suddenly shift their allegiances – including philosopher C. E. M. Joad, Labour MP Philip Noel-Baker and Storm Jameson, novelist and president of English PEN (Laursen op cit: 24). Following the evacuation from Dunkirk and the appointment of Winston Churchill as Prime Minister, Britain begins to execute a policy of 'area' bombing 'in which the RAF deliberately targeted large areas, whole cities, for indiscriminate attacks' (ibid: 27). As Laursen comments: 'No other nation had ever adopted such an approach, not even the Axis powers in Spain; the Luftwaffe's attacks on Britain never reached the same intensity' (ibid). In May 1942, the RAF Bomber Command launches its first – unsuccessful – attempt to wipe out a whole city, Cologne. Operation Gomorrah in August against Hamburg kills up to 40,000 people 'almost as many as the entire German Blitz over England – although the final death toll will probably never be known' (ibid: 28). In total, some 600,000 European civilians are killed and more than a million seriously injured as a result of British and American air raids, with 7.5 million left homeless. During the conflict, the war cabinet will even contemplate area attacks using mustard gas on civilians. When reports emerge in 1943 that the Nazis may be planning to use biological weapons, the US begins to produce such weapons as well. Moreover, the tight blockade imposed on the Nazi-occupied Continent by the British navy leads to famine in Greece while food shortages kill thousands of Jews confined to ghettos in Warsaw and other cities.

Yet Laursen is always careful to 'balance' his reporting. Here he records the Luftwaffe dropping more than 57,000 tons of high-explosive incendiary bombs on British cities killing over 43,000 civilians and leaving up to 139,000 injured. According to the RAF, the bombing campaign was not gratuitous but a matter of desperate necessity while the naval blockade, it could be argued, helped reduce the duration of the war – perhaps by years (ibid: 34-35).

ORWELL'S CHANGING RESPONSE TO THE BRITISH WAR EFFORT

By 1941, Orwell is already confiding to his diary concerns over the lack of self-criticism among the patriotic clergy. 'God is asked "to turn the hearts of our enemies, and to help us to forgive them, to give them repentance for their misdoings and a readiness to make amends". Nothing about our enemies forgiving us' (ibid: 35). Later, he writes in his diary: 'The authorities in Canada have now chained up a number of German prisoners equal to the number of British prisoners chained up in Germany. What the devil are we coming to?' (ibid: 40). And in an unpublished letter to *The Times*, he argues that this sort of response only shows how Britain is prepared to 'descend to the level of our enemies'.

ORWELL REVIEWS COMFORT FOR THE FIRST TIME

It is only now that Orwell comes into contact with Alex Comfort – reviewing his first novel, *No Such Liberty*, for *Adelphi*, the journal edited by Orwell's friend Sir Richard Rees which has published some of Orwell's earliest essays and which has recently taken up a pacifist position. As Laursen indicates, Comfort was the sole child of lower middle class parents, only able to send him to Highgate School, then to Cambridge and his medical training 'with the help of scholarships and a good deal of scrimping and saving' (ibid: 22). By the 1940s he becomes part of the New Romantics group of young poets – including Nicholas Moore, John Bayliss, George Barker and Henry Treece – who oppose the 'insanity' of a political system that instigates the mass slaughter of war (ibid: 20). *No Such Liberty* is the story of a young pathologist and his wife who flee Nazi Germany only to face persecution in Britain. In his review, Orwell says it's a 'good novel as novels go at the moment' but is essentially a tract pushing the message of pacifism. In any case, he argues, the pacifist is objectively pro-Nazi.

He follows this up with a letter in the March-April 1942 issue of *Partisan Review*, in which he attacks 'quisling intellectuals' including Comfort ('a "pure" pacifist of the other-cheek school'). Comfort responds in the September/October issue challenging Orwell's insinuation that pacifists would make peace with a German occupation. Rather, pacifists would be 'the only people likely to hold genuinely anti-fascist values'. And so the controversy between the two men continues. Orwell now acknowledges that Comfort has written a poem he values greatly ('The atoll of the mind') but rejects totally his argument in a recent letter to *Horizon* that 'adversity tends to produce great literature'. Laursen sums up the two positions astutely:

> Orwell hoped, at least faintly, that the government-directed wartime economy would become a stepping-stone to socialism, the overthrow of the class system, and the marginalization of the Right. ... Comfort and the other anarcho-pacifists were far more cynical. Who were the people directing the war effort? they asked. What were their aims and why should people on the left suddenly trust them? (ibid: 51).

Laursen goes on to criticise Orwell's position: 'Other than occasionally voicing vague hopes for a libertarian-socialist revolution, he seems never to have thought through the implications of allowing Churchill and his companions to lead the nation in its fight against the very regimes many of them had tolerated before the war' (ibid: 51).

VITRIOL IN VERSE

Following the *Partisan Review* exchanges, Comfort and Orwell send respectful letters to each other. Orwell explains some references he had made to 'Jew-baiting of a mild kind' in an *Adelphi* article while Comfort compliments Orwell on his essay 'The art of Donald McGill' and even thanks him for the negative review of his novel. Then, on 4 June 1943, *Tribune* publishes Comfort's 15-stanza poem 'Letter to an American visitor' in which he mocks Churchill's stirring speeches as 'the dim productions of his bulldog brain', condemns the Church's willingness to preach that 'bombs are Christian when the English drop them' and even suggests – in a direct jibe at Orwell's BBC arts programmes – that the country's literary giants are willing to turn out propaganda in exchange for avoiding military service (ibid: 60). Two weeks later, on 18 June, Orwell responds with his own Byronic satire 'As one non-combatant to another (A letter to "Obadiah Hornbrooke")'. Laursen suggests that at the heart of the poem 'is an almost anguished attempt to justify his own decision to offer his services and his reputation to a government he knew was trafficking in lies and propaganda, and to distinguish himself from the professional liars' (ibid: 63). He writes:

> It doesn't need the eye of a detective
>
> To look down Portland Place and spot the whores
>
> But there are men (I grant, not the most heeded)
>
> With twice your gifts and courage three times yours

Who do that dirty work because it's needed;
Not blindly, but for reasons they can balance,
They wear their seats out and lay waste their talents.

Orwell, ever ready to surprise, moves ever closer to Comfort after this intriguing poetic tiff. In a letter he praises Comfort's poetic gifts and says he is reconsidering his views on literature and the war. Laursen comments:

> It was easier, perhaps, for Orwell's thoughts to turn in this direction in the summer of 1943 when the German army was being driven, agonizingly, from Russia and the Allied invasion of occupied Europe was in the planning stage. ... Additionally, Orwell was clearly tired of defending his decision to work for the government. Two months later, he resigned from the BBC 'after wasting 2 years in it' (ibid: 65).

On becoming literary editor of *Tribune*, Orwell invites Comfort to contribute articles. So the following June, he sends – mischievously – a poem titled 'The little apocalypse of Obadiah Hornbrook' in which he again satirises wartime propagandists. The poem draws furious letters from readers. In response, Orwell reassures them that he does not agree with poet's sentiments but stresses the journal's open policy towards contributors – though they would never print an article in favour of anti-Semitism, for instance. He even takes on some of Comfort's argument: 'I should be the last to claim that we are morally superior to our enemies and there is quite a strong case for saying that British imperialism is actually worse than Nazism' (ibid: 69).

The strength of Laursen's book is that it unearths the fascinating story of Orwell's ongoing debates with Comfort – largely ignored in previous biographies – which reveal the depth, complexity and ever-changing nature of Orwell's positions on war-fighting and pacifism. After Comfort, in January 1944, issues a manifesto to subscribers of *Poetry Folios* protesting at the ways in which modern warfare relegates the principles of international law 'in favour of the unreserved pursuit of total warfare', the pacifist campaigner Vera Brittain publishes *Seed of Chaos: What Mass Bombing Really Means* comprising eye-witness accounts of the saturation bombing of German cities. In his 19 May 1944 'As I Please' column in *Tribune*, Orwell responds to Brittain and suddenly shifts away from his neo-Comfortian line, backing – appallingly – the strategy of indiscriminate bombing. All talk of limiting and humanising warfare is sheer humbug, he says. And in a column two months later he argues ('bizarrely', according to Laursen) that it is 'probably somewhat better to kill a cross-section of the population than to kill only young men...' (ibid: 80).

OUTRAGE OVER ATTACK ON FREEDOM PRESS

In November 1944, Special Branch raids the premises of the anarchist Freedom Press in response to a manifesto published in *War Commentary* calling on members of the armed forces to practise mass disobedience once the war is over, if not before. Immediately, a Freedom Press Defence Committee is formed with Orwell as vice-chair (the only office he ever accepts), Herbert Read, chair, and George Woodcock as secretary. Laursen comments perceptively: 'The Freedom Press raid must have had an especially powerful effect on Orwell, given his experience of political persecution in Spain' (ibid: 85). In an August 1944 'As I Please', he writes:

> War damages the fabric of civilisation, not by the destruction it causes … not even by the slaughter of human beings but by stimulating hatred and dishonesty. … By hating [your enemy], by inventing lies about him and bringing children up to believe them, by clamouring for unjust peace terms which make further wars inevitable, you are striking not at one perishable generation but at humanity itself (ibid).

Orwell moves increasingly closer to his anarchist/pacifist colleagues. The two writers he attacked in his 1942 *Partisan Review* column, Woodcock and Julian Symons, become close friends; in January 1946 he accepts an invitation to address the London Anarchist Group on 'Trends in Russia's foreign policy', and he allows the anarchists Vernon Richards and his wife Marie Louise Berneri to take photographs of him at his home relaxing with his son, Richard. Laursen comments: 'This is not as paradoxical as it might seem. Whatever Orwell's objections to anarchism, anarchists themselves were an important component of the anti-communist left with which he generally identified himself, starting in Spain, and he couldn't help but notice their viewpoints overlapped with his' (ibid: 86).

Orwell next joins his pacifist/anarchist colleagues in condemning the nuclear bombing of Hiroshima and Nagasaki in August 1945. Writing in *War Commentary*, Comfort says bluntly that 'the men who did this are criminal lunatics'. For his part, Orwell, in *Tribune*, argues that the discovery of the atomic bomb would intensify trends apparent over the last dozen years with a few superpowers dominating the world. 'The Bomb, because of the industrial resources needed to produce it, would reinforce and speed up this grim trend which foreshadowed the dystopia he was already turning into compelling fiction in his manuscript of *Nineteen Eighty-Four*' (ibid: 89-90).

In a comprehensive account of the launch of the book at the Golden Notebook bookstore in Woodstock, New York, Carol Biederstadt reports Laursen as suggesting that 'Orwell won the battle' with Comfort for it 'was clearly necessary to oppose Hitler'.[1] Believing there exists a 'need to take the activist role that Comfort envisaged', however, he felt Comfort had ultimately won their 'ideological war'. Biederstadt continues:

He elaborates on this in the final pages of *The Duty to Stand Aside*, where he draws attention to the fact that whether or not current governments label a military action a 'war', modern assaults continue to sacrifice civilians. He cites, for example, Associated Press statistics that claim there were between 9,000 and 11,000 civilian casualties in the 2017 'assault against Islamic State forces in Mosul, Iraq'. But neither the Iraqi government, the US-led coalition, nor the Islamic State itself would acknowledge the numbers, even though most of them came from Mosul's morgue. ... If Comfort were alive, these revelations would have shocked but not surprised him, registering as yet another example of the irresponsibility of the State, carrying us one step further in the decline of sociability and another step toward barbarism. His answer would doubtless be the same one he offered during World War II and the nuclear build-up of the post-war decades: Be responsible. Disobey (Laursen 2018: 151-152).

DYSTOPIA AND AFTER

Laursen criticises Orwell's dystopian masterpiece for saying little about how the elites of the three superstates come into being other than through the simple lust for power. He suggests that Comfort offers a 'partial answer' in his treatise which appears shortly after Orwell's death in January 1950 titled *Authority and Delinquency: A Criminological Approach to the Problem of Power*. His strategy for ending the regime of delinquents in authority has six elements: education, experiments in communal living; increasing workers' control of production; 'propaganda' and 'instruction' of both children and adults to make sociability a more prominent part of character formation; psychiatry to help the individual to reject and resist 'bad institutions' – plus public resistance and the willingness to disobey. Overall, Laursen is in sympathy with these views. 'Comfort's proposals were rooted in a belief, shared by others on the left, not only that human nature could be improved, but that such improvement was now necessary to keep the human race from destroying itself' (ibid: 105).

Comfort's later fame with the publication of *The Joy of Sex* in 1972 is mentioned but Laursen strangely fails to take this as a cue to explore the ideas about sexuality and sex repression which play such an important role in *Nineteen Eighty-Four* – particularly in the descriptions of the secret, passionate affair between Winston Smith and Julia. In *Barbarism and Sexual Freedom* (1948), Comfort argues that coercion or institutions sponsored by the state and other religious or civil bodies have no place in sexuality – and any necessary revolution in the individual's sexuality will equally require a revolution in the social order (see Marshall 2008 [1992]: 596).

ORWELL'S 'LITTLE LIST'

Having developed this friendship with Comfort his final act is, astonishingly, to betray him. In May 1949, Orwell sends a list of 38 names of crypto-communists to his friend, the glamorous Celia Kirwan, who has taken a job at the government's recently set-up secret propaganda unit, the Information Research Department. One of these – alongside such names as Charlie Chaplin, historians E. H. Carr and Isaac Deutscher, J. B. Priestley, Paul Robeson, Orson Welles, Upton Sinclair – is Alex Comfort. On his potential to collaborate with the communists, he writes: 'Potential only.' Worse is to come: 'Is pacifist-anarchist. Main emphasis anti-British. Subjectively pro-German during the war, appears temperamentally pro-totalitarian. Not morally courageous. Has crippled hand. Very talented' (ibid: 105). Laursen is rightly highly critical of Orwell's action. While his coverage is again deliberately 'balanced' giving the 'understanding' reactions of Christopher Hitchens and Timothy Garton Ash, he ends with these strong words:

> Though Orwell's submission to the IRD was not a blacklist – he wasn't seeking to get anyone fired from their job – it brought Comfort and dozens of other individuals to the attention of a state intelligence apparatus that might abuse that information. And while many of these individuals were already strongly identified as leftists, being tagged as unreliable by another prominent writer of the left could only have put them at greater risk, given the atmosphere of the time (ibid: 121-122).

FINAL REFLECTIONS

One of the many strengths of Laursen's book is to highlight Comfort's anarcho/pacifist views – views which are so rarely considered in the mainstream media – nor even in the academy. Yet there are long and highly significant traditions of both anarchism and pacifism. As Peter Marshall stresses in his 818-page, comprehensive history of anarchism: 'Although often associated with violence, historically anarchism has been far less violent than other political creeds. ... Moreover, a tradition which encompasses such thoughtful and peaceable men as Godwin, Proudhon, Kropotkin and Tolstoy can hardly be dismissed as inherently terroristic and nihilistic' (Marshall 2008 [1992]: ix). Mohandas Gandhi, the leader of Indian Independence, was a kind of pacifist anarchist, always opposed to the centralised state and the violence it engendered. He was particularly inspired by the writings of Leo Tolstoy, Henry David Thoreau's essay on *Civil Disobedience* (1849) and John Ruskin's *Unto This Last* (1860). Carissa Honeywell, for her part, places Comfort within a modern tradition of pacifist theory and practice which embraces the work of Herbert Read, Paul Goodman, Colin Ward and Murray Bookchin (Honeywell 2014). Given more space, Laursen would probably have sought to situate the Comfort/Orwell spat in this broader historical context.

The study is also useful for highlighting the ways in which Orwell's thoughts shifted, often dramatically, over time. One moment he is fervently opposed to the approaching war with the Nazis; then suddenly following a dream he switches to an equally firm commitment to supporting the war effort. And this allegiance shifts down many contrasting lanes – he even supports indiscriminate bombing. But then, after the raid on the anarchist Freedom Press, he shakes off a habit of a lifetime and actually joins a committee set up to defend it. Orwell was, after all, a journalist and author determined to bash out as many words as possible in his short life. Not surprisingly, given the pressures, his views shifted as his moods changed.

The spat with Comfort also highlights the dark side of Orwell's complex, contradictory personality. There is no excusing those nasty few words he wrote about Comfort in his secret list to British intelligence. It is all the more shocking given the friendship which appears to have developed between the two men. Orwell was certainly no saint. But then he never claimed to be one. And no wonder he asked for no biography to be written. He had a lot of secrets which he clearly wanted the world never to know.

NOTE

[1] https://orwellsociety.com/the-comfort-of-pacifism/, accessed on 22 June 2020

REFERENCES

Honeywell, Carissa (2014) Bridging the gaps: Twentieth-century Anglo-American anarchist thought, Kinna, R. (ed.) (2012) *The Bloomsbury Companion to Anarchism*, London: Bloomsbury pp 111-139

Marshall, Peter (2008 [1992]) *Dreaming the Impossible: A History of Anarchism*, London: Harper Perennial

- **This essay originally appeared as 'Throwing light on Orwell's crucial quarrel with Comfort',** *George Orwell Studies*, **Vol. 5, No. 1 pp 120-128**

Chapter Eight

Down But Not Out: 'The Spike' – And Orwell As (An Always Ambivalent) Radical Campaigner for Social Justice

This chapter examines 'The spike', one of George Orwell's earliest essays – about his time spent with street beggars and tramps. It places the essay in the context of the personal, political and journalistic development of Eric Blair (as he then was) and of the tradition of socially concerned journalistic investigations of poverty in the UK from the mid-Victorian period up until Blair's largely overlooked contemporaries in the 1930s. In stressing the importance of identifying the political economy of the media in any analysis of the ethics of literary journalism, it focuses on the *Adelphi*, the journal which carried 'The spike' highlighting its political/ethical stance and the preoccupations of its targeted readership. In examining the literary elements of 'The spike', the essay explores such aspects as narrative flow, the narrator's voice, mixing compassion and disgust, and the descriptions of characters. The conclusion, however, challenges John Rodden's over-literary analysis of Orwell's early writings and argues that his journalism is best seen as one element of his *life as a politically engaged writer*.

BIOGRAPHICAL BACKGROUND

Journalism persisted as an activity for Orwell from the start of his writing career until ill-health forced him to stop in 1949 – while newspapers, censorship, freedom of speech, propaganda and language were subjects for constant study and critique. Resigning after five years as an Imperial Policeman in Burma in 1927, Eric Blair (as he then was) returns to England and (much to the horror of his family) determines to make his way as a journalist and writer. So he decides to spend months on end with the tramps in London's East End, with the hop pickers of Kent and as a *plongeur* in an up-market hotel in Paris. All this is part of his efforts (as he points out in the autobiographical, second section of *The Road to Wigan Pier*, of 1937) to exorcise his guilt for having been part of an illegitimate system of imperial oppression – but at the same time he is fully aware that his experiences can form the basis for journalistic copy. 'The spike' is one of a series of works based on his time spent with tramps – the most substantial being *Down and Out in Paris and London* (1933), to which he attaches for the first time the pseudonym George Orwell.

The essay appears at a time of deep economic and political crisis for Britain. In May 1926, British workers engage in a nine-day General Strike (see https://spartacus-educational.com/TUgeneral.htm). Following the Wall Street crash in 1929 and the consequent global depression, Britain's trade slumps so that by 1932 registered unemployed number 3.5 million with many more reduced to part-time employment. A minority Labour government takes office in May 1929 but Big Business panics and withdraws capital from the country. In response, Labour leader Ramsay Macdonald is forced to form a National Government in 1931 with Conservative and Liberal support. One dissatisfied Labour government minister, Oswald Mosely, resigns and goes on to form the British Union of Fascists (Bowker 2003: 127). Led by communists, the National Unemployed Workers' Movement continues its series of 'hunger marches' on London. Between 1920, when the depression begins to bite, and 1936, six national marches are organised, with protestors demanding 'work or full maintenance at trade union rates'. Protests over unemployment are held in many cities throughout the country, often leading to pitched battles with police. Indeed, the unemployed are far from apathetic (Gardiner 2011 [2010]: 149-181). And in January 1933, Adolf Hitler becomes German Chancellor.

PUTTING THE SPOTLIGHT ON THE 'LUMPENPROLETARIAT'

In focusing his attention on down-and-outs, street beggars and tramps, Orwell is deliberately adopting a radical political/ethical approach, highlighting the plight of those too often rendered invisible by society. Karl Marx and Friedrich Engels set the trend, in effect, in a range of works where they direct not concern but venom at the members of the underclass they call the 'lumpenproletariat'. For instance, in *The Communist Manifesto* (1848: 20), they are described as 'the dangerous class, the social scum, that passively rotting mass thrown off by the lowest layers of the old society which may, here and there, be swept into the movement by a proletarian revolution; its conditions of life, however, prepare it far more for the part of a bribed tool of reactionary intrigue'. However, the anarchist Mikhail Bakunin celebrates the revolutionary potential of the 'lumpenproletariat' which he dubs 'that great mass, those millions of the uncultivated, the disinherited, the miserable, the illiterates, whom Messrs Engels and Marx would subject to their paternal rule' (see Ingram n.d). Contrasting attitudes towards the underclass amongst social justice theorists continue into the 1930s when Orwell is reporting on the plight of the down-and-outs. As Philip Bounds comments (2016: 38).

> With the exception of Wilfred Macartney, whose prison memoir *Walls Have Mouths* was reviewed admiringly by Orwell in November 1936, there were practically no communist intellectuals who wrote sympathetically about the 'lumpenproletariat'. This was probably because the genuinely dispossessed were often regarded as politically unreliable, usually on the grounds that their desperate circumstances made them susceptible to the appeal of fascism.

But drawing on the research of H. Gustav Klaus (2003), Bounds goes on to highlight a group of working class writers who, in the Bakunin/anarchist tradition, portray the tramp as a sort of walking protest against the dull conformities of bourgeois life. They include Liam O'Flaherty, R. M. Fox and James Hanley who write for radical publications such as *Sunday Worker*, the *Worker* and *Forward* (Bounds 2016: 38-39).

SOCIAL JUSTICE CAMPAIGNERS

Equally important to an understanding of Blair/Orwell's reporting on the poor and outcasts is the tradition of social justice action and reportage associated in the 19th and early 20th centuries with slumming. *The People of the Abyss* (1903), Jack London's account of his journeys to the poorest areas of London's East End, had a substantial impact on Orwell – inspiring him to conduct his own investigations into the underclass. And his dystopian novel, *The Iron Heel* (1908), is also to exercise a major influence on Orwell's later *Nineteen Eighty-Four* (1949).

But London is just one of a group of journalists and social justice campaigners who venture into the slum districts around Whitechapel and Shoreditch. For instance, novelist and journalist Charles Dickens (1812-1870) and Henry Mayhew (1812-1887), author of *London Labour and the London Poor* (1851), trawl the backstreets of the capital in search of scenes of destitution to reproduce for their indignant readers. But, as Seth Koven stresses (2004: 26), they remain 'sympathetic outsiders and observers of life among the poor'. In contrast, *Pall Mall Gazette* reporter James Greenwood (1832-1929) ventures into London's netherworlds masquerading as one of the poor and publishes a series of articles in 1866 that causes an immediate sensation. According to Koven, Greenwood's articles 'made the degrading conditions in the casual wards of workhouses an instant *cause célèbre*' (ibid). In the September 1888 issue of *Nineteenth Century*, Beatrice Potter (1858-1943) publishes her 'Pages of a workgirl's diary', recording her experiences going undercover as a Jewish trouser fitter and in an East London sweatshop. London-based American journalist Elizabeth L. Banks (1872-1938) and trade unionist Clementina Black (1853-1922) also highlight the plight of labouring girls and women, matchbox makers and servants around this time (ibid: 155-180). And in November 1883, Samuel Barnett launches the 'university settlement' movement, inspiring Oxford University students (in particular, those at Keble College) to commit to philanthropic work amongst the destitute of London (ibid: 237-276).

THE INFLUENCE OF THE SUPER-TRAMP

Another inspiration was W. H. Davies's *The Autobiography of a Super-Tramp* (1908) which Orwell read while at Eton from 1917-1921 (Bowker n. d). Davies, born in Newport, Monmouthshire, in 1871, the son of an iron moulder, describes the six years he spends living as a tramp while crossing North America 1883-1899. They take in the terrible accident in Canada which leaves him with one leg, the later years he becomes a beggar and would-be poet in England and Wales – and the eventual publication of his poetry. He is encouraged to publish his autobiography by fellow Welsh poet Edward Thomas while George Bernard Shaw, who suggests the title (somewhat analogous to the title of his play *Man and Superman*), praises it in a preface as 'an amazing book'.

ON THE WILDE SIDE

In his early study of Orwell, *The Crystal Spirit*, his anarchist friend George Woodcock highlights the possible influence of Oscar Wilde on the decision to go tramping. Wilde's *The Picture of Dorian Gray* always fascinates Orwell – from his time at Eton. 'Dorian Gray also descended into the lower depths of London society …. In search of opium, Orwell of another kind of forgetfulness, but each had his guilt, each picked a disguise, each set off with a touch of fear for the darknesses of London's dockland subworld where, in the ugliness of misery, the diamond of reality might be found' (Woodcock 1966 [1984]: 93-94).

Yet Orwell's sustained interest in Wilde's novel 'was most probably due to the fact that it described a double life centring around the creation of a new persona, and this was precisely what concerned Orwell at the time he was making his expeditions into the slums' (ibid: 95).

ORWELL NOT ALONE IN FOCUS ON UNEMPLOYED AND THE 'HUNGRY 1930S'

Orwell was far from alone in writing about the plight of the unemployed during the 1930s. Wal Hannington, leader of the National Unemployed Workers' Movement wrote a number of books – *Never on Our Knees, Ten Lean Years, Unemployed Struggles* – some of which were published by Victor Gollancz's Left Book Club. Walter Greenwood's *Love on the Dole* (1933) was probably the best known novel of the Depression (in 1936, the British Board of Film Censors twice banned the film version, one reason being that it featured a scene in which unemployed men fought the police, and it only reached the screen in 1941). Walter Brierley's harrowing *Means-Test Man* (1935) sold 6,000 copies in its first year of publication. Other books included James Hanley's *Grey Children*, Roger Dataller's *Steel Saraband*, Lewis Jones's *Cwmardy*, Lewis Grassic's *A Scots Quair*, B. L. Coombes's *These Poor Hands* (1937) and A. J. Cronin's *The Stars Look Down* (1935) and *The Citadel* (1937) (see Gardiner 2011 [2010]: 64-65).

The Pilgrim Trust, after surveying 1,000 unemployed men, published their findings in *Men Without Work*; Hubert Llewellyn Smith's team at the London School of Economics examined the changes since Booth's turn-of-the century survey, *Life and Labour of the People in London*; J. P. Priestley set out on a journey across England, determined not to be one of those who 'never poked [their noses] outside Westminster, the City and Fleet Street'; journalist J. L. Hodson titled his survey *Our Two Englands* (1936), drawing on Benjamin Disraeli's notion of two nations; American professor of English Mary Ellen Chase published *In England Now* (1937) while in *Hungry England* (1932) Fenner Brockway (later, as leader of the Independent Labour Party, to help Orwell secure access to the Spanish Civil War frontline in 1936) writes of 'hunger gnawing at the stomach, hunger making one dizzy and weak, hunger destroying one's body and destroying one's mind'. John Brown, Max Cohen and George Tomlinson, a Nottingham coalminer, wrote memoirs of their time unemployed. In 1931, the BBC broadcast a series on unemployment, with speakers including Herbert Morrison, the economist John Maynard Keynes, Seebohm Rowntree and Conservative leader Stanley Baldwin. BBC journalist S. P. B. Mais travelled the country interviewing the jobless for his *Time to Spare* series in January 1933. And a second series of *Time to Spare*, produced by Felix Greene, brought unemployed workers to Broadcasting House in London to tell their stories (ibid: 60-64).

ORWELL AND THE PROGRESSIVE PRESS

While in Paris, Blair exploits the contacts his radical feminist aunt Nellie and her partner Eugène Adam have with Henri Barbusse, the communist editor of the journal *Monde*, to contribute an article 'La censure en Angleterre'. As a result of his connection with Barbusse, Orwell comes to the attention of a section of British intelligence who follow him closely for the rest of his life. His follow-up articles on an eclectic range of topics – unemployment in Britain, a day in the life of a tramp, beggars in London, and the British Empire in Burma – are published by another progressive French journal *Le Progrès Civique*. Significantly, his first published piece in the UK, 'A farthing newspaper' (for Chesterton's review *G. K's Weekly*) focuses on *Ami du Peuple*, costing just ten centimes, which has recently been launched in Paris with a manifesto claiming it is 'uncontaminated by any base thoughts of gain'. Blair comments ironically:

The proprietors, who hide their blushes in anonymity, are emptying their pockets for the mere pleasure of doing good by stealth. Their objects, we learn, are to make war on the great trusts, to fight for a lower cost of living and above all combat the powerful newspapers which are strangling free speech in France (1970 1 [1931]: 34-35).

He proceeds to deconstruct, with polemical vigour, the paper's pretensions – noting that its proprietor is M. Coty – a 'great industrial capitalist and also proprietor of the *Figaro* and the *Gaulois*'. In other words, it is merely putting across 'the sort of propaganda wanted by M. Coty and his associates' (see Keeble 2020). According to D. J. Taylor, Blair's early essay is missing a conspicuous personal voice approximating more to what a commissioning editor today would call a 'think piece' (Taylor 2003: 95)

Yet Eric Blair's decision to target his first articles, including his next essay, 'The spike', to alternative, progressive journals reflects a crucial commitment to translate his *understanding* of the political economy of the press into journalistic *practice*. And this commitment was to remain throughout his career – right up until his final writings in 1949. The *Adelphi*, which publishes 'The spike' in 1931, was launched by John Middleton Murry in 1923 to promote the ideas of his friend, the novelist D. H. Lawrence (Marks 2011: 22). But in 1930, Max Plowman and fellow old-Etonian, pacifist and millionaire Richard Rees take over the editorship and the journal moves to the radical left, even affiliating to the anti-war Independent Labour Party in October 1932 and promoting anti-Soviet Marxist views. The political allegiances Orwell forms in the early 1930s are to last throughout his life: the pacifist Plowman supports Blair until his death in 1941; Rees becomes a close friend and co-executor of Orwell's will. Jack Common, a proletarian author from Newcastle, who works as the journal's circulation manager, also becomes a lifelong friend after being initially suspicious of Blair's public school mannerisms (Bowker 2003: 123). Indeed, Orwell is to direct a great deal of his journalism throughout his short career not to the corporate press which he considers propaganda for the wealthy but to dozens of social justice, human rights, leftist, anarchist, pacifist, trade union journals.

NARRATIVE FLOW

The narrative of 'The spike' (Orwell 1970 1 [1931]: 58-66), starts late one Saturday afternoon – and we follow the narrator in the spike (a doss house for down-and-outs, one of many dotted about the country) until he leaves at 10 am the following Monday. Throughout, the chronology is spelled out with unusual precision. The essay begins in typical Orwellian style locating the narrative right from the start in the 'who, when, what, where, why and how' of a traditional news introductory section (intro, in the jargon). So while the style throughout is distinctly 'literary' (incorporating many of the techniques often associated with fiction) Orwell adopts the conventions of 'hard news reporting' (normally considered unliterary) both imaginatively and provocatively to launch into his 'story'. Let us examine the opening section:

'It was late afternoon' captures the 'when' element; 'Forty-nine of us, forty-eight men and one woman' the 'who'; 'lay' the 'what'; 'on the green' provides the 'where' element; and the 'why' is in 'waiting for the spike to open' (ibid: 58). Indeed, this stress on the leading Ws is to become a recurring motif of Orwell's novel writing reflecting an underlying 'literary journalistic' style. For instance, In *Burmese Days* (1934), he writes:

- *Who*: U Po Kyin, sub-divisional magistrate of Kyauktada, in Upper Burma
- *What*: was sitting
- *Where*: on his veranda
- *When*: It was only half past eight, but the month was April.

In *A Clergyman's Daughter* (1935), there's:

- *When*: As the alarm clock on the chest of drawers exploded like a horrid little bomb of bell metal
- *Who*: Dorothy
- *What*: awoke ….. and lay on her back
- *How*: with a start … looking into the darkness in extreme exhaustion.

In *Keep the Aspidistra Flying* (1936):

- *When*: The clock struck half past two
- *Where*: in a little office at the back of Mr McKechnie's bookshop
- *Who*: Gordon Comstock
- *What*: lounged
- *Where*: across the table.

In *Coming Up For Air* (1939):

- *Subject*: The idea
- *What*: really came to me
- *When*: the day I got my new false teeth.

And in *Nineteen Eighty-Four* (1949):

- *When*: It was a bright cold day in April and the clocks were striking thirteen.
- *Who*: Winston Smith
- *What*: slipped
- *How*: quickly
- *Where*: through the glass doors of Victory Mansions.

'The spike' starts with the narrator waiting outside. The next major event happens at six when 'the gates swung open and we shuffled in'. Next: 'When we had bathed our own clothes were taken away from us and we were dressed in the workhouse shirts. ... Then we were sent to the dining room...' (ibid: 60). 'Then the Tramp Major [the man running the spike] served us with three cotton blankets each and drove us off to our cells for the night.' In the morning: 'The Tramp Major came marching down the passage with his heavy tread, unlocking the doors and yelling to us to show a leg. ... We hurried into our clothes and then went to the dining room to bolt our breakfast' (ibid: 60-61). 'After breakfast we had to undress again for the medical inspection.' This being a Sunday, 'we were to be kept in the spike over the weekend. As soon as the doctor had gone we were herded back to the dining room and its door shut upon us. Already at eight o'clock in the morning we were bored with our captivity' (ibid: 62).

The narrator says he is much luckier than the others 'because at ten o'clock the Tramp Major picked me out for the most coveted of all jobs in the spike, the job of helping in the workhouse kitchen' (ibid: 63). Then, at three 'I left the workhouse kitchen and went back to the spike. ... At last six o'clock did come and the Tramp Major and his assistant arrived with supper. ... When we had finished, the blankets were served out immediately and we were hustled off once more to the bare, chilly cells' (ibid: 65). Thirteen hours go by. 'At seven we were awakened and rushed forth to squabble over the water in the bathroom and bolt our ration of bread and tea. Our time in the spike was up, but we could not go until the doctor had examined us again for the authorities have a terror of smallpox and its distribution by tramps. The doctor kept us waiting two hours this time, and it was ten o'clock before we finally escaped' (ibid).

In effect, the narrative flow (precisely outlined) provides the structural base on which the essay can build.

NARRATOR'S VOICE

The voice of the narrator is, above all, ambivalent – mixing fascination and empathy with disgust (so probably reflecting not only Blair's attitudes but also those of the journal's largely middle class readers) and in the writing combining a matter-of-fact 'realism' with literary lyricism. He blends a sense of solidarity with the tramps (particularly when he adopts the 'we' voice) with a critical distance and aloofness from them.

According to Peter Marks, the narrator remains 'an empathetic observer never truly part of the environment' (Marks 2011: 26). Indeed, Orwell never claims to be a down-and-out. He had preferred his first book to be titled *Confessions of a Dishwasher in London and Paris* but his publisher, Victor Gollancz pressed for the final version as better for selling purposes. As Peter Davison comments (1996: 33), Orwell wrote about the poor 'from an intimate knowledge but from a detached viewpoint'. Davison quotes Orwell's friend Michael Meyer who wrote that he lived among the destitute 'to find out at first-hand how poverty and near starvation conditioned people's outlook. He felt that there had been too much theorising about the feelings of the poor' (ibid).

Michael Amundsen (2016) describes Blair/Orwell as an autoethnographer combining subjective responses, sociological enquiries, an engaging narrative and truth-seeking with a sense of moral urgency. The narrator in 'The spike' is also a 'newcomer' so witnesses the scenes with the special intensity of someone new to the life of the tramp. Near the start, he says he accepts the advice of 'the old hands' to bury his eightpence in a hole under the hedge – since it was forbidden to take money, matches and tobacco into the skip (Orwell op cit: 59). He is also concerned early on to stress how he is socially superior to the down-and-outs. In the process, he gives a clear indication of his insecurity. The Tramp Major who runs the spike 'gave the tramps no more ceremony than sheep at the dipping pond shoving them this way and that and shouting oaths in their faces' (ibid). But when he comes to the narrator 'he looked hard at me' and this dialogue follows:

> 'You are a gentleman?'
>
> 'I suppose so,' I said.

Blair continues: 'He gave me another long look. "Well, that's bloody bad luck, guv'nor," he said, "that's bloody bad luck, that is." And thereafter he took it into his head to treat me with compassion, even with a kind of respect.'

In effect, Blair/the narrator makes no attempt to disguise his 'upper classness'. In *Down and Out in Paris and London* (1933) Orwell details how he sells his normal clothes for a shilling at a 'rag shop' in exchange for the clothes of a tramp: these were 'a coat, once dark brown, a pair of black dungaree trousers, a scarf and a cloth cap; I had kept my own shirt, socks and boots, and I had a comb and razor in my pocket' (Orwell 1970 1 [1933]: 115). As John Sutherland comments (2016: 130), Orwell becomes an 'Etonian in rags'. Orwell adds:

> It gives one a very strange feeling to be wearing such clothes. I had worn bad enough things before, but nothing at all like these; they were not merely dirty and shapeless, they had – how is one to express it? – a gracelessness, a patina of antique filth, quite different from mere shabbiness (op cit: 115).

But even though his clothes give him the appearance of a tramp, Orwell realises that his old-Etonian voice, his body language, even the way the tramp rags fall over his tall, thin body confirm his 'gentlemanly' status.

Interestingly, the scene with the Tramp Major is reproduced in *Down and Out*, but with significant changes. Here, the Tramp Major asks sharply: 'Which of you is Blank? (I forget what name I had given).' And Orwell continues:

> 'Me, sir.'
>
> 'So you are a journalist?'
>
> 'Yes, sir,' I said, quaking. A few questions would betray the fact that I had been lying, which might mean prison. But the Tramp Major only looked me up and down and said:
>
> 'Then you are a gentleman?'
>
> 'I suppose so.'
>
> He gave me another long look. 'Well, that's bloody bad luck, guv'nor,' he said, 'bloody bad luck that is.' And thereafter he treated me with unfair favouritism and even with a kind of deference (ibid: 173).

So in this version, Blair/Orwell is sufficiently unsure in his role as an undercover reporter that he even lets slip his cover. Which of these two versions is closer to the 'truth' we will never know. But considered together they confirm the narrator's ambivalent stance – combining both journalistic insecurity and clear class identity.

Intriguingly also, the geographical location of the spike – unnamed in the essay – is Lower Binfield in *Down and Out* – the name Orwell gives the village Gordon Comstock revisits in a (fruitless) bid to recapture the Golden Age of his idyllic youth in his novel *Coming Up For Air* (of 1939).

DISGUST AND CLASS

One particularly prominent feature of the narrator's voice is his disgust and squeamishness (perhaps also reflecting the assumed response of his imaginary middle class audience). Even in the opening paragraph, the narrator evokes the beauty of nature only then to stress how the earth-bound reality of the tramps 'defiles' the scene: 'Overhead the chestnut branches were covered with blossom and beyond that great woolly clouds floated almost motionless in a clear sky. Littered on the grass, we seemed dingy urban riff-raff. We defiled the scene, like sardine-tins and paper bags on the seashore' (Orwell 1970 1 [1931]: 58). Later on, he dwells at length on the 'disgusting sight' in the bathroom:

> All the indecent secrets of our underwear were exposed: the grime, the rents and patches, the bits of string doing duty for buttons, the layers upon layers of fragmentary garments, some of them mere collections of holes, held together by dirt. The room became a press of steaming nudity, the sweaty odours of the tramps competing with the sickly, sub-faecal stench native to the spike (ibid: 59-60).

As the men line up for the medical inspection, the narrator mixes cool observation with disgust (the adjectives piling on one after another):

> It was an instructive sight. We stood shivering naked to the waist in two long ranks in the passage. ... No one can imagine, unless he has seen such a thing, what pot-bellied, degenerate curs we looked. Shock heads, hairy, crumpled faces, hollow chests, flat feet, sagging muscles – every kind of malformation and physical rottenness were there (ibid: 61).

Significantly, the essay ends on a climactic note of intense disgust. One of the tramps, little Scotty, runs after him after the spike is closed.

> He pulled a rusty tin box from his pocket. He wore a friendly smile, like a man who is repaying an obligation.
>
> 'Here y'are mate,' he said cordially. 'I owe you some fag ends. You stood me a smoke yesterday…'
>
> And he put four sodden, debauched, loathly cigarette ends into my hand (ibid: 61).

Indeed, as Beci Dobbin (2012: 68) stresses, Blair's tendency towards squeamishness betrays a distinct 'class specific sensibility'. Nathan Waddell actually sees Orwell's preoccupation with filth, nausea and disgust culminating in *Nineteen Eighty-Four* where his creation of a literary dystopia helps him to 'think through the complexities and inconsistencies of a politics built on the logic of filth' (Waddell 2020: 180).

CHARACTER DESCRIPTIONS

Central to Blair's literary technique is his stress on describing some of the characters he meets – giving identities (however slender), names and occasionally nick-names to those normally rendered invisible. There's old 'Daddy' who is described as 'aged seventy-four, with his truss, and his red watering eyes: a herring gutted starveling, with sparse beard and sunken cheeks, looking like the corpse of Lazarus in some primitive picture…' (op cit: 61). There's George 'a dirty old tramp notorious for the queer habit of sleeping in his hat'; Bill, 'the moocher, the best built man of us all, a Herculean sturdy beggar who smelt of beer even after twelve hours in the spike'; William and Fred: 'two young ex-fishermen from Norfolk' and there's Scotty, whose tobacco has been seized and so to whom the narrator 'stood him the makings of a cigarette' (ibid: 62).

Significantly, again betraying his class background, the narrator devotes the longest description to the tramp he stresses is 'rather superior … a young carpenter who wore a collar and tie and was on the road, he said, for lack of a set of tools. He kept himself a little aloof from the other tramps and held himself more like a free man than a casual. He had literary tastes, too, and carried one of Scott's novels on all his wanderings' (ibid: 64). The narrator enters an argument with this posh tramp – who denounces the down-and-outs as 'scum' – and goes on to ponder the class basis of this attitude:

> It was interesting to see how subtly he disassociated himself from his fellow tramps. He has been on the road six months but in the sight of God, he seemed to imply, he was not a tramp. His body might be in the spike, but his spirit soared far away, in the pure aether of the middle classes (ibid).

Looming over everything there's the Tramp Major who is represented as a monster: a sort of human manifestation of the monstrous, degrading system he runs: 'He was a devil, everyone agreed, a tartar, a tyrant, a bawling, blasphemous, uncharitable dog. You couldn't call your soul your own when he was about, and many a tramp had he kicked out in the middle of the night for giving a back answer.' Later on, he is described as 'a gruff, soldiery man of forty' (ibid: 59).

CONCLUSION

In a major study of 'A hanging', the story of the execution of a man in Burma (1931), John Rodden highlights Blair/Orwell's literary techniques and themes. He suggests it represents not only a 'literary breakthrough in stylistic terms' but also anticipates many of his later themes such as the nightmare of authoritarian power and totalitarian dictatorship, the hypocrisy and cruelty of respectable 'authority', the ruthless exploitation of the powerless. In comparison, Rodden dismisses 'The spike' as a 'pedestrian effort that utterly lacks the sophistication' of 'The hanging'. But Rodden, in his assessment, concentrates entirely on the literary techniques and themes and so fails to take into account the partisan, social justice stance of 'The spike' which adds the crucial political edge to the writing.

Orwell's writings are to take in a vast range of genres: memoir, novels (though, interestingly, no short stories), war reporting, radio plays and commentaries, column writing, book, film and theatre reviewing, essays, political analysis and polemic, poetry, press analysis, investigative reporting, profiles, humorous sketches, social documentaries, letters, cultural criticism, diaries and so on.

Yet these genres are forever overlapping. As Lynette Hunter stresses on Orwell (1984: 4): 'The divisions between subject and object, fiction and fact, novel and documentary and the whole field of static genre became subordinate to stance.' Journalism, then, for Orwell, is not to be seen as a discreet activity but one element of his *life as a politically engaged writer*. Thus he directs much of his journalism to journals of the left (many of which survive for just a few issues) such as *The Adelphi, Commentary, Controversy, For Anarchism, Forward, Fortnightly Review, Gangrel, Left News, Left Forum, Left Review, New English Weekly,* New York's *New Leader, New Republic, The Highway, New Road, New Statesman and Nation, New Saxon Pamphlets, Polemic, Politics and Letters, Tribune.* These are to play a crucial role in the intellectual and political debates within the alternative public sphere of the 1930s and 1940s.

Indeed, in his radical, social justice journalism, Orwell is engaging in the crucial political dialogue with people who matter to him. They are an authentic audience compared with what Stuart Allan (2004: 84) calls the 'implied reader or imagined community of readers' of the mainstream media. And through this dialogue emerges some of the greatest journalism of the twentieth century.

REFERENCES

Allan, Stuart (2004) *News Culture*, Maidenhead: Open University Press

Amundsen, M. (2016) George Orwell's ethnographies of experience: *The Road to Wigan Pier* and *Down and Out in Paris and London*, *Anthropological Journal of European Cultures*, Vol. 25, No. 1 pp 9-25

Bowker, Gordon (n.d.) Orwell's reading. Available online at https://www.orwellfoundation.com/the-orwell-foundation/orwell/library/gordon-bowker-orwells-library/

Bowker, Gordon (2003) *George Orwell*, London: Little, Brown

Davison, Peter (1996) *George Orwell: A Literary Life*, Houndmills, Basingstoke: Macmillan

Dobbin, Beci (2012) Orwell's squeamishness, Keeble, Richard Lance (ed.) *Orwell Today*, Bury St Edmunds: Abramis pp 62-76

Gardiner, Juliet (2011 [2010]) *The Thirties: An Intimate History*, London: HarperPress

Hunter, Lynette (1984) *George Orwell: The Search for a Voice*, Milton Keynes: Open University Press

Ingram, J. D. (n.d.) Lumpenproletariat. Available online at https://krisis.eu/lumpenproletariat/

Keeble, Richard Lance (2020) The myth of freedom: Orwell and the press, *Journalism Beyond Orwell*, London: Routledge pp 15-22

Klaus, H. G. (2003) Introduction, Klaus, H. G. (ed.) *Tramps, Workmates and Revolutionaries: Working-class Stories of the 1920s*, London: Journeyman Press pp 1-4

Koven, Seth (2004) *Slumming: Sexual and Social Politics in Victorian London*, Princeton and Oxford: Princeton University Press

Marks, Peter (2011) *George Orwell the Essayist: Literature, Politics and the Periodical Culture*, London: Continuum

Marx, Karl and Engels, Friedrich (1848) *Communist Manifesto*. Available online at https://www.marxists.org/history/erol/spain/manifesto.pdf

Orwell, George (1970 1 [1928]) A farthing newspaper, Orwell, S. and Angus, I. (eds) *The Collected Essays, Journalism and Letters of George Orwell, Vol. 1: An Age Like This, 1920-1940*, Harmondsworth, Middlesex: Penguin pp 34-37; originally published in *G. K.'s Weekly*, 29 December

Orwell, George (1970 1 [1931]) The spike, Orwell, S. and Angus, I. (eds) *The Collected Essays, Journalism and Letters of George Orwell, Vol. 1: An Age Like This, 1920-1940*, Harmondsworth, Middlesex: Penguin pp 58-66; originally published in the *Adelphi*, April

Orwell, George (1983 [1933]) *Down and Out in Paris and London*, Harmondsworth, Middlesex: Penguin Books; originally published London: Gollancz

Orwell, George (1970 1 [1946]) Why I write, Orwell, S. and Angus, I. (eds) *The Collected Essays, Journalism and Letters of George Orwell, Vol. 1: An Age Like This, 1920-1940*, Harmondsworth, Middlesex: Penguin pp 23-30; originally published in *Gangrel*, summer

Rodden, John (2014) A hanging: George Orwell's unheralded literary breakthrough, *Concentric: Literary and Cultural Studies*, Vol. 40, No. 1 pp 19-33

Sutherland, John (2016) *Orwell's Nose: A Pathological Biography*, London: Reaktion Books

Taylor, D. J. (2003) *Orwell: The Life*, London: Chatto & Windus

Waddell, Nathan (2020) Oceania's dirt, filth, nausea and disgust in Airstrip One, Waddell, Nathan (ed.) *The Cambridge Companion to* Nineteen Eighty-Four, Cambridge: Cambridge University Press pp 168-180

- This essay was originally published as 'Down but not out: "The spike" and Orwell as an (always ambivalent) campaigner for social justice', *Ethical Space*, Vol. 17, No. 2 pp 38-44

Chapter Nine

The Pleasures and Politics of Food

Food – and drink – occupy surprisingly prominent places in George Orwell's life and writings. His first published book, *Down and Out in Paris and London* (1933), revolves entirely around the theme of food and its absence while some of the most important scenes in his novels occur in cafés, canteens or restaurants. In *The Road to Wigan Pier* (1937), he goes to great lengths to highlight the impact of unemployment on the diet of the poor; and during a break with his wife, Eileen, in Marrakech just before the outbreak of the Second World War, he writes in his diary about the vegetables grown and agricultural techniques he witnesses in the North African country. Towards the end of his life he composes not only a series of wonderfully light and witty essays on such diverse topics as cups of tea, English cooking, the Christmas feast and the ideal pub but also an extraordinary, unpublished, little-known, 6,000-word essay on British cooking. And at the heart of many of his writings is a desire to highlight the plight of the poor and the under-nourished – and an acute awareness of the politics of food production and consumption.

'A STATE OF NEAR STARVATION' AND THE NEED FOR RADICAL CHANGE

Significantly, the plight of the poor and their appalling diet – together with a radical political analysis – are the subjects of one of Orwell's first pieces of journalism, published under the byline of Eric Blair, for the French journal, *Le Progrès Civique*, on 29 December 1928 (*CWGO* X: 124). How can one live on 18 shillings 'dole' a week? he asks. 'The reply is simple: one does not live, one just avoids dying.' An unemployed married man with a wife and two young children has a total weekly income amounting to 25 shillings (150 francs). They probably pay 7 shillings (42 francs) a week in rent alone. The remainder must suffice to feed and keep four people. 'Given this sort of income, what can their meals consist of? Bread and tea, tea and bread, week in, week out. ... This is wretched sustenance: bad bread, white and lacking nutriment, and very strong tea is the staple diet for very poor people in England. ...' So 'idleness in luxury', as the Conservative newspapers say in righteous indignation, turns out to mean, on closer inspection 'a state of near starvation'.

Blair next highlights the plight of the single unemployed man who takes up residence in one of the enormous barracks known as 'lodging houses'. These are run by large companies, which make a significant income for them. The lodgers spend their days in underground kitchens, built under the street, where they can cook their food, if they have any, in a frying pan on a coke fire. In the lodging house 'the unemployed man takes his meals, consisting of bread and tea. He sits in a blank stupor in front of the fire for those long hours when he is not searching for some kind of work'. He adds: 'Efforts will be made to prevent most of these poor creatures from actually dying of hunger. For example, no government would dare to make a stand against half-a-million starving miners. Whatever happens, to avoid revolution they will make sure that the unemployed can receive subsidies from somewhere' (ibid: 127).

And he concludes: 'For the moment, the English worker is the scapegoat. He will no doubt continue to suffer until there is radical change in the present economic system' (ibid). In other words, well before his supposed 'conversion' to socialism while fighting with a Republican militia during the Spanish Civil War in 1937, Orwell is expressing radical, economically grounded, socialist attitudes.

DOWN AND OUT AND THE CENTRALITY OF FOOD

All the events narrated in Orwell's first published book, the part memoir/part fictional *Down and Out in Paris and London*, revolve in some way around food – or its absence. At the start, the narrator and his friend Boris are very short of money. 'I had given up the pretence of going out to restaurants, and we used to eat in my room, one of us sitting on the bed and the other on the chair. Boris would contribute his two francs and I three or four francs, and we would buy bread, potatoes, milk and cheese and make soup over my spirit lamp. We had a saucepan and coffee-bowl and one spoon; every day there was a polite squabble as to who should eat out of the saucepan and who out of the coffee-bowl (the saucepan held more), and every day to my secret anger Boris gave in first and had the saucepan' (1980 [1933]: 30).

The narrator lands a job as a *plongeur*/dish-washer at the posh Hotel X. With its 'elaborate caste system' amongst the 110 employees, the hotel comes to symbolise the society outside its walls where the poor live side-by-side with the obscenely rich and where people compete within hierarchical structures. At the top is the manager, then the *maitre d'hôtel*, next the head cook, then the *chef du personnel*, the waiters and finally, symbolically, right at the bottom, the *plongeurs* (ibid: 48-49). Orwell writes: 'It was amusing to look round the filthy little scullery and think that only a double door was between us and the dining room. There sat the customers in all their splendour – spotless table-clothes, bowls of flowers, mirrors and gilt cornices and painted cherubins; and here, just a few feet away, we in our disgusting filth' (ibid: 48-49).

Moving over to London, the narrator joins the tramps walking the streets of the capital, scavenging for food. For instance, on one occasion they drift into a church service, simply with the aim of getting a cup of tea. 'We ranged ourselves in the gallery pews and were given our tea; it was a one-pound jam-jar of tea each, with six slices of bread and margarine. As soon as tea was over, a dozen tramps who had stationed themselves near the door bolted to avoid the service; the rest stayed, less from gratitude than lacking the cheek to go' (ibid: 104). Towards the end of the book, the narrator says there are two major 'evils' in the life of a tramp. 'The first is hunger, which is the almost general fate of tramps. The casual ward gives them a ration which is probably not even meant to be sufficient, and anything beyond this must be got by begging – that is, by breaking the law. The result is that every tramp is rotted by malnutrition. ... The second great evil ... is that he is entirely cut off from contact with women' (ibid: 115). In other words, sexual hunger...

AVERTING REVOLUTION: THE POOR AND THE POLITICS OF CHEAP FOOD

Significantly, Orwell's investigation into poverty in the north of England, *The Road to Wigan Pier*, begins in the kitchen of the Brookers' family in Wigan. He writes, with typical disgust:

> In front of the fire there was almost always a line of damp washing and in the middle of the room was the big kitchen table at which the family and all the lodgers ate. I never saw this table completely uncovered, but I saw its various wrappings at different times. At the bottom there was a layer of old newspapers stained by Worcester Sauce; above that a sheet of sticky white oil cloth; above that a green serge cloth; above that a course linen cloth, never changed and seldom taken off. Generally the crumbs from breakfast were still on the table at supper. I used to get to know individual crumbs by sight and watch their progress up and down the table from day to day (1980 [1937]: 126).

Whilst examining at close hand miners at work, Orwell focuses on their eating rituals: 'From what I have seen I should say that the majority of miners prefer to eat their meal first and wash afterwards, as I should do in their circumstances. It is the normal thing to see a miner sitting down to his tea with a Christy-minstrel face, completely black except for very red lips which become clear by eating' (ibid: 139).

He continues:

> If he is on the night shift he gets home in time for breakfast, on the morning shift he gets home in the middle of the afternoon, and on the afternoon shift he gets home in the middle of the night; and in each case, of course, he wants his principal meal of the day as soon as he returns. I notice that the Rev. W. R. Inge, in his book *England*, accuses the miners of gluttony. From my own observation, I should say that they eat astonishingly little. Most of the miners I stayed with ate slightly less than I did. Many of them declare that they cannot do their day's work if they have had a heavy meal beforehand, and the food they take with them is only a snack, usually bread-and-dripping and cold tea. They carry it in a flat tin called a snap-can which they strap to their belts (ibid: 140).

Orwell also cleverly places his observations of the miners' everyday activities in the context of a broader critique of the economic system. For instance, he now stresses the way in which capitalism deliberately serves up cheap 'luxury' foods for the underprivileged as one way of keeping them 'pacified'. He writes: 'Trade since the war has had to adjust itself to meet the demands of underpaid, underfed people, with the result that a luxury is nowadays almost always cheaper than a necessity. One pair of plain solid shoes costs as much as two ultra-smart pairs. For the price of one square meal you can get two pounds of cheap sweets. You can't get much meat for threepence, but you can get a lot of fish-and chips. Milk costs threepence a pint and even "mild" beer costs fourpence, but aspirins are seven a penny and you can wring forty cups of tea out of a quarter-pound packet' (ibid: 164).

Julian Symons speaks of Orwell's talk being like his journalism – 'a mixture of brilliant perception, common sense and wild assertion' (Meyers 2000: 168). And Orwell, always the pamphleteer and controversialist, here adds one of his typical, deliberately provocative generalisations and wild assertions: 'It is quite likely that fish and chips, art silk stockings, tinned salmon, cut-price chocolate (five two-ounce bars for six-pence), the movies, the radio, strong tea and Football Pools have between them averted revolution' (ibid: 165). Discuss…

THE CRUCIAL – AND TOO OFTEN FORGOTTEN – PLACE OF DIET IN HISTORY

Orwell indulges in another provocative generalisation, arguing with journalistic élan that the importance of diet has been too often forgotten in the conventional histories.

> A human being is primarily a bag for putting food into; the other functions and faculties may be more godlike, but in point of time they come afterwards. … I think it could be plausibly argued that changes of diet are more important than changes of dynasty or even of religion. The Great War, for instance, could never have happened if tinned food had not been invented. And the history of the past four hundred years in England would

have been immensely different if it had not been for the introduction of root-crops and various other vegetables at the end of the Middle Ages, and a little later the introduction of non-alcoholic drinks (tea, coffee, cocoa) and also distilled liquors to which the beer-drinking English were not accustomed. Yet it is curious how seldom the all importance of food is recognized. You see statues everywhere of politicians, poets, bishops, but none to cooks or bacon-curers or market-gardeners (ibid: 165-166).

Clearly determined to base his findings on the collection of 'objective' data, Orwell lists meticulously the various items on a typical week's budget of an unemployed miner with a wife and two children – at a cost of thirty-two shillings. He concludes: 'The basis of their diet, therefore, is white bread and margarine, corned beef, sugared tea and potatoes – an appalling diet' (ibid: 168).

In this context, he understands the appeal of junk food. 'When you are unemployed, which is to say when you are underfed, harassed, bored and miserable, you don't *want* to eat wholesome food. You want something a little bit "tasty". There is always some cheaply pleasant thing to tempt you. Let's have three pennorth of chips. Run out and buy us a twopenny ice-cream. Put the kettle on and we'll all have a nice cup of tea. ... Unemployment is an endless misery that has got to be constantly palliated, and especially with tea, the Englishman's opium' (ibid, italics in the original).

But this diet has a terrible impact on the nation's health. In particular, he notices the appalling state of people's teeth. In fact, very few people, apart from children, are left with their natural teeth. And on the over-industrialisation of food production, he comments: 'We may find in the long run that tinned food is a deadlier weapon than the machine gun' (ibid: 169). Again, discuss...

SPAIN – AND THE POLITICS OF FOOD

Late in December 1936, Orwell joins a Republican militia fighting Franco's fascist forces in the Spanish Civil War. In his account of the conflict and his time on the frontline, *Homage to Catalonia*, food features prominently. For instance, he comments: 'In trench warfare five things are important – firewood, food, tobacco, candles and the enemy. In winter on the Zaragoza front they were important in that order, with the enemy a bad last' (1980 [1938]: 245). He adds: 'The food was good enough and there was plenty of wine. Cigarettes were still being issued at the rate of a packet a day, matches were issued every other day, and there was even an issue of candles' (ibid: 250).

When Orwell arrives in Barcelona he is profoundly inspired by the revolutionary situation he sees all around him – which he considers 'worth fighting for'. 'Every shop and café had an inscription saying it had been collectivized ... Waiters and shop-walkers looked you in the face and treated you as an equal. ... Tipping was forbidden by law' (ibid: 236). But when he returns to the city after two and a half months at the front, he notices deep changes: '... the people – the civil population – had lost much of their interest in the war' and 'the normal division of society into rich and poor, upper class and lower class, was reasserting itself' (ibid: 293). The changes in cafés and restaurants are particularly noticeable:

> Now things were returning to normal. The smart restaurants and hotels were full of rich people wolfing expensive meals while for the working class population food-prices had jumped enormously without any corresponding rise in wages. ... The restaurants and hotels seemed to have little difficulty in getting whatever they wanted but in the working class quarters the queues for bread, olive oil, and other necessities were hundreds of yards long. Previously in Barcelona I had been struck by the absence of beggars; now there were quantities of them. Outside the delicatessen shops at the top of the Ramblas gangs of barefooted children were always waiting to swarm around anyone who came out and clamour for scraps of food (ibid: 294).

In a world where affluence exists side-by-side with appalling poverty, Orwell astutely avoids adopting a superior tone. 'A day or two after the street fighting I remember passing through one of the fashionable streets and coming upon a confectioner's shop with a window full of pastries and bon-bons of the most elegant kinds, at staggering prices ... And I remember feeling a vague horror and amazement that money could still be wasted upon such things in a hungry war-stricken country. But God forbid that I should pretend to any personal superiority. After several months of discomfort I had a ravenous desire for decent food and wine, cocktails, American cigarettes, and so forth and I admit to having wallowed in every luxury that I had money to buy' (ibid: 295).

Orwell returns to the front line, luckily survives being shot in the neck by a fascist sniper, and with the communists keen to capture them – and maybe even later kill – Orwell and his wife, Eileen, go on the run, frequenting posh restaurants as part of their disguise before they escape into France. 'It was an extraordinary, insane existence that we were leading. By night we were criminals, but by day we were prosperous English visitors – that was our pose, anyway. Even after a night in the open, a shave, a bath and a shoe-shine do wonders with your appearance. The safest thing at present was to look as bourgeois as possible. We frequented the fashionable residential quarter of the town where our faces were not known, went to expensive restaurants and were very English with the waiters' (ibid: 355).

THE IMPORTANCE OF TEA IN ORWELL'S *OEUVRE*

In 1933, Orwell's sister, Avril, opens a teashop, the Copper Kettle, in Southwold. His aunt Nellie even suggests he joins her as an assistant, Orwell being at the time out of a job, his post at The Hawthorns, a boys' private school at Hayes, Middlesex, having just ended. Biographer Gordon Bowker comments: 'The picture of tall and spindly Eric Blair serving afternoon teas to fat ladies in large hats would have made an excellent *Punch* cartoon, and one can only imagine his chuckles at the very suggestion' (2003: 151).

But thereafter Orwell has a lot of fun in his novels using the teashop as a symbol of failure and the commercialism and hypocrisy of modern life in which workers are ruthlessly exploited. For instance, in *Keep the Aspidistra Flying*, Gordon Comstock, the central character, ponders his relatives. 'They were all more or less alike – grey, shabby, joyless people, all rather sickly in healthy and all perpetually harassed by money-worries which fizzled along without ever reaching the sensational explosion of bankruptcy' (1976 [1936]: 600). Significantly, his sister, Julia, takes a cookery course and gets a job in a 'nasty, ladylike, little teashop near Earl's Court Underground Station'. A few years later 'Julia was nearly thirty now, and looked much older. She was thinner than ever, though healthy enough, and there was grey in her hair. She still worked twelve hours a day and in six years her wages had only risen by ten shillings a week. The horribly ladylike lady who kept the teashop was a semi-friend as well as an employer, and thus could sweat and bully Julia to the tune of "dearest" and "darling"' (ibid: 606).

One of the central scenes later in the novel is to occur in a restaurant. Gordon and Rosemary go for a romantic walk in the countryside around Burnham Beeches and end up – extremely hungry – in Crickham-on-Thames. The only place open appears to be the rather expensive-looking Ravenscroft Hotel. But the meal, perhaps inevitably, is a disaster. 'The beef and salad were corpse-cold and did not seem like real food at all. They tasted like water. The rolls, also, though stale, were damp. The reedy Thames water seemed to have got into everything. It was no surprise that when the wine was opened it tasted like mud' (ibid: 663). To cap it all, the meal is expensive. So Gordon, ever obsessive about money, has to fork out just about all the cash he is carrying to pay for it. Crucially, his male pride is hurt.

Indeed, the humiliation Gordon experiences in the restaurant prepares the way for the disastrous love-making that follows: 'It dismayed him to find how little, at this moment, he really wanted her. The money-business still unnerved him. How can you make love when you have only eightpence in your pocket and are thinking about it all the time?' (ibid: 665).

A teashop also appears at a significant moment in Orwell's 1939 novel *Coming Up For Air*. After service in the war, the parents of the central character, George Bowling, die. One day, walking down Charing Cross, in central London, a poster proclaiming 'KING ZOG'S WEDDING POSTPONED' together with the sound of traffic and smell of horse-dung bring back memories of his childhood – and he resolves to lie to his wife, take time off work and spend some time back in Lower Binfield rediscovering the Golden Age of his youth (1976 [1939]: 445). But as Bowker summarises: 'The journey is doomed – the small town had been engulfed by suburbia and his woodland paradise infested with fruit juice-drinking, sandal-wearing, nudist vegetarians and Garden City cranks. The Golden Age is done for...' (2003: 250).

Bowling books himself into a hotel and has lunch. But then, symbolising the degeneracy of modern life, he returns to the shop where he grew up and is horrified to find it is now Wendy's Teashop, serving morning coffee and home-made cakes. He enters and asks for tea. The waitress is ten minutes getting it. 'You know the kind of tea – China tea, so weak that you could think it's water till you put the milk in. I was sitting almost exactly where Father's armchair used to stand...' He tells her he used to live in the village. But she is not the slightest bit interested – so he leaves (1976 [1939]: 542).

A café is even the site for the crucial final scene in *Nineteen Eighty-Four*. However, the Chestnut Tree does not serve up tea and cakes but Victory Gin – the absence of tea symbolising the death of the pre-revolution, capitalist civilisation. Winston Smith has survived the torture in Room 101 and thinks back on his chance meeting in a park with Julia – with whom he had a passionate secret affair. 'When he woke, seldom before eleven hundred, with gummed-up eyelids and fiery mouth and a back that seemed to be broken, it would have been impossible even to rise from the horizontal if it had not been for the bottle and teacup placed beside the bed overnight. Through the mid-day hours he sat with glazed face, the bottle handy, listening to the telescreen' (1976 [1949]: 914).

'A NICE CUP OF TEA'

During some of the darkest days of the war, Orwell writes a polemical study of the English character to help promote the patriotic spirit, *The Lion and the Unicorn: Socialism and the English Genius* (1941), and the pub and 'nice cup of tea' – along with the football match, the back garden, the fireside – are depicted as essential features of the nation's communal spirit (*CWGO* XII: 394).

Tea is also to be the subject of one of Orwell's light, brilliantly witty, journalistic – and much neglected – features about English life and customs he contributes to the London *Evening Standard* in 1945-1946. He begins highlighting the fact that, while cook books rarely mention tea, it is actually 'one of the mainstays of civilization in this country, as well as in Eire, Australia and New Zealand' while 'the best manner of making it is the subject of violent disputes' (*CWGO* XVIII: 33).

The clarity of the expression and the attention to detail are particularly striking in the essay. Read it aloud to any group of people and they will be in stitches throughout – I can guarantee it. It's a wonderful example of Orwell's 'plain' style of writing, incorporating, as George Woodcock stresses in his celebrated study, *The Crystal Spirit*, 'its firmness, its colloquial vigour, its unpretentious vividness and, above all, its limpid clarity' (1984 [1966]: 229-230). V. S. Pritchett sees Orwell essentially as a pamphleteer in the tradition of Cobbett and Defoe, writing in 'lucid, conversational' prose (Bowker 2003: 275). And for Jeffrey Meyers, Orwell's plain style 'appeals to readers' common sense and persuades them of his honesty and good faith. At the same time his arguments are sophisticated, provocative and entertaining' (2000: 266).

According to Alex Woloch (2016), this style can also be deceptively complex. Typically, Orwell begins highlighting what's missing in cook books. Indeed, Woloch suggests that Orwell's focus in a range of his writings – such as *Wigan Pier*, *Down and Out*, his essay 'A hanging' and in his regular 'As I Please' columns for *Tribune* – on what we are 'liable to miss' 'reveals a strange blankness, or emptiness, at the deliberate heart of Orwell's work' (ibid: 23). Later Woloch describes this 'withholding at the center of his style' as 'the poetics of exclusion' (ibid: 67).

Orwell next lists carefully his 11 rules for making the perfect cup of tea – all of which he regards as 'golden'. 'First of all, one should use Indian or Ceylonese tea. China tea has virtues which are not to be despised nowadays – it is economical and one can drink it without milk – but there is not much stimulation in it. One does not feel wiser, braver or more optimistic after drinking it. Anyone who uses that comforting phrase, "a nice cup of tea" invariably means Indian tea' (*CWGO* XVIII: 33). So Orwell proceeds through his points – jokingly listing them as fifthly, sixthly, seventhly and so on.

Each point usually begins with a short and snappy phrase summarising the particular argument and driving the feature forward. For instance, there's 'tea should be made in small quantities – that is, in a teapot', 'the pot should be warmed beforehand', 'the tea should be strong', 'the tea should be put straight into the pot' and so on. Thereafter, Orwell expands on the individual point in a few sentences. He ends with five, mainly humorous paragraphs. For instance: 'There is also the mysterious social etiquette surrounding the teapot (why is it considered vulgar to drink out of your saucer, for instance?) and much might be written about the subsidiary uses of tea leaves, such as telling fortunes, predicting the arrival of visitors, feeding rabbits, healing burns and sweeping the carpet' (ibid: 35).

The feature is interesting for a number of other reasons. A great deal of Orwell's journalism is directed at the alternative press (see Keeble 2020). Here, he is writing for a right-wing, mass-selling evening newspaper. Perhaps this is why he makes no mention, even simply in passing, of the slave conditions tea workers were facing in India and Ceylon (as, indeed, they still do today).[1]

As for Orwell's actual favourite tea brew, according to George Woodcock, it was 'as dark and almost as thick as treacle'. He would also take a 'boyish pleasure in imitating a few working class habits'. 'For example, he would often pour his tea into his saucer and blow on it vigorously before he drank it, and if anyone appeared to be shocked, he would be delighted and regard it all as a great joke' (1984 [1967]: 26).

Tea also features, rather poignantly, in Orwell's last moments. The Canadian poet Paul Potts was the last person to see Orwell alive in University College Hospital, in January 1950. Finding him asleep he leaves his present – a packet of tea – at his door. 'He died soon after that and I often wonder who got the tea,' Potts comments (Wadhams 2012).

'IN DEFENCE OF ENGLISH COOKING'

Just a month earlier, on 15 December 1945, Orwell has devoted another pleasure-packed *Evening Standard* column to defending English cooking. He begins by saying it is simply not true that English cooking is the worst in the world. Rather, 'there is a whole host of delicacies which it is quite impossible to obtain outside the English-speaking countries' (*CWGO* XVIII: 446). He proceeds, in impressive detail, to list these delicacies, displaying an impressive knowledge of the matters of the cuisine: 'First of all kippers, Yorkshire pudding, Devonshire cream, muffins and crumpets. Then the list of puddings that would be interminable if I gave it in full: I will pick out for special mention Christmas pudding, treacle tart and apple dumplings. Then an almost equally long list of cakes: for instance, dark plum cake (such as you used to get at Buszard's before the war), shortbread and saffron buns. Also innumerable kinds of biscuit which exist, of course, elsewhere, but are generally admitted to be better and crisper in England.' Special ways of cooking potatoes are highlighted – and the various sauces peculiar to England, English cheeses such as Stilton and Wensleydale and apples such as the Cox's Orange Pippin. 'What else? Outside these islands I have never seen a haggis, except one that came out of a tin, nor Dublin prawns, nor Oxford marmalade, nor several other kinds of jam (marrow jam and bramble jelly, for instance), nor sausages of quite the same kind as ours.'

But he admits there is a snag from the foreign visitor's point of view: good English cooking is to be found in private houses and not in restaurants. Pubs, at the time, sold no food other than crisps and 'tasteless sandwiches'. So the solution – restaurant meals must improve.

CELEBRATING THE BRITISH KITCHEN

In 1946, Orwell is commissioned by the British Council to write an essay on British cooking (Orwell 1946). They probably expect him to laud the nation's restaurants while adding some astute critiques of British cuisine. This is not what they are sent. Orwell, typically, praises home-made meals and downplays the delights of restaurants. Thus, he begins saying British cooking 'is best studied in private houses, and more particularly in the homes of the middle-class and working-class masses who have not become Europeanised in their tastes. Cheap restaurants in Britain are almost invariably bad, while in expensive restaurants the cookery is almost always French, or imitation French'. Perhaps, inevitably, Orwell is sent a rejection note on 3 May 1946, which, while it stresses it's an 'excellent essay', adds that 'it would be unfortunate and unwise to publish it for the continental reader'. All the same, he is sent the payment – 30 guineas.

In the extraordinary 6,000-word essay, Orwell displays a remarkable knowledge – indeed, love – of cooking.

He starts with some typical Orwellian, provocative generalisations to attract the attention of the reader. For instance: 'One may say that the characteristic British diet is a simple, rather heavy, perhaps slightly barbarous diet, drawing much of its virtue from the excellence of the local materials, and with its main emphasis on sugar and animal fats. It is the diet of a wet northern country where butter is plentiful and vegetable oils are scarce, where hot drinks are acceptable at most hours of the day, and where all the spices and some of the stronger-tasting herbs are exotic products.' Continuing, he painstakingly goes through the typical contents of each meal eaten through the day beginning with the breakfast – all in impressive detail. There are problems in considering the mid-day meal which he confronts head-on, highlighting intriguing social, regional and class factors:

> The richer classes have their midday meal at one-thirty in the afternoon and call it 'luncheon'. At about half-past four in the afternoon they have a cup of tea and perhaps a piece of bread-and-butter or a slice of cake, which they call 'afternoon tea' and they have their evening meal at half-past seven or eight, and call it 'dinner'. The others, perhaps ninety percent of the population, have their midday meal somewhat earlier – usually about half-past twelve – and call it 'dinner'. They have their main evening meal at about half-past six and call it 'tea' and before going to bed they have a light snack – for instance, cocoa and bread-and-jam – which they call 'supper'. The distinction is regional as well as social. In the North of England, Scotland and Ireland many well-to-do people prefer to follow the working-class time scheme, partly because it fits in better with the working day, and partly, perhaps, from motives of conservation: for our ancestors of a century ago also had their meals at approximately these hours.

As for the content of the meal, he writes: 'The British midday meal consists essentially of meat, preferably roast meat, a heavy pudding, and cheese. And here one comes upon the central institution of British life, the "joint": that is, a large piece of meat – round of beef or leg of pork of mutton – roasted whole with its potatoes round it, and preserving a flavour and a juiciness which meat cooked in smaller quantities never seems to attain.' Orwell moves on to consider the delights of British sauces:

> Here also we may mention the special sauces which are so regularly served with each kind of roast meat as to be almost an integral part of the dish. Hot roast beef is almost invariably served with horseradish sauce, a very hot, rather sweet sauce made of grated horseradish, sugar vinegar and cream. With roast pork goes apple sauce, which is made of apples stewed with sugar and beaten up into a froth. With mutton or lamb there usually goes

mint sauce, which is made of chopped mint, sugar and vinegar. Mutton is frequently eaten with redcurrant jelly, which is also served with hare and with venison. A roast fowl is always accompanied by bread sauce, which is made of the crumb of white bread and milk flavoured with onions, and is always served hot. It will be seen that British sauces have the tendency to be sweet, and some of the pickles that are eaten with cold meat are almost as sweet as jam.

And so on through cooking birds and fish, puddings, pastry, a vast range of sweet dishes including of jellies, blancmanges, custards, soufflés, ice puddings, meringues and pancakes. Tea, he says, is invariably drunk with the evening meal. 'It is very unusual to drink any alcohol at this meal. British working-people, in any case, do not often drink alcohol in their own homes. They like to bring home a few bottles of beer for midday dinner on Sundays, but for the most part their drinking is done in the public house, which serves as a kind of club.'

Towards the end, he lists 'the foodstuffs, natural or prepared, which are especially good in Britain and which any foreign visitor should make sure of sampling'. First mentioned are apples. 'The best are the Cox's Orange pippin, the Blenheim Orange, the Charles Hoss, the James Grieve and the Russet. These are all eaten raw. The Bramley: Seedling is a superlative cooking apple.' Then there are fish and drinks – and finally a word in praise of British bread. 'It is a good general rule that small, old-fashioned shops make the best-flavoured bread. Throughout a great deal of the North of England the women prefer to bake their bread for themselves.'

As a final flourish, Orwell ends by presenting a set of recipes – for Welsh rarebit, Yorkshire pudding, treacle tart, orange marmalade, plum cake and Christmas pudding – complete with cooking directions.

Blake Perkins, in a highly considered essay in the specialist cooking journal, *Petits Propos Culinaires*, argues that in 'British cookery' Orwell is displaying above all his gloomy side while much of it 'bears scant resemblance to the traditional foodways of the archipelago' (Perkins 2014: 74). He writes: 'The overall tenor of "British Cookery" is so grim (even, perhaps, "Orwellian") that it would not only deter the most intrepid traveller from hazarding a journey to Britain but would also depopulate the islands of the indigenes if true.' I would tend to totally disagree. But then, I guess it's all a question of different tastes in writing…

ENJOYING XMAS PUD

Later, just before Christmas in 1946, Orwell devotes another wonderfully inventive, witty and joyous 'As I Please' column in *Tribune* to considering the four necessary ingredients for a successful Christmas: a roast turkey, Christmas pudding, a dish of mince pies and finally a tin of –'s Liver Salt (*CWGO* XVIII: 517). But this time, given the progressive views of his expected readership, he does not ignore the plight of the poor and hungry in Europe, India and China. 'In India there are, and always have been, about 100 million people who only get one square meal a day. In China, conditions are no doubt much the same. In Germany, Austria, Greece and elsewhere, scores of millions of people are existing on a diet which keeps breath in the body but leaves no strength for work...' (ibid).

Before this sobering point, Orwell has had a great deal of fun celebrating the joys of the Xmas feast. He writes: 'The whole point of Christmas is that it is a debauch – as it was probably long before the birth of Christ was arbitrarily fixed at that date. Children know this well. From their point of view Christmas is not a day of temperate enjoyment, but of fierce pleasures which they are quite willing to pay for with a certain amount of pain' (ibid: 518). And he proceeds with delight to detail the elements of an imaginary, pleasure-packed Xmas day:

> The awakening at about 4 a.m. to inspect your stocking, the quarrels over toys all through the morning, and the exciting whiffs of mincemeat and sage-and-onions escaping from the kitchen door; the battle with enormous plateloads of turkey, and the pulling of the wishbone; the darkening of the windows and the entry of the flaming plum-pudding; the hurry to make sure that everyone has a piece on his plate while the brandy is still alight; the momentary panic when it is rumoured that Baby has swallowed the threepenny bit; the stupor all through the afternoon; the Christmas cake with icing an inch thick; the peevishness next morning and the castor oil on 27 December – it is an up-and-down business, by no means all pleasant, but well worth while for the sake of its more dramatic moments (ibid).

Typically, Orwell shifts his attention to writings about Christmas – again focusing on what's 'missing'. 'How enormous is the literature of eating and drinking, especially drinking, and how little that is worth while has been said on the other side! Offhand I can't remember a single poem in praise of water, i.e. water regarded as a drink. It is hard to imagine what one could say about it. It quenches thirst: that is the end of the story.' He continues in the same comical vein: 'Curiously enough, I can't remember a poem in praise of stout, not even draught stout, which is better than the bottled variety, in my opinion. There is an extremely disgusting description in *Ulysses* of the stout-vats in Dublin. But there is a sort of back-handed tribute to stout in the fact that this description, though widely known, has not done much towards putting the Irish off their favourite drink' (ibid: 519).

He moves on to consider the literature about eating. And he concludes: 'In all the writers who have enjoyed describing food, from Rabelais to Dickens and from Petronius to Mrs Beeton, I cannot remember a single passage which puts dietic considerations first. Always food is an end in itself.'

Having highlighted the plight of the global poor, Orwell concludes, promoting, as ever, the pleasure principle: 'In such circumstances we could hardly have a "proper" Christmas, even if the materials for it exist. But we will have one sooner or later, in 1947, or 1948, or maybe even in 1949. And when we do, there may be no gloomy voices of vegetarians or teetotallers to lecture us about the things that we are doing to the linings of our stomach.'

ORWELL'S TASTE FOR THACKERAY

Is it not interesting, now, that in his brief essay, 'Oysters and brown stout' on the novels of Thackeray (in *Tribune*, 22 December 1944), Orwell should praise, in particular, his depiction of food – so much part of the 'characteristic flavour' of his collected works? He writes: 'Partly it is the atmosphere of surfeit which belongs to the early nineteenth century, an atmosphere compounded of oysters, brown stout, brandy and water, turtle soup, roast sirloin, haunch of venison, Madeira and cigar smoke, which Thackeray is well able to convey because he has a good grip on physical detail and is extremely interested in food' (Orwell 1980 [1944]: 676).

Relishing the food theme, Orwell goes on to suggest Thackeray 'writes about food perhaps more often even than Dickens, and more accurately'. 'His account of his dinners in Paris – not expensive dinners, either – in "Memorials of gormandizing" is fascinating reading. "The ballad of the bouillabaisse" is one of the best poems of that kind in English.' 'A little dinner at Timmins's', he even asserts, is 'one of the best comic short stories ever written, though it is seldom reprinted' (ibid).

THE PERSONAL: 'HE LIKED GOOD FOOD'

In his personal life, Orwell constantly expresses an interest in food and in agricultural techniques, sets up a shop to sell food to the local villagers – is a keen vegetable-grower and raises animals (he even has chickens in the garden of his London apartment).

In a letter composed when he is just 12, while a pupil at St Cyprian's prep school, in Eastbourne, dated mid-July 1916, he writes: 'Darling mums, Thanks for your letter. Today there was a whole holiday, and we took our dinner out to East Dean and went to have tea at Jevington. The tea was unspeakably horrible, though it did cost 1/6' (*CWGO* X: 21).

Significantly, when he moves into a house with Rayner Heppenstall and Michael Sayers, in Lawford Road, Kentish Town in August 1935, it is Orwell who cooks and does the washing up (Crick 1980: 274). In a letter to his life-long friend Brenda Salkeld, of 7 May 1936, he even spells out in detail a recipe he fancies: 'I have hit on a wonderful recipe for a stew which is the following: half a pound of ox-kidney chopped up small; half a pound of mushrooms, sliced; one onion chopped very fine; two cloves of garlic, four skinned tomatoes, a slice of lean bacon chopped up, and salt, the whole stewed very gently for about two and a half hours in a very little beef stock. You eat it with spaghetti or rather coquillettes. It is a good dish to make as it cooks itself while you are working' (ibid: 386).

Later in the year, he marries Eileen O'Shaughnessy. And it appears she ends up doing most of the cooking during their time at the Stores, Wallington. In her biography of Eileen, Sylvia Topp writes: 'Every morning Eileen would make one of those huge English breakfasts they both loved. … She was an inventive cook and besides making delicious breakfasts in her tiny kitchen, she would concoct creative dinners worthy of compliments from friends' (2020: 153).

Orwell is the designated goat-milker and bacon slicer in the shop. In gaps between his writing, he also spends many hours working in the garden – planting rows of vegetables, as well as apple and plum trees and gooseberry and loganberry bushes. 'Soon they were able to grow much of the food they needed from day to day, banishing for good their initial simple diet of spuds and eggs' (ibid: 146). And Orwell, it seems, always tries to dress specially for dinner when they have guests. Topp quotes one visitor, saying Orwell would 'go around looking like a tramp during the day, but when dinnertime came he'd go upstairs and he'd wash himself and do his hair and he'd dress, and you'd sit down to the linen and all the rest' (ibid: 155).

According to Topp, the shop has little success in selling groceries and food, the villagers preferring to go to nearby Baldock to shop. Eileen ends up selling mainly sweets to children (ibid: 148).

In 1938, Orwell and Eileen travel to Marrakech – paid for by an anonymous donor – to restore their health in the sunshine. And Orwell's diary is packed with details about their vegetable growing and rearing of animals such as hens and goats. And he lists precisely the crops grown by the locals: 'palms, olives, pomegranates, maize, chillis, lucerne, most of the European vegetables (beans, cabbages, tomatoes, marrows, pumpkins, peas, radishes), brinjals, oranges and some cereals, I do not yet know which' (Davison 2009: 105). He is also interested in how the vegetables are cultivated: 'No spades or European forks, only hoes of the Indian style. Cultivation is made much more laborious by the lack of water, because every field has to be partitioned off into tiny plots with earth banks between, to conserve water. Not only small children but very old women work in the fields, women who must be at least 60, probably 70, clearing roots etc. with pick-axes' (ibid).

In 1941, Orwell joins the BBC as a talks producer for the Eastern Service broadcasting to India and one colleague, Mulk Raj Anand, becomes a particular friend and he cooks Indian meals specially for him and Eileen at their Langford Court apartment (Bowker 2003: 286). Later, he also befriends Michael Meyer, a 21-year-old Oxford undergraduate and poet and invites him to their new flat in Mortimer Crescent. Of those visits Meyer remembers particularly the tea – 'always black and strong, with large leaves floating on top, poured by George from a huge metal pot which must have held the best part of a gallon' (ibid: 298). The Canadian Paul Potts speaks of high tea with Orwell on a winter's evening – 'a huge fire, the table crowded with marvellous things, Gentlemen's Relish and various jams, kippers, crumpets and toast' (Meyers 2000: 231). When Geoffrey Gorer, the social anthropologist, is invited for a meal he is served liver and bacon – which unfortunately does not go down well (Crick 1980: 265). But when soon afterwards he revives his Etonian friendship with Cyril Connolly he cooks him '*bifteck aux pommes*' it's a success (ibid). Another meal with H. G. Wells and Inez Holden ends in a terrible shouting match between the two men (ibid: 430).

Orwell, like most of the other BBC employees working close to Portland Place, uses the corporation's canteen. Here Orwell is often found most days – and sometimes at night (ibid: 285). The Ministry of Truth, in *Nineteen Eighty-Four*, is said to be based on Orwell's experience at the BBC – and significantly a 'low-ceilinged canteen, deep underground' features in a number of important scenes. In the first, Winston Smith chats to his friend Syme who raves about Newspeak and the destruction of words (Orwell 1976 [1949]: 773). In the second, Winston finally manages to have a few furtive words with Julia, 'the girl from the Fiction Department' – and they agree to meet at nineteen hours in Victory Square, near the monument (ibid: 810). So begins their fateful, passionate, secret affair.

When, in 1942, Orwell befriends the old-Etonian and *Observer* journalist, David Astor, they share their liking for good food. Astor has security service links dating back to 1939 and he introduces Orwell to the Shanghai dining group (named after the Soho restaurant where they meet). A number of its members are old-Etonians including Guy Burgess (later exposed as a Soviet spy), Frank Pakenham (later Lord Longford) and John Strachey (Keeble 2019: 11).

During his reporting assignment on the Continent in 1945, in the final months of the Second World War, Orwell meets another fellow old-Eonian A. J. 'Freddie' Ayer, in Paris. Ayer at the time is working for the Secret Intelligence Service (MI6), who are particularly concerned about the danger of a communist coup in the French capital. Ayer comments: 'There is a legend that Orwell was a very austere man, very much of the puritan. It's not borne out at all by my experience of him in Paris. He used to like going to good restaurants. He liked good food, liked drink. In fact he was a lively, gay companion' (Wadhams 1984: 168).

Also while in Paris, Orwell is introduced to P. G. Wodehouse by Malcolm Muggeridge, who is keeping an eye on the great comic novelist for British intelligence. Wodehouse is under some form of house arrest having been accused of treachery for broadcasting for the Nazis from Berlin. Not surprisingly, Orwell – who had written the essay 'In defence of P. G. Wodehouse' just before leaving for the Continent – takes him out for dinner at a good restaurant near les Halles. But his dinner date at Les Deux Magots with the novelist and editor of the Resistance journal, *Combat*, Albert Camus, has to be called off after the Frenchman falls ill with his tuberculosis (Meyers 2000: 233). As Dorian Lynskey comments, this 'could have been a remarkable meeting between two natural rebels who put principles before political expediency and turned political writing into an art. Orwell later sent Camus a copy of the French translation of *Animal Farm*' (Lynskey 2019: 131).

In 1946, Orwell goes – with son Richard and sister Avril – to live on the remote Scottish island of Jura and compose what was to become his last major work, the dystopian masterpiece *Nineteen Eighty-Four*. When not writing, he enjoys planting a vegetable garden, looking after the geese and hens, going fishing and setting lobster traps, shooting rabbits and butchering venison (Meyers 2000: 261). The meals, prepared largely by Avril, can be Spartan. Bill Dunn, who lives locally and goes on to marry Avril, remembers Orwell coming down from his workroom upstairs. He would 'seem to be a wee bit hungry, but he wouldn't really eat anything substantial. He would eat something like brown bread and Marmite and he would seem to enjoy it. Then he would go back upstairs and go on writing away' (Wadhams 1984: 185). Jane, daughter of Orwell's recently deceased sister Marjorie, who comes to stay at Barnhill, comments: 'Eric always came in for meals, but he worked hard and had his routine. He'd have his breakfast and then he'd go up and write; then he always came down at lunchtime and we had the main meal in the middle of the day. … He liked pudding, I remember. And so did his father. I think Eric must have inherited that' (ibid: 188).

ORWELL AND THE PERFECT PUB

When Orwell was living with Eileen in Wallington after their marriage, they would go to the Plough next door for drinks and occasionally to the nearby Derby (Topp 2020: 156). But he was a stickler for his own preferences in alcohol. '… one of Eileen's friends remembered how, even when she had specifically ordered lager, Orwell would always bring her dark ale' (ibid).

Moving to London in 1940, Orwell plunges into literary society meeting at Soho pubs and cafés among others Richard Crossman, Aneurin Bevan, Michael Foot, George Strauss, Tosco Fyvel, H. G. Wells, Anthony Powell, Kay Dick, Malcolm Muggeridge, Hugh Kingsmill, Dylan Thomas, T. S. Eliot, Michael Sayers, Rayner Heppenstall, the Labour MP Patrick Gordon-Walker and Graham Greene. Occasionally, he makes forays into more glamorous haunts such as the Café Royal where he meets, for example, the young artist Lucian Freud (Taylor 2003: 329). According to Bowker (2003: 277): 'The Barcelona in Beak Street is his favourite restaurant, the Wheatsheaf his favourite pub.' Other favourite pubs are the Dog and Duck, in Bateman Street – where there is today a George Orwell Bar – the Fitzroy Tavern, in Rathbone Place, and the Marquis of Granby, in Rathbone Street (Young 2016: 16). His friend, George Woodcock, also mentions Victor Berlemont's York Minster (the 'French hose') near the bombed ruin of St. Anne's, Soho, and the Swiss tavern in Old Compton Street (1984 [1966]: 24).

As for his favourite restaurants, they are the Bodega, Czardas and Elysée (Meyers 2000: 231). The Akropolis, in Percy Street, is also a favourite until he is ejected for removing his jacket (Bowker 2003: 309). George Woodcock relates how soon afterwards Orwell takes him to a restaurant opposite and very conspicuously hangs his jacket over the back of his chair. 'With a look he challenged me to follow his example: I did. At that time, wartime restrictions of restaurant meals were beginning to relax and the lunch was an excellent and lavish one, with aperitifs, wine and brandy; it was a far cry from the boiled cod and turnip tops in the Strand a few years before, and Orwell seemed to enjoy the change' (1984 [1966]: 34). After the war, he meets Vernon Richards and other pacifists in pubs near Conway Hall (Crick 1980: 449).

Orwell's favourite pub, The Moon Under Water, is the subject of his last *Evening Standard* Saturday Essay (of 9 Febuary 1946). It's typically witty, wonderfully inventive, conversational, down-to-earth. The pub is 'only two minutes from a bus stop, but it is on a side street, and drunks and rowdies never seem to find their way there, even on Saturday nights' (*CWGO* XVIII: 98). And thereafter Orwell carefully goes over the various aspects of the pub that appeal to him – the Victorian architecture, there's a good fire burning in at least two of the bars, it's always quiet enough to talk, it sells tobacco and good, solid lunches upstairs – and so on. Only towards the end does he reveal that The Moon Under Water actually does not exist – it's his ideal. 'I have mentioned above ten qualities that the perfect pub should have and I know one pub that has eight of them. Even there, however, there is no draught stout and no china mugs' (ibid: 100). Richard Young reports John Thompson, in his book *Orwell's London*, of 1984, thinking that the Canonbury Tavern, which is close to where Orwell was living at the time, is the inspiration for The Moon Under Water (Young 2016: 16).

Young also highlights a little-known, unsigned review of the book, *The Pub and the People*, which Orwell pens in January 1943 for the *Listener*. It is the first of a series which Victor Gollancz commissions from Mass Observation – and is based on interviews with people in pubs in 'Worktown' (actually Bolton). Orwell is clearly fascinated by the book. And while it highlights the decline in pub-going and the general trend in people's leisure 'from active and communal forms to those that are passive and individual', Orwell is more concerned to stress that the Mass Observers have 'no difficulty in showing that there was extraordinarily little drunkenness in the period they were studying' (ibid: 17).

A major new study of *The Pub and the People*, by academics Jennie Taylor and Simon Prince, largely confirms Orwell's conclusions. Writing in *The Historical Journal*, they point out that the Mass Observers tended to idealise the world of the pub, representing it as largely socially harmonious and egalitarian with individuals generously buying drinks for their companions. Looking into the pub study's archive, Taylor and Prince discover material that contradicts the published findings (2020). Observers actually turned in reports focusing on 'authoritarian conduct, hierarchical power structures' and heated discussions about contemporary politics. *The Pub and the People* does describe a fight between 'Jack', 'Peter' and 'Peter's woman' and one heated argument at Waterloo Tavern. And occasionally observers became involved in heated discussions. But, as Orwell stresses, these moments of tension are, remarkably, very much the exceptions.

Taylor and Prince are clearly unaware of Orwell's review. They merely quote the main organiser of the 'Worktown' project, Tom Harrisson, dismissing Orwell as a member of an 'old Eton group slumming' (ibid: 9).

PUBS IN THE NOVELS

Not surprisingly, pubs feature in Orwell's novels. In *Keep the Aspidistra Flying*, there are two contrasting scenes involving the central character, Gordon Comstock. He is alone, with little money in his pockets, walking through London's streets – in Lambeth, across Trafalgar Square, past the cinema showing Greta Garbo in *The Painted Veil,* past the prostitutes up to Tottenham Court Road and Camden Road. Finally, dreadfully thirsty, he enters the Crichton pub. In a private room the Buffaloes are singing but in the saloon bar he sees Flaxman, the outrageously confident, fellow lodger of Mrs Wisbeach, in Willowbed Road, NW. 'One elbow on the bar, his foot on the rail, a beer-streaked glass in the other hand, he was swapping backchat with the blonde cutie barmaid' (Orwell 1976 [1936]: 623). Comstock leaves and heads home.

The next time Gordon visits a pub he's with Ravelston, the aristocratic editor of *Antichrist*, who is loosely based on Sir Richard Rees, Orwell's life-long friend, fellow old-Etonian and editor of the *Adelphi*. Bowker highlights the 'Eton tradition of ruthless criticism within a continuing friendship' (2003: 288) which Orwell gleefully maintains in a number of his relationships. Here Ravelson is the butt of Orwell's satirical pen – a man who spouts Marx and socialist ideas but when confronted with a working class pub recoils. He only enters when he thinks that 'pubs are genuinely proletarian. In a pub you can meet the working class on equal terms'. Young comments astutely: 'I suspect this was part of the fascination that Orwell had in real life for pubs' (Young 2016: 16). Comstock pays for the first round, mocks his friend's commitment to socialism and ends up moaning about having no money. Ravelson thinks about the unemployed in Middlesbrough 'seven in a room on twenty-five bob a week', feels guilty – and then they leave (op cit: 638).

There is also an important scene in *Nineteen Eighty-Four* (1976 [1949]: 793-797) when Winston Smith follows an old man into a 'dingy little pub' in the prole district – hoping to find out about life before the revolution that removed the capitalists and installed the Party. But the old man talks largely nonsense. The scene follows shortly after Orwell intones in the novel: 'But if there was hope, it lay in the proles.' Thus, Orwell cleverly avoids the temptation to sentimentalist the proles with an idealistic picture of their 'humanity'. Instead, he paints a very negative picture – the message clearly being: the revolution will be led by the proles but it won't be easy and not without its problematics.

CONCLUSION: ORWELL, FOOD AND THE PLEASURE PRINCIPLE

In the spring of 1940, Orwell writes a short piece about his life, likes and dislikes for an American writers' directory. Food features prominently: 'Outside my work the thing I care most about is gardening, especially vegetable gardening. I like English cookery and English beer, French red wines, Spanish white wines, Indian tea, strong tobacco, coal fires, candle light and comfortable chairs.' Amongst his dislikes is 'tinned food' (Bowker 2003: 263). And significantly, in his masterpiece, *Nineteen Eighty-Four* (1949), amongst the illicit pleasures Winston Smith and Julia enjoy in the room above Mr Charrington's shop – away from all the dystopian horrors – along with sex are chocolate, real coffee and sugar (Kerr 2020: 45).

Orwell is perhaps too often associated with the gloom and doom of *Nineteen Eighty-Four*. Typically, Jason Cowley, in an introduction to a new edition of *Animal Farm* in 2020, writes that 'Orwell is not renowned for his humour' (2020: 41). P. G. Wodehouse described him as 'a gloomy sort of chap' (Dwan 2018: 198). Michael Ayrton even nicknames him 'Gloomy George'. Yet there is another side to Orwell which this essay has sought to highlight. For food and drink are incredibly important to Orwell – and his love of them is all part of the optimistic, pleasure-seeking, life-affirmative, Sancho Panza aspects of his personality which so often shine through.

ACKNOWLEDGEMENT

The author would like to thank Richard Young for alerting him to the existence of Orwell's unpublished essay, 'English cookery'.

NOTES

[1] See https://www.dw.com/en/sri-lanka-tea-workers-and-a-legacy-of-exploitation/a-55006963

REFERENCES

Bowker, Gordon (2003) *George Orwell*, London: Little, Brown

Cowley, Jason (2020) The road to revolution, *New Statesman*, 11 December-7 January pp 39-41

CWGO (1998) – *The Complete Works of George Orwell*, XX Vols, Davison, Peter (ed.) London: Secker & Warburg

Davison, Peter (ed.) (2006) *George Orwell Diaries*, London: Penguin

Dwan, David (2018) *Liberty, Equality and Humbug: Orwell's Political Ideals*, Oxford: Oxford University Press

Keeble, Richard Lance (2019) The 'invisible masonic network of support': Orwell and Eton, Davidson, Russ (ed.) *George Orwell: His Enduring Legacy*, Albuquerque: University of New Mexico pp 8-14

Keeble, Richard Lance (2020) The myth of freedom: Orwell and the press, *Journalism Beyond Orwell*, London: Routledge pp 15-32

Kerr, Douglas (2020) The virtual geographies of *Nineteen Eighty-Four*, Waddell, Nathan (ed.) *The Cambridge Companion to* Nineteen Eighty-Four, Cambridge: Cambridge University Press pp 37-50

Lynskey, Dorian (2019) *The Ministry of Truth: A Biography of George Orwell's* 1984, London: Picador

Meyers, Jeffrey (2000) *Orwell: Wintry Conscience of a Generation*, New York: W.W. Norton & Company

Orwell, George (1980 [1933]) *Down and Out in Paris and London*, in the *Collected Non-Fiction*, London: Secker & Warburg/Octopus pp 15-120

Orwell, George (1976 [1936]) *Keep the Aspidistra Flying*, in the *Collected Fiction*, London: Secker & Warburg/Octopus pp 577-737

Orwell, George (1980 [1937]) *The Road to Wigan Pier*, in the *Collected Non-Fiction*, London: Secker & Warburg/Octopus pp 125-231

Orwell, George (1976 [1939]) *Coming Up For Air*, in the *Collected Fiction*, London: Secker & Warburg/Octopus pp 431-571

Orwell, George (1980 [1944]) Oysters and brown stout, in the *Collected Non-Fiction*, London: Secker & Warburg/Octopus pp 675-677

Orwell, George (1946) British cookery. Available online at https://www.orwellfoundation.com/the-orwell-foundation/orwell/essays-and-other-works/british-cookery

Orwell, George (1976 [1949]) *Nineteen Eighty-Four*, in the *Collected Fiction*, London: Secker & Warburg/Octopus pp 743-925

Orwell, Sonia and Angus, Ian (eds) (1970) *The Collected Essays, Journalism and Letters of George Orwell, Vol. 1: An Age Like This*, Harmondsworth: Middlesex: Penguin

Perkins, Blake (2014) George Orwell and the defence of English food, *Petits Propos Culinaires*, No. 106 pp 68-86. Available online at https://prospectbooks.co.uk/products-page/ppc/ppc-101-october-2014/

Taylor, D. J. (2003) *Orwell: The Life*, London: Chatto & Windus

Taylor, Jennie and Prince, Simon (2020) Temporalities, ritual and drinking in Mass Observation's Worktown, *The Historical Journal*. Available online at https://www.cambridge.org/core/journals/historical-journal/article/temporalities-ritual-and-drinking-in-mass-observations-worktown/E05E24232A5358C588294FD0287C37D1

Topp, Sylvia (2020) *Eileen: The Making of George Orwell*, London: Unbound

Wadhams, Stephen (1984) *Remembering Orwell*, Harmondsworth: Middlesex: Penguin

Wadhams, Stephen (2012) Orwell's crystal chandelier, orwellsociety.com, 14 January. Available online at https://orwellsociety.com/orwells-crystal-chandelier-by-steve-wadhams/

Woloch, Alex (2016) *Or Orwell: Writing and Democratic Socialism*, Cambridge, Massachusetts: Harvard University Press

Woodcock, George (1984 [1966]) *The Crystal Spirit: A Study of George Orwell*, London: Fourth Estate

Young, Richard (2016) The pub and George, Orwell Society *Journal*, No. 8 pp 16-17

- This essay is based on four articles which were originally published on The Orwell Society website as Orwell – The politics and pleasures of food, 21 March 2021, https://orwellsociety.com/food-for-thought-i/; 27 March 2021, https://orwellsociety.com/food-for-thought-ii/; 18 April, https://orwellsociety.com/food-for-thought-iii/ and 25 April, https://orwellsociety.com/food-for-thought-iv/8

Chapter Ten

'Seeing What is In Front of One's Nose': The Importance and Delights of the Domestic Diaries

Amongst Orwell's greatest obsessions is gardening. He once said: 'Outside my work the thing I care most about is gardening.' Yet this aspect of his personality has been downplayed or totally ignored by his biographers and academics studying his writings. Why?

Similarly, Orwell's domestic diaries have drawn little attention. They are usually seen as dull and dreary since they record in meticulous detail the ordinary everyday aspects of gardening and husbandry – observations about nature and the weather, vegetable growing, raising chickens and goats, the numbers of eggs produced by his chickens each day and so on. His anarchist friend, George Woodcock, in his otherwise brilliantly insightful, early study of Orwell, damns the 'disappointing poverty' of the diaries (Woodcock 1984 [1966]: 184). Yet the domestic diaries can be seen as some of his most important and fascinating writings. For they offer crucial insights about his personality, his literary style, his love of the simple life, his emphasis on the constant struggle to see clearly 'what is in front of one's nose' – and the complexities of the creative process of writing more generally.

Is it not symbolically significant that in his dystopian masterpiece, *Nineteen Eighty-Four*, Winston Smith's ultimate act of rebellion is the secret writing of a personal diary? Away, he thinks, from the gaze of the Thought Police and surveillance telescreens, in an alcove in his apartment, on 4 April (significantly the day after the funeral of Orwell's first wife, Eileen, in 1945), he takes a pen – 'an archaic instrument, seldom used even for signatures' – and begins writing: 'Last night to the flicks. All war films…' (Orwell 1976 [1949]: 747). The act of writing is a pleasure in itself. As Douglas Kerr comments, it's an activity 'to be enjoyed for its own sake'. 'But the act of writing is also the key that unlocks all of his interior world in a flood of words, the secret life of his buried memories as well as his anger and rebellion' (Kerr 2020: 46). For Diletta De Cristofaro (2020: 59), 'the diary functions as a repository of Winston's scattered memories and, thus, as the sign of the Party's not entirely successful control of the individual archive. That is why the Party cannot but severely punish the act of keeping a diary'.

The collection of Orwell's diaries edited by Peter Davison (2010) incorporates those for 9 August-5 September 1938 when Orwell is living with his new wife Eileen O'Shaughnessy at the Stores, Wallington, in deepest Hertfordshire; from 10 April-26 May 1939 when the Blairs return to the UK after a six-month break convalescing in Morocco; from 27 May 1939-2 July 1939 and 5 September-29 April 1940 at Wallington again. Then when Orwell surprises everyone and retires to Jura, a remote Scottish island, he resumes his domestic diary writings – from 7 May 1946-29 October and again from 21 March 1949-September of the year. Days later, in January 1950, Orwell dies – aged just 46.

Intriguingly, Orwell writes a number of kinds of diary. While in Morocco, he writes one in which he notes newspaper coverage, observations about the natural environment, local customs, overheard conversations, food provisions, changes in the weather, agricultural equipment (accompanied by little sketches) and so on. From 2 July-3 September he composes a diary of events leading up to the Second World War – mostly summarising reports from a wide variety of newspapers – both mainstream and left-wing. And during the war, he writes two diaries: from 28 May 1940-28 August 1941 and 14 March 1942-15 November 1942 incorporating the major political developments, his opinions and those of friends, newspaper coverage etc.

Orwell is constantly at his desk bashing out novels, journalism, letters to family members, lovers, work colleagues, political friends and adversaries, reviews, journal columns, polemics, poems and so on. Yet, amazingly, he still finds the time to write diaries. Why? Orwell, in effect, is making important points about the purpose of writing – and the deeper purposes, challenges and joys of living.

WHY WRITE A DIARY?

Orwell only once writes about diaries. In his essay, 'In front of your nose', published in *Tribune* on 22 March 1946, he comments: 'One thing that helps is to keep a diary or, at any rate, to keep some kind of record of one's opinions about important events. Otherwise, when some particularly absurd belief is exploded by events, one may simply forget that one ever held it' (Orwell 2006 [1946a]: 305). Here he is clearly referring to the kind of political diary he writes during the war years. Yet that notion of seeing 'what is in front of one's nose' lies at the heart of his domestic diaries. Orwell has travelled to Burma, to the north of England to report on the plight of the poor, to Spain to fight in the civil war in 1937, to Morocco. But in the domestic diaries, Orwell 'self-isolates' and celebrates what is close at hand: the simple joys of *working on the land*, the aesthetic pleasures of gardening and the wonders of nature. And the act of recording all this in his diary is, itself, a joy. As Irene and Alan Taylor say in the Introduction to their 686-page collection of 170 diaries (significantly not including Orwell's): 'The best diaries are those in which the voice of the individual comes through untainted by self-censorship or a desire to please. First and foremost, the diarist must write for himself, those who do not, who are already looking towards publication and public recognition, invariably strike a phoney note' (Taylor and Taylor 2000: ix).

Let us take one, quite arbitrary, example. On 14 March 1940, he writes: 'Heavy snow in the night & during a good deal of the day. Nasty slush snow which will not lie long, but makes everything very nasty. Impossible to do anything out of doors. Began water-glassing some eggs, experimentally. It appears you should use eggs 5-12 hours old, as if they have been laid a day or two it takes several months off the time they will stay good. Put 20-30 older eggs (laid about 6 days) in a glass jar, & these can be used first. Am using a large enamelled pan for newer eggs, & shall put in none more than 24 hours old. 16 eggs' (Orwell 2010: 235). So, typically, normal grammar rules do not apply and he uses '&' always for 'and'. He begins by recording the weather; then shifts to describing in some laborious detail water-glassing eggs and ends, again typically, with his egg count for the day.

In a fascinating section of his book on Orwell's political ideals, David Dwan focuses on the domestic diaries. In one entry he considers goats ('Saw 3 wild goats. They were about 400 years away, & at that distance looked definitely black. Somewhat heavy moments, compared with the deer'). In another, he reflects on wild birds ('Large hovering hawk of some kind – in style of flight somewhat like a larger edition of a kestrel, but flaps its wings more slowly – always about behind the house. Presumably some kind of buzzard'). Dwan concludes: '… underneath his endless botanizing is a clear sense of wonder' (Dwan 2018: 199).

THE DIARY'S EVER CHANGING STYLE AND FUNCTION

On one level all this seems banal. The contents are highly selective, of course. There is no mention of his wife; later, while writing the Jura diaries, Orwell is devoted to bringing up his son, Richard, but he is nowhere mentioned – though he appears regularly in his letters of this period. Without the support of his sister, Avril, nothing could have been achieved in Jura, according to Richard Blair.[1] Nowhere is she mentioned, either.

Yet, for Orwell writing the domestic diary is both psychologically and creatively important. In 'Why I write', the essay he contributes to the short-lived alternative journal, *Gangrel*, Orwell stresses: 'What I have most wanted to do throughout the past ten years is to make political writing an art' (Orwell 1970 1 [1946b]: 28) and these 'artistic' aspects add to both the challenges and constraints of communicating to an audience and writing for publication. In contrast, the diary, as the French theorist Philippe Lejeune, argues, is 'only secondarily a text or a literary genre' while 'keeping a diary is a way of living before it is a way of writing' (see Millim 2010).

THE DIARY IN DYSTOPIAN TIMES

Let us look at Winston Smith's diary items in *Nineteen Eighty-Four*. Notice how, initially, their *writing style* is radically unconventional, encapsulating a sort of James Joycean stream of consciousness (see Mullen 2020: 106). The first opens with the dateline, 4 April 1984. Then three relatively short, journalistically 'punchy' sentences: 'Last night to the flicks. All war films. One very good one of a ship full of refugees being bombed somewhere in the Mediterranean' (Orwell 1976 [1949]: 747). The use of the phrase 'very good one' is strange. Is Winston being ironic? Or is he, in bravely launching into the essentially seditious act of diary writing, starting out cautiously – mouthing the uncaring rhetoric expected by the Thought Police? The next sentence, as Winston begins to throw off literary constraints, is 45 words long incorporating six clauses, two of them linked by using 'then'; another two by 'and'. Thereafter, there are no capital letters to begin sentences. Three times 'then' is used as the changing contents of the 'flick' and the reactions of the audience are hastily recorded. Towards the end of the diary entry, Winston loses all sense of punctuation and spelling and drifts into slang and repetition as a woman shouts out: 'they didn't oughter of showed it not in front of kids they didn't it aint right not in front of kids it aint until the police turned her turned her out …' (ibid).

This totally free style of writing is remarkably modernist, avant-garde even. Inspired by Freud's method of 'free association', in 1920, André Breton and Philippe Soupault publish their first volume of automatic writing, *Les Champs Magnétiques*. The idea is to 'write without thinking'. In Paris at the same time, the Chilean artist, Roberto Matta, adopts this creative technique for painting (Manguel 2001: 26). This is the kind of creative daring that fires Winston's first diary entries.

His next diary entry is entirely without any conventional punctuation and grammar – as Winston dares to utter anti-state slogans: 'theyll shoot me i don't care theyll shoot me in the back of the neck i don't care down with big brother they always shoot you in the back of the neck i don't care down with big brother' (ibid: 753). The use of the lower case in 'big brother' even serves as a mark of disrespect to the great leader of the Party.

Yet Winston is unsure of his audience in his first diary entries. Is he writing purely for the sake of it, to emote, to express – in the only way he knows possible – all his secret hatred of Big Brother? Perhaps this uncertainty partly accounts for the radically free style of the ungrammatical, unpunctuated early diary entries. But for his third entry, Winston develops some sense of purpose: it is important to carry on 'the human heritage'. So now the writing follows punctuation, spelling and grammar conventions. Ideas are now separated in paragraphs – and he actually addresses, with striking irony, his imaginary audience:

To the future or to the past, to a time when thought is free, when men are different from one another and do not live alone – to a time when truth exists and what is done cannot be undone:

From the age of uniformity, from the age of solitude, from the age of Big Brother, from the age of doublethink – greetings! (ibid: 758).

For Lisa Mullen, Winston moves from an unfiltered stream of consciousness into a 'tone of self-conscious pomposity'. 'These two modes of writing seem to satirize two strands of Orwell's literary predecessors, first puncturing the unpunctuated modernist experiments of Joyce and others, and then lancing the overblown histrionics of the futuristic fiction of the past' (Mullen 2020: 106-107).

After reflecting on death ('He was already dead'), Winston goes on to realise that, in writing the diary, in expressing his hatred of Big Brother, he inevitably is going to be killed – since the 'consequences of every act are included in the act itself'. And having ritualistically dipped his pen in ink, the physicality of the process being part of its pleasure, he writes: 'Thoughtcrime does not entail death, thoughtcrime is death' (op cit: 758).

Winston becomes ever more daring in the content of his diary, though stylistically he remains conventional. In the next entry, writing becomes an erotic substitute, a sort of psychological therapy, as he tries to capture the sexually charged, guilty and subversive intensity of the moments he spends with a prostitute. There is an almost journalist attention to detail. The 'when' ('It was three years ago. It was a dark evening…') followed by the 'where' ('in a narrow side-street near one of the big railway stations. She was standing near a doorway in the wall, under a street lamp that hardly gave any light') and then the 'who' ('She had a young face, painted very thick. It was really the paint that appealed to me, the whiteness of it, like a mask, and the bright red lips') (ibid: 780). 'She said two dollars. I …' and at this point Winston, torn between pleasure and pain, is overwhelmed with guilt and violent self-hatred. 'He had an almost overwhelming temptation to shout a string of filthy words at the top of his voice. Or to bang his head against the wall, to kick over the table, and hurl the inkpot through the window – to do any violent or noisy or painful thing that might black out the memory that was tormenting him' (ibid).

Winston reflects on how something as basic as the human nervous system becomes an 'enemy' in Big Brother society. The diary writing serves to provoke memories – of a man he has passed in the street, a Party member with a tic in his face. 'He remembered thinking at the time: That poor devil is done for. And what was frightening was that the action was quite possibly unconscious. The most deadly danger of all was talking in your sleep.' Winston returns to his erotic narrative: 'I went with her through the doorway and across a backyard into a basement kitchen. There was a bed against the wall, and a lamp on the table, turned down very low. She …' As the sexual tension mounts, he reflects on his sexless relationship with his separated wife Katharine. And this leads remorselessly to the guilt-ridden climax in the narrative: 'She threw herself down on the bed, and at once, without any kind of preliminary, in the most coarse, horrible way you can imagine, pulled up her skirt. I ...' He ponders the Party women in whom chastity is deeply ingrained making the sex act, in effect, an act of rebellion. He writes: 'I turned up the lamp. When I saw her in the light.... ' (ibid: 783).

The writing is now out of control. There is massive guilt but even more a burning desire to record the event. 'It had got to be written down, it had got to be confessed.' Sexuality in Orwell's novels usually involve attempts at the sexual 'possession' of a woman and the affirmation of manhood (Patai 1984: 248). For instance, of the sex between Winston and Julia, he writes: 'He had pulled her down to the ground, she was utterly unresisting, he could do what he liked with her.' Here in the diary entry, the horror of the event for Winston is not so much in its brutal, instant, impersonality but in the ugliness and old age of the prostitute: 'The paint was plastered so thick that it looked as though it might crack like a cardboard mask. ... She had no teeth at all.' And the diary entry culminates in the sex act – completely divorced from any humanity: 'When I saw her in the light she was quite an old woman, fifty years old at least. But I went ahead and did it just the same' (Orwell 1976 [1949]: 783). According to Nathan Waddell, the whole meeting with the prostitute 'is a matter of dirt and of being dirtied', the seediness of the old woman's room contrasting with the 'literal and symbolic chastity of the women of the Party' (Waddell 2020: 177, 178).

In his essay, 'Why I write' (Orwell 1970 [1946b]: 29), Orwell, ever aware of the limitations of language, writes that all books are failures. Here, Winston's attempt to use the diary writing to dampen his anger, guilt and self-hatred also fails: 'He had written it down at last but it made no difference. The therapy had not worked. The urge to shout filthy words at the top of his voice was as strong as ever' (Orwell 1976 [1949]: 783).

But immediately after that 'failure', Orwell has Winston writing one of the most important lines in the text: 'If there is hope it lies in the proles.' That short phrase encapsulates an enormous amount of Winston's thinking and reflections which are not, significantly, included in the diary. Is Orwell suggesting that, in writing, what is missing/left out can be important – and maybe even more important – than what is actually conveyed? Winston goes on to ponder at some length the plight of the 'swarming disregarded masses, 85 per cent of the population of Oceania'. If only they realised their strength in numbers 'they could blow the Party to pieces tomorrow morning' (ibid: 784). He remembers walking down a crowded street, hearing a tremendous shout of hundreds of women's voices, and thinking that an anti-Party riot had broken out. But instead the women were scrabbling over saucepans. Winston now sums up his thinking with this appalling, concise paradox: 'Until they become conscious they will never rebel, and until after they have rebelled they cannot become conscious.' In fact, it's doublespeak.

As Winston reflects, that 'might almost have been a transcription from one of the Party textbooks' (ibid: 784).

He goes on to ponder the proles' plight in more detail: 'Heavy physical work, the care of home and children, petty quarrels with neighbours, films, football, beer and, above all, gambling, filled up the horizon of their minds. ... The sexual puritanism of the Party was not imposed upon them. Promiscuity went unpunished, divorce was permitted. ... As the Party put it: "Proles and animals are free"' (ibid: 785). And now he goes on to simply copy 283 words from a children's history textbook about 'the old days ... before the Glorious Revolution'. It's all about children working 12 hours a day for cruel masters, rich men living in a few great big beautiful houses, and ordinary people having to cringe and bow when talking to capitalists.

So Winston has moved from the anti-Big Brother, free, radical writing style of the first diary entry to the expression of a kind of Party-line doublethink and now to a basic copying of a Party text. The diary writing is currently mirroring the fate of Winston – from secret, Brotherhood-supporter to, in the end, a 'lover' of Big Brother.

Winston now reflects on the fate of three men, Jones, Aaronson and Rutherford. In 1965 they had all confessed to being traitors and were then reinstated to the Party. But they engaged in new conspiracies, were tried and finally executed. While working at his desk at the Ministry of Truth, Winston spots in *The Times* from ten years earlier a photograph of the three men disproving the evidence they gave in their confessions. 'Very likely the confessions had been rewritten and rewritten until the original facts and dates no longer the smallest significance. The past not only changed but changed continuously.' Winston takes up his pen and writes briefly: 'I understand HOW: I do not understand WHY.' In other words, he is shifting from docile, Party-line plagiarism to a highly focused questioning stance. In the end, he ponders, the Party would announce that two and two make five and you would have to believe it. The Party told you to reject the evidence of your eyes and ears. And he pens his final diary entry, the 'important axiom': 'Freedom is the freedom to say that two plus to make four. If that is granted, all else follows' (ibid: 790).

But a deep and shocking irony underlies this episode. Since every act of communication implies some kind of audience, real or imagined, every diary writer has to consider the question – for whom is it being written? The awareness of the audience normally brings with it some kind of constraint on the writing. But when the diary is solely for the author, then perhaps it's the purist form of writing. Here, Winston resolves the crucial question over audience by convincing himself he is writing it for O'Brien, whom he currently believes, is involved in the rebellious Brotherhood (ibid: 803). The uncertainty over the audience which influenced the radical, free style of writing in the first diary entry is now resolved.

But later, O'Brien is to turn torturer of Winston in Room 101 – forcing him to admit, with terrible irony, that two and two actually do make five.

DIARY WRITING AS A COLLABORATIVE PROJECT

There is another fascinating aspect of Orwell's own domestic diaries. Writing is seen very much as an individual pursuit in the dominant Western tradition. In contrast, in Japan, for instance, rengas are poems composed collaboratively – by two or more people, even entire villages (Miner 1979). At times, Orwell's domestic diaries become a collaborative project. Thus, when he is away from Wallington in September 1939, Eileen Blair fills in the diary and during the winter of 1947-1948 when he is away in hospital, his sister, Avril, jots down entries on his behalf. Both closely follow his style so incorporate basic information about the weather and work undertaken around their houses. In other words, while the obsessive diary entries may seem an idiosyncratic feature of Orwell's personality and writing process, it is understood by his closest family members. And so they willingly join him in the exercise – making the diaries ultimately a sort of intimate celebration of their life together.

Orwell, then, as an exponent of 'close' travel, exploring the near-at-hand as a way of embracing a creative and more ethically nuanced notion of travel and travel writing, is following in a long tradition. At the end of the 18th century, in Turin, for instance, Xavier de Maistre writes *A Journey Around My Room* (1794) while imprisoned in his bedroom for six weeks after being caught fighting a duel in the north Italian city in 1790. As a way of coping with his imprisonment he decides to compose a travel book about the contents of his chamber (see de Botton 2002: 243-247). As Alain de Botton comments: 'De Maistre's work springs from a profound and suggestive insight: that the pleasure we derive from journeys is perhaps dependent more on the mindset with which we travel than on the destination we travel to. If only we could apply a travelling mindset to our own locales, we might find these places becoming no less interesting than the high mountain passes and butterfly-filled jungles of Humboldt's South America' (ibid: 246).

In a similar vein, the French Oratorian priest Abbé Perreyve (1831-1865) writes that 'within all journeys it is the hermit and those who look closer at things who attain the real value from travel'. And Henry David Thoreau, in *Walden* (1854), tells of the time he lives alone in a remote log cabin at Walden Pond, Massachusetts, focusing on simple experiences and on slowing down as an antidote to the stresses he sees being created by modern industrialism (see Stubbs 2020). Like Orwell, Thoreau is an obsessive diary writer, tracking the seemingly trivial aspects of his 'simple living' in meticulous detail.

Significantly, *Walden* is among the list of books Orwell owns at the time of his death that Peter Davison carries towards the end of the last volume of the twenty *Complete Works* (1998). Orwell had an ambivalent attitude to the simple life (as, indeed, to many other topics). As David Dwan notes (2018: 193): 'Orwell had little time for the "shallow pantheism" of committed nature-worshippers.' George Bowling, the anti-hero of his novel, *Coming Up For Air* (1939), similarly dislikes those who preach the simple life and 'roll in the dew before breakfast'.

Yet Orwell, in practice, loved the simple life. Sylvia Topp highlights in her biography of Eileen Blair the primitive state of the Stores. The two-storey building was tiny – just eleven feet deep. The corrugated iron roof, recently added since the original thatch was rotting, made a colossal racket every time it rained which was often. The ceiling downstairs was so low Orwell – at 6ft 3ins – had to bend double all the time (Topp 2020: 126-127). There was no internal water supply, lighting was by oil lamp and heating and cooking by oil stove. The chimney was constantly blocked so any fire was likely to fill the cottage with smoke (Bowker 2003: 185). As Topp writes of the Blairs (op cit: 155): 'Some saw their cottage life as masochistic. Certainly they pushed themselves to the extreme, wanting to fill each day completely with fulfilling work. … They got pleasure from the rewards of accomplishment: the garden grew, the eggs and milk fed them, the books and articles were perfected and appreciated.' Similarly, in moving to the remote Scottish island of Jura at the end of his life, Orwell was indulging in his love of the simple life.

THE PASSION FOR LIFE

Better than anything else, it is the domestic diaries – with their copious entries about work done, animals caught copulating, hedges planted, the changing weather and moods of the sea, fishing exploits and the spraying of fruit trees (apples, plums, cherries, black currants, red currants and gooseberries) – that capture Orwell's passion not only for gardening but for life.

NOTE

[1] Speaking during an Orwell Society George Talk via Zoom on 21 February 2021

REFERENCES

Bowker, Gordon (2018) *George Orwell*, London: Little, Brown

De Botton, Alain (2002) *The Art of Travel*, London: Hamish Hamilton

De Cristofaro, Diletta (2018) The politics of the archive in *Nineteen Eighty-Four*, Waddell, Nathan (ed.) *The Cambridge Companion to* Nineteen Eighty-Four, Cambridge: Cambridge University Press pp 51-63

Dwan, David (2018) *Liberty, Equality and Humbug: Orwell's Political Ideals*, Oxford: Oxford University Press

Kerr, Douglas (2020) The virtual geographies of *Nineteen Eighty-Four*, Waddell, Nathan (ed.) *The Cambridge Companion to* Nineteen Eighty-Four, Cambridge: Cambridge University Press pp 37-50

Millim, Anne-Marie (2010) The Victorian diary: Between the public and the private, *Literature Compass*, Vol. 7, No. 10 pp 977-988

Miner, Earl (1979) *A History of Japanese Literature*, Princeton: Princeton University Press

Mullen, Lisa (2020) Orwell's literary context: Modernism, language and politics, Waddell, Nathan (ed.) *The Cambridge Companion to* Nineteen Eighty-Four, Cambridge: Cambridge University Press pp 95-108

Orwell, George (2006 [1946a]) *Orwell in* Tribune, Anderson, Paul (ed.) London: Politico's

Orwell, George (1970 1 [1946b]) Why I write, Orwell, Sonia and Angus, Ian (eds) *The Collected Essays, Journalism and Letters of George Orwell, Vol. 1*, Harmondsworth, Middlesex: Penguin Books pp 23-30; first published *Gangrel*, No. 4

Orwell, George (1976 [1949]) *Nineteen Eighty-Four*, in the *Collected Fiction*, London: Secker & Warburg pp 743-925

Orwell, George (2010) *Diaries*, London: Penguin

Patai, Daphne (1984) *The Orwell Mystique: A Study in Male Ideology*, Amherst: University of Massachusetts Pres

Stubbs, Ben (2020) Close travel: On the ethics of writing about the near-at-hand, *Ethical Space: The International Journal of Communication Ethics*, Vol. 17, No. 1 pp 11-17

Taylor, Irene and Taylor, Alan (eds) (2000) *The Assassin's Cloak: An Anthology of the World's Greatest Diarists*, Edinburgh: Canongate

Topp, Sylvia (2020) *Eileen: The Making of George Orwell*, London: Unbound

Woodcock, George (1984 [1966]) *The Crystal Spirit: A Study of George Orwell*, London: Fourth Estate

Waddell, Nathan (2020) Oceania's dirt: Filth, nausea and disgust in Airstrip One, Waddell, Nathan (ed.) *The Cambridge Companion to* Nineteen Eighty-Four, Cambridge: Cambridge University Press pp 168-180

- The author writes four diaries – a personal one, a political one (drawing on newspaper and website reports), one in which he records his dreams, and a cheap, slim-line, day-to-day diary in which he notes meetings to attend, dates of library book renewals, Nottm Forest/Notts County/Gainsborough Trinity/England football and Notts CCC and England cricket results, films watched – basic things like that – though none of them are for publication. This essay is based on 'Seeing what is in front of one's nose' Orwell's Domestic Diaries, orwellsociety.com 7 April 2020, available online at https://orwellsociety.com/seeing-what-is-in-front-of-ones-nose/

Chapter Eleven

The Play's the Thing

George Orwell is best known as the author of the novels *Animal Farm* (1945) and *Nineteen Eighty-Four* (1949); as an essayist, journalist, poet, letter and diary writer and broadcaster– but rarely as someone with a deep connection to drama. In fact, he acts in a school theatre production, writes a play while at school, another one while serving as an Imperial Policeman in Burma and a third, now totally forgotten, for children at a school where he is teaching. Drama features prominently in his novel, *A Clergyman's Daughter* – and he works for a number of months as a theatre and film critic during the Second World War. In addition, he composes some highly original 'dramatic dialogues' when at the BBC in the early 1940s, adapts *Animal Farm* as a drama for radio in 1947, writes dramatic versions of *Little Red Riding Hood* and the *Voyage of the Beagle* – while William Shakespeare and Oscar Wilde are constantly referenced in his essays. Orwell really is a man of the theatre.

BLAIR THE ACTOR
Orwell gives a highly damning account of his time spent at St Cyprian's prep school, in Eastbourne (from 1911-1917), in his essay 'Such, such were the joys' (1970 4 [1952]: 379-422). The extent to which the essay should be considered as either 'fact' or 'fiction' is a subject of some considerable debate (see Keeble 2018). But it contains no mention of the fact that in 1916, Eric Blair (as he then was) performs in a 'dramatic entertainment' 'Mr Jingle's wooing' based on a Charles Dickens excerpt. The *St Cyprian's Chronicle*, of Christmas 1916, records Blair, playing Mr Wardle, as 'exceedingly good in a difficult part'. His friend, Cyril Connolly – later, as editor of *Horizon*, to publish some of Orwell's most celebrated essays – playing Miss Wardle 'showed himself to be an artist of exceptional merit' (Daly 1981).

THE FIRST ATTEMPTS AT WRITING PLAY

While still a youth, Orwell composes a three-act play, 'The man and the maid'. Peter Davison dates it while he is still at St Cyprian's or shortly after he leaves at Christmas 1916 (*CWGO* X: 31-44). Robert Colls summarises the plot: it's 'about a bunch of useless intellectuals who live on roots and herbs and think that righteousness lies in the acquisition of a black skin. Their leader, the youthful Lucius, son of Mireldo, feels the "desire for adventure and romance". He also wishes "to be quit of this island"' (Colls 2013: 14).

In her remarkable memoir of her times spent with Orwell while he is on holiday, first from St. Cyprian's and then from Eton, which he leaves in December 1921, Jacintha Buddicom (2006 [1974]) tells of their voracious reading together. Here, Orwell's love of the theatre and, in particular, Shakespeare's plays and sonnets is born.[1]

So it is perhaps not surprising that while serving as an Imperial Policeman in Burma, from 1922-1927, Orwell (then Eric Blair) attempts to write a play (*CWGO* X: 104-110). Francis and Lucy Stone are desperate: their four-year-old child needs an operation – but it is costly and they have only debts. Then Stone is offered a job composing advertisements (just like Gordon Comstock in his later novel, *Keep the Aspidistra Flying*, of 1936). But when he ends up promoting a medicine which he knows to be a swindle he refuses. Lucy is appalled by his action – saying she may as well work as a prostitute to earn the money. The second scene is set in a prison with the cast made up of Stone, The Christian, The Poet, The Poet's Wife and The Jailer, a particularly violent, obnoxious character. Prisoners are being executed in the next cell; off stage, the sounds of revolution can be heard. Peter Davison comments (1996: 23): 'The plotting and characterisation are stilted and possibly influenced by Expressionist drama. It is not difficult to see why Orwell abandoned writing the play but he maintained his interest in writing drama.'

Indeed, while teaching at The Hawthorns High School for boys in Hayes, Middlesex (earning money to subsidise his writing activities), Orwell writes a play, *King Charles II* (*CWGO* X: 277-294) which is performed at Christmas 1932 in St Mary's Church nearby – and at Hayes on 4 April 1992 by Compass Arts Theatre.[2] As Peter Davison records, the play survives because one of the participants, Geoffrey W. Stevens, kept his copy. The typescript was purchased by Bill Blair (no relation) of Connecticut in 1988 (ibid: 277).

It is perhaps Orwell's attempt to re-create the excitement, violence and tensions of Shakespeare's history plays. The first act, on the night of the Battle of Worcester, 23 August 1651, is set in an inn and features the landlord, Mr Giles, the oldest inhabitant of the village, his granddaughter Lucy (the name being carried over, then, from his Burma play) and George Burton, a labourer (intriguingly P. S. Burton is one of the pseudonyms he toys with before settling on George Orwell for the publication of his first book, *Down and Out in Paris and London*, in 1933).

Suddenly King Charles appears, pronouncing: 'Alone, weaponless and on foot/ My horse is dead. My sword is snapped in two./My men are scattered through the countryside./I am a penniless and landless king./True subjects must you be who would serve such.' As Captain Chambers, of the 17th Roundheads Regiment, bangs on the inn's door demanding to arrest the traitor king, the plot then takes a typical Shakespearean twist – involving disguise and subterfuge – with Charles putting on the clothes of Will Hodge, the 'prentice boy', and escaping leaving Will, dressed in Charles's apparel, to be taken away.

Act 2 moves to Bristol where Will is being guarded over by two soldiers. As he manages, somewhat incredibly, to escape, news comes in that the king has successfully fled to France. So the play ends with a celebratory song: 'Good people all, this is a joyous time/When our good king, long in most dangerous plight,/Is safe at sea and bound for friendly France./We'll honour it with song, and silver too.' But, as Davison comments (ibid: 278): 'In fact, Charles was hunted for nearly six weeks, hiding, according to a legend Orwell ignores, in an oak tree near Worcester while Cromwell's troops searched for him in nearby fields.'

DRAMA AND *A CLERGYMAN'S DAUGHTER*

Intriguingly, this play appears as *Charles 1* which Dorothy Hare produces in Orwell's novel, *A Clergyman's Daughter* (1976 [1935]). Dorothy is the daughter of the overbearing vicar of St. Athelstan's Church, Knype Hill, Suffolk, and constantly overwhelmed by her many responsibilities. The production and stage management are in the hands of Victor Stone (another name carried over from the Burma play), the church school headmaster. Orwell continues (ibid: 289): 'It was horribly hot in the conservatory and there was a powerful smell of glue and the sour sweat of children. Dorothy was kneeling on the floor, with her mouth full of pins and a pair of shears in her hand, rapidly slicing sheets of brown paper into long narrow strips.' As the rehearsal descends into chaos, Orwell cleverly and wittily shifts the narrative into dramatic dialogue:

> A GIRL: Please Miss, Mother said I was to tell you, Miss –
>
> DOROTHY: Keep still, Percy! For goodness' *sake* keep still!
>
> CROMWELL: 'Alt! I 'old a pistol in my 'and!
>
> A SMALL GIRL ON THE BENCH: Mister! I've dropped my sweetie! [*Snivelling*] I've dropped by swee-e-etie!

And so on. The chaos continues: 'Victor, gesticulating with his sword and shouting to overcome the din of galloping horses, was personating in turn Oliver Cromwell, Charles 1, Roundheads, Cavaliers, peasants, and court ladies. The children were now growing restive and beginning to yawn, whine and exchange furtive kicks and punches' (ibid: 290).

In the course of the novel, Dorothy is sexually abused by the seedy Mr Warburton, has a breakdown, ends up a down-and-out in Trafalgar Square, goes hop picking in Kent, teaches for a while in a dreadful private school – only to be finally rescued by Warburton and brought back to the church. Significantly, her return to the humdrum drudgery of everyday is symbolised in her resuming her work on the costumes for the next play: 'The glue had liquefied. Dorothy took two fresh sheets of brown paper, sliced them into narrow strips and – rather awkwardly, because of the difficulty of keeping the breastplate convex – pasted the strips horizontally across it, back and front. By degrees it stiffened under her hands. When she had reinforced it all over she set it on end to look at it. It wasn't half bad!' (ibid: 425).

All this is actually based on Orwell's own experiences. Davison even picks up a term Orwell uses in a review of two works by William Hale White to describe the novel as 'pseudo-autobiography' (1996: 63). As Orwell tells his friend Eleanor Jaques in a letter on 18 November 1932, he is making armour for the school play and 'I have been suffering untold agonies with glue and brown paper etc. Also painting a cigarette box for the Church Bazaar, which I very rashly undertook to gild' (Orwell and Angus 1970 1: 130-131). To his agent, Leonard Moore, he writes, on 23 December 1932: 'The miserable school play over which I had wasted so much time went off not badly' (ibid: 134). Davison comments (1996: 31): 'Despite himself, Orwell may have enjoyed writing and producing his little play.'

In Chapter 3 of the novel, Dorothy spends a night with the down-and-outs in Trafalgar Square (Orwell clearly milking his experiences as a tramp) and the whole episode appears in the form of a pastiche of the 'Nighttown' sequence of James Joyce's *Ulysses* (see Myers 1991: 60). To give a flavour, here is the opening (Orwell (1976 [1935]: 343):

> CHARLIE [*singing*]: 'Ail Mary, 'ail Mary, 'a-il Ma-ary – *[Big Ben strikes ten.]*
>
> SNOUTER [*mimicking the noise*]: Ding dong, ding dong! Shut you – noise, can't you? Seven more hours of it on this – square before we get the chance of a setdown and a bit of sleep! Cripes!
>
> MR TALBOYS [*to himself*]: *Non sum quails eram boni sub regno Edwardi*! In the days of my innocence, before the Devil carried me up into a high place and dropped me into the Sunday newspapers – that is to say when I was Rector of Little Fawley-cum-Dewsbury …
>
> DEAFIE [*singing*]: With my willy will, *with* my willy willy –

Critics have been generally very critical. Jeffrey Meyers (2000: 119), for instance, describes the chapter as a 'feeble imitation' of Joyce. Orwell, himself, came to dislike the novel as a whole damning it as 'bollix' and asking for it never to be reprinted in his lifetime (Taylor 2003: 139). Yet the 'dramatic scenario' is interesting on many counts. It reflects Orwell's intent to be experimental in his novel writing and his life-long admiration for Joyce but, above all, it underlines his fascination with dialogue and dramatic text. As Tim Crook comments on Chapter 3: 'This has all the hallmarks of a post-World War Two Theatre Workshop drama script developed through social immersion and observation, and the transcription of improvisation by actors. Of course, Orwell's ear and appreciation for the language of this sub-culture as well as the realism of its social reality had been honed by direct experience' (Crook 2015: 196). Biographer Bernard Crick also has some complimentary words, saying that Dorothy's life as a schoolmistress 'is another compelling creation of a closed world, the remorseless detail of which was drawn, like the tramping scenes, directly from his own experience' (Crick 1980: 259).

ORWELL THE FORGOTTEN THEATRE CRITIC

Between May 1940 and August 1941 Orwell does a stint as film and theatre reviewer for *Time and Tide* (the vaguely right-of-centre journal edited by Margaret, Lady Rhondda). But it has drawn little attention. It receives no mention in Robert Colls's *George Orwell: English Rebel* (2013). John Sutherland (2016: 195) dismisses his output as 'low-grade pap on literature and film' while Gordon Bowker comments (2003: 268-269): 'Reviewing plays and films he felt was somehow demeaning…' Jeffrey Meyers devotes three pages to a useful, critical overview of his film reviewing but describes it as 'a little-known aspect of his career'. There is no mention of his theatre reviewing (2000: 201-2013). Undoubtedly the best appreciation of Orwell's film reviews was penned by my late friend and University of Lincoln colleague John Tulloch (2012: 79-101). Tulloch concludes even-handedly:

> He shared in many of the standard prejudices of the Thirties intellectual against film – it was a mass art, machine-made by capitalism, producing low-grade rubbish for working class consumption. … Nevertheless, the reviews contain some valuable insights and embody a developing vision of the possibilities of film, both in its degraded form as a mass-produced mechanism for propaganda and escapism and an agency through which contrary, humane perceptions can be articulated. Orwell made heroic efforts to overcome his inbuilt class prejudices, and cultivated a belief in the innate human values of ordinary people and their capacity to remake society (ibid: 98).

But then what of the 38 theatre reviews? While a lot of the writing is, indeed, pedestrian, it still offers unique insights into Orwell's preoccupations and theatrical interests.

Given that his own play was titled *King Charles II* it is quite a coincidence that the first performance he reviews, on 18 May 1940, is of Bernard Shaw's *In Good King Charles' Golden Days* (*CWGO* XII: 162-163). Particularly interesting, given

Orwell's life-long fascination with dress (see Keeble 2020a and Chapter 1.), is his criticism of the costumes: 'There is one serious fault in the present production of the play and that is the hideousness of the costumes. In a seventeenth-century play this is quite inexcusable. The women's clothes are just bearable but the men's seem to have been designed by someone who is colour-blind' (ibid: 163). A week later he reviews two productions in which his determination is to confront prudery and puritanism – begun in his very first article, 'La censure en Angleterre', in Henri Barbusse's *Monde*, in 1928, where he suggests the censorship of Joyce's *Ulysses* and Radclyffe Hall's *The Well of Loneliness*, is a result of 'that strange English puritanism which has no objection to dirt but which fears sexuality and detests beauty' (see Keeble 2020b: 17). *Les Parents Terribles*, by Jean Cocteau, involves a convoluted plot with incest at its core (which Orwell outlines in too much tedious detail so robbing any prospective audience of any surprise) while in his review of *Palladium*, at the Garrison Theatre, he praises Jack Warner's 'gloriously vulgar bandinage' with his 'little gel' Joan Winters and the Three Aberdonians 'who enliven a good acrobatic display with mild obscenities' (*CWGO* XII: 166).

His reviews of Shakespeare's *The Tempest*, at the Old Vic, and *Portrait of Helen*, by the now long-forgotten Audrey Lucas,[3] are brief and witty. Shakespeare's tragedies are the most successful with audiences, he argues, because they are 'chock-full of murders'; but the comedies and histories are 'hopeless, because nine-tenths of the people watching don't know the text and can be counted on to miss the point of any joke that is not followed up by a kick on the buttocks' (ibid: 180). Ariel, he says, 'was horribly whimsical and indulged in exaggeratedly homosexual mannerisms, a sort of Peter Pansy' (ibid). Of *Helen*, he says that 'Under a thin veneer of sophistication it has the mental atmosphere of a fourpenny novelette' (ibid: 181). In Noel Coward's *I'll Leave it to You*, which he reviews on 15 June 1940, it's the humour that particularly appeals to him: 'It may be hard to believe that such nonsense can be charming, but it is so, because of the easy dialogue which sometimes rises to the level of real funniness' (ibid: 185).

Chu Chin Chow, by Oscar Asche, which he reviews on 13 July 1940, is 'tripe' but he still tries to account for its original success during the First World War, highlighting, as in his film reviews, the important role of fantasy in the public imagination. 'The charm lay in the fantastic unreality of the whole thing, and the droves of women, practically naked and painted to an agreeable walnut-juice tint. It was a never-never land, the "gorgeous East" where, as is well-known, everyone has fifty wives and spends time lying on a divan, eating pomegranates. In this vulgar spectacle [Orwell mixing here both irony and ambivalence] a doomed generation of boys got a sort of dreamlike glimpse of all the ease and pleasure that they would never have' (ibid: 216).

His review of Vernon Sylvaine's farce, *Women Aren't Angels*, on 27 July 1940, revels in the bawdy humour. The 'adultery-and-underwear motif is pushed to the extreme limit of decency, and sometimes a little beyond it, to the delight of the audience' while Robertson Hare at one point wears a kilt 'incidentally solving the famous problem of "whether they wear anything underneath"' (ibid: 221). And his review of Shaw's *The Devil's Disciple*, on 3 August 1940, ends by highlighting the humour. Mr Milton Rosmer, as General Burgoyne, has all the best lines: 'His remark, "The British soldier can stand up to anything except the British War Office" was much appreciated by an audience well sprinkled with uniforms' (ibid: 224).

Orwell's limitations as a theatre critic appear particularly in his review of Clifford Odet's *Till the Day I Die*, on 17 August 1940. It would have been helpful for his English readership to outline briefly Odet's career as a radical, American, left-wing actor and playwright – by 1940 the author already of nine plays including the acclaimed *Waiting for Leftie* and *Awake and Sing!*, of 1935. But Orwell provides no context and simply dives in – outlining the plot. While discussing Orwell's 1944 essay, 'Benefit of clergy' on Salvador Dali's scurrilous autobiography, Gordon Bowker highlights his sometimes fascination with the gruesome: 'Orwell himself had confessed on numerous occasions to childhood cruelties – wasps cut in half, toads inflated with bicycle pumps – and some adult ones – beating his Burmese servants – and was capable of making art out of sadistic cruelty as he would demonstrate in *Nineteen Eighty-Four*' (2003: 314-315). So it is interesting that in the review of Odet's play, he writes (*CWGO* XII: 236): 'There is only one piece of physical brutality in the whole play but it happens early on and the memory of it haunts all the other scenes. This is when the Brownshirt captain makes the Jew lay his fingers on the table and then suddenly smashes them to pulp with a rifle butt. A little too horrible, perhaps, but not more horrible than other things that are enacted on the stage (the gouging-out of Gloucester's eyes in *King Lear*, for instance) and Heaven knows how many such things have happened in real life in the last seven years' (Orwell perhaps thinking here of both the Spanish Civil War and the current conflict).

Occasionally, Orwell provides striking insights into the somewhat stoical public reactions to the dangers of warfare in his reviews. For instance, at the end of his comments on J. B. Priestley's *Cornelius*, on 7 September 1940, he records: 'About half way through the performance ... the air-raid sirens sounded. Mr Stephen Murray, acting the part of Cornelius, stepped forward and said that the lights would be turned on to allow any of the audience who wishes to go out. No more than three or four people did so, and the play proceeded normally. After only a week of bombing an air raid has ceased to be a serious interruption' (ibid: 252).

And in his review of *Applesauce*, on the same day, the germ of his 1941 *Horizon* essay on Donald McGill's sexy seaside postcards appears with its celebration of 'vulgarity'. He enjoys Doris Hare's 'skit on a strip-tease act', the 'startling obscenities' in the show and, in particular, Max Miller 'one of a long line of English comedians who have specialized in the Sancho Panza side of life, in real *lowness*' (ibid: 253, italics in the original). Max Miller is, indeed, to be celebrated in 'The art of Donald

McGill' (Orwell 1980 [1941a]: 576) where he also writes: 'If you look into your own mind, which are you, Don Quixote or Sancho Panza? Almost certainly you are both. There is one part of you that wishes to be a hero or a saint, but another part of you is a little fat man [Orwell here assuming his reader is male] who sees very clearly the advantages of staying alive with a whole skin. He is your unofficial self, the voice of the belly protesting against the soul' (ibid: 577).

He goes on in his review to suggest that the 'utter baseness' of the jokes of Miller and Little Tich are distinctly English. 'They remind one how closely-knit the civilization of England is, and how much it resembles a family, in spite of its out-of-date class distinctions. The startling obscenities which appear in *Applesauce* are only possible because they are expressed in *double entendres* which imply a common background in the audience' (*CWGO* XII: 253). Orwell is to develop this idea of England being a 'family' in his celebrated essay *The Lion and the Unicorn*, of 1941, where he writes: 'England is not the jewelled isle of Shakespeare's much-quoted passage, nor is it the inferno depicted by Dr Goebbels. More than either it resembles a family, a rather stuffy Victorian family, with not many black sheep in it but with all its cupboards bursting with skeletons. It has rich relations who have to be kow-towed to and poor relations who are horribly sat upon, and there is a deep conspiracy of silence about the source of the family income' (Orwell 1980 [1941b]: 536). Is Orwell pondering here the fact that his Scottish ancestors did, indeed, prosper on the back of slavery in Jamaica (Moore 2020)?

A strikingly original – perhaps tongue-in-cheek – interpretation of Falstaff appears in his review of Shakespeare's *The Merry Wives of Windsor*, on 4 January 1941. Falstaff, he says, is fat, dishonest and cowardly. 'But he is nevertheless highly intelligent man, one of the very few among Shakespeare's characters who can be described as "intellectual". It would be wonderful if some actor would some day recognize this and act Falstaff with as much care as is usually given to Hamlet' (*CWGO* XII: 361).

Much of the rest of his theatre reviewing is dreary – and clearly Orwell was not getting much fun out of it. In his diary of 17 June 1940, he confides: 'Nowadays when I write a review, I sit down at the typewriter and type it straight out. Till recently, indeed till six months ago, I never did this and would have said that I could not do it. Virtually all that I wrote was written at least twice and my books as a whole three times – individual passages as many as five or ten times. It is not really that I have gained in facility, merely that I have ceased to care, so long as the work will pass inspection and bring in a little money. It is a deterioration directly due to the war' (*CWGO* XII: 187). But he comes to life in his review of Shakespeare's *King John*, on 19 July 1941, where he draws out some contemporary connections: 'The Papal legate, inciting France to attack England, is curiously reminiscent of the League of Nations. … There is a scene which would have delighted Marx in which everyone decides to obey or disobey the Pope according to his own economic interest. Even the Quisling motif is represented by the three English aristocrats who turn traitor when the French invade England, hurriedly changing sides again at the last moment' (ibid: 532).

DRAMATIC TIMES AT THE BBC

While working as a talks assistant and later talks producer in the Indian section of the BBC's Eastern Service from August 1941 until November 1943, Orwell composes a number of original dramatic dialogues. They include adaptations of 'Crainquebille' by Anatole France (on 11 August 1943), 'The fox', by Ignazio Silone (on 9 September 1943), 'A slip under the microscope', by H. G. Wells (on 6 October 1943) and 'The emperor's new clothes', by Hans Andersen (on 18 November) (West 1985a: 130-167). Their international scope is particularly striking. Biographer Michael Shelden singles out 'The fox' for special praise, describing it as 'excellent' (Shelden 1991: 374). He continues: 'There is a hint in it of his future work in *Animal Farm*. The adaption begins in a pig-sty, and one newborn pig is christened Benito Mussolini.'

On the Wells adaptation, Tim Crook comments: 'It has an orthodox exposition of traditional narrator and dialogue through characterisation. The narrative voice is deployed as a lens for the listener and indirect focus for a character's thoughts and feelings. … Orwell was a radio dramatist who preferred to write with clarity rather than play with his listener's cognitive perception' (Crook 2015: 205).

The adaptations are produced along with his other work which includes providing political commentaries: 56 for India, 30 for occupied Malaya and 19 for occupied Indonesia (Davison 1996: 116; West 1985b). Indeed, drawing on his experiences teaching in the early 1930s, he presents a wide range of topics in an always accessible language and format. There was an element of 'cultural imperialism' in the series since there was no attempt to highlight any aspect of Asian culture for the Indian audience. But elsewhere in his talks programmes Asians – such as K. Shelvankar, Mulk Raj Anand, Cedric Dover and R. R. Desai – were well represented. Crook comments: 'Orwell became an expert in making radio for news, editorial propagandizing, and education through entertaining sound dramatization and cultural discussion. It was the equivalent of devising a multimedia syllabus for an Open University of the Air' (Crook 2015: 194).

Of the six commentaries he gives on writers, three of them are dramatists. The talk on Bernard Shaw, given on 22 January 1943, focuses on *Arms and the Man*, first performed in 1894. The play clearly ties in with Orwell's long-lasting preoccupations with a host of issues; for instance, those relating to war, peace and violence in general, comedy and satire, politics and the theatre. He begins by providing a critical overview: 'It is probably the wittiest play he ever wrote, the most faultless technically and, in spite of being a very light comedy, the most telling' (West 1985a:118).

Then, after describing the plot in detail, he explores its major themes and 'message'. For Orwell, seeming to draw on his experiences fighting alongside a Republican militia during the Spanish Civil War in 1937: 'Shaw is saying, in effect, that war, though sometimes necessary, is not glorious, not romantic. Killing and being killed isn't the heroic, picturesque business that the propagandists make it out to be…' (ibid: 119). Orwell next personalises the talk telling of the two, contrasting occasions when he has seen the play performed. The first was in 1918 and the theatre was full of soldiers just back from the front in France. At one point they all 'burst into a laugh which almost lifted the roof off' when Shaw mocks heroism during a cavalry charge. The second time was with a highbrow audience in 1935. This time there was no laughter at that point in the play. 'War was far away and very few people in the audience knew what it was like to have to face bullets' (ibid).

According to Orwell, Shaw's plays today lack their original freshness 'because in them he is attacking illusions which no one any longer believes in'. This comment sends Orwell off into a critical overview of Shaw's other plays. *Mrs Warren's Profession* deals with prostitution suggesting its causes are largely economic. 'This idea was a novelty in the eighteen-nineties, but now, when everyone has read Marx, it seems a commonplace, hardly worth uttering.' *Widowers' Houses* is an attack on slum landlordism. 'Slums still exist and people still make a profit out of them, but at least no one thinks this normal and proper any longer.' The satire in *John Bull's Other Island* depends largely on Ireland being under English rule 'a state of affairs which has long ceased to exist'. And even *Major Barbara* and *Androcles and the Lion* depend on orthodox religious belief 'being very much more general than it is today' (ibid: 119-120).

Orwell next, rather brilliantly, examines Shaw's brand of satire in its political, economic and historical contexts. 'For the background, the springboard as it were, of his witticisms, Shaw needed the solidity, the power and the self-righteousness of the late-Victorian society in which he first lived and worked' (ibid: 120). In other words, the world of late Victorian England was 'easy meat for a satirical writer'. That world has now disappeared. 'No one, nowadays, could make his reputation as a "shocker". What is there any longer to be shocked at? … The self-satisfied, prudish, money-ruled world that Shaw made fun of has been washed away by the spread of scepticism and enlightenment; and for that scepticism and enlightenment Shaw himself, as much as any one writer of our time, is responsible' (ibid: 121).

Orwell returns at the end to *Arms and the Man*, praising it as 'a miracle of stage technique' in which Shaw's genius 'reached its high water mark'. 'There are not even any verbal fireworks; brilliant as the dialogue is, every word of it helps the action along.' He rates it as highly as *The Devil's Disciple*, and just beneath these two in quality he places *Captain Brassbound's Conversion, Ceasar and Cleopatra, Androcles and the Lion* and *The Man of Destiny* 'all of them brilliantly witty comedies'.

Orwell's love of Shakespeare, born in his youth, shines through his talk on *Macbeth*, given on 17 October 1945. As with the Shaw talk, he begins with a general comment, spends some time carefully outlining the plot and finally explores the play's central themes.

For Orwell, *Macbeth* is his most perfectly constructed play. Its theme is ambition. His focus is entirely on Macbeth the man so the crucial role of Lady Macbeth – and the terrible darkness of her personality – is missed. He compares it to other plays, perhaps over-simplifying in the process – in *Antony and Cleopatra* the theme is the power which a worthless woman can establish over a brave and gifted man; in *Hamlet* it's the divorce between intelligence and practical ability; in *King Lear*, it's the difficulty of distinguishing between generosity and weakness. But the power of *Macbeth* comes because it is 'the nearest of all to normal experience'. 'If you like, *Macbeth* is the story of Hitler or Napoleon. But it is also the story of any bank clerk who forges a cheque, any official who takes a bribe, any human being in fact who grabs at some mean advantage which will make him feel a little bigger and get a little ahead of his fellows' (ibid: 160).

In conclusion, Orwell argues that *Macbeth* is the only Shakespeare play in which the hero and villain is the same character. 'Nearly always in Shakespeare you have the spectacle of a good man, like Othello or King Lear, suffering misfortune; or of a bad man, like Edgar or Iago, doing evil out of sheer malice. In *Macbeth* crime and misfortune are one; a man whom one cannot feel to be wholly evil is doing evil things. It is very difficult not to be moved by this spectacle' (ibid: 161).

Orwell's commentary on *Lady Windermere's Fan* reflects his life-long interest in Wilde. As Kristian Williams comments, Orwell loaned *Dorian Gray* to his friend, Cyril Connolly, at Eton, read at least two biographies, reviewed the *Soul of Man* for the *Observer*, alluded to Wilde in *A Clergyman's Daughter* and *Coming Up For Air* while amongst his readings during his last year were two accounts of Wilde's trials and his prison letter 'De Profundis' (Williams 2017: 42). Williams further suggests that as a young man, disgusted by his experience of imperialism in Burma, Orwell adopted the Wildean, anarchist theory 'that all government is evil, that the punishment always does more harm than the crime and that people can be trusted to behave decently if only you will let them alone' (ibid).

Moreover, according to Philip Bounds, Orwell acknowledges his debt to Wilde by deliberately overturning his ideas in his novel *Keep the Aspidistra Flying*. 'Where Wilde speaks of altruism as a universal duty under capitalism, Orwell evokes a flyblown aesthete whose sympathy lies only with his own class. Where Wilde regards aesthetic relativism as a precondition of personal liberation, Orwell sees it as a nightmarish source of uncertainty. And where Wilde insists that the socialist society of the future must be libertarian or nothing, Orwell sympathises with a character for whom the planned economy is a synonym for tyranny' (Bounds 2016 [2009]: 190). In addition, Bounds suggests there are Wildean overtones to the section in

Nineteen Eighty-Four in which Winston Smith gazes at the old paperweight which he buys from Mr Charrington's junk shop. Simply by illustrating the aesthete's maxim that a work of art should always create a world of its own, the paperweight defies 'the crushing sameness of a totalitarian culture' (ibid: 91).

Orwell begins his talk on *Lady Windermere's Fan* by highlighting Wilde's contradictions. While arguing that every work of art is completely useless, he contradicts this 'by making nearly everything that he writes turn upon some point of morals' (West 1985a: 168). Moreover, he is never certain whether he is attacking current morality or defending it.

Just as Orwell placed Shaw's comedy, critically, in its broader political, economic, cultural and social context, he now does the same with Wilde's play suggesting that it has lost some of its impact because of changing social mores: when it was written 'it was an accepted fact that a divorced woman must become almost an outcast; she was practically debarred from decent society for the rest of her life'. Now, a divorced woman is no longer ruined for life (ibid: 169). Having outlined the plot, Orwell argues that it draws on a number of popular themes of the Victorian stage – the situation in which someone is the child of somebody else, the parent being aware of it, the child not, the mother sacrificing herself for her child and the unjustly suspected person suffering in silence rather than reveal some deadly secret were all favourites.

With his life-long interest in humour (Keeble 2015), Orwell next focuses on Wilde's witticisms. 'These are stuck all over his writings as arbitrarily as the decorations on top of a cake. Nearly always they the form of debunking of something that his contemporaries believed in, such as religion, patriotism, honour, morality, family loyalty, public spirit and so on and so forth' (West 1985a: 170). His dialogue remains charming, even when it has ceased to seem wicked or iconoclastic. But Orwell concludes suggesting Wilde won an easy fame 'by pushing over an idol that was toppling already. In its fall the idol killed him, for Wilde never recovered from the shock of his trial and imprisonment, and died soon after he was released' (ibid: 171).

Orwell's inventiveness while at the BBC does not stop with the dramatic dialogues. On one occasion he engages in an imaginary interview with Jonathan Swift (one of my favourites in the whole Orwellian *oeuvre*). Swift, like Shakespeare, was a favourite of Orwell since his prep school days. As Meyers writes (2000: 14): 'He stole and devoured *Gulliver's Travels*, intended as a present, just before his eighth birthday. Taking a hint from Swift's rational horses, Orwell idealized the horse in *Animal Farm* and transformed Swift's Floating Island of Laputa into the Floating Fortress in *Nineteen Eighty-Four*.' In 1940, Orwell listed amongst the authors he most cared about Shakespeare, Swift, Fielding, Dickens, Zola, Flaubert, Joyce, T. S. Eliot and D. H. Lawrence – all of them interestingly male (ibid: 100). While at the BBC, he launches a talks series called 'Books that have changed the world' and begins it, significantly, with Narayana Menon on *Gulliver's Travels* (West 1985:

39). And in 1946, in his long essay, 'Politics vs. literature' for *Polemic*, he examines at length *Gulliver's Travels*. It's influence on the horrifying, dystopian world of *Nineteen Eighty-Four* is clear when he writes (Orwell 1976 [1946]: 774): 'Swift's greatest contribution to political thought, in the narrower sense of the words, is his attacks, especially in Part III, on what would now be called totalitarianism. He has an extraordinarily clear prevision of the spy-haunted "police State" with its endless heresy hunts and treason trials, all really designed to neutralize popular discontent by changing it into war hysteria.'

And on a personal note, he says that while he is against Swift 'in a political and moral sense': 'Yet curiously enough he is one of the writers I admire with least reserve and *Gulliver's Travels*, in particular, is a book which it seems impossible for me to grow tired of. … If I had to make a list of six books which were to be preserved when all others were destroyed I would certainly put *Gulliver's Travels* among them' (ibid: 779).

It is not then surprising that Orwell's delight in Swift should shine through his wonderfully inventive and witty BBC 'interview'. Take this section, for instance, where Orwell, a constant critic of the mass media throughout his life (Keeble 2020b) cleverly inserts yet another jibe at the newspapers of his day: ORWELL: Tell me candidly, do we stink as we used to? SWIFT: Certainly the smells are different. There was a new one I remarked as I came through the streets – (*sniffs*) – ORWELL: It's called petrol. But don't you find that the mass of the people are more intelligent than they were, or at least better educated? How about the newspapers and the radio? Surely they have opened people's minds a little? There are very few people in England now who can't read. SWIFT: That is why they are so easily deceived… (West op cit: 115). And Orwell is able to conclude with this typical celebration of human decency: 'His vision of human society is so penetrating, and yet in the last analysis it's false. He couldn't see what the simplest person sees, that life is worth living and human being, even if they are dirty and ridiculous, are mostly decent' (ibid: 116). Desmond Avery comments (2017: 80): 'There is a note of sadness in this public parting with his oldest and favourite teacher, as if he felt he was on his own now.'

In the end, Orwell grows tired of the heavy censorship regime at the BBC (which he describes as 'something half way between a girls' school and a lunatic asylum') and resigns on 23 November 1943 to take up the post of literary editor at *Tribune*. He is typically self-deprecatory over his BBC experience damning it as 'two wasted years'. But according to Crook: 'Far from being a bureaucratic grind of exhaustion and disillusionment, Orwell's experiences at the BBC were predominantly a process of positive creativity and cultural enlightenment both for himself and his audience. The contrasting roles of scripting both factual and fictional programming for the radio served a writer who had the mind of a robust and independent public intellectual and the feelings of the common person' (op cit: 206).

DRAMA AT THE BBC: THE NEXT ACT

Orwell's work for the BBC is not to end in November 1943. For through his friendship with Rayner Heppenstall, a producer at the corporation, he goes on to write two fine dramatic adaptations – of Darwin's *Voyage of the Beagle*, for the Home Service on 29 March 1946 (*CWGO* XIII: 179-201). The second, too often neglected, is of *Little Red Riding Hood* (ibid: 345-354). Just like the earlier adaptation of Andersen's 'The emperor's new clothes' for the BBC's Eastern Service, this reflects Orwell's deep interest in the fairy story genre – which finds its most famous flowering in *Animal Farm – A Fairy Story*, in 1945. And Orwell is to adapt his famous satire on the Russian revolution for the BBC in 1947. Crick describes it as 'very stilted' (1980: 493) while Orwell told his friend, Mamaine Paget: 'I had the feeling that they had spoilt it but one nearly always does with anything one writes for the air' (Lynskey 2019: 157).

LEAR, TOLSTOY, SHAKESPEARE AND ORWELL

Orwell's fascination with the theatre and Shakespeare in particular culminates in his remarkable essay, 'Lear, Tolstoy and the fool', published in *Polemic*, in March 1947. It has been strangely missed, or its significance downplayed, by the biographers. There is no mention of the essay at all in either Shelden (1991) or Meyers (2000) while D. J. Taylor (2003) and Bowker (2003) only comment on it *en passant*. Crick (op cit: 438, 520, 522) first focuses on Orwell's critique of anarchism and pacifism; in the third reference he points out Orwell's 'tempered pessimism'; only in the second reference is there any mention of Shakespeare as he describes it as 'a profound comparison of the didacticism of Tolstoy with the tolerant humanism of Shakespeare'.

Orwell bases his critique of Tolstoy on an obscure pamphlet in which he has damned *King Lear* as 'stupid, verbose, unnatural, unintelligible, bombastic, vulgar, tedious' etc. (1980 [1947]: 793). Tolstoy fails to consider Shakespeare as a poet. 'Those who care most for Shakespeare value him in the first place for his use of language, the "verbal music" which even Bernard Shaw, another hostile critic, admits to be "irresistible"' (ibid: 796). Tolstoy sees no justification for the presence of the Fool. But for Orwell it's crucial. 'He acts not only as a sort of chorus, making the central situation clearer by commenting on it more intelligently than the other characters, but as a foil to Lear's frenzies. His jokes, riddles and scraps of rhyme, and his endless digs at Lear's high-minded folly … are like a trickle of sanity running through the play … ' (ibid: 797).

But Tolstoy's essential 'anti-human' stance draws Orwell's special venom. Indeed, what Tolstoy probably most dislikes about Shakespeare 'is a sort of exuberance, a tendency to take – not so much a pleasure as simply an interest in the actual process of life' (ibid). In other words, it's a 'quarrel between the religious and humanist attitudes towards life'.

The plot of *King Lear*, Orwell argues, is essentially about renunciation. And this clearly resonates with Tolstoy's own history. 'In his old age he renounced his estate, his title and his copyrights and made an attempt – a sincere attempt though it was not successful – to escape from his privileged position and live the life of a peasant. … Ultimately, therefore, Tolstoy renounced the world under the expectation that this would make him happier. But there is one thing certain about his later years, it is that he was *not* happy' (ibid: 799, italics in the original). Indeed, one of the morals of the play is that 'to make yourself powerless is to invite an attack'.

In contrast, all of Shakespeare's later tragedies 'start out with the humanist assumption that life, although full of sorrow, is worth living and that Man is a noble animal – a belief which Tolstoy in his old age did not share'. Against Tolstoy's 'other-worldliness', Orwell celebrates Shakespeare's worldly vitality, his love of life which he conveys, above all, in the 'music of language'.

Orwell next moves on to Tolstoy's pacifism – criticising it, along with anarchism, for being intolerant. 'For if you have embraced a creed which appears to be free from the ordinary dirtiness of politics – a creed from which you yourself cannot expect to draw any material advantage – surely that proves you are in the right? And the more you are in the right, the more natural that everyone should be bullied into thinking likewise' (ibid: 802).

In many respects, Orwell is presenting a very slanted view of Tolstoy. For instance, Peter Marshall offers a totally different picture of him in his monumental history of anarchism: 'Although Tolstoy condemned the passions of greed, anger and lust as vigorously as any tub-thumping Puritan, he was no other-worldly moralist. He recommended the happiness which is to be found in a life close to nature, voluntary work, family, friendship and a painless death.' Moreover, Tolstoy's promotion of anarchistic pacifism stresses its impact on people's well-being here and now. 'He rejects the charge that without government there will be chaos or a foreign invasion. His experience of Cossack communities in the Urals had shown him that order and well-being are possible without the organized violence of government' (Marshall 2008 [1992]: 370, 374).

Yet Orwell is using his picture of Tolstoy for essential rhetorical purposes – and as a foil against which he can deliver his wonderfully profound celebration of life – and the music of words of his hero, William Shakespeare.

In a strikingly perceptive analysis of the essay, George Woodcock tries to explain Orwell's particular fascination with Tolstoy. Just as Orwell highlights the resemblance between Tolstoy and Lear in experiencing the failures of renunciation, so he, in his turn, 'was fighting against a half-recognized similarity' in attempting a major act of renunciation (Woodcock 1984 [1966]: 242). 'He gave up his career in the Indian service, which was probably no great sacrifice, but he followed it up by his deliberate descent into the lower depths of destitution. Afterwards, like Tolstoi [sic], he realized that he had acted on mistaken motives and that the impression he had first gained of having crossed the great gulf of caste was an illusion.' Thus, 'what appears to be violent disagreement is really an unwilling and unadmitted recognition of moral affinity' (ibid: 242-243).

Moreover, in Orwell's critique of pacifism in the *Lear* essay, Woodcock, an anarchist and personal friend, sees Orwell struggling with his own ambivalent attitudes. '… he was trying to discipline his own strong emotional feeling for a doctrine which his realistic and rational self recognized to be, at least in its pure form, impractical in any foreseeable future' (ibid: 244).

CONCLUSIONS

Orwell's love of the theatre begins in his childhood and remains constant throughout his life. Theatrical plot lines are dotted about – often wittily and imaginatively – *A Clergyman's Daughter*. For instance, when Dorothy, while recovering from her breakdown, teaches at Mrs Creevy's appalling school, Orwell has a great deal of fun describing the hoo-ha and parental protests that follow her class on *Macbeth* with its oh so controversial/shocking line 'Macduff was from his mother's womb/ Untimely ripp'd' (1976 [1935]: 387). 'I do so adore *Macbeth*,' he writes to his friend Eleanor Jaques, on 18 November 1932 and is keen to take her to see a production at the Old Vic (Orwell and Angus 1970 1: 130-131).

Orwell does not particularly distinguish himself during his stint as drama critic (1940-1941) but many of his reviews capture his sense of humour, his love of bawdy, Max Miller-ish jokes and show him playing with ideas later to be taken up in longer essays. Then while working at the BBC, his drama interests inevitably spill over into his output. Along with all his often inventive and highly original arts feature programmes and political commentaries, he designs thirteen courses based on Calcutta and Bombay University syllabuses in English and American literature, science, medicine, agriculture and psychology and runs a series introducing drama and the mechanics of production, backed up with shortened versions of Indian plays. According to Peter Davison: 'This had a direct effect in that two participants, Balraj and Damyanti Sahni, set up a travelling drama company in India on their return' (1996: 117).

Interestingly, his fascination with fairy stories is reflected in two dramatic adaptions he writes for the BBC – of 'The emperor's new clothes' and 'Little Red Riding Hood' while his own version of *Animal Farm* is broadcast in 1947.

Moreover, the work of dramatists such as Oscar Wilde and William Shakespeare is constantly reflected upon during his writing career (though D. H. Lawrence's short stories and poems especially interest him rather than the plays). The *Complete Works* indicate more than 120 references to Shakespeare and around 30 to Wilde. Davison even suggests that the concept of 'doublethink' (the ability to hold two contradictory ideas at the same time) of *Nineteen Eighty-Four* could have been drawn from *Macbeth*. In this play, the Porter refers satirically to equivocation.

Standing at the Door of Hell, the Porter asks who knocks: 'Faith, here's an equivocator that could swear in both the scales against either scale, who committed treason enough for God's sake, yet could not equivocate to Heaven: O come in [to Hell] equivocator' (Davison 1996: 132). An intriguing idea.

One thing is certain, however: for it's the Bard's sexiness and love of life that Orwell, the theatre man, celebrates so movingly and memorably in his essay 'Lear, Tolstoy and the Fool'.

NOTES

[1] In addition, his friendship at these schools with Cyril Connolly – later to be the distinguished editor of *Horizon* and publisher of many of Orwell's greatest essays – is largely based on their joint passion for reading

[2] The Hawthorns today is the Fountain House Hotel. There is a plaque to Orwell on the front of the building, sponsored by the Hayes Literary Society

[3] There is an incredibly detailed and fascinating profile of Audrey Lucas, author, playwright and one-time lover of Evelyn Waugh at http://www.evelynwaugh.org.uk/styled-44/index.html

REFERENCES

Avery, Desmond (2017) *George Orwell at the BBC in 1942*, Wellingore: The Garth Press

Bounds, Philip (2016 [2009]) *Orwell & Marxism: The Political and Cultural Thinking of George Orwell*, London: I. B. Tauris

Bowker, Gordon (2003) *George Orwell*, London: Little, Brown

Buddicom, Jacintha (2006 [1974]) *Eric & Us*, Chichester: Finlay Publisher, postscript edition edited by Venables, Dione

Crick, Bernard (1980) *George Orwell: A Life*, Harmondsworth, Middlesex: Penguin

Colls, Robert (2013) *George Orwell: English Rebel*, Oxford, Oxford University Press

Crook, Tim (2015) George Orwell and the radio imagination, Keeble, Richard Lance (ed.) *George Orwell Now!* New York: Peter Lang pp 193-208

CWGO (1998) *The Complete Works of George Orwell*, XX Vols, Davison, Peter (ed.) London: Secker & Warburg

Daly, Georgina (1981) Cold bath before breakfast, *Eastbourne Herald*, 7 March

Davison, Peter (1996) *George Orwell: A Literary Life*, Houndmills, Basingstoke: Macmillan

Keeble, Richard Lance (2015) 'There is always room for one more custard pie': Orwell's humour, Keeble, Richard Lance and Swick, David (eds) *Pleasures of the Prose: Journalism and Humour*, Bury St Edmunds: Abramis pp 10-25

Keeble, Richard Lance (2018) 'Such, such were the joys' and the journalistic imagination, *George Orwell Studies*, Vol 2, No. 2 pp 69-90

Keeble, Richard Lance (2020a) Orwell and dress: The naked truth? *George Orwell Studies*, Vol. 4, No. 2 pp 78-94 and Chapter 1

Keeble, Richard Lance (2020b) The myth of freedom: Orwell and the press, in *Journalism Beyond Orwell: A Collection of Essays*, London: Routledge pp 15-32

Lynskey, Dorian (2019) *The Ministry of Truth: A Biography of George Orwell's* 1984, London: Picador

Marshall, Peter (2008 [1992]) *Demanding the Impossible: A History of Anarchism*, London: Harper Perennial

Meyers, Jeffrey (2000) *Orwell: Wintry Conscience of a Generation*, New York/London: W. W. Norton and Company

Moore, Darcy (2020) Orwell's Scottish ancestry and slavery, *George Orwell Studies*, Vol 5, No. 1 pp 6-19

Myers, Valerie (1991) *George Orwell*, London: Macmillan

Orwell, George (1976 [1935]) *A Clergyman's Daughter*, in the *Collected Fiction*, London: Secker and Warburg/Octopus pp 255-425

Orwell, George (1980 [1941a]) The art of Donald McGill, in *Collected Non-Fiction*, London: Secker & Warburg/Octopus pp 571-578

Orwell, George (1980 [1941b]) The Lion and the Unicorn, in *Collected Non-Fiction*, London: Secker & Warburg/Octopus pp 527-564

Orwell, George (1980 [1946]) Politics vs. literature: An examination of *Gulliver's Travels*, in *Collected Non-Fiction*, London: Secker & Warburg/Octopus pp 769-781

Orwell, George (1970 4 [1952]) Such, such were the joys, Orwell, Sonia and Angus, Ian (eds) *The Collected Essays, Journalism and Letters Vol. 4: In Front of Your Nose, 1945-1950*, Harmondsworth, Middlesex: Penguin Books pp 379-422; *Partisan Review*, September-October

Orwell, Sonia and Angus, Ian (eds) (1970 1) *The Collected Essays, Journalism and Letters, Vol. 1: An Age Like This, 1920-1940*, Harmondsworth, Middlesex: Penguin

Sutherland, John (2016) *Orwell's Nose: A Pathological Biography*, London: Reaktion Books

Taylor, D. J. (2003) *Orwell: The Life*, London: Chatto & Windus

West, W. J. (ed.) (1985a) *Orwell: The War Broadcasts*, London: Gerald Duckworth & Co/BBC Productions

West, W. J. (ed.) (1985b) *Orwell: The War Commentaries*, London: Gerald Duckworth & Co/BBC Productions

Williams, Kristian (2017) *Between the Bullet and the Lie: Essays on Orwell*, Chico, CA: AK Press

Woodcock, George (1984 [1966]) *The Crystal Spirit: A Study of George Orwell*, London: Fourth Estate

- **Originally published as 'The play's the thing: Orwell and drama', Orwellsociety.com. 6 September 2020, https://orwellsociety.com/the-plays-the-thing-orwell-and-drama-1-3/, part 1; 12 September 2020, https://orwellsociety.com/the-plays-the-thing-orwell-and-drama-2-3/, part 2; 19 September 2020, https://orwellsociety.com/the-plays-the-thing-orwell-and-drama-3-3/, part 3**

Chapter Twelve

Philip Bounds: On Marxism and Much More

Philip Bounds's *Orwell & Marxism: The Political and Cultural Thinking of George Orwell* (2016 [2009])[1] is one of the most original and yet seriously under-valued contributions to Orwellian scholarship of recent years.

Bounds is always acutely sensitive to the ambiguities and contradictions in Orwell's stances and to the ways in which his writings can take issue with Marxist tenets or, at other times, endorse them. His book is massively researched and packed with penetrating insights into Orwell's personality and writings. Orwell has a deep distrust of abstract ideologies. As Robert Colls comments: 'A key feature of his writing was a desire to put himself as far away from abstraction and as close to experience as he could, followed by a meticulous attention to the detail of what he saw, heard, touched, tasted, smelled, and reasonably assumed to be the case. For Orwell, this was the first test of truth.'[2] And because of Orwell's clear loathing of Soviet communism, it is tempting to think that he had little interest in Marxism.

Yet Richard Rees, Orwell's closest friend, recalls a meeting in the 1930s when he astonished everybody, including Marxist theoreticians, 'with his breath-taking Marxist paradoxes and epigrams, in a way as to make the sacred mysteries seem almost too obvious and simple'.[3] And John Rodden comments: 'It is likely that Orwell knew more about Marxism than he let on in *The Road to Wigan Pier* and *Homage to Catalonia*. In both books he assumed the stance of the intellectual naïf and earthy sceptic, probably for rhetorical effect. By portraying himself as a man of common sense and by exaggerating the suddenness and force of his conversion to socialism when confronted by the suffering English miners and unemployed.'[4]

Bounds, a journalist, historian and critic who died last year, expands on these points and painstakingly demonstrates the substantial and complex influence of

Marxism on his novels, journalism and cultural criticism. Moreover, given the originality and depth of research in Bound's text, it worth devoting some time to exploring some of its many fascinating insights.

He introduces his study by stressing that during the 1930s and 1940s Orwell studied intensely the cultural writings of young literary intellectuals who were either members of or closely associated with the Communist Party of Great Britain such as Alick West, Ralph Fox, Christopher Caudwell, Edgell Rickwood, Jack Lindsay and T. A. Jackson. According to Bounds, 'their influence on Orwell was so profound that his cultural writings can in one sense be interpreted as a sort of dialogue with them' (op cit: 3). He also made frequent references to communist newspapers and journals such as *Left Review*, *Labour Monthly*, the *Daily Worker* and the *Modern Quarterly*.

ORWELL'S 'MISCHIEVOUS DELIGHT' WITH THE UNDERCLASS

Bounds's first chapter examines Orwell's attitudes to the 'common people' and the underclass of tramps and beggars. He writes: 'Although Orwell is often portrayed as the most morally incorruptible of men, he clearly took a mischievous delight in the behaviour of what we might call the underclass antinomians – those cheerfully amoral men and women who fend for themselves in difficult circumstances by resorting to all kinds of larceny, dishonesty and petty crime' (ibid: 31). Reviewing 'Hop-picking diary', of 1931, and *Down and Out in Paris and London*, of 1933, he suggests that Orwell admired the way 'the underclass's immorality was accompanied by a supreme indifference to the disdain of other people'. And he often portrays their culture as a sort of miniature welfare system in which people behaved compassionately to others through choice rather than compulsion. 'By focusing on the unwillingness of the tramps to make pompous moral judgements, Orwell was perhaps implying that a ruthless capacity to be honest about one's own faults is an essential feature of the good society' (ibid: 33).

Orwell's early socialist friends were all associated in some way with John Middleton Murry's *Adelphi* which published some of his most celebrated essays between the early 1930s and late 1940s – and as Bounds points out, the journal's circulation manager Jack Common, a proletarian author from Newcastle, took a special interest in tramping and encouraged him to regard the destitute as 'kickers against authority' (ibid: 39).

In a fascinating section looking at Orwell's ambivalent attitudes to science, Bounds outlines the activities of the Social Relations of Science group of Marxist and *Marxisant* intellectuals which included the eminent J. D. Bernal. In a flurry of publications such as *The Social Function of Science* (1939), Bernal argued that capitalism tends to undermine scientific research by creating an intellectual climate in which 'pure' science is better regarded than 'applied' science and preventing scientists from fully co-operating with experts in other fields. The anti-scientific strain in Orwell's thinking is most evident in the second, idiosyncratic and highly personal section of *The Road to Wigan Pier* in which he lambasts – with a sort of D. H. Lawrentian venom – what he calls the 'machine civilisation'. 'Orwell's biggest anxiety was that technological progress would end up reducing human beings to a state of "soft" and "flabby" torpor. Against the argument that socialism inevitably restores what John Ruskin had famously called joy in "labour", Orwell insisted that the tendency of modern technology is to rationalise production to the point where all traces of intellectual and aesthetic significance have been stripped from the experience of work' (ibid: 53).

But on the few occasions when Orwell spoke positively about science, he presented arguments which the SRS movement had done much to popularise. One of his main reasons for wanting socialism was that the free market had become a brake on technological development. Moreover, Orwell recognised that machines in the future would go a long way towards liberating human beings from unpleasant work 'though he glumly acknowledged that they might never free us from the gruesome business of doing the dishes' (ibid: 54).

Orwell is well known for his interest in the middle class – as reflected in his 'England your England' and in certain sections of *The English People* – and this is often seen as distinguishing him from the rest of British left which was more obsessed with the 'progressive' potential of the working class. Bounds adds astutely, drawing on his vast knowledge of radical, progressive, left-wing texts: 'Yet this is to overlook the fact that a concern with winning middle class support had been a central feature of Marxist politics at the time of the People's Front. Indeed, there were some striking parallels between *The Lion and the Unicorn* and Alec Brown's *The Fate of the Middle Classes* (1936), a rather breathless communist text which Orwell reviewed on two separate occasions in the months following its publication' (ibid: 56-57). For instance, Orwell adopted a similar position on bourgeois culture, ascribing the 'decay of the ability in the ruling class' to the fact that the dynamic entrepreneurs of the past had been transformed into 'mere owners, their work being done for them by salaried managers and technicians' (ibid: 57-58). And both men illustrate their arguments about the middle class with critical references to the work of H. G. Wells.

THOSE GROUND-BREAKING WRITINGS ON MASS COMMUNICATION

Moving on to consider Orwell's writings on mass communication, Bounds highlights their ground-breaking qualities. For instance, in his essay on the boys' weeklies, *Gem* and *Magnet*, he points out how nearly every scene, character or episode is painstakingly evoked in the most verbose and repetitive manner imaginable while the extravagant use of stereotypes reduces each character to a handful of easily identified features – Bunter's corpulence, D'Arcy's monocle, Inky's Anglo-Indian solecisms and so on. 'Nearly twenty years before the emergence of

Cultural Studies in Britain, Orwell had thus anticipated two major theoretical insights (one about the textual function of stereotypes and the other about the "hyper-real" status of media representations) which his successors would explore with rather less essayistic flair' (ibid: 68).

Bounds also takes a neo-Marxian approach to Orwell's essay 'In defence of P. G. Wodehouse', stressing the way in which he extracts a political message from ostensibly 'non-political' texts. 'By demonstrating that such unlikely characters as Jeeves, Wooster and PSmith were all the bearers of conservative ideology, Orwell showed that there is no such thing as "simple entertainment" and that all popular texts convey a political message of one sort or another' (ibid: 73). Orwell's ideas in 'The detective story' (1943) and 'Raffles and Miss Blandish' (1944), according to Bounds, are very similar to those of the communist writer Alick West who contributed a two-part article on 'The detective story' to *Left Review* in 1938.

Moreover, while Bounds acknowledges that Orwell's remarkable essay on sexy seaside postcards, 'The art of Donald McGill' (1946), is held in high regard, he points out that it has generally been overlooked that he was actually contributing to an important debate on the left concerning the role of vulgarity and sensationalism in the popular media. In 1937, for instance, the communist intellectual Charles Madge, whom Orwell knew as the co-founder of the Mass Observation movement, had published an essay, 'Press, radio and social consciousness', highlighting the element of political ambiguity in popular newspapers. On the one hand, given that newspapers are owned by large commercial organisations, the ideas they express will be those of the ruling class. Yet, to secure a mass readership the popular press cultivates the 'vulgar and sensational' which, in part, subverts those ideas. In contrast, Orwell sees the 'obscene' jokes of McGill's postcards as reaffirming the dominant morality. Bounds comments perceptively: 'As a writer who was always suspicious of the doctrine of human perfectibility, not least because it had infected the socialist movement with the sort of intolerance that ultimately gave rise to Stalinism, Orwell perhaps saw the element of working class fatalism in seaside postcards as a useful anti-dote to utopian illusions' (ibid: 83).

Bounds comments are particularly perceptive when he considers the ideas which informed Orwell's critical essays and broadcasts highlighting, again, his ambivalence. For while Orwell argued – along with the Marxists – that all works of literature were intrinsically political, he was also suspicious of the excessively partisan approach of some of his Marxist contemporaries and concerned over the 'invasion of literature by politics'. Bounds locates this ambivalence in the residual influence of the art-for-art's sake movement – led by the aesthetes Walter Pater and Oscar Wilde who stressed three main principles: a political writer is likely to be worthless unless he commands a high level of literary skill, aesthetic pleasure can be derived even from works whose political message one disagrees with and, finally, the best political writers are those who view their particular movement from the perspective of the outsider.

Interestingly, Bounds highlights the fact that Orwell's celebrated essay 'Charles Dickens' (1940) was a direct response to *Charles Dickens: The Progress of a Radical* (1937) by the communist T. A. Jackson while in 'Politics vs literature*:* An examination of *Gulliver's Travels*' (1946), he answered the communists' claim that none of the great writers of the past had displayed fascist or proto-fascist ideas with the argument that Swift, in his novel, was exploring right-wing authoritarianism *from the inside* (ibid: 92, italics in the original).

ORWELL'S UNDER-RESEARCHED STANCE ON MODERNISM

Orwell's stance towards the modernist movement – incorporating writers as diverse as D. H. Lawrence, T. S. Eliot, Virginia Woolf, Ezra Pound and W. B. Yeats – is a fascinating subject though seriously under-researched. Here Bounds devotes a substantial section to the topic, highlighting Orwell's argument that their belief in aesthetic autonomy had essentially condemned them to a species of political obscurantism. 'Disillusioned by human nature and the naive optimism of their literary forebears, the modernists had arrived at a state of complete political irrelevance by way of a pointless belief in the opacity of language' (ibid: 106-107). Bounds actually underestimates the influence of Lawrence on Orwell. Throughout his writing career, Lawrence, particularly as a short story writer, was constantly referenced – always in positive terms. Indeed, in the index to the *Collected Works of George Orwell*, edited by Peter Davison in 1998, Lawrence is mentioned 71 times.[5]

But Bounds is seen at his best when he considers Orwell's ideas about language – placing them in a highly original yet crucial historical context. Thus, essays such as 'Propaganda and demotic speech' (1944), 'Politics and the English language' (1946) and 'The English language' section of *The English People* (1947) are understood as part of a debate 'about the linguistic virtues of the lower orders' beginning at the start of the nineteenth century when Wordsworth announced in his Preface to *Lyrical Ballads* (1800) that poetry could only be revived by resorting to the 'language of the middle and upper classes of society'. During the 1930s a number of Marxists, such as the novelist Alec Brown, Montagu Slater, Douglas Garman, the critic J. M. Hay and the poet Hugh MacDiarmid explored contrasting ideas relating to working class speech, ruling class 'jargon' and the rejection of abstract terms. It is within this context of lively debate on the left that Orwell's ideas on language emerge.

Similarly, Bound's detailed analysis of *Nineteen Eighty-Four* comes within the context of Orwell's fierce polemical disagreement with the communist poet Randall Swingler over freedom of speech in the columns of the journal, *Polemic*. Following on from Orwell's 'The prevention of literature' in the second issue, Swingler argues – in the fifth issue of 1946 – that since 'absolute truth' can never be realistically attained, the intellectual's main social function is not so much to state a particular view but to 'show people how to deal with evidence'. In response, Orwell maintains that relativist assumptions are peculiarly vulnerable to totalitarian appropriation. As Bounds concludes: 'There are obvious parallels between … Orwell's reply to Swingler and the philosophical opinions which were later ascribed to O'Brien [Winston's torturer in *Nineteen Eighty-Four*]' (ibid: 155).

In another section of striking originality, Bounds sees Winston Smith as being deliberately portrayed as a sort of negative caricature of the 'positive heroes' of the Socialist Realist novel. He fails to fit in with any of Oceania's established classes or groups and subverts the formula for the positive physical hero being prematurely decrepit and continually suffering from coughing fits. 'Whereas the socialist novel traded righteous anger as a means of undermining the status quo, Orwell grimly implies that the only rational response to Stalinist tyranny is one of resignation and detachment' (ibid: 169).

EXPLORING NOVELS IN ORIGINAL WAYS

Bounds, in true *Nineteen Eighty-Four* style, ends his text with a wonderfully rich Appendix in which he explores the ideas in Orwell's novels in many original ways. Focusing first on *Burmese Days*, he suggests that John Flory is effectively trying to solve the problems of empire in much the same way that young Orwell tried to solve the problems of the British class system – by reaching out to oppressed groups and relating to them as equals. Yet Flory's idealism is stymied more from the Burmese side than from the British. Faced with Flory's stress on the British in Burma having no purpose 'except to steal', Veraswami argues that the imperial ruling class brings modernity to an inferior people. In contrast, the ruthless U Po Kyin, Kyauktada's sub-divisional magistrate, drives Flory to suicide and destroys Veraswami's reputation. 'When a colonial state seeks to absorb a native elite into the machinery of power, Orwell seems to be saying, those who are chosen will defer and those who are excluded will destroy. There is no middle ground between imperialism and national self-determination' (ibid: 180).

Moving on to *Keep the Aspidistra Flying*, he suggests a crucial scene is when Gordon Comstock sees tramps in Westminster and makes no secret of his contempt for them – and this reawakens his sympathy for the class he has tried to abandon. 'Weighed down by self-pity, still obsessed with keeping up appearances, he makes no attempt to resist as his bohemian contempt for the philistine middle classes suddenly mutates into a sort of sickly compassion' (ibid: 186). Moreover, at the heart of the novel is Orwell's debate with the art-for-art's sake movement of aesthetes such a Baudelaire, Pater and Wilde. When Comstock returns to his job at the New Albion Publicity Company, Orwell implies that the impulse to create alternative realities is better served by mainstream hacks in high-tech offices than by bohemian aesthetes in garrets. 'It is almost as if Orwell can be cast as a plain speaking precursor to Jean Baudrillard, anxious to show how the rise of consumerism has divorced the means of signification from the real world in which they were once anchored' (ibid: 188).

Bounds also suggests that Orwell in the novel is deliberately taking issue with Oscar Wilde's *The Soul of Man Under Socialism* (1891). In effect, Orwell stands Wilde's arguments on their head. 'Where Wilde speaks of altruism as a universal duty under capitalism, Orwell evokes a flyblown aesthete whose sympathy lies only with his own class. Where Wilde regards aesthetic relativism as a precondition of personal liberation, Orwell sees it as a nightmarish source of uncertainty' (ibid: 190).

Again, Bounds's observations on Orwell's *Coming Up For Air* are both profound and original. While George Bowling aims to capture the atmosphere of his idyllic childhood in his secret trip to Lower Binfield, the memoir of his actual time there is, paradoxically, littered with images of disorder. Market day is spoilt by bitter commercial rivalry and widespread drunkenness, a drunken man falls to the ground and is left there for ages during a General Election, weak parents fail to discipline naughty brats. But what helps form the citizens of Lower Binfield into a relatively stable community is their unobtrusive but genuine sense of piety. Significantly, Lower Binfield is 'shaped roughly like a cross with the market-place in the middle'. In addition, 'The ethical benefits of rural labour are brought home with disconcerting power in the chapters on fishing, especially in the scenes in which the infant Bowling accompanies his brother's gang on a trip to Brewer's stream. As long as the boys are preoccupied with snaring carp, their thuggishness is held at bay and they behave like adults in the making. It is only when Brewer chases them off his land that they resort to barbarous type...' (ibid: 193).

Bounds concludes highlighting Orwell's use of traditional narrative forms – with his 1930s novels' critique of aestheticism reflecting the severe disapproval of 'fashionable pansies' which had entered English culture at the time of Wilde's imprisonment in 1895. 'In seeking to bend the middlebrow novel to his own purposes ... Orwell surrendered to precisely the sort of commonsensical nostrums which he otherwise opposed' (ibid: 196).

DEEP INTELLECTUAL DEBT TO THE COMMUNISTS

A few years after the publication of the first edition of *Orwell and Marxism*, in 2009, Bounds contributed a chapter on a parallel theme to *Orwell Today*, a collection of eclectic essays I edited in 2012 and published by Abramis, of Bury St Edmunds. He argues that while Orwell distrusted the communists, he never shrank from appropriating, reworking or challenging what he took to be their most distinctive assumptions. He ends with typical élan: 'It is taken for granted in some circles that the left is almost pathologically fissiparous and that members of various parties, sects and factions are utterly scornful of rival forms of radical thinking. George Orwell's deep intellectual debt to the communists suggests that the culture of the left is not always so sectarian. Although the capacity of left-wingers to fall out with each other should never be underestimated, Orwell's work shows that at least some of them are willing to learn from their rivals.'

In 2015, I had the pleasure of reviewing for the Orwell Society's *Journal* Bounds's witty and self-deprecatory political memoir *Notes for the End of History: A Memoir of the Left in Wales*, Merlin Press, London. In it, he tells of how reading *Nineteen Eighty-Four* when a 15-year-old schoolboy had such a transformative effect on his life and outlook. 'As I held the book in my hands I got the unnerving feeling that past, present and future had somehow been conflated. In one way or another that relic of history was telling me how to live now.'

While in 2019, Bounds contributed another strikingly original essay on Orwell and the paranormal to this journal (Vol. 4, No. 1: 57-70). Indeed, his immense contribution to Orwell Studies will live on in his many writings – for us and future generations to enjoy and learn from. Thank you, Philip.

NOTES

[1] Published by I. B. Taurus, London

[2] Colls, Robert (2013) *George Orwell: English Rebel*, Oxford: Oxford University Press p. 11

[3] See Rodden, John (2003) *Scenes from an Afterlife: The Legacy of George Orwell*, Wilmington, Delaware: ISI Books p. 179

[4] Ibid: p. 180

[5] See https://orwellsociety.com/orwells-love-of-lawrence/. And Chapter 5

- **This tribute was originally published in** *George Orwell Studies*, **Vol. 5, No. 2, 2021 pp 157-164**

Chapter Thirteen

On the 'Unreality' of Royal Coverage

Given the recent, unprecedented avalanche of complaints to the BBC over its wall-to-wall coverage of Prince Philip's death, it's interesting to consider George Orwell's views on the press handling of the royals of his day.

On 7 April 1944, in one of the 80 'As I Please' columns he writes for *Tribune* between 1943 and 1947, Orwell meticulously deconstructs the *Daily Mirror* issue of 21 January 1936 containing the announcement of the death of George V (*CWGO* XVI: 145-148; see also Keeble 2020).

First, he provides a detailed quantitative analysis, highlighting the unreality of the world as manufactured by the press and, equally significantly, important events and perspectives missed by the media. He then moves on to make more general qualitative comments, comparing press output with that of the radio. He opens by providing background to the column (establishing the wry, critical tone which is to persist throughout):

> Sometimes, on top of a cupboard or at the bottom of a drawer, you come on a pre-war newspaper, and when you have got over your astonishment at its enormous size, you find yourself marvelling at its almost unbelievable stupidity (ibid: 145).

He admits it may be dangerous to draw too many inferences from this one edition since the *Daily Mirror* is the 'second silliest paper' after the *Sketch*. But, he argues (addressing his readers directly as 'you'), it is still worth analysing: 'If you want to know why your house has been bombed, why your son is in Italy, why the income tax is ten shillings in the pound and the butter ration is only just visible without a microscope, here is part of the reason' (ibid).

Most of the 28 pages, he calculates, are devoted to the Royal Family: the first 17 being entirely focused on the dead King and the other royals. 'There is a history of the King's life, articles on his activities as a statesman, family man, soldier, sailor, big and small game shot, motorist, broadcaster and what-not, with, of course, photographs innumerable.' Pages 18-23 feature 'amusement guides, comic articles and so forth'. On page 24, 'some news begins to creep in': a highway robbery, a skating contest, the forthcoming funeral of Rudyard Kipling and details about a snake at the Zoo which is refusing food.

Then, on page 26 comes 'the sole reference to the real world' with the headline: 'Bombing pledge by Duce: No more attacks on Red Cross.' The article underneath says il Duce 'deplores' the attacks on the Red Cross and adds that the League of Nations has just turned down Abyssinia's requests for assistance and refused to investigate the charges of Italian atrocities. Orwell continues ironically: 'Turning to more congenial topics the *Daily Mirror* then follows up with a selection of murders, accidental deaths and the secret wedding of Earl Russell' (ibid). The last page is headed 'LONG LIVE KING EDWARD VIII' and contains 'a short biography and a highly idealised photograph of the man whom the Conservative Party were to sack like a butler a year later' (ibid: 145-146). Orwell goes on to highlight important omissions: the two or three million unemployed, Hitler, the progress of the Abyssinian war, the political situations in France and Spain. He adds:

> And though this is an extreme instance, nearly all newspapers of those days were more or less like that. No real information about current affairs was allowed into them if it could possibly be kept out. The world – so the readers of the gutter Press were taught – was a cosy place dominated by royalty, crime, beauty-culture, sport, pornography and animals (ibid: 146).

Orwell's contempt for the *Daily Mirror* is to persist. At the end of *Animal Farm*, the pigs take out subscriptions to *John Bull*, *Tit-Bits* and the *Mirror* – symbolically marking their ultimate betrayal of the revolution! (Orwell 1976 [1945]: 63).

Monarchy has also featured in *The Lion and the Unicorn*, Orwell's stirring celebration of socialism and the English genius composed in 1941 when defeat by the Nazis appeared a distinct possibility (1970 2 [1941]). He suggests that any future English Socialist government will be neither doctrinaire, nor even logical. 'It will abolish the House of Lords, but quite probably will not abolish the Monarchy. It will leave anachronisms and loose ends everywhere, the judge in his ridiculous horsehair wig and the lion and unicorn on the soldier's cap buttons' (ibid: 125-126). And in a special section on the monarchy in one of the 'London Letters' he writes for the American leftist journal, *Partisan Review*, during the war, in spring 1944, he suggests the abdication of Edward VIII 'must have dealt royalism a blow from which it may not recover' (Orwell 1970 3 [1944]: 101). But Orwell is not an anti-monarchist. He continues: 'I do not defend the institution of monarchy in an absolute sense, but I think that in an age like our own it may have an inoculating effect, and certainly it does far less harm than the existence of our so-called aristocracy. I have often advocated that a Labour government, i. e. one that meant business, would abolish titles while retaining the Royal family' (ibid: 103).

ORWELL AND THE INVENTION OF JOURNALISM/MEDIA STUDIES

The critique of the 1936 royal coverage is not the only occasion when Orwell enjoys deconstructing the contents of newspapers and magazines. Let's look at just a few other examples. Significantly, his first published piece in the UK, 'A farthing newspaper' (for Chesterton's review *G. K's Weekly*) adopts a political economy approach that he is to maintain throughout his writing career (Orwell 1970 1 [1928]: 34-37). *Ami du Peuple*, costing just ten centimes, has recently been launched in Paris with a manifesto claiming it is 'uncontaminated by any base thoughts of gain' (ibid: 34). Blair adds, ironically:

> The proprietors, who hide their blushes in anonymity, are emptying their pockets for the mere pleasure of doing good by stealth. Their objects, we learn, are to make war on the great trusts, to fight for a lower cost of living and above all combat the powerful newspapers which are strangling free speech in France (ibid: 34-35).

He proceeds to deconstruct, with polemical vigour, the paper's pretensions – noting that its proprietor is M. Coty 'a great industrial capitalist and also proprietor of the *Figaro* and the *Gaulois*'. In other words, it is merely putting across 'the sort of propaganda wanted by M. Coty and his associates'.

At the heart of *Homage to Catalonia*, his eye-witness account of fighting in a Republican militia during the Spanish Civil War, is Orwell's anger at the coverage of the conflict by both mainstream and alternative/left newspapers – and his desire to put the record straight. As he writes: 'One of the dreariest effects of this war has been to teach me that the Left-wing press is every bit as spurious and dishonest as that of the Right' (though he excludes the *Manchester Guardian* from this criticism) (Orwell 1962 [1938]: 64). With typical wry humour, he tells of the 'fat Russian agent' at the Hotel Continental, in Barcelona: 'I watched him with some interest, for it was the first time that I had seen a person whose profession was telling lies – unless one counts journalists' (ibid: 135).

In another 'As I Please' column of 1944, he uses a serious critique of women's papers – such as *Lucky Star*, the *Golden Star* and *Peg's Paper* – to explore the ways in which press proprietors and the ruling class in general promote the notion of the moral superiority of the poor as 'the deadliest form of escapism' (*CWGO* XVI: 305). He argues that it is all 'a sublimation of the class struggle' and adds, with typical dry irony: 'The vast majority of the people who will see a film are poor and so it is politic to make the poor man a hero. Film magnates, Press lords and the like amass quite a lot of their wealth by pointing out that wealth is wicked' (ibid).

In his lengthy essay, *The English People* (also written in 1944 but only published in 1947), Orwell's critique again focuses on the press (*CWGO* XVI: 199-228): 'It is a fact that the much-boasted freedom of the British press is theoretical rather than actual. To begin with the centralised ownership of the press means in practice that unpopular opinions can only be printed in books or in newspapers with small circulations.'

Orwell's reflections on the press culminate in his creation of Winston Smith, the anti-hero of his dystopian masterpiece *Nineteen Eighty-Four* – published in 1949 just months before he died. For Winston is a media worker at the Ministry of Truth altering the records of *The Times* to conform to the current dogma. So Orwell's damning critique of the press persists to the very end.

Orwell is becoming well-known as, in effect, the founder of Cultural Studies with his essays on boys' weeklies, American crime novels, sexy seaside postcards, junk shops, cups of tea, women's fashion magazines, public houses and so on. His role in inventing Journalism/Media/PR Studies is yet to be acknowledged (see Keeble 2020).

REFERENCES

CWGO (1998) *The Complete Works of George Orwell*, Davison, Peter (ed.) XX Vols, London: Secker & Warburg

Keeble, Richard Lance (2020) The myth of freedom: Orwell and the press, in *Journalism Beyond Orwell*, London: Routledge pp 15-32

Orwell, George (1970 1 [1928]) A farthing newspaper, Orwell, Sonia and Angus, Ian (eds) *The Collected Essays, Journalism and Letters of George Orwell, Vol. 1: An Age Like This, 1920-1940*, Harmondsworth, Middlesex: Penguin pp 34-37; *G. K.'s Weekly*, 29 December

Orwell, George (1962 [1938]) *Homage to Catalonia*, Harmondsworth, Middlesex: Penguin

Orwell, George (1970 2 [1941]) *The Lion and the Unicorn*, Orwell, Sonia and Angus, Ian (eds) *The Collected Essays, Journalism and Letters of George Orwell, Vol. 2: My Country Right or Left, 1940-1943*, Harmondsworth, Middlesex: Penguin pp 74-134

Orwell, George (1970 3 [1944]) London Letter to *Partisan Review*, Orwell, Sonia and Angus, Ian (eds) *The Collected Essays, Journalism and Letters of George Orwell, Vol. 3, As I Please, 1943-1945*, Harmondsworth, Middlesex: Penguin pp 95-103

Orwell, George (1976 [1945]) *Animal Farm*, in the *Collected Fiction*, London: Secker & Warburg/ Octopus pp 13-66

- This essay is based on 'Orwell and the "unreality" of royal coverage', available online at https://orwellsociety.com/orwell-and-the-unreality-of-royal-coverage/

SECTION 2
Eileen Blair: Inspiration, Wife, Mother

Chapter Fourteen

The Wedding – Through Her Eyes

Sylvia Topp's life of Eileen O'Shaughnessy, George Orwell's first wife (Unbound, 2020), follows in a tradition of studies of the wives and lovers of famous artists who have been largely ignored in the conventional biographies. These include Brenda Maddox's *Nora: A Biography of Nora Joyce* (1988), Claire Tomalin's *The Invisible Woman: The Story of Nelly Ternan and Charles Dickens* (1990), Stacy Schiff's *Vera (Mrs Vladimir Nabokov)* (1999), Sally Cline's *Zelda Fitzgerald* (2003) and Suzanne Fajence Cooper's *The Passionate Lives of Effie Gray, Ruskin and Millais* (2010).

The conventional dismissal of these women – which their biographers have sought to counter – appears in Rachel Cooke's review of *Eileen* in the *Guardian*, of 10 March 2020. According to Cooke, the book is a 'dispiriting read'. She even questions whether Eileen deserves such a lengthy biography at all. Topp argues that Eileen had a significant influence on his writings – far more than his male biographers have so far allowed. But Cooke rejects this idea bluntly. 'Her arguments are unconvincing. I don't buy her suggestion that Orwell based Julia in *Nineteen Eighty-Four* on Eileen (that was surely Sonia). Nor do I believe she was behind what some regard as the major improvement in his work with the publication of *Coming Up For Air* in 1939. He was getting better anyway, as writers do over time' (Cooke 2020).

Topp, in fact, provides many original and important insights into Eileen's personality and psychology which certainly justify the biography – and yet Cooke fails to acknowledge them. As an example, it's interesting to focus on Eileen's decision to marry George Orwell. Why would a highly intelligent, lively young woman – an Oxford graduate then studying for a Master's in Educational

Psychology at University College London – give up her chance of a successful career and devote the rest of her life to a largely unknown writer?

How do the biographers treat this crucial moment? D. J. Taylor is somewhat bemused. 'Not very much is known of the circumstances of Orwell's marriage. … One wonders what Eileen, a bright, spirited woman who had given up her Master's degree for a life spent selling shillings' worth of groceries and watching her husband type, expected from her marriage. … Whatever Eileen may have thought of the rushing East Anglian winds and smoking chimneys is beyond recreation' (2003: 186, 188).

Bernard Crick is light on Eileen's psychology: 'They were not to be perfect together, but always a good match. She fought his fights and looked after him as well as he would allow – although she was a woman careless of creature comforts herself' (1980: 268). And Crick's wedding account concentrates on the event itself – George vaulting over the churchyard wall, the lunch in the pub afterwards – while no attention is given to exploring the feelings behind Eileen's momentous decision (ibid: 303).

Gordon Bowker is brief on the subject but typically highly sensitive. '… she had chosen to live a life which, in many ways, was far more to her taste than that of a professional psychologist – married to a writer with a fellow-feeling for literature, whom she would have liked to help more than he allowed, but with whom, through her sharp wit and ready sense of humour, soon established a highly relaxed and stimulating rapport. … She could have pursued an independent career but chose to partner a man whose strange brilliance deeply attracted her' (2003: 190).

Michael Shelden, in the authorised biography, makes no attempt to ponder Eileen's feelings about the marriage. He does focus on their initial attraction to each other. 'She could appreciate his dry wit, and she was capable of matching it with her own quips. She was not intimidated by him, and she was not the kind of woman whom he could easily shock with his unconventional remarks' (1991: 230). But for the actual marriage, Shelden concentrates on the concerns of family members and friends over Eileen's rash decision 'to throw away a chance of a good career in order to live in a primitive cottage [the Stores, Wallington], far from any major towns with an "author" who wanted to be a shopkeeper and whose literary earnings were modest and insecure' (ibid: 266).

Eileen is, intriguingly, largely absent from Robert Colls's account of the lead-up to the wedding, warranting just one passing reference: 'Though his girlfriend Eileen O'Shaughnessy came from South Shields, a town built on collieries, railways and shipyards, and his friend at the *Adelphi* Jack Common was another Tynesider, Orwell showed no interest in going there and there is no evidence that he ever did go there except to bury his wife and visit her grave' (2013: 47). The wedding comes after Colls's account of Orwell's trip to the north of England, examining the plight of the poor. He says simply: 'In the meantime, he got married like any ordinary man should, dug his garden over the autumn, and wrote *The Road to Wigan Pier* as the Jarrow Marchers made their way to London' (ibid: 71).

Jeffrey Meyers, like Shelden, briefly attempts to explain Eileen's attraction to Orwell. '… she had a deep affinity with him, a shared idealism, and he brought out the warm, loving, maternal side of her character' (2000: 122). But on the decision to marry – nothing.

Compare all this with Topp's treatment. Acknowledging the significance of the decision, she devotes a substantial section to exploring – empathetically – Eileen's complex feelings on the matter. And she is able to draw on her deep knowledge of Eileen's life leading up to the Big Event – largely missing in the conventional biographies – on 9 June 1936. Why, then, would Eileen suddenly decide to give up her chances for a career of her own? Topp comments (2020: 117): 'Eileen had already turned down other possibilities for success. She had also rejected the ideas of marrying a man who could have given her the type of family life and home she had grown up with. She had always known – and this belief was increasingly reinforced in those eight years after she graduated from Oxford – that such traditional goals had no interest for her. Since her teenage years, perhaps influenced by her aunt, she'd been intrigued by missionaries and saints, and the rewarding life choices they had made. Instead of being tempted by comfort and common pleasures, she admired the values of self-denial, rejection of worldly greed and devotion to moral causes.'

Topp acknowledges that Eileen was 'not a true feminist'. 'She shared with Orwell a more traditional understanding of marriage. However, since she had by then spent over ten years making her own life decisions, it was impossible for her to become a complete second fiddle to him. And, at any rate, that wasn't really what he wanted. They were both social rebels, uninterested in a mundane marriage.' And she adds, perceptively: 'Although her choice might be criticised by young women of today, Eileen was acting in a very defiant manner.' She continues: 'She could see that Orwell would be a difficult man to live with but life with him promised the thrills and surprises for which many women constantly yearn. And Eileen was old-fashioned enough to want to help her husband succeed instead of being admired for excelling on her own.'

Returning to the women marginalised in the conventional biographies of famous artists, perhaps the one I would link most closely to *Eileen* is Rosie Jackson's wonderful life of *Frieda Lawrence* (Pandora, 1994). Frieda shocks all her friends and family by suddenly, in 1912, leaving her husband, Professor Ernest Weekley, of University College, Nottingham, and three young children and eloping with the relatively unknown novelist and poet D. H. Lawrence. Here is Frieda, the daughter of a German count, Friedrich von Richthofen, running off with the son of a Nottinghamshire miner. What a scandal!

The rest of their lives together are to be mainly on the move – between England, Europe, Australia and Mexico. Frieda also comes in for an enormous amount of criticism from the biographers. According to F. R. Leavis, in his highly influential *D. H. Lawrence: Novelist* (1955), Frieda is the Earth mother, the body, coarse matter, while Lawrence is mind, soul and intelligence. 'Moreover, she had none of his delicate moral discrimination. Unlike Lawrence, she was all crude instinct and blind passion' (Jackson 1994: 12). Keith Sagar describes her as 'amoral, disorderly, wasteful, utterly helpless in the house, lying in bed late, lounging about all day with a cigarette dangling from her mouth, expecting service and deference from everyone as her birthright' (ibid: 14). Elaine Feinstein's portrait in *Lawrence's Women* (1993) is laden with disdain (ibid). And in his profile of Lawrence, R. P. Draper sees the relationship entirely through the man's eyes: 'After her divorce from Professor Weekley in 1914, Frieda married Lawrence. Their life together was far from unruffled, since Lawrence did not believe in the "leprous forbearance which we are taught to practise in our intimate relationships" but in "open antagonism" and the free venting of "real hot rage". But the marriage proved a lasting one and gave Lawrence a centre of stability which his intensely individualistic nature required' (Draper 1969: 4).

Why would Frieda suddenly give up everything for a man, like Orwell, condemned by many for his misogyny – famously by Simone de Beauvoir in *The Second Sex* (1949) and Kate Millet, in *Sexual Politics* (1970)? Jackson carefully examines her motivations. 'After her etiolated and repressed existence with Weekley, Frieda found Lawrence vital and alert. He enabled her to live life more fully and her youthful exuberance returned' (Jackson 1994: 30). At the opening of her memoir, *Not I, But the Wind*, Frieda writes: 'I wanted to give Lawrence my silence.' Jackson comments: 'It is not that she thinks women cannot or should not speak, rather that the life to which she wanted writing to lead … could not be put fully into language. It was the deeper life, and not critical commentary for against it, that Frieda wanted to find and realize' (ibid: 62). Jackson adds:

> Frieda, far from encouraging or supporting Lawrence's reactionary views on male supremacy, violently opposed them. If Kate Millet was fighting Lawrence on gender issues in the late 1960s, Frieda was doing so throughout their time together. The difference is that Frieda had no feminist framework in and through which to articulate her struggle, nor did she feel the need for one. She wanted to find her identity and particular form of female integrity *within* and *through* a heterosexual relationship: separatism was not part of her agenda (ibid: 65, italics in the original).

Sylvia Topp returns to the question of Eileen's 'feminism' while examining one of the final, long letters she wrote to Orwell just before her operation – which was to prove tragically fatal, in March 1945. Topp comments astutely: 'Throughout this letter it becomes abundantly clear that Eileen cannot be described as a feminist.

Although she often revealed her strong will, she had accepted the role of a wife as secondary to the husband, something Orwell needed since he believed his writing was more important than anything or anyone' (op cit: 399).

In other words, both Eileen Blair and Frieda Lawrence had their very individual ways, to a certain extent constrained by the mores of their times, to assert forcefully their notions of female identity. These two biographies help explain the complex factors behind their decisions to commit to Orwell and Lawrence – which makes reading them so particularly moving.

REFERENCES

Bowker, Gordon (2003) *George Orwell*, London: Little, Brown

Colls, Robert (2013) *George Orwell: English Rebel*, Oxford: Oxford University Press

Cooke, Rachel (2020) *Eileen* – review, *Guardian*, 10 March. Available online at https://www.theguardian.com/books/2020/mar/10/eileen-the-making-of-george-orwell-sylvia-topp-review

Crick, Bernard (1980) *George Orwell: A Life*, Harmondsworth, Middlesex: Penguin

Draper, R. P. (1969) *D. H. Lawrence*, London: Routledge & Kegan Paul

Jackson, Rosie (1994) *Frieda Lawrence*, London: Pandora

Meyers, Jeffrey (2003) *Orwell: Wintry Conscience of a Generation*, New York/London: W. W. Norton & Company

Taylor, D. J. (2003) *Orwell: The Life*, London: Chatto & Windus

Topp, Sylvia (2020) *Eileen: The Making of George Orwell*, London: Unbound

- **Originally published as 'The wedding through Eileen's eyes', Orwellsociety.com, 21 May 2020. https://orwellsociety.com/the-wedding-through-eileens-eyes/**

Chapter Fifteen

How Eileen Saved His Life During 1938 Flu Epidemic

Flu epidemics have been a constant feature of British history – and the one in 1937-1938 impacted massively on George Orwell and his newly-married wife, Eileen. At the time, the Blairs were living in a ramshackle cottage in Wallington, deep in rural Hertfordshire. Orwell caught a cold, then started haemorrhaging from his mouth and nearly died. During the following July, Eileen had to go to bed with a serious cold – just before the country was hit by an even more serious flu epidemic.

MISSING IN THE CONVENTIONAL BIOGRAPHIES

Yet looking at the various biographies of Orwell, the crucial role played by Eileen – who had suffered a serious case of flu during the appalling Spanish Flu pandemic in 1919 – in saving Orwell's life is really only highlighted in Sylvia Topp's biography of Orwell's first wife (2020). Indeed, focusing on the handling of this one event by the biographers provides a fascinating case study in the ways in which the vital role played by women tends to be either ignored or marginalised in the conventional histories – and highlights the importance of Topp's biography in finally setting the record straight for Eileen.

She plays no active role in Michael Shelden's account in the authorised biography: 'In early March [Orwell] had been afflicted with a bad cough and in a few days his condition had worsened to the point where he was coughing up an alarming amount of blood. "The bleeding seemed prepared to go on for ever," Eileen later remarked. Her brother examined him and arranged for an ambulance to take him to Preston Hall Sanatorium in Kent' (1991: 316).

Jeffrey Meyers similarly downplays Eileen's role: 'On March 8, [Orwell's] three bouts of pneumonia and wounds in Spain finally caught up with him, when he began to hemorrhage [sic] and blood from an old lesion in his lung poured out of his mouth. Eileen was horrified, for the "bleeding seemed prepared to go on forever".' Next, Eileen's brother, Laurence O'Shaughnessy, is said to examine Orwell and decide to send him by ambulance to Preston Hall Sanatorium in Aylesford, Kent, where he was a consulting and thoracic surgeon (2000: 179-180).

D. J. Taylor, in his award-winning biography, similarly shows Eileen as having little influence on the events: 'Orwell's condition worsened to the extent that his life was in danger. A letter of 15 March from Eileen to Jack Common talks about "the drama of yesterday" – Common had apparently been summoned to help from his neighbouring village – and bleeding that seemed to go on for ever. Orwell was admitted to Preston Hall on 15 March which, given the distance involved, suggests an emergency trip by ambulance late on the previous day' (2003: 251). No indication is given as to who actually 'summoned' help.

Bernard Crick's handling of the event is interesting. He reports: 'On 8 March, a tuberculous lesion on Orwell's left lung suddenly began to bleed badly. Eileen got her brother, Laurence O'Shaughnessy, to see him. O'Shaughnessy was friendly with the director of a sanatorium in Kent where he was himself a consultant surgeon. After some debate about the risk of moving him, the director, Dr J. B. McDougal, took him into Preston Hall, Aylseford, Kent' (1980: 359). Crick next goes on to carry, in full, Eileen's letter to Jack Common, written shortly afterwards, describing the event in detail. This leads Crick to reflect on how similar the Blairs were: 'They shared a deep reluctance to accept help even from families, certainly felt ashamed to admit it, especially to someone like Jack Common in case he regard it as middle class nepotism' (ibid). So no reflection about Eileen's crucial support for Orwell – in this case even helping save his life in a highly stressful situation – and how terrifying the event must have been for her in a remote cottage in the dead of night.

Robert Colls ignores the event entirely in the main body of the text and simply reports: 'Orwell was diagnosed with TB in 1938. In September 1938, the Blairs went to Marrakech, so that he might recover his health' (2013: 109). Colls displays vast and impressive reading on the relevant political, social, cultural and literary background in the extensive notes at the end of the biography and here one spells out in more detail the drama of Orwell's transfer to the Aylesford sanatorium and the Blairs' departure for Morocco. But still Eileen's crucial role in saving her husband is missed (ibid: 265).

Gordon Bowker stresses how the event was 'extremely frightening' for Eileen but in no way indicates her crucial, active role in saving Orwell, reporting simply: 'Laurence O'Shaughnessy saw him and had him transferred immediately to Preston Hall Village…' (2003: 238).

TOPP'S INSIGHT AND COMPASSION

Compare all that with Sylvia Topp's account. She rightly draws attention to Eileen's prompt handling of the 'disaster' all alone, in the middle of the night, in an isolated cottage – without any neighbours to rush to. She quickly phones Jack Common to come and help her. Topp adds insightfully and compassionately: 'It's not hard to imagine her utter panic' (op cit: 208). Eileen next calls her brother who agrees 'that Eric must be taken somewhere where really active steps could be taken if necessary – artificial pneumothorax to stop the blood or transfusion to replace it'. And Topp concludes: 'Then somehow, terrified but with her brother's instructions and perhaps helped by Orwell's constant belief that "I've no doubt they'll find as before that I'm OK", Eileen managed to reach the right people who could help her save his life. But without her being there and without her brother's connections, it's entirely possible that Orwell would have died that night' (ibid).

In other words, without Eileen, Orwell would now be remembered as no more than a minor left-wing novelist and journalist who died of TB during a flu epidemic at a tragically young age.

Then, the following June, just before an even worse flu epidemic hit the country, Eileen herself had to retire to bed with a cold (Topp op cit: 220). Indeed, while the other biographies highlight the importance of the trip to Morocco (between September 1938 and March 1939) to helping Orwell recuperate after his health crisis, they omit to say how Eileen so desperately needed a break – since her health was deteriorating seriously too.

Topp's treatment of the March 1938 'disaster' is just one among many others in her biography of Eileen that highlights the ways in which women's roles are constantly marginalised or erased from the historical record. So *Eileen: The Making of George Orwell* is not only opening up new areas in Orwellian scholarship – it is also likely to occupy an important place in the development of gender studies more generally.

REFERENCES

Bowker, Gordon (2003) *George Orwell*, London: Little, Brown

Colls, Robert (2013) *George Orwell: English Rebel*, Oxford: Oxford University Press

Crick, Bernard (1980) *George Orwell: A Life*, Harmondsworth, Middlesex: Penguin

Meyers, Jeffrey (2000) *Orwell: Wintry Conscience of a Generation*, New York: W. W. Norton

Taylor, D. J. (2003) *Orwell: The Life*, London: Chatto & Windus

Topp, Sylvia (2020) *Eileen: The Making of George Orwell*, London: Unbound

- Originally published as 'How Eileen saved Orwell's life during 1938 flu epidemic', Orwellsociety.com, 28 March, 2020. https://orwellsociety.com/how-eileen-saved-orwells-life-during-1938-flu-epidemic/

Chapter Sixteen

Eileen – and Orwell's Shifting Attitudes on Gender Issues

Sylvia Topp's new biography of Eileen O'Shaughnessy, the first wife of George Orwell (Unbound, 2020), is focusing attention on how much influence she may well have had on Orwell's writings – from their marriage in 1936 until her untimely death aged just 39 in 1945.

Indeed, Orwell's views were constantly changing and there is substantial evidence (easily missed) that during the 1940s Orwell displayed what some might describe as even 'feminist' views – and Eileen's influence could have been substantial.

Feminist critics unite in condemning Orwell as a misogynist. According to Beatrix Campbell (1984: 131): 'Part of the problem is that Orwell's eye never comes to rest on the culture of women, their concerns, their history, their movements. He only holds women to the filter of his own desire – or distaste.' According to Deirdre Beddoe (1984: 140): 'Orwell was not only anti-feminist but he was totally blind to the role women were and are forced to play in the order of things.' And for Daphne Patai, author of the seminal *The Orwell Mystique: A Study in Male Ideology* (1984), Orwell cultivated 'a traditional notion of masculinity, complemented by a generalized misogyny' (ibid: 15). He 'polarizes human beings according to sex roles and gender identity and legitimizes male displays of dominance and aggression' (ibid: 17). John Newsinger is also critical of Orwell's attitudes to women. He writes (2018: 154): 'He regularly dismissed both "feminists" and "feminism". He was unfortunately one of those male socialists who were opposed to every oppression, except that of women.' Even Christopher Hitchens, hardly noted as a feminist, argues (2002: 105): 'Every one of the female characters [in his novels] is practically devoid of the least trace of intellectual or reflective capacity.'

MAN WITH MANY SIDES TO HIS PERSONALITY

Yet, Orwell was a complex man with many sides to his personality – and one was distinctly un-misogynistic. As Topp stresses (op cit: xiv), many of the women he is associated with (Jacintha Buddicom, aunt Nellie, Stevie Smith, Inez Holden, Mabel Fierz, Celia Kirwan – not to mention his two wives Eileen O'Shaughnessy and Sonia Brownell) are forceful characters who would hardly have tolerated a misogynist. As a father to Richard Horatio, whom he and Eileen adopted in June 1944, Orwell certainly confounded the expectations of his day, displaying considerable affection for the child, taking him for walks in the pram – and even changing his nappies (though with a cigarette in his mouth) (Crick 1980: 483).

Between 1943 and 1947 Orwell contributed 80 'As I Please' columns to the leftist journal, *Tribune*, where he became literary editor after two unhappy years at the BBC. The subject matter was vast: writers and writing, critiques of the mainstream press, the war effort, language, personal reminiscence and experiences, media censorship and the promotion of free speech, the BBC, post-war reconstruction, racism/anti-racism/anti-Semitism, the love of nature, socialism, the ruling classes, the handling of collaborators and so on. And in a number of columns, Eileen's influence appears considerable.

CONFOUNDING FEMINIST CRITICS

On 28 April 1944, Orwell certainly confounds his feminist critics by following up the comments of Basil Henriques, chairman of the East London juvenile court, who has attacked girls of 14 for dressing and talking like those of 18 and 19 and putting 'filth and muck on their faces' (Anderson 2006: 132). The polymath Orwell (and probably helped by Eileen) proceeds to offer a potted history of women's make-up – of all things (see Chapter 1.).

In another column, responding to a reader's letter, he uses a serious critique of women's papers – such as *Lucky Star*, the *Golden Star* and *Peg's Paper* (completely ignored by the intellectuals of his day) – to explore the ways in which press proprietors and the ruling class in general promote the notion of the moral superiority of the poor as 'the deadliest form of escapism' (*CWGO* XVI: 305). He argues that it is all 'a sublimation of the class struggle' and adds, with typical dry irony: 'The vast majority of the people who will see a film are poor and so it is politic to make the poor man a hero. Film magnates, Press lords and the like amass quite a lot of their wealth by pointing out that wealth is wicked' (ibid).

Yet, he argues, reality enters these papers through the correspondence columns where you can read harrowing tales of 'bad legs' and haemorrhoids 'written by middle-aged women who give themselves such pseudonyms as "A Sufferer", "Mother of Nine" and "Always Constipated"': 'To compare these letters with the love stories that lie cheek by jowl with them is to see how vast a part mere day dreaming plays in modern life' (ibid).

In 1945, Orwell reviews Virginia Woolf's seminal feminist text, *A Room of One's Own*, 'a discussion of the handicaps which have prevented women, as compared with men, from producing literature of the first order'. There is no condemnation. Rather, he suggests that 'almost anyone of the male sex could read it with advantage' (Newsinger 2018: 134-135). Significantly, John Newsinger identifies 'some shift in his attitudes' towards women in his writings in the mid-1940s, becoming 'more sensitive in his arguments regarding gender issues'. Eileen's influence was, no doubt, profound.

INFLUENCE PERSISTS AFTER EILEEN DIES

After Eileen dies suddenly in 1945, Orwell returns to composing his 'As I Please' columns for *Tribune* – and Eileen's influence seems to persist.

For instance, on 8 November 1946, he begins his column: 'Someone has just sent me a copy of an American fashion magazine which shall be nameless' (*CWGO* XVII: 471). In fact, it was *Vogue* containing, amidst its many photographs of glamorous women, a short profile of Orwell – along with a photograph of him. Biographer Michael Shelden comments (1991: 455):

> Orwell must have felt a mixture of pride and embarrassment to see his personal life described in the breezy style of the *Vogue* correspondent: 'Nowadays, Orwell lives in a top-floor flat in London, with his twenty-odd-months-old son. The stuff around his rooms – a Burmese sword, a Spanish peasant lamp, the Staffordshire figures, show something of his foreign life and his strong English solidity. Educated at Eton, Orwell has since then had the kind of picaresque life that is so superb in English autobiographies.'

Orwell proceeds to deconstruct the magazine, noting: 'One striking thing when one looks at these pictures is the overbred, exhausted, even decadent style of beauty that now seems to be striven after. Nearly all of these women are immensely elongated.' On the prose style of the advertisements, he says it's 'an extraordinary mixture of sheer lushness with clipped and sometimes very expressive technical jargon'. And, typically, Orwell focuses on what's missing:

> A fairly diligent search through the magazine reveals two discreet allusions to grey hair, but if there is anywhere a direct mention of fatness or middle age I have not found it. Birth and death are not mentioned either: nor is work, except that a few recipes for breakfast dishes as given. The male sex enters directly or indirectly into perhaps one advertisement in twenty and photographs of dogs and kittens appear here and there. On only two pictures out of about three hundred, is a child represented (op cit: 472).

Alex Woloch actually highlights Orwell's habit – in his 'As I Please' columns and other essays – to focus on what we are 'liable to miss'. This, he suggests 'reveals a strange blankness, or emptiness, at the deliberate heart of Orwell's work' (2016: 23).

In conclusion, during the 1940s, Orwell – probably influenced by Eileen – displays what some might describe as 'feminist' views – and it's easy to miss that important shift in his attitudes.

REFERENCES

Anderson, Paul (2006) *Orwell in* Tribune, London: Politico's

Beddoe, Deirdre (1984) Hindrance and help-meets: Women in the writings of George Orwell, Norris, Christopher (ed.) *Inside the Myth: Orwell: Views from the Left*, London: Lawrence and Wishart pp 139-154

Campbell, Beatrix (1984) Orwell: Paterfamilias or Big Brother?, Norris, Christopher (ed.) *Inside the Myth: Orwell: Views from the Left*, London: Lawrence and Wishart pp 128-136

Crick, Bernard (1980) *George Orwell: A Life*, Harmondsworth, Middlesex: Penguin

CWGO (1998) *The Complete Works of George Orwell* Davison, Peter (ed.) XX Vols, London: Secker & Warburg

Hitchens, Christopher (2002) *Orwell's Victory*, London: Allen Lane, The Penguin Press

Newsinger, John (2018) *Hope Lies in the Proles: George Orwell and the Left*, London: Pluto Press

Patai, Daphne (1984) *The Orwell Mystique: A Study in Male Ideology*, Amherst: University of Massachusetts Press

Shelden, Michael (1991) *Orwell: The Authorised Biography*, London: William Heinemann

Topp, Sylvia (2020) *Eileen: The Making of George Orwell*, London: Unbound

Woloch, Alex (2016) *Or Orwell: Writing and Democratic Socialism*, Massachusetts, London: Harvard University Press

- This essay first appeared on the website of The Orwell Society, 6 March 2020. https://orwellsociety.com/eileen-and-orwells-shifting-attitudes-on-gender-issues/

SECTION 3

George Orwell:
The Man

Chapter Seventeen

Warburg and the Making of Orwell

Animal Farm: A Fairy Story, Orwell's great damning satire on the Russian Revolution, first appeared on 17 August 1945. The publisher was Fredric Warburg (1898-1981) whose role in promoting Orwell's writings over many years and in the development, more broadly, of progressive ideas in post-war Europe cannot be understated.

Warburg was a scholarship boy at Westminster School. Intriguingly, after he visited Orwell at Cranham sanatorium in June 1949, Orwell decided to enrol his son, Richard, to this school. Previously, he had enrolled him to Eton but grew to detest their dress code. 'They have abandoned their top hats, I learn. It is a day school, which I prefer & I think has other good points,' Orwell wrote to Julian Symons about Westminster (*CWGO* XX: 137).

Warburg describes Secker & Warburg, formed with Roger Senhouse in 1935, in his autobiography, *All Authors Are Equal* (1973), as 'a midget firm, fragile as bone china'. He adds: 'My revolutionary urges were to be expressed in the publishing sphere, for I never joined any political group or party.' And around the company he assembled 'a miscellaneous collection of socialists, anarchists, radicals, independent socialists, pacifists and eccentrics' (ibid).

In its early years, the firm is consistently unprofitable but quickly publishes H. G. Wells, Thomas Mann, André Gide and Lewis Mumford. In 1937, it buys out *This Was Their Youth*, the second novel by Ralph Fox who goes on to fight with the International Brigades in Spain and who dies fighting in the defence of Madrid.

Then in 1938, after Orwell's publisher Victor Gollancz, objecting to his support for the leftist POUM militia and the anarchists during the Spanish Civil War, turns down *Homage to Catalonia*, his remarkable eye-witness account of fighting on the frontline, Warburg steps in. He is recommended to Orwell by Fenner Brockway, a leader of the Independent Labour Party, who has earlier given him the accreditation to serve with the POUM militia. The relationship Orwell develops with Warburg and Senhouse is to prove one of the most important and fruitful of his writing life.

SENHOUSE: NOT TO BE UNDER-ESTIMATED

Senhouse's role should not be under-estimated. He runs the company with Warburg for almost 30 years, so yet another old-Etonian (along with David Astor, A. J. Ayer, Cyril Connolly, Andrew Gow, Denys King-Farlow, L. H. Myers and Richard Rees) at the heart of Orwell's career. Warburg says of him in his autobiography: 'At times he seemed larger than life, buoyant, audacious and hyper-active. His rages, when he was roused, were uninhibitedly magnificent. ... He was one of the best copy editors and proof readers I have ever known. Above all, he had the important ability to convince many that Secker & Warburg was a distinguished firm with a future' (ibid).

Warburg takes a brave gamble with *Homage* (personally, one of my Orwellian favourites) and in the short term it does not pay off. Of the 1,500 copies printed, around 700 are sold so there are still copies in stock when it is reprinted in 1951 as part of the Uniform Edition. And it is not brought out in the US until 1952.

Warburg serves in the same Civil Guard unit based in St John's Wood, London, as a corporal under Sergeant Blair during the war years – and actually turns down publication of his *War Diaries*. But he introduces Orwell to a wide range of contacts – including Tosco Fyvel, Arthur Koestler and H. G. Wells – some of them to become important friends and colleagues. For instance, Fyvel and Orwell become joint editors of a series of Secker & Warburg pamphlets called 'Searchlight Books' – Orwell's contribution being *The Lion and the Unicorn*, in 1941, which sells over 10,000 copies. The first part 'England your England' (the title a deliberate variant of D. H. Lawrence's 'England my England') begins, famously: 'As I write, highly civilized human beings are flying overhead, trying to kill me.' Other books in the series are by Sebastian Haffner, Ritchie Calder, T. C. Worsley, Arturo Barea, Joyce Carey, Bernard Causton, Olaf Stapledon and Stephen Spender. But after Warburg's printers in Portsmouth are destroyed in a 1942 bomb attack, the series is closed down.

HOW *ANIMAL FARM* IS RESCUED

Warburg's role, next, in the publication of *Animal Farm* is to prove crucial. In 1944, the manuscript is rejected by four publishers concerned over its implicit attack on the Soviet Union, then a close ally in the war against the Nazis. The Ministry of Information turns down Jonathan Cape's request – but it emerges that the chief censor there is Peter Smollett, later revealed to be a Soviet spy. At Faber, T. S. Eliot (who in 1931 rejected *Down and Out in Paris and London*) objects, somewhat obtusely, to the representation of the animals: 'What was needed was not more communism but more public-spirited pigs' (Taylor 2003: 338). After rejection letters arrive from publishers William Collins and André Deutsch, Orwell turns to his friend Paul Potts who runs the Whitman Press, a small anarchist imprint. For this edition, Orwell pens an eight-page Introduction. But then Warburg agrees to publish in March 1945 and the Introduction is ditched. The Introduction is later to be discovered by Senhouse buried amongst his papers and published in 1972 with the ironic title 'The freedom of the press'.

The question remains: why did not Orwell take the manuscript to Warburg in the first place? According to biographer Bernard Crick: 'The answer must lie in Orwell's confidence in the merit of the book and his desire to see it published by one of the two best publishing houses in England. ... Secker & Warburg, before their faith in Thomas Mann, Franz Kafka and Orwell had paid off, looked a very different house – small, lively but precarious and still nicknamed, however unfairly, because of their courage and persistence in bringing out difficult left-wing books "the Trotskyite publisher"' (Crick 1980: 459-460).

Moreover, at the time of the publication of *Animal Farm*, Warburg gives Orwell important personal support. As biographer Gordon Bowker comments: 'Warburg wrote later that as soon as he read the book he realised that he had a major work on his hands. Orwell was less certain and quite apprehensive about how his old enemies the Stalinists would react to it' (Bowker 2003: 319).

Orwell's commitment to accuracy is perhaps best shown in a letter about *Animal Farm* – just about to be published – he sends to Senhouse in March 1945 from Paris, where he is reporting on the final days of the war for Astor's *Observer* and the *Manchester Evening News*. When in Chapter 8 the windmill is destroyed, Orwell originally writes: '... all the animals including Napoleon flung themselves on their faces'. He now asks for this to be changed to 'all the animals except Napoleon...' since he wants to be fair to Stalin who did stay in Moscow during the German advance. Warburg comments: 'To me this single sentence throws as much light on Orwell's character as any I know' (op cit).

Orwell's *Critical Essays*, including those on Charles Dickens, W. B. Yeats, Koestler, the sexy seaside postcards of Donald McGill and P. G. Wodehouse, is published by Warburg in 1946. According to Bowker, this book 'aroused more interest in literary circles than *Animal Farm*. It was widely reviewed by many leading thinkers of the day, including some of Orwell's friends' (Bowker op cit: 345).

PUBLISHING THE DYSTOPIAN MASTERPIECE

Warburg is probably best known for his support to Orwell in his final years – and in the publication of his dystopian, best-selling masterpiece *Nineteen Eighty-Four*. It first appears in bookshops on 8 June 1949, a first edition of 25,575 copies with further printings of 5,000 in the following March and August. Indeed, it is Warburg and his wife who recommends a friend of theirs, Dr Andrew Morland, a consultant physician at University College Hospital and expert on tuberculosis, to treat Orwell while he stays at Cranham sanatorium, in the Cotswolds, from January to September 1949. Morland was one of the last doctors to be seen by D. H. Lawrence in the south of France in 1929-1930.

At Orwell's funeral service, at Christ Church, Albany Street, London NW1, on 26 January 1950, Warburg greeted the mourners at the door. Biographer Michael Shelden records Inez Holden remembering him saying over and over: 'How good of you to come' (Shelden 1991: 485).

With its financial position devastated by paper shortages during and after the war, Secker & Warburg join the Heinemann publishing group in 1952. Warburg's list continues to be innovative and daring including authors such as Simone de Beauvoir, Colette, Alberto Moravia, Günter Grass and Angus Wilson. He even publishes in 1956 *The Third Eye*, supposedly written by Tuesday Lobsang Rampa about his mystical experiences while growing up in Tibet. It becomes a global best-seller but in the following year the author is revealed to be none other than Cyril Henry Hoskin, the son of a village plumber in Devon.

BRAVERY IN THE FACE OF LEGAL THREATS: BACKING *THE PHILANDERER*

Perhaps Warburg's courage as a progressive intellectual is best seen in 1953 with his publication of *The Philanderer*, by the American Stanley Kauffmann. A brilliant dissection of the Don Juan complex, with all its misogyny, emotional poverty and self-hatred, it is judged obscene on the Isle of Man and banned. A scandal ensues, predictably, in the British press with the editor of the *Daily Express* describing it, for instance, as 'calculated and deliberate pornography ... as degraded an essay in salacity as I have ever read'. Warburg is duly charged with obscene libel – and risks jail if he loses the case.

Most publishers faced with such a charge admitted guilt, paid a token fine, withdrew the book and moved on. Not Warburg. He chooses to send the case to trial by jury at the Old Bailey. There the prosecution presents the jury with all the allegedly salacious sections of the novel typed out on a sheet of paper. But then, in an unprecedented move, Mr Justice Stable orders all jury members to be given a copy of the book and sends them away to read it in three days. In summing up, the Judge says pornography certainly exists: any adult can recognise it. But because it exists, should non-pornographers be restrained from writing as fully and as well as they can about contemporary life? Such a summing up is unprecedented. The jury spend 50 minutes in discussion and then rule 'not guilty'.

The importance of this case for freedom of expression and reforming the obscenity law in the UK has been totally overshadowed by the 1960 watershed trial of D. H. Lawrence's *Lady Chatterley's Lover*, when the charge of obscenity is thrown out. But Warburg's remarkable courage over *The Philanderer* is typical of the man.

Thus, while Sylvia Topp's recent excellent biography of Orwell's first wife throws new light on Eileen Shaughnessy and her role in the making of the author of *Nineteen Eighty-Four*, it is perhaps useful to remember that Orwell's success would not have been possible without support from a wide range of friends, relatives and colleagues. So as we celebrate the anniversary of the publication of *Animal Farm*, let's not forget Fred Warburg.

REFERENCES

Bowker, Gordon (2003) *George Orwell*, London: Little, Brown

Crick, Bernard (1980) *George Orwell: A Life*, Harmondsworth, Middlesex: Penguin

CWGO (1998) *The Complete Works of George Orwell*, XX Vols, Davison, Peter (ed.) London: Secker & Warburg

Shelden, Michael (1991) *Orwell: The Authorised Biography*, London: William Heinemann

Taylor, D. J. (2003) *Orwell: The Life*, London: Chatto & Windus

Warburg, Fredric (2015 [1973]) *All Authors Are Equal*, Lexington, Massachusetts: Plunkett Lake Press. Available online at https://www.google.co.uk/books/edition/All_Authors_Are_Equal/4dGpDwAAQBAJ?hl=en&gbpv=1&kptab=overview

- **Originally published as 'Warburg and the Making of George Orwell'. Orwellsociety.com, 11 August 2020. https://orwellsociety.com/warburg-and-the-making-of-george-orwell/**

Chapter Eighteen

Angling for the Truth: The Enduring Passion for Fishing

OBSESSION BEGINS IN YOUTH

Fishing is one of George Orwell's many obsessions. It begins in his youth and continues right up until his final years on the remote Scottish island of Jura.
Fishing comes to serve as a powerful metaphor for the 'Golden Country' of England's lost civilisation. And it is deeply entangled in his attempts to deal with the guilt over a terrible tragedy that occurs while he is a pupil at Eton.

As a child in Henley, out with Humphrey Dakin's gang, fishing first becomes a passion for Orwell. And fishing – along with their shared love of literature and writing poetry – also features in Jacintha Buddicom's remarkable memoir of her times with Orwell in Shiplake, from 1914-1920. Orwell, then Eric Blair, regularly goes on 'not-too-long' country walks with her brother Prosper and sister Guiny where they develop an intimate knowledge of nature – particularly birds.

Buddicom continues: 'On very many occasions in the spring and summer, we went down to the river fishing. ... The site we liked best was one of the little sandy bays along the river bank of the gently sloping meadows on the way to Shiplake Court' (Buddicom 2006 [1974]: 28).

According to biographer Gordon Bowker, fishing becomes 'a sacred pastime', its magic symbolising for Orwell the Golden Country of his past which is about to be swept away (Bowker 2003: 25). And fish live in rivers – hence the appeal of the name Orwell.

Not surprisingly, 'smell specialist' and apparently keen angler John Sutherland highlights the fact that, for Orwell, fishing being an extremely smelly sport adds to its attractions (Sutherland 2016: 191). He writes: 'Coarse fishing has a rich menu for the nose. For example, the primitive bread-paste bait (no roach or gudgeon can resist it), moistened with spittle for those at the bent-pin entry level, then kneaded into a ball in a handkerchief with thumb and index finger. You smell it, and by the end of the day your hands smell of it … There is the dangerous toxic taste of the lead weights which you bite onto the catgut' (ibid).

MEDITATIONS ON FISHING IN *COMING UP FOR AIR*

Large parts of Orwell's 1939 novel *Coming Up For Air* (the title alluding to the movement of fish to the water's surface to breathe) are meditations on fishing as his central character, George Bowling, escapes his missus and work for a secret break in Lower Binfield. But the adventure to recapture the joys of youth is doomed to failure. As Bowling ponders: 'The civilisation which I grew up in … is now, I suppose, just about at its last kick. And fishing is somehow typical of that civilization. As soon as you think of fishing you think of things that don't belong to the modern world. The very idea of sitting all day under a willow tree beside a quiet pool – and being able to find a quiet pool to sit beside – belongs to the time before the war, before the radio, before aeroplanes, before Hitler' (Orwell 1976 [1939]: 473).

Later on Bowling remembers how, as a soldier in 1916, just before being wounded, he slips away from the frontline with some mates to do some fishing. He muses: 'Fishing is the opposite of war' (ibid: 478).

HOW FISHING IS ENTANGLED IN ETON TRAGEDY

Orwell spends two weeks fishing in June 1942, staying at Beauchamp Court Farm at Callow End, Worcestershire – where the Severn and Stour rivers converge – and the trip is probably deeply entangled in his guilt over a tragedy many years previously. The land belongs to Lord Beauchamp, an Eton contemporary and friend of Philip Yorke, whose family home, Madresfield, is close by. While at Eton, Eric Blair, as he then was, helps his friend, Steven Runciman, take revenge on Yorke for insulting him. Dabbling in a bit of childish magic, they create an image of Yorke from candle wax and break off a leg. To their horror not only does Yorke break his leg but, shortly afterwards, dies of leukaemia. According to Bowker, guilt over Yorke's sudden death plays a part in Blair's decision to quit England in 1922 to serve as an Imperial Policeman in Burma. The guilt has to be expiated and a 'remote region among strangers offered the chance to begin again with a clear conscience and a clean sheet' (2003: 478). The ghost of Yorke may also have drawn Orwell to Callow End on the 25th anniversary of his death.

With a typical attention to detail, Orwell records his catch over the two weeks – 18 dace (though one may have been a roach), one perch and two eels; on five days he catches nothing (*CWGO* XIII: 384-385). Bowker also adds astutely: 'In view of the novel about an animal revolution Orwell was still gestating, it is worth noting that at Callow End there was not only a Manor Farm but a farmer called Jones and a family called Pilkington' (2003: 478).

PASSION – RIGHT TO THE VERY END

Not surprisingly, Orwell's domestic diary for his time living on the remote Scottish island of Jura after 1946 is littered with references to fishing.[1] And significantly, when he dies in January 1950, rods stand in the corner of his room at University College Hospital. According to John Sutherland: 'It was the only luxury (it cost a whopping eight quid) we know him to have bought himself' (2016: 191). For he is determined that when he recovers he will take them to Switzerland – and there, once again, indulge his great passion for fishing.

NOTE

[1] Jura appears in a number of novels: Ian Rankin's *Question of Blood* (2003), *The Careful Use of Compliments*, by Alexander McCall Smith (2007), Anne Michaels' *The Winter Vault* (2008), *Eric is Awake*, by Dom Shaw (2012), Andrew Ervin's *Burning Down George Orwell's House* (2015) and Norman Bissell's *Barnhill: A Novel* (2019).

REFERENCES

Bowker, Gordon (2003) *George Orwell*, London: Little, Brown

Buddicom, Jacintha (2006 [1974]) *Eric & Us*, Chichester: Finlay Publisher, with a postscript by Dione Venables

CWGO (1998) *The Complete Works of George Orwell*, XX Vols, Davison, Peter (ed.), London: Secker & Warburg

Orwell, George (1976 [1939]) *Coming Up For Air*, in the *Collected Fiction*, London: Secker & Warburg/Octopus pp 431-571

Sutherland, John (2016) *Orwell's Nose: A Pathological Biography*, London: Reaktion Books

- **This essay first appeared in The Orwell Society *Journal*, 2021 pp 15-16**

Chapter Nineteen

The 'Invisible Masonic Network of Support': The Eton Factor

George Orwell attended Eton as a King's Scholar from May 1917 until December 1921 while the ghost story writer, M. R. James, was Provost of the college. This essay will explore the few comments Orwell made in various essays about his years at the college, the numerous old-Etonian friends and contacts – an 'invisible masonic Etonian network', according to biographer John Sutherland (2016) – who played such significant roles in his later career, and his ambivalent attitudes to public schools as expressed in his political writings – and in his will.

THE ETONIAN WALL OF SILENCE

Orwell devoted a major, 15,000-word essay towards the end of his life reflecting on his experiences at St Cyprian's prep school in Eastbourne, East Sussex, which he attended between 1911 and 1917. The extent to which 'Such, such were the joys' blends fact and fiction is open to debate (Orwell 1970 4 [1952]: 379-422). The picture Orwell gives of the school is somewhat nightmarish (with beatings, humiliations over wetting in the bed, disgusting food, bullying teachers and so on). Completed around 1947, though possibly begun as early as 1938, it was so critical of the married couple named Wilkes who ran the school that it was considered libellous, only being published after Orwell's death, in 1952 in America, with UK publication delayed until 1968 (Taylor 2019).

Orwell significantly wrote no similar essay reflecting on his years at Eton which he began after spending nine unhappy weeks at Wellington College. But there are a number of references to Eton dotted about his writings. He mentions his surprisingly uninterested approach to the First World War in the essay, 'My country right or left', of 1940: 'It is an instance of the horrible selfishness of children that by 1917 the war had almost ceased to affect us, except through our stomachs. In the school library a huge map of the Western Front was pinned on an easel, with a red silk thread running across on a zigzag of drawing pins. Occasionally the thread moved half an inch this way or that, each movement meaning a pyramid of corpses. I paid no attention' (Orwell 1998 [1940a]: 270).[1]

And in his essay, 'Wells, Hitler and the world state', of 1941, Orwell describes the excitement he experienced reading Wells's books at Eton: 'There you were, in a world of pedants, clergymen and golfers ... and your dull-witted schoolmasters sniggering over their Latin tags; and here was this wonderful man who could tell you about the inhabitants of the planets and the bottom of the sea, and who *knew* that the future was not going to be what respectable people imagined' (Orwell 1970 2 [1941]: 166-172, italics in the original).

For a 1940 brief, biographical entry in *Twentieth Century Authors*, he writes: 'I was educated at Eton, 1917-1921, as I had been lucky enough to win a scholarship, but I did no work there and learned very little, and I don't feel that Eton has been much of a formative influence in my life.' Five years later, for the American journal *Commentary*, he stresses: 'I was only at Eton because I had a scholarship and I don't belong to the social structures of most people who are educated there' (Taylor 2003: 41). And in an Introduction to a Ukrainian edition of *Animal Farm*, he writes: 'I was educated at Eton, the most costly and snobbish of the English Public Schools. But I had got in there by means of a scholarship, otherwise my father could not have afforded to send me to a school of this type' (ibid).

Eric Arthur Blair, as he then was, plays the Wall Game competently and even wins his Wall colour in the autumn of 1921 (Shelden 1991: 81). But he does not distinguish himself academically at Eton, ending 117th out of the 140 boys in his year in 1920 and 137th out of 168 in his final year. In his essay, 'Inside the whale', of 1940, he describes his time at the college as 'five years in a lukewarm bath of snobbery'. Eight years later, in an *Observer* review of *Eton Medley*, by B. J. W. Hill, he praises the college's 'one great virtue ... and that is a tolerant and civilised atmosphere which gives each boy a fair chance of developing his individuality' (Orwell 2003: 225-226). But in the review, he makes no mention of ever having attended Eton.

ANDREW GOW: THE ETONIAN MYSTERY DEEPENS

After Eton, Eric Blair surprises many of his contemporaries by not going up to either Oxford or Cambridge. Instead, he follows the tradition set by his father, Richard Walmesley Blair, who worked in the Opium Department, in India. And so for five years from 1922 Blair serves in the Indian Imperial Police force in Burma where his mother, Ida, has relatives. During his time in Burma, Blair grows to detest the exploitation and brutality at the core of British imperialism. As he later comments: 'I felt that I had got to escape not merely from imperialism but from every form of man's dominion over man' (Orwell 1980 [1937]: 192).

Thus, while on leave at his parents' home in Southwold, Suffolk, in 1927, he decides to resign prematurely on the pretext (fabricated) of illness (Sutherland op cit: 109). Then, strangely, one of the first men he meets after making his decision to quit the Imperial Police is Andrew Gow, his Classics tutor at Eton, now installed as a fellow of Trinity College, Cambridge. Nicknamed 'Granny Gow' because of his effeminacy, Gow had been the subject of a scurrilous poem written by the young Blair. It begins: 'Then up waddled Wog [Gow backwards] and he squeeked in Greek/'I've grown another hair on my cheek.' According to Sutherland: 'The lines are an illusion to the outrageously homosexual Cleisthenes tearing the hair out of his rump in Aristophanes' *The Frogs*' (ibid: 74). Gow had also stressed to Blair's father, after the college's final examination results were announced, that it would be a 'disgrace' for Eton even to allow Eric to apply for Oxbridge.

So how can we account for Gow's invitation to Blair to stay with him for a couple of days in 1927? It's impossible to say with any certainty. According to Peter Stansky and William Abrahams (1972: 91), Blair, privately, was fond of Gow but in public 'he took the patronizing tone that would be expected from him'. John Sutherland comments on Gow: 'He was a friend of fellow fellows such as [the poet] Housman in the 1920s and master spy Anthony Blunt in the 1930s, and his favourite student was that other master spy, Guy Burgess. In short, was Gow sounding Blair out for something in behind-the-scenes intelligence? If so it went nowhere. But at least Orwell met his idol, A. E. Housman' (Sutherland op cit: 111).

Intriguingly, Orwell offers a portrait of Gow as 'Porteous', the unofficial mentor to the anti-hero, George Bowling, in his novel *Coming Up For Air* (1939). As Sutherland comments (2016: 75): 'The actual name is borrowed from the tutor who gets Kit into college in *Sorrell and Son* [by Warwick Deeping], a novel Orwell loathed for its grovelling worship of the English class system.'

Mystery continues to follow in Gow's wake. In the spring of 1946, he writes to Blair out of the blue. His letter has not survived. But it is clear from Orwell's response that he is presuming Gow knows nothing of his life or writings in the last ten years. Yet, in fact, Gow published a book in 1945 mentioning several of Orwell's publications. Moreover, between 1939 and 1944, Gow writes letters to his former Eton and Cambridge students. And in these, Orwell is mentioned a number of times (Hurst 2020: 18).

Then, as Orwell lies dying in University College Hospital, in 1949, one of the last people to visit him is Gow. Bernard Crick, in his biography of Orwell, says he used 'the excuse for his visit that he was in UCH to see a Trinity man and happened to hear that Blair was there too. Years afterwards he could not remember the name of that Trinity man…' (Crick op cit: 577). L. J. Hurst highlights the fact that Gow mentored at Trinity Anthony Blunt and through him, the Cambridge spies, Burgess, Maclean and Philby (Hurst op cit):

> That is, Gow was the connection between the anti-Stalinist Orwell and the Cambridge ring. Gow made contact with Orwell at two significant times in his adult life: 1946 when Orwell's work began to be used as anti-communist propaganda by front organisations for the CIA and then in Orwell's last months he visited Orwell unexpectedly in University College Hospital. Not long before, Orwell had given Celia Kirwan advice for the Attlee government via his 'list' on who should be deprecated as government spokesman due to their communist sympathies. These would be the periods when Orwell's opponents would most like to know what he was doing and thinking.

Then, to add to the mystery, the art critic, Brian Sewell, names Gow as the final member of the 'Cambridge Five' Soviet spy ring in his memoir, *Outsider II* (Luck 2012). In 2016, however, Andrew Lownie, author of *Stalin's Englishman: The Lives of Guy Burgess*, identifies another man as the fifth Cambridge spy and files a Freedom of Information request to have the crucial document, held in the National Archive, released. The request is refused and that decision is upheld by a judge (Fitsanakis 2016).

RICHARD REES: AT THE START AND END OF ORWELL'S WRITING CAREER

Old-Etonian Sir Richard Lodowick Edward Montagu Rees, 2nd Baronet, was a British diplomat, writer, painter, pacifist, millionaire – and editor (with Max Plowman) of the *Adelphi* which crucially published some of Blair's earliest writings. Rees is to remain close to Orwell until his dying days. Blair's first contributions to the journal in 1930 are book reviews. Then, in the following year, it publishes 'The spike', based on his months of tramping with the down-and-outs in the East End of London (Orwell 1970 1: 58-66). The much-anthologised essay, 'A hanging' (drawing on his experiences while a policeman in Burma: see ibid: 66-71) followed in August of the same year. (His 1936 essay 'Shooting an elephant', also based on his Burma experiences, is published in *New Writing*, edited by old-Etonian John Lehmann: see below).

Despite all the encouragement Rees gives him, George Orwell (the pseudonym he adopts for his first published book, the part memoir, part fictional *Down and Out in Paris and London,* of 1933) goes on to satirise him in *Keep the Aspidistra Flying* (1936) in his portrait of Ravelston. He's a wealthy, socialist editor of a 'middle to high-brow monthly' who is acutely aware of his upper class background and defensive about his unearned income. But this in no way damages their friendship. Bowker highlights the 'Eton tradition of ruthless criticism within a continuing friendship' (2003: 288) which Orwell gleefully maintains in a number of his relationships – including that with Rees.

Jeffrey Meyers comments perceptively: 'The two men shared similarities of background as well as temperament. Both had fathers who'd worked in India; both were old-Etonians and would serve in the Spanish War. Both wore threadbare clothes, which failed to disguise their true social class' (Meyers 2000: 94). But there was also a deeply sensitive side to Orwell. Blair was one of seventy King's Scholars or Collegers. The other Etonians were Oppidans who paid high fees and tended to look down on Collegers they dubbed 'Tugs' (from toga). Rees, an Oppidan, recounts in his memoir/biography, *Fugitive from the Camp of Victory* (1961: 134), how one day in 1948, he cautiously used the word 'Tug' and although Orwell 'was too polite to say anything, he winced as if I had trodden on his tenderest corn'.

Rees introduces Orwell to other writers – such as the poet Dylan Thomas and Rayner Heppenstall who goes on to compose a moving memoir of Orwell and Thomas in *Four Absentees* (1988 [1960]). And he suggests *Adelphi* contacts whom Orwell could meet while researching poverty in the north of England in 1936 – the results later published as *The Road to Wigan Pier* (1937). Rees visits Orwell while he is composing *Nineteen Eighty-Four* on the remote Scottish island of Jura in the last years of his life; pays for livestock and farming equipment; travels part of the way with him to the sanatorium in Cranham, Gloucestershire, in 1949, and is named as executor of his literary estate (with his second wife, Sonia) in Orwell's final will (Shelden op cit: 466). As Orwell describes 'Dicky Rees' to Anthony Powell: 'Scrupulously painstaking and much more than that, of course: astonishing integrity and devotion' (Bowker 2003: 332).

L. H. MYERS: THE SECRET BENEFACTOR

In 1938, Orwell is treated for his serious lung disease at Preston Hall sanatorium, near Aylesford, in the Medway valley. Max Plowman, editor of the *Adelphi*, visits one day with his wife and novelist L. H. Myers. Biographer D. J. Taylor says of Myers: 'An immensely wealthy old-Etonian who inherited a fortune in his early twenties, he lived what his friend and novelist L. P. Hartley called a "leisured and uneventful" life' (Taylor 2003: 255). He adds: 'A depressive hypochondriac, at this point of his life obsessed with communism, his novels tended to turn on the conflict between the material and spiritual worlds. His tetralogy *The Near and the Far* (1929), for example, though set in an imaginary sixteenth-century India, is full of contemporary shadings' (ibid).

Orwell and Eileen O'Shaughnessy, whom he has married in 1936, are hoping to spend six months in a warmer climate and are saving up to rent a cottage in the south of France. Myers admires Orwell enormously and so arranges for the Plowmans to give him £300 (about £10,000 in modern currency) as an anonymous gift to help the Orwells with their travel plans. In the end, they travel to Morocco where he works on his novel *Coming Up For Air* (eventually published by Gollancz in 1939).

From 24 August to 3 September 1939, just before the outbreak of World War Two, Orwell stays at Myers' house at Ringwood, Hampshire – but Myers never reveals that he is the anonymous benefactor (Crick 1980: 377). It is at this house where Orwell dreams that the war has already begun. When he learns next day of the Soviet/Nazi pact, he believes conflict is inevitable and decides, suddenly, to shake off his pacifism of the previous two years and back the war effort – thus surprising his ILP and anarchist friends (Taylor 2003: 272). Myers and Orwell keep in touch during the war, and Orwell writes approvingly in his diaries of Myers' occasional pronouncements on the political situation. Myers sadly commits suicide in 1944 – and Orwell never knows who has given him the anonymous gift.

CHRISTOPHER HOLLIS AND ERIC SEELEY: BURMESE DAYS TOGETHER

Hollis, a contemporary in College though never a close friend, later meets up with Blair when he is passing through Rangoon in the summer of 1925 following an Oxford Union debating tour of Australasia with Malcolm Macdonald and Christopher Woodruff. They have dinner together on two occasions and Hollis reports Assistant Superintendent Blair as having distinctly racist reactionary opinions – hating particularly the Buddhist priests against whom he thinks violence is wholly desirable. Bowker quickly deconstructs the event – suggesting that Blair is carefully avoiding expressions of disaffection in the restaurant where he can have been easily over-heard. 'Probably what Hollis found was Blair in devil's advocate mood, ironically assuming his old Socratic role' (Bowker 2003: 86). But Hollis also learns that Blair has befriended a near contemporary old-Etonian, Eric Seeley, who has been ostracised by Rangoon society for marrying an Indian woman, Leila Das (Moore 2021). Intriguingly, in their path-breaking biography of Orwell, Stansky and Abrahams protect Seeley, giving him the pseudonym 'Lawrence' (1972: 158). They comment: 'It was precisely the oddness of his behavior and the disapproving reaction to it that would have excited Blair's sympathy and interest' (ibid). Bowker adds:

> Hollis must have been a reminder of what he had missed by not trying for university, and no doubt he brought news of his contemporaries' onward progress – Connolly at Oxford, the hated Majoribanks President of the Oxford Union, Harold Acton with a book of poems already published, and [Steven] Runciman on a visit to China, inside the Forbidden City teaching the last Chinese Emperor to play the piano. No doubt this visitation from the past further reanimated the writer he had all but suppressed since coming to Burma (Bowker op cit: 87).

Hollis, a Roman Catholic convert and brother of Roger Hollis, director general of MI5 from 1956-1965, is significantly mentioned by Orwell in his wide-ranging critical overview of literary trends, 'Inside the whale' (Orwell 1998 XII [1940b]: 2). After stressing how important it is for people to have something to believe in, he continues: 'There had been a sort of false dawn a few years earlier when numbers of young intellectuals, including several quite gifted writers (Evelyn Waugh, Christopher Hollis and others), had fled into the Catholic Church. It is significant that these people went almost invariably to the Roman Church and not, for instance, to the C. of E., the Greek Church or the Protestant sects. They went, that is, to the Church with a world-wide organisation, the one with rigid discipline, the one with power and prestige behind it' (ibid).

Hollis publishes a major study of Orwell in 1956. Seeley, for his part, goes on – somewhat notoriously – to quote Blair telling him that he frequents the waterfront brothels. Stansky and Abrahams respond astutely: 'Perhaps he did. Or perhaps he did not, and claimed that he did, out of pride and for effect, to impress a fellow Etonian whose experience in sexual matters was so much greater than his' (op cit; 158).

CYRIL CONNOLLY: THE ATTRACTION OF OPPOSITES?

Cyril Connolly, Blair's contemporary at both St Cyprian's and Eton, is to become a loyal friend and the eminent editor of the literary journal *Horizon* which publishes some of Orwell's most celebrated and brilliant essays. To a large extent, his essay 'Such, such were the joys' can be considered as a riposte to Connolly's autobiographical *Enemies of Promise* (1961 [1938]) in which he remembers his times at both St Cyprian's (called St Wulfric's to avoid any libel hassles) and Eton. Connolly actually mentions Blair very positively: 'I was a stage rebel, Orwell a true one. ... The remarkable thing about Orwell was that alone among the boys he was intellectual and not a parrot for he thought for himself, read Shaw and Samuel Butler and rejected not only St Wulfric's but the war, the Empire, Kipling, Sussex and Character' (ibid: 178, 179).

Jeremy Lewis (1998), in his biography of Connolly, records how Orwell, in his essay on the British intelligentsia 'Inside the whale' (1940), refers 'somewhat scathingly' to the 'Theory of Permanent Adolescence' and continues:

> Cultured middle class life has reached a depth of softness at which a public school education – five years in a lukewarm bath of snobbery – can actually be looked upon as an eventful period. To nearly all the writers who have counted during the thirties, what more has ever happened than Mr Connolly records in *Enemies of Promise*? It is the same pattern all the time: public school, university, a few trips abroad, then London. Hunger, hardship, solitude, exile, war, prison, persecution, manual labour – hardly even words (ibid: 95).

The two men get in touch for the first time since their schooldays after Connolly reviews *Burmese Days* (1934) in the *New Statesman*, in July 1935, describing it an 'admirable novel' (ibid: 289). Both men travel separately to Spain to report the civil war in 1936/1937. But while Orwell's *Homage to Catalonia* (1938) amounts to a wonderful celebration of his new-found commitment to radical socialism, the war has exactly the opposite impact on Connolly. 'The defeat of the Spanish republic shattered my faith in political action. I doubt if I have written a single political article since,' he declares in 1969 (ibid: 291).

Connolly moves into book reviewing for a range of publications: the *New Statesman and Nation*, the *Daily Telegraph* and *Sunday Times* and helps Orwell secure reviewing assignments at the *New Statesman*. Then in December 1939, after T. S. Eliot closes down his journal, the *Criterion*, in July of the same year, Connolly launches *Horizon* (with financial backing from old-Etonian Peter Watson). For a decade, it is to become one of the most celebrated literary journals of the period. Orwell becomes a regular reviewer for the journal – and it also publishes some of his most innovative essays examining aspects of contemporary culture usually ignored by literary journals aimed at the middle class: 'Boys weeklies' (March 1940), 'The art of Donald McGill', about sexy seaside postcards (September 1941), 'Raffles and Miss Blandish' (1944) and 'Politics and the English language' (1946).

Moreover, it is through frequenting the *Horizon* offices in London that Orwell becomes acquainted with Sonia Brownell, Connolly's extremely glamorous editorial assistant. Crick writes:

> She was always vague and evasive when asked when they first met or got to know each other well. Sometimes she talked of a continuous friendship since 1940 when she had first copy-edited his contributions to *Horizon*, at other times it was 'the end of the war'; but always it was 'when everyone was talking about *Burmese Days*' (which would be the Penguin reprint of 1944, although a friend claims to have given her an old Gollancz copy in 1940) (Crick op cit: 449).

After Eileen dies suddenly, aged just 39, in March 1945, Orwell spends a great deal of effort looking for a new wife who, amidst other roles, may help bring up his newly-adopted son, Richard Horatio. Various women are propositioned (including Celia Paget and Anne Popham). Finally, and much to everyone's surprise, on 13 October 1949, in University College Hospital, in central London, Sonia weds Orwell. The couple plan a honeymoon in Switzerland; on 18 January 1950, Orwell makes a new will making Sonia his sole beneficiary. Then Orwell's lung haemorrhaged on the night of 21 January 1950 and he dies before Sonia can be found (ibid: 579). He is never to enjoy the amazing worldwide success achieved with his final masterpiece, *Nineteen Eighty-Four*, which has been published just a few months earlier.

DENYS KING-FARLOW: WEDDING DAY SURPRISE

King-Farlow works with Orwell on *Election Times* and *College Days* while at Eton and both are members of the prestigious Debating Society. Michael Shelden records how one issue of the *College Days* co-incided with the annual Harrow v Eton cricket match and through advertising he claimed they made a profit of over one hundred pounds (Shelden op cit: 77-78). They also accuse the Master in College, J. F. Crace, of a 'tendency to be overfond of some boys'. He is unable to do anything about it 'because he had been compromised' (ibid: 78). Both youths share a tent during an OTC field exercise on Salisbury Plain (Stansky and Abrahams 1972: 115).

King-Farlow begins Eton in 1916 with that name but changes it to Nettleton three years later. He then reverts back to King-Farlow in 1935. In 1936, he writes to Orwell out of the blue saying he is intrigued by his decision to use a pseudonym. The letter is received by Orwell on the day of his wedding – and typically Orwell responds saying he is busy but invites him to the Stores, Wallington (Crick op cit: 303). In the end, he visits more than once and remembers Orwell following the events in revolutionary Spain closely – and being well informed about them (ibid: 308; Bowker op cit: 240).

This, then, may well support the view of John Rodden about Orwell's representation of himself as an intellectual naïf in *The Road to Wigan Pier* and *Homage to Catalonia*: 'By portraying himself as a man of common sense and by exaggerating the suddenness and force of his conversion to socialism when confronted by the suffering English miners and unemployed, Orwell depicted his former self as that of a skeptic and truth seeker. He thereby disposed the average reader to identify more readily with his dramatic conversion' (Rodden 2003: 180).

ROGER SENHOUSE: METICULOUS EDITOR OF COPY

In 1935, Roger Senhouse (1899-1970), another contemporary of Orwell at Eton, forms the publishing company Secker & Warburg with Fredric Warburg, rescuing it from receivership – and they run it together for almost 30 years. In its first years, the firm is consistently unprofitable but quickly publishes H. G. Wells, Thomas Mann, André Gide and Lewis Mumford. Then, in 1938, the company takes on Orwell's *Homage to Catalonia*, his eye-witness account of his time fighting with a neo-Trotskyist militia and alongside anarchists in the Spanish Civil War after Victor Gollancz, the ever loyal communist, turns it down on political grounds.

During Orwell's final years, Secker & Warburg publish *Animal Farm* (1945), *Critical Essays* (1946) and *Nineteen Eighty-Four* (1949). In contrast to *Homage*, which sells around 700 copies during Orwell's lifetime, the final two novels achieve immediate international acclaim. The role of Senhouse, the one-time lover of Lytton Strachey, in the making of Orwell should not be under-estimated. He serves as the meticulous editor of his copy. For instance, Peter Davison carries the corrections and queries he sends on the *Nineteen Eighty-Four* proof, on 22 February 1949 – together with Orwell's answers – and their detail is extraordinary (Orwell 1998 XIX [1948a]: 58-60).

ANTHONY POWELL: NOVELIST AND CONFIDANT

The novelist, Anthony Powell, is a close friend of Orwell throughout the 1940s – a regular dining companion, they visit each other's homes for meals and they correspond while Orwell is on Jura and in hospital and sanatoria in his final years. During the war, Powell serves for a while in Military Intelligence (Liaison), dealing with the Czechs, Belgians and French. In the first of his four volumes of autobiography, *Infants of the Spring*, he is particularly concerned to explore Orwell's personality, often with a dash of old-Etonian critique: he had 'a mixture of down-to-earth scepticism with a dash of self-dramatization. ... With all his honesty, ability to face disagreeable facts, refusal to be hoodwinked, there was always about him a touch of make-believe, the air of acting a part' (Powell 1961: 140).

In the late 1940s, he becomes principal reviewer at the *Times Literary Supplement*, and Orwell acquires some (anonymous) reviewing assignments there, too. For instance, on 17 April 1948, he reviews *Spearhead: Ten Years' Experimental Writing in America*, edited by James Laughlin (Orwell 1998 XIX [1948b]: 312-317) while on 7 August 1948, he reviews *The Novelist as Thinker*, edited by B. Rajan (ibid: 416-418).

And it is Powell, who, with Malcolm Muggeridge, finds him a smoking jacket for his marriage to Sonia Brownell in Room 65, University College Hospital, London, on 13 October 1949 – just days before he dies in January 1950. Bernard Crick comments on Orwell (1980: 576): 'He looked unexpectedly grand and military in a smoking jacket as if, son of a poor gentleman, he had pursued his natural career in Burma to a successful end and had never become a political writer. Powell remembers the jacket as crimson corduroy, but Muggeridge as mauve velvet. Memory is so fallible.'

JOHN LEHMANN: EDITOR WHO HELPS LAUNCH ORWELL'S CAREER

It is Lehmann who records in his autobiography Blair/Orwell's heroics in the Wall Game at Eton: 'I had witnessed that extremely rare event, a goal scored in the Wall Game, and what made it more exciting for me it had been scored by my fagmaster Bobbie Longden with the aid of Eric Blair' (Bowker 2003: 69).

After Eton and Trinity College, Cambridge, Lehmann (1907-1987) becomes a journalist in Vienna. Returning to the UK in the mid-1930s he launches *New Writing*, a magazine committed to anti-fascism and promoting working class authors and progressive middle class writers. Contributors include Christopher Isherwood, W. H. Auden, Edward Upward and the miner writer, B. L. Coombes. In the autumn of 1936, Orwell's much anthologised essay 'Shooting an elephant' based on his experiences as a despised Imperial Policeman in Burma, is published in *New Writing*. And in 1940, *New Writing* publishes Orwell's 'My country right or left' with its patriotic, radical, revolutionary call to arms: 'I dare say the London gutters will have to run with blood ... But when the red militias are billeted in the Ritz I shall feel that the England I was taught to love so long ago and for such different reasons is somehow persisting' (see Crick 1980: 380). Lehmann also contributes to programmes while Orwell works as a talks producer at the BBC's Eastern Service between 1941 and 1943.

DAVID ASTOR: *OBSERVER* EDITOR, VITAL FRIEND – AND THE SPOOKS

Cyril Connolly also introduces Orwell in 1941 to fellow old-Etonian, millionaire and editor David Astor who becomes, after Eileen dies, arguably the most important influence on his life. Astor has a largely undistinguished career at Eton in the late 1920s – though he claimed to have invited the novelist P. G. Wodehouse to the school (Lewis 2016: 22). Then, after reading Orwell's *The Lion and the Unicorn* (1941), he determines to contact its author. And following their meeting at the Langham Hotel, near Broadcasting House, where Orwell is working as a producer in the Indian Section of the BBC's Eastern Department, the two immediately become friends (ibid: 116). Astor's family own the *Observer;* he becomes its highly distinguished editor between 1948 and 1975 – and, from March 1942, Orwell makes regular contributions such as profiles and book reviews to the newspaper until his death.

Astor, one of the richest men in England (Sutherland 2016: 57), also introduces Orwell to the world of intelligence. Astor's intelligence ties go back as far as 1939, when he does 'secret service stuff', according to his cousin, Joyce Grenfell (Macintyre 2014: 201). He serves in the early part of the Second World War in naval intelligence alongside Ian Fleming (author of the James Bond spy novels) and later with the covert Special Operations Executive (SOE) (see Cabel 2008: 12; Knightley 1986: 131).[2] Thereafter, he maintains close links with intelligence.

Knightley records that when, in July 1939, Col. Count Gerhardt von Schwerin, of the German General Staff, arrives in the UK as a spokesman for the German opposition to Hitler, he is met by David Astor. According to Cabell, Astor and Fleming work alongside Dennis Wheatley (specialising in deception plans), later to become the occult/adventure novelist (op cit: 29, 49). Cabell also reports that Fleming may well play a central role in luring Rudolf Hess to Scotland in May 1941 (ibid: 40-52). Astor introduces Orwell to other intelligence friends through the Shanghai dining group (named after the Soho restaurant where they meet) which he has created with his friend and old-Harrovian Edward Hulton. Old-Etonians in the group include Guy Burgess (later exposed as a Soviet spy), Frank Pakenham (later Lord Longford) and John Strachey.

Most intriguingly, Orwell serves as a referee for his friend Georges Kopp – his extraordinarily brave and somewhat mysterious commander in the POUM militia in Spain in 1937 – when he seeks employment as 'an agent in the field' with MI5 in June 1942. Following an initiative by MI5's Anthony Blunt – friend of Burgess, Gow and Astor, later exposed as a Soviet spy and member of the Cambridge ring

– Orwell (described, in positive terms by MI5, as 'the well-known political writer') is interviewed by Courtenay Young (Davison 2006: 86-87).³ Orwell says Kopp, after staying in Greenwich in 1939, 'apparently joined the Foreign Legion'. He is 'not deeply interested in politics although mildly Left Wing. He was physically courageous and resolute and, generally speaking, an adventurer. He had a tendency, however to embellish things…' (ibid: 87).

How do we account for Orwell's involvement with intelligence in 1942 when he was also at the same time being followed by MI5 and Special Branch as a political subversive (Keeble 2020; Smith 2013)? It is perhaps important always to view British intelligence not as a monolithic body with a single view and strategy but as site of many conflicting interests and groupings. Indeed, many of the celebrated scoops of the intelligence specialist Chapman Pincher rely on representatives of one group spilling the beans – anonymously, of course – on another faction and its members (Pincher 1978, 1984, 2014; Andrew 2009: 627-645; Moran 2013). Perhaps one section of intelligence – linked to Astor, Blunt and Co. – is looking more favourably on Orwell than another group. After all, Orwell's wife, Eileen, works for a time in the Press and Censorship Bureau of the Ministry of Information at the start of the war – and must have passed a security vetting procedure to secure the post (Topp 2020: 279-280). And similarly Orwell has to pass security vetting before joining the BBC in 1941 as a talks producer on the Eastern Service (Bowker op cit: 282).

After leaving the BBC in November 1943, Orwell plans to report for the *Observer* from Algiers and Sicily following the Allied landings but the authorities turn him down on health grounds. A previous application to join the army in May 1940 was also turned down on health grounds. Orwell then quickly acquires the post of literary editor at the leftist weekly *Tribune*, which he holds until February 1945 when he resigns to take on the war reporting assignment for Astor's *Observer* and the *Manchester Evening News*.⁴ Is this a cover for an intelligence mission? Orwell is ill – he even has to go to a military hospital in Cologne following a serious bronchitis attack while on the assignment – but still this time appears to have either passed or by-passed a medical test. Did he receive special clearance because of the importance of his assignment?

Intriguingly, most of the men he meets in Paris on his assignment are either old-Etonians, working for intelligences services of one kind or another – or both. Most evenings, Orwell dines with Harold Acton, whom he has known vaguely at Eton and who is working as a press censor for SHAEF (the Supreme Headquarters Allied Expeditionary Force) (Bowker op cit: 324). Acton was also a close friend of Roger Hollis, future head of MI5, and Dick White, later head of both MI5 and MI6, while at Oxford University in the mid-1920s.

Orwell also meets the philosopher (old-Etonian and former pupil of Andrew Gow) A. J. 'Freddie' Ayer⁵ who is in Paris for the Secret Intelligence Service (MI6), at that time particularly concerned about the danger of a communist coup (see

Ayer 1978: 286-287; Rogers 1999: 192). By April 1946, Orwell is able to describe Ayer in a letter to Andrew Gow as 'a great friend of mine' (Orwell 1998 [1946]: 242). In another letter, in August 1946, to Celia Kirwan, later to work – as we shall see – for the secret propaganda unit, the Information Research Department, he describes him affectionately as 'Freddie' and jokes, in a postscript: 'You might ask Freddie from me, now that he has a chair in Mental Philosophy, who has the chair in non-mental philosophy' (ibid).

Another writer Orwell sees in Paris is Ernest Hemingway whom he has previously met in Barcelona during the Spanish Civil War. The American novelist, who is serving as a war correspondent and staying at the Paris Ritz, has close links with members of the Office of Strategic Services (forerunner of the CIA) and his son, Jack, is a member of the OSS's military arm (Whiting 1999: 104).

Carlos Baker's account of the meeting with Orwell in his biography of Hemingway (1972 [1969]: 672-673), based on a letter he wrote to the critic Hervey Breit on 16 April 1952, only adds to the mystery: 'Orwell looked nervous and worried. He said he feared that the Communists were out to kill him and asked Hemingway for the loan of a pistol. Ernest lent him the .32 Colt that Paul Willerts had given him in June. Orwell departed like a pale ghost.' Andrew Belsey raises some intriguing questions about this incident: Why did Paul Willerts give a pistol to Hemingway? Where did the pistol come from? Was Willerts authorised to give away weapons that presumably belonged to the military? What happened to the pistol after it was lent to Orwell? Was it returned, or did Orwell retain it?[6] Belsey comments: 'Group-Captain Paul Willerts was Air Attaché in Paris at the time. He was the son of Sir Arthur Willerts, previously head of the press office at the FO, and before that *Times* correspondent in Washington. No doubt both were familiar with the magic circle of intelligence.'[7]

Yet another spook Orwell meets in Paris is Malcolm Muggeridge (Selwyn College, Cambridge) who introduces him to P. G. Wodehouse (Dulwich College) (see Wolfe 1995: 215; Muggeridge 1975: 256-257). Muggeridge, who previously served in the intelligence corps in Mozambique and Algiers, has been assigned to keep watch on the comic novelist who is suspected of having Nazi sympathies following his broadcasts in the summer of 1941 from Berlin for the American CBS network (Donaldson 1982: 259-260). Orwell has written an article in defence of Wodehouse in February just before leaving on his assignment (though it is not published until July in the *Windmill* magazine) and may simply have wanted to express his admiration to the creator of Jeeves and Bertie Wooster (Keeble 2001). Muggeridge goes on to win the Croix de Guerre from the French government. He is assigned by Orwell's widow, Sonia, to write the 'official' biography of the author of *Nineteen Eighty-Four*, but according to his biographer, Richard Ingrams, he abandons it 'saying that he found out too much about Orwell that he would rather not have known' (Ingrams 1995: 180). However, according to Bowker: 'Privately she [Sonia] said that she considered him too slothful ever to finish the job, and in this case her judgement proved sound. After a few years of gathering material in a desultory fashion, Muggeridge, true to form, grew bored and gave up. One of Sonia's friends thinks it foundered when her relationship with Muggeridge ended' (op cit: 424).

Returning to Orwell's Paris assignment, Dorril certainly reports that in 1944 Astor was transferred to a unit liaising between SOE and the Resistance throughout Europe (Dorril 2000: 457). While in the French capital, perhaps inspired by Astor, Orwell attends the first conference of the Committee for European Federation, bringing together Resistance groups from around Europe. The French novelist and editor of *Combat*, Albert Camus, is amongst those present – though they fail to meet. Astor is later adamant that Orwell had no intelligence links[8] and Peter Davison, editor of Orwell's twenty-volume *Complete Works*, comments: 'I doubt if Orwell would be involved with intelligence – but that by no means says he wasn't.'[9]

Could Orwell have been attending the Paris conference as an 'unconscious agent' of the intelligence services? Such agents help intelligence – without actually being aware of it – delivering a message, say, attending a meeting and so on. But Astor is unlikely to have deceived his friend; and Orwell is too alert to be compromised in this way.

All this suggests that Orwell's controversial decision – on 2 May 1949 – to submit a 'little list' of 38 'crypto-communists' (briefly and somewhat crudely) to his friend, the sister-in-law of the author Arthur Koestler, Celia Kirwan (née Paget) when she is working as Robert Conquest's assistant for the secret state's newly-formed propaganda unit, the Information Research Department, may well not be an aberration (as generally thought).[10] Rather, it could have been an action consistent with his attitudes and behaviour as they developed during the 1940s – particularly through his friendship with David Astor and others in the intelligence community.[11]

Moreover, during Orwell's final years, Astor plays an enormously important role. It is he who persuades Aneurin Bevan, Orwell's old *Tribune* editor, by now Secretary of State for Health in the Attlee government, to allow the special importation of the very expensive drug, streptomycin, from the United States to treat his friend's TB.[12] It is he who owns land on the remote Scottish island of Jura where Orwell spends his final days bashing out the *Nineteen Eighty-Four* manuscript. Astor also pays for the private room (No. 65) at University College Hospital where Orwell is to marry (with Astor as Best Man) and spend his last days. It is he who hosts the lunch at the Ritz following the wedding (Orwell is too ill to attend). And after Orwell, the atheist and unpredictable to the very end, asks in his will to be buried in a churchyard, Astor finds a plot at All Saints, Sutton Courtenay, Oxfordshire, close to his family estate (Crick op cit: 580).

STEVEN RUNCIMAN: THE MYSTERY OF THE LOST FRIENDSHIP

One of Blair's closest friends at Eton is Steven Runciman, a fellow King's Scholar in the same Election who later becomes a distinguished historian with works including *A History of the Crusades*, *The Sicilian Vespers* and *The Fall of Constantinople*. It remains a mystery why the friendship does not continue after Eton. Gordon Bowker may have located the reason. In correspondence with Bowker while he is composing his biography of Orwell, Runciman reveals for the first time an extraordinary story from their time together at the college. Runciman is insulted by Philip Yorke and together with his friend Blair they devise a peculiar form of revenge. 'As Runciman recalled, they fashioned an image of Yorke from candle wax. Blair wanted to pierce it through with a pin but Runciman thought that too drastic. Instead they simply broke off a leg. To their horror, shortly afterwards, Yorke not only broke his leg but in July died of leukaemia' (Bowker 2003: 56).

Both boys must have felt profoundly guilty – and the tragedy appears to have damaged their friendship. Bowker even suggests that Orwell's decision to opt for the Imperial Police force in India rather than Oxbridge was one way of expiating the guilt (ibid: 74). Certainly, at the end of June 1942, Orwell takes a two-week break from his duties at the BBC Eastern Service fishing in Worcestershire on land belonging to Lord Beauchamp, an Eton contemporary and friend of Philip Yorke. Bowker comments: 'The ghost of Yorke might well have drawn him there, July 1942 being the twenty-fifth anniversary of his untimely death' (ibid: 294; see also Chapter 18).

In this context, is it not interesting that when Richard Rees asks him why he changed his name from Eric Blair, he says it gives him an unpleasant feeling to see his name in print because 'how can you be sure your enemy won't cut it out and work some black magic on it?' (Rees 1961: 39).

Runciman clearly never forgets his friendship with Blair. For he keeps a letter Blair sends him in August 1920, written from Grove Terrace, Polperro Railway Sorting Office, Cornwall. In it, Blair tells of his adventure as an 'amateur tramp' after missing the train at Seaton Junction. 'The corner [of a field] had a large tree for shelter, & bushes for concealment, but it was unendurably cold; I had no covering, my cap was my pillow. ... When I got to Looe I was forced to walk 4 miles in the hot sun; I am very proud of this adventure, but I would not repeat it' (Orwell 1998 X [1920]).

Runciman also maintains a clear memory of Blair at Eton. When interviewed by Stephen Wadhams for his collection *Remembering Orwell*, of 1984, he speaks warmly of his close friend. 'I thought he was very good company. He was very bright, and I think he found me a good listener perhaps. They were always amusing – and rather stringent. ... I knew him always as a rather sardonically cheerful sort of boy – I mean loving the irony, loving to have a slight grievance against masters and older boys but enjoying it' (Wadhams 1984: 20). Many of the boys had treated

Aldous Huxley, a master at the college at the time, 'appallingly badly' because of his bad eyesight. But Blair and others appreciated his use of words: 'You felt you were with someone who enjoyed words, and compared to the ordinary Eton master it was a rare, rare joy to listen to him' (ibid: 21).

ORWELL AND THE POLITICS OF PUBLIC SCHOOLS

Orwell views on public schools – as one many other issues – are ambivalent: somehow managing to mix criticism with support. On the one hand, he calls for the 'democratisation' of education in his wartime polemic *The Lion and the Unicorn* which so impresses David Astor. In it, he calls for the nationalisation of mines, railways, banks and major industries, limitation of incomes, immediate dominion status for India, the formation of an Imperial General Council, 'in which the coloured people are to be represented', and the declaration of 'a formal alliance with China, Abyssinia and all other victims of the Fascist powers'. In addition, he advocates the abolition of 'the autonomy of the public schools and the older universities and flooding them with State-aided pupils chosen simply on grounds of ability'. He continues: 'At present, public-school education is partly a training in class prejudice and partly a sort of tax that the middle classes pay to the upper class in return for the right to enter certain professions.'[13] In 1948, reviewing a book on Eton for the *Observer* (mentioned above), he comments: 'Whatever may happen to the great public schools when our educational system is reorganised, it is almost impossible that Eton should survive in anything like its present form, because the training it offers was originally intended for a landowning aristocracy and had become an anachronism long before 1939' (Orwell 2003: 225).

After his publisher, Fredric Warburg, a former scholarship boy at Westminster, visits Orwell at Cranham sanatorium in June 1949, Orwell decides to enrol his son, Richard, to Westminster. Previously, he had enrolled him to Eton but grew to detest their dress code. 'They have abandoned their top hats, I learn. It is a day school, which I prefer & I think has other good points,' Orwell writes to Julian Symons about Westminster (Orwell 1998 [1949]: 137). In the end, however, Richard goes to the Loretto private school, near Edinburgh.[14]

ETON AND ORWELL'S FINAL READINGS

Eton features prominently in his reading during his last months of life reflecting 'a mind infused with a sense of nostalgia' (Bowker op cit: 410). He reads a humorous novel by his Eton headmaster, Cyril Alington, and Connolly's *Enemies of Promise* with its chapter on the college. Orwell also reads two novels by Henry Green, the youngest brother of Philip Yorke over whose death he possibly still feels guilty. As Bowker comments (ibid): 'The past was always a powerful presence in Orwell's mind – the source of unforgotten terrors, guilt feelings and resentments. It was also a country from which he felt his greatest sense of exile.'

CONCLUSION

Orwell wrote an estimated 2 million words over his short, 20-year career (1929-1949). Yet relatively few focused on his years at Eton. Crick highlights the fact that, on being invited to an Eton reunion dinner on 7 July 1938 he chose not to go. 'Afterwards guests sent him a signed menu card: "Greetings and regrets you were not here"' (Crick op cit: 368). Yet Crick is perhaps over-generous when he comments: 'Blair made no attempt to use old-Etonian connections to further his literary career' (ibid: 212). Rather, given the importance of the old-Etonian network to Orwell, as stressed in this essay, Sutherland is probably correct to comment: 'In his later career, Orwell might as well have had the old school tie tattooed on his chest' (Sutherland op cit: 79).

NOTES

[1] Is it not interesting, also, that Orwell makes no mention of the devastating Spanish Flu pandemic which rages while he is at Eton

[2] In 1956, Astor was persuaded to offer cover for the SIS agent (later to be revealed as a Soviet spy), Kim Philby, as a journalist in Beirut. According to Stephen Dorril, after Astor is appointed editor of the *Observer* in 1947 he takes on various anti-communist emigrés with ties to propaganda and intelligence such as the German socialist, Richard Lowenthal, and Terence Kilmartin who has been employed by the MI6-sponsored Arab radio station, Sharq Al-Adna, and who, in 1949, launches the covertly-funded Foreign News Service (Dorril 2015)

[3] Courtenay Young is described as a 'counter espionage specialist' by Chapman Pincher (1984: 126). It is also Young who interviews Anthony Blunt after he makes 'limited, informal admissions' to British intelligence of being a Soviet spy in June 1951 (Davenport-Hines 2018: 414). It is interesting also that in his biography of William J. Donovan, head of OSS during the final years of the Second World War, Richard Dunlop (1982: 214) reports him meeting Orwell during a visit to London. They talked about 'how British institutions were standing up under the strain of war'. Orwell fails to record this meeting in his diaries

[4] *Tribune* was later to be distributed to British missions abroad by the Information Research Department

[5] From October 1941 to March 1943, Ayer worked as a Special Operations Executive agent within British Security Co-ordination with cover symbol G.246, in the Political and Minorities Section. He worked on intelligence relating to Latin America, particularly Argentina and Chile. In 1950, he attended the Berlin Congress for Cultural Freedom as a member of the British delegation, which was funded by the Foreign Office through the Information Research Department. See http://www.spinprofiles.org/index.php/A.J._Ayer

[6] Email to author, 22 July 2011

[7] Ibid

[8] In an interview with the author, London, November 1999

[9] In a letter to the author, 7 December 1999

[10] Some 29 names are listed in the *Complete Works*, in 1998. More names appear in *The Lost Orwell*, edited by Peter Davison (2006: 141-151) after Kirwan's daughter finds in her papers a photostat of Orwell's original list. They include Labour MPs, the future Poet Laureate Cecil Day-Lewis, authors J. B. Priestley and John Steinbeck; journalists Richard Crossman, Tom Driberg, Alaric Jacob, Cedric Dover, John Beavan; actors Michael Redgrave, Charlie Chaplin and Paul Robeson, actor and director Orson Welles, and the historians A. J. P. Taylor, E. H. Carr and Isaac Deutscher. By 1950, MI5 had amassed 250,000 files on the Communist Party and its fellow travellers (Callaghan 2021: 77)

[11] It is ironic, then, that Orwell was followed closely by a section of British intelligence from the time of his first publication in *Monde*, edited by the communist Henri Barbusse, in Paris, in 1929 until his death

[12] Taylor 2003: 392. The treatment unfortunately did not work

[13] See https://www.orwellfoundation.com/the-orwell-foundation/orwell/essays-and-other-works/the-lion-and-the-unicorn-socialism-and-the-english-genius/. Also cited in Green, Francis and Kynaston, David (2019) *Engines of Privilege: Britain's Private School Problem*, London: Bloomsbury p. 30

[14] See https://orwellsocietyblog.wordpress.com/2011/10/27/richard-blair-on-life-with-my-aunt-avril/

REFERENCES

Andrew, Christopher (2009) *The Defence of the Realm: The Authorised History of MI5*, London: Penguin

Ayer, A. J. 'Freddie' (1978) *Part of My Life*, Oxford and London: Oxford University Press

Baker, Carlos (1972 [1969]) *Ernest Hemingway: A Life Story*, Harmondsworth, Middlesex: Penguin Books

Bowker, Gordon (2003) *George Orwell*, London: Little, Brown

Cabell, Craig (2008) *Ian Fleming's Secret War*, Barnsley, South Yorkshire: Pen and Sword Books

Callaghan, John (2021) Doris Lessing: A person of interest, *Socialist History*, No. 59 pp 76-100

Connolly, Cyril (1961 [1938]) *Enemies of Promise*, Harmondsworth, Middlesex: Penguin Books

Crick, Bernard (1980) *George Orwell: A Life*, Harmondsworth, Middlesex: Penguin Books

Davenport-Hines, Richard (2018) *Enemies Within: Communists, the Cambridge Spies and the Making of Modern Britain*, London: William Collins

Davison, Peter (2006) *The Lost Orwell*, London: Timewell Press

Donaldson, Frances (2005 [1982]) *P. G. Wodehouse: A Biography*, London: Carlton Publishing Group

Dorril, Stephen (2000) *MI6: Fifty Years of Special Operations*, London: Fourth Estate

Dorril, Stephen (2015) Russia accuses Fleet Street: Journalists and MI6 during the Cold War, *The International Journal of Press/Politics*, Vol. 20, No. 2 pp 204-227

Dunlop, Richard (1982) *Donovan: America's Master Spy*, New York: Rand McNally and Company

Fitsanakis, Joseph (2016) British judge denies request to name alleged new member of Cambridge spy ring, *intelnews.org*, 20 September. Available online at https://intelnews.org/2016/09/20/01-1980/

Heppenstall, Rayner (1988 [1960]) *Four Absentees*, London: Cardinal

Hurst, L. J. (2020) Letters from Cambridge, surveillance too? Orwell Society *Journal*, No. 16 pp 17-18

Ingrams, Richard (1995) *Muggeridge: The Biography*, London: HarperCollins

Keeble, Richard (2001) Orwell as war correspondent: A reassessment, *Journalism Studies*, Vol. 2, No. 3 pp 393-406

Keeble, Richard Lance (2020) *Nineteen Eighty-Four* and the spooks, in *George Orwell, the Secret State and the Making of* Nineteen Eighty-Four, Bury St Edmunds: Abramis pp 26-38

Knightley, Phillip (1986) *The Second Oldest Profession: The Spy as Bureaucrat, Patriot, Fantasist and Whore*, London: André Deutsch

Lewis, Jeremy (1998) *Cyril Connolly: A Life*, London: Pimlico

Lewis, Jeremy (2016) *David Astor*, London: Jonathan Cape

Luck, Adam (2012) Orwell's Eton tutor is named as Fifth Man as art critic reveals Andrew Gow was Cambridge Five spymaster, *Daily Mail*, 20 October

Macintyre, Ben (2014) *A Spy Among Friends: Philby and the Great Betrayal*, London: Bloomsbury

Meyers, Jeffrey (2000) *Orwell: Wintry Conscience of a Generation*, New York: W. W. Norton & Company

Moran, Christopher (2013) *Classified: Secrecy and the State in Modern Britain*, Cambridge: Cambridge University Press

Muggeridge, Malcolm (1975) *Chronicles of Wasted Time, Vol 2: The Infernal Grove*, London: Fontana

Orwell, George (1980 [1937]) *The Road to Wigan Pier*, London: Secker & Warburg

Orwell, George (1998 X [1920]) Letter to Steven Runciman, *The Complete Works of George Orwell*, Davison, Peter (ed.) London, Secker & Warburg pp 76-77

Orwell, George (1998 XII [1940a]) My country right or left, *The Complete Works of George Orwell*, Davison, Peter (ed.) London, Secker & Warburg pp 69-72; *Folios of New Writing*, No. 2, Autumn

Orwell, George (1998 XII [1940b]) Inside the whale, *The Complete Works of George Orwell*, Davison, Peter (ed.) London, Secker & Warburg pp 86-115

Orwell, George (1970 2 [1941]) Wells, Hitler and the world state, Orwell, Sonia and Angus, Ian (eds) *Collected Essays, Journalism and Letters of George Orwell, My Country Right or Left, 1940-1943*, Harmondsworth, Middlesex: Penguin Books pp 166-172; *Horizon*, August

Orwell, George (1998 XVII [1946]) Letter to Andrew S. F. Gow, *The Complete Works of George Orwell*, Davison, Peter (ed.) London, Secker & Warburg pp 241-243

Orwell George (1998 XIX [1948]) It is What I Think, *The Complete Works of George Orwell*, Davison, Peter (ed.) London, Secker & Warburg

Orwell, George (1998 XX [1949]) Letter to Julian Symons, 16 June, Davison, Peter (ed.) *The Complete Works of George Orwell, Our Job is to Make Life Worth Living*, London: Secker & Warburg

Orwell, George (1970 4 [1952]) Such, such were the joys, Orwell, Sonia and Angus, Ian (eds) *The Collected Essays, Journalism and Letters, Vol. 4: In Front of Your Nose 1945-1950*, Harmondsworth, Middlesex: Penguin Books pp 379-422; *Partisan Review*, September-October

Orwell, George (2003) *The* Observer *Years*, London: Atlantic

Pincher, Chapman (1978) *Inside Story*, London: Sidgwick and Jackson

Pincher, Chapman (1984) *Too Secret Too Long*, London: Sidgwick and Jackson

Pincher, Chapman (2014) *Dangerous to Know: A Life*, London: Biteback Publishing

Rees, Richard (1961) *George Orwell: Fugitive from the Camp of Victory*, Carbondale: Illinois University Press

Rodden, John (2003) *Scenes from an Afterlife: The Legacy of George Orwell*, Wilmington, Delaware: ISI Books

Rogers, Ben (1999) *A Life: A. J. Ayer*, London: Chatto & Windus

Shelden, Michael (1991) *Orwell: The Authorised Version*, London: Heinemann

Smith, James (2013) *British Writers and MI5 Surveillance 1930-1960*, Cambridge: Cambridge University Press

Stansky, Peter and Abrahams, William (1972) *The Unknown Orwell*, Constable: London

Sutherland, John (2016) *Orwell's Nose: A Pathological Biography*, London: Reaktion Books

Taylor, D. J (2003) *Orwell: The Life*, London: Chatto & Windus

Taylor, D. J. (2019) *On Nineteen Eighty-Four: A Biography*, New York: Abrams Press

Topp, Sylvia (2020) *Eileen: The Making of George Orwell*, London: Unbound

Wadhams, Stephen (1984) *Remembering Orwell*, Harmonsworth, Middlesex; Markham, Ontario; New York; Ringwood, Victoria; Aukland, New Zealand: Penguin

Whiting, Charles (1999) *Hemingway Goes to War*, Stroud: Sutton

Wolfe, Gregory (1995) *Malcolm Muggeridge: A Biography*, London: Hodder and Stoughton

- **This essay is based on 'The "invisible masonic network of support" Orwell and Eton', in *George Orwell: His Enduring Legacy*, Catalogue for Exhibition at University of New Mexico Honors College/University of New Mexico Libraries, edited by Russ Davison, 2019 pp 8-14. Thanks to university for allowing republication here**

Chapter Twenty

From the Beginning to the End: The Amazing Compton Mackenzie

One man who played a major role in George Orwell's life is Compton Mackenzie. Yet he is largely marginalised in most of the conventional biographies. He is mentioned *en passant* by Michael Shelden (1991) and Jeffrey Meyers (2000) but not at all by D. J. Taylor (2003) and Robert Colls (2013) – nor by Sylvia Topp in her biography of Eileen O'Shaughnessy, Orwell's first wife (2020). Only Bernard Crick (1980) and Gordon Bowker (2003) give any hint of his importance.

Yet Mackenzie's novel *Sinister Street* is one of Orwell's favourites while he is a pupil at St Cyprian's prep school in Eastbourne and significantly it is amongst the books he owns at the time of his death in 1950. It may well help inspire him to explore the world of tramps and beggars when he returns from five years' of service as an Imperial Policeman in Burma (1922-1927).

Moreover, Mackenzie provides significant support to Orwell early on in his writing career giving favourable reviews in the *Daily Mail*. And most crucially, it is Mackenzie who helps plant the idea in Orwell's mind of retreating to a Scottish island. This is to culminate with Orwell withdrawing with his son, Richard, and sister, Avril, to the remote isle of Jura in the Inner Hebrides. And here he spends what are to prove the last years of his short life composing his dystopian masterpiece, *Nineteen Eighty-Four*.

A PREP SCHOOL PASSION

In a letter to Julian Symons in 1948, Orwell remembers his childhood admiration for H. G. Wells as a writer and recalls while at St Cyprian's (from 1911-1917) he and his friend Cyril Connolly (later as editor of *Horizon*, in the 1940s, to publish some of Orwell's most celebrated essays) read with delight *Sinister Street*. 'We also got into severe trouble (and I think a caning – I forget) for having a copy' of the novel (Crick 1980: 87). Mackenzie's biographer Andro Linklater reports that the 15-year-old Connolly kept a copy hidden by his bed and could quote it by the page. 'It may well be that some of its aura of wickedness came from the opinion of schoolmasters, but without doubt for four or five decades it ranked high on the index of forbidden adolescent literature' (Linklater 1987: 128; see also Lewis 1998: 34). Bowker comments astutely on its likely appeal to the young Eric Blair:

> It's hero, Michael Fane, is studying classics at a prep school and moves with his mother from the countryside to Kensington (close to where Aunt Nellie lived). He spends holidays in Cornwall (as the Blairs did), visits Bournemouth (where Uncle Charlie lived), and meets a girl from an Anglo-Indian family whose father is away in Burma. He visits Eastbourne and thinks what a lovely place (hollow laughter from Blair and Connolly, no doubt). Fane envies a wild-looking, unkempt boy he sees wandering down Kensington High Street and longs to be a 'raggle-taggle wanderer'. He is bullied on his first day at school but stands up to the bullies (Bowker 2003: 46).

The novel achieves a *succès de scandale* when published in two parts in 1913 and 1914, being banned by the powerful circulating libraries – hence the reaction of St Cyprian's headmistress, Mrs Wilkes (nicknamed Flip – apparently because of her floppy breasts) and headmaster, Mr Wilkes (nicknamed Sambo). They are to be the target of Blair/Orwell's vitriol in his memoir of his years at St Cyprian's, 'Such, such were the joys', published only after his death because of libel worries. John Sutherland suggests that the Wilkes probably found its satire of the prep school (Randell House) the hero of *Sinister Street* attends particularly offensive (Sutherland 2016: 68).

Today, it's difficult to understand the outrage that greets the novel – a monster, 829-page, semi-autobiographical, 200,000-word *bildungsroman*. There are hints of homosexuality at Oxford. In the final part, Fane does descend into what is described as 'London's evil underworld' of seedy prostitution, dancing girls and grinding poverty in his desperate attempts to find the love of his life, Lily. And this may have been one of the many influences – along with Jack London's *People of the Abyss* (1903) and W. H. Davies's *The Autobiography of a Super-Tramp* (1908) – behind Orwell's later tramping expeditions, captured so colourfully in his part memoir/part fictional *Down and Out in Paris and London* (1933). Fane mixes fascination, detachment and disgust towards the (sometimes violent) scenes he witnesses. And while, in one scene, he ends up in the bedroom of a prostitute he merely asks about her life and plight and quickly leaves. There is never any hint of sex.

And in his novel, *Coming Up For Air* (1976 [1939]: 501-502), Orwell acknowledges his continuing admiration for *Sinister Street*, listing it – along with H. G. Wells's *The History of Mr Polly*, Conrad's *Victory* and Wilde's *A Picture of Dorian Gray* (all of them, perhaps not surprisingly, amongst Orwell's favourites) – among the books, George Bowling, the anti-hero, devours during a tedious two years spent in a non-job for the West Coast Defence Force during the war.

PRAISE FOR EARLY NOVELS

Following the publication of *Down and Out in Paris and London*, under the pseudonym George Orwell for the first time, he commits himself entirely to the life of a 'man of letters' – writing over the next few years novels, poetry, literary essays, reviews and an investigation into poverty in the north of England. One reviewer who remains consistently positive about his writings over this period is the *Daily Mail's* Compton Mackenzie. On *Down and Out*, he comments: 'A clearly written human document which at the same time is written with so much simple force that in spite of the squalor and degradation thus unfolded, the result is curiously beautiful with the beauty of an accomplished etching on copper' (Crick 1980: 236).

And on *Down and Out*, *Burmese Days* (1934), and *A Clergyman's Daughter* (1935), Mackenzie, again in the *Mail*, offers these striking words of praise: 'I have no hesitation in asserting that no realistic writer during the last five years has produced three volumes which can compare in directness, vigour, courage and vitality with these volumes from the pen of Mr Orwell' (Linklater 1987: 258). But, on *Keep the Aspidistra Flying* (1936), he adds: 'Among the aspidistra, Mr Orwell seems to lose touch with reality ... There is some searching talk, and one or two ideas are given an airing which, though not strictly fresh, will pass as original. A novel, however, needs something more than this.' Orwell would have probably agreed – he later dismisses the novel as one of his 'silly potboilers' (Lucas 2003: 30).

Orwell is later able to repay the compliment to Mackenzie. Much of Orwell's early journalism is published in *Adelphi*, edited by his friend and fellow old-Etonian Sir Richard Rees. And reviewing *Walls Have Mouths*, W. F. R. Macartney's gruelling account of his ten years in Parkhurst Prison, in November 1936, he is able to highlight approvingly Mackenzie's contribution. Orwell writes that 'the cold, rigid discipline of a modern English jail, the solitude, the silence, the everlasting lock-and-key ... is more cruel and far more demoralising than the barbarous punishment of the Middle Ages' (*CWGO* X: 514). He ends: 'Mr Compton Mackenzie's prologue and comments might appear at first sight to be unnecessary, but actually they have the effect of pulling the book together and supplying useful corroboration. Probably without Mr Mackenzie's help the book would not have been published, in which case everyone who cares for decency must be deeply grateful to him' (ibid: 515).

THE CRUCIAL MEETING

One of Orwell's most celebrated essays focuses on the writings of Charles Dickens which appears in the collection *Inside the Whale*, of 1940. Soon after its publication, on 25 May, Orwell addresses the thirty-fourth annual conference of the Dickens Fellowship at the Comedy Restaurant, Panton Street, London. He says he has been reading Dickens's principal novels since early childhood – with *David Copperfield* his favourite (*CWGO* XII: 167). And he argues that Dickens's tradition 'moves outside the realm of literature'. According to a report of the meeting: 'Mr Orwell said that ten years ago he had been among the hop-pickers and there he had met men who, although they had not read the book, nevertheless knew about Oliver Twist; they knew it instinctively and felt that the author had struck a memorable blow on their behalf' (ibid).

Most importantly, Mackenzie, who proposes the toast to the Immortal Memory of Dickens, and Orwell meet here for the first time. As Bowker comments (2003: 263), it is to prove a 'fateful meeting'. For in their chat a seed is planted that is to flower in Orwell's decision a few years later to withdraw to the remote Scottish island of Jura. According to Bowker: 'It was Mackenzie who excited Orwell – always fascinated by Robinson Crusoe – with the prospect of one day living the self-reliant island life, remote from the horrors of the modern world, its streamlined falsity and genocidal wars' (ibid).

MACKENZIE 'THE MAN WHO LOVED ISLANDS'

Today largely forgotten, Mackenzie (1883-1972) is one of the most extraordinary characters of the last century. A child prodigy who reads *Don Quixote* when only four, he goes on to write fiction, biography, children's stories, ten volumes of memoir, reviews, satires, poetry, cultural commentaries and spy stories though he is best known for his best-selling comic novels set in Scotland, *The Monarch of the Glen* (1941) and *Whisky Galore* (1947).

During the First World War, he is a master spy running British intelligence operations in Greece. For his wartime services he is awarded an OBE in 1952, while the French grant him the Legion of Honour, the Serbs the Order of the White Eagle, and the Greeks the Order of the Redeemer. But following the publication of his no-holes-barred account of his spying years in *Greek Memories*, in 1932, he is prosecuted at the Old Bailey under the Official Secrets Act for quoting from supposedly secret documents. He is fined and has to pay substantial costs. As Paul Lashmar points out (2020: 45): 'He got his own back by writing the satirical novel *Water on the Brain* [of 1933], which lampooned the SIS [British foreign intelligence] under the name MQ9 (E), the Directorate of Extraordinary Intelligence.'

A man of varied interests, a Roman Catholic convert, Rector of Glasgow University from 1931-1934, keen gardener, celebrated raconteur, a popular broadcaster for the BBC and lover of Siamese cats, in 1923, he and his brother-in-law Christopher Stone launch the still-surviving *Gramophone* magazine.

He also loves living on islands. While on Capri, in 1919, he finds a flat for D. H. Lawrence and his wife, Frieda, whom he has known since meeting them in Buckinghamshire in 1914 (Worthen 2005: 220). And the two men spends hours together sharing their dreams of living in the South Pacific. Nothing comes of their plans and Lawrence leaves for Sicily. But Mackenzie's island obsession continues. So in 1920 he purchases two tiny Channel Islands, Herm and Jethou. Then, in the early 1930s, dissatisfied with his Channel Islands adventure, he purchases the Shiant Islands in the Western Isles for the knockdown price of £500, flaunts his Scots ancestry and identity and becomes a fervent advocate of Scottish Nationalism. Lawrence never forgets Mackenzie – and Cathcart, the central figure of his short story, 'The man who loved islands', of 1926, is loosely based on him. But as John Worthen comments in his biography of Lawrence: 'It is a story which draws on so many of the tendencies and potentialities in Lawrence's life and temperament that it goes far beyond the elements of Mackenzie's life which had been its starting point' (2005: 346).

ORWELL AND THE JURA DREAM

Having met Mackenzie, Orwell confides to his diary on 20 June 1940: 'Thinking always of my island in the Hebrides, which I suppose I shall never possess nor even see. Compton Mackenzie says even now most of the islands are uninhabited (there are 500 of them, only 10 per cent inhabited at normal times), and most have water and a little cultivable land, and goats will live on them' (*CWGO* XII: 188). Bowker comments astutely: 'The dream would one day come true, but only when it was rather too late for him fully to savour the idyll' (2003: 263).

In 1944, Orwell learns that his friend and *Observer* journalist, David Astor, owns land on Jura, a sparsely populated island off the west coast of Argyllshire, and he sets off in September to explore. He immediately falls in love with the island. His wife, Eileen, dies tragically in March 1945 – just months after they adopt baby Richard – while he is away on the Continent reporting on the final days of the war for the *Observer* and *Manchester Evening News*. He returns to Jura the following September for a two-week break, discovers a large deserted farmhouse, Barnhill, near the northern tip of the island, and applies to the Laird, old-Etonian Robin Fletcher, to lease it. The deal is quickly done. And so Orwell's final years are to be spent living his island dream – discussed all those years ago with Mackenzie.

Indeed, Orwell never forgets Mackenzie. Significantly in the list of 144 books he reads, amazingly, during 1949 when he is suffering terribly from TB and close to death, *Sinister Street* appears between J. Langdon-Davies's *Russia Puts the Clock Back* and Agatha Christie's *Sparkling Cyanide* (*CWGO* XX: 222). And in the list of 389 books owned by Orwell at his death, it falls between A. E. Macglagen's *The*

Bayeux Tapestry and A. M. Maclennan's *A Pronouncing and Etymological Dictionary of Gaelic Language* (ibid: 294). In a way, then, Mackenzie has been with Orwell – from the beginning right to the end.

REFERENCES

Bowker, Gordon (2003) *George Orwell*, London: Little Brown

Colls, Robert (2013) *George Orwell: English Rebel*, Oxford: Oxford University Press

Crick, Bernard (1980) *George Orwell: A Life*, Harmondsworth, Middlesex: Penguin

CWGO (1998) *The Complete Works of George Orwell*, XX Vols, Davison, Peter (ed.) London: Secker & Warburg

Lashmar, Paul (2020) *Spies, Spin and the Fourth Estate*, Edinburgh: Edinburgh University Press

Lewis, Jeremy (1998) *Cyril Connolly: A Life*, London: Pimlico

Linklater, Arno (1987) *Compton Mackenzie: A Life*, London: Chatto & Windus

Lucas, Scott (2003) *Orwell*, London: Haus Publishing

Meyers, Jeffrey (2000) *Orwell: Wintry Conscience of a Generation*, New York and London: W. W. Norton and Company

Orwell, George (1976 [1939]) *Coming Up For Air*, in the *Collected Fiction*, London: Secker & Warburg/Octopus pp 431-571

Shelden, Michael (1991) *Orwell: The Authorised Biography*, London: Heinemann

Sutherland, John (2016) *Orwell's Nose: A Pathological Biography*, London: Reaktion Books

Taylor, D. J. (2003) *George Orwell: The Life*, London: Chatto & Windus

Topp, Sylvia (2020) *Eileen: The Making of George Orwell*, London: Unbound

Worthen, John (2005) *D. H. Lawrence: The Life of An Outsider*, London: Allen Lane

- **Originally published as 'From the beginning to the end: The extraordinary Compton Mackenzie', 29 November. https://orwellsociety.com/from-the-beginning-to-the-end/**

Chapter Twenty-one

Homage and the Forgotten Memoir of the Spanish Civil War

Orwell's eye-witness account of his time fighting alongside Republican militiamen in the Spanish Civil War, *Homage to Catalonia*, of 1938, sold only 700 copies during his lifetime. Yet two years earlier, Secker & Warburg, the publishers of *Homage*, had brought out John Langdon-Davies's *Behind the Spanish Barricades: Reports from the Spanish Civil War* and it had been a best-seller.

Langdon-Davies's text is now largely forgotten (though it was republished in 2007 by the now sadly defunct Reportage Press). But it is well worth re-visiting. And while both men quarrelled bitterly over their analyses of the fighting that broke out between factions of the left in Barcelona in May 1937 (and which both witnessed first-hand), it is interesting to note that amongst the 144 books Orwell listed as having read in 1949 – the year before he died – is Langdon-Davies's *Russia Puts the Clock Back: A Study of Soviet Science and Some British Scientists*.

Unlike Orwell, who arrived in Spain in December 1936 largely ignorant of its language, culture and politics, Langdon-Davies, by this time, was well-acquainted with the country. Born in South Africa in 1897, he came to England at the age of six and was jailed after refusing to wear a military uniform when called up in 1917. He first settled in Catalonia with his wife and two young sons in 1921 – and developed contacts with left-wing intellectuals and nationalists. In 1923, he reported for the *Daily News* from Barcelona on the coup by Miguel Primo de Rivera. Returning to the Catalan coast in 1926, he wrote *Dancing Catalans*, a study of the national dance, the *sardana*. In 1927, his *A Short History of Women* was published – and Virginia Woolf comments on it approvingly in her seminal *A Room of One's Own*, of 1929.

233

In *Behind the Spanish Barricades*, he recounts the time he spends in Spain – first in May 1936 when reporting on the May Day celebrations in Madrid for the *News Chronicle* and then in August of the same year when he covers the civil war.

There are, in fact, some striking similarities with *Homage*. Orwell's account begins, memorably, with the description (with certain homo-erotic undertones) of his meeting with an Italian militiamen at the Lenin Barracks and of the revolutionary spirit which he finds so inspiring in the streets of Barcelona. 'It was the first time that I had ever been in a town where the working class was in the saddle. .... There was much in it that I did not understand, in some ways I did not even like it, but I recognized it immediately as a state of affairs worth fighting for. Also I believed that things were as they appeared, that this was really a workers' State and that the entire bourgeoisie had either been killed, or voluntarily come over to the workers' side; I did not realize that great numbers of well-to-do bourgeois were simply lying low and disguising themselves as proletarians for the time being' (Orwell 1962 [1938]: 9).

'A CITY GIVEN OVER TO THE PROLETARIAT'

Reporting the 1 May demonstration in Madrid, Langdon-Davies writes colourfully (2007 [1936]: 1): 'A city given over to the proletariat. Those members of the bourgeoisie who have not driven away the night before to some country retreat, are staying in bed or peeping with distaste from behind closed shutters. ... The banners are innumerable and for those willing to understand they are warnings of the storm which will break ere long. As each banner passes, the crowd salutes, clenched fist, bent left or right arm, the salute of the Popular Front or, less frequently, but too frequently for the pleasure of those who may be peeping from behind the closed shutters, a straight arm with the first stretched skywards. The trees themselves, pollarded into gaunt skeletons, are raising their boughs in the communist salute.'

Langdon-Davies is at pains throughout the book to stress that the poor in Spain are revolting quite independently against the appalling oppression they suffer – not assisted by any Moscow gold as Fleet Street was claiming. 'No Moscow Jew had trudged those Extremaduran wastes with a pail of red paint to put up on every broken wall the sickle and hammer of angry hope. The writing on the wall has come from men and women grown tired of waiting for the redress of centuries-old wrongs' (ibid: 17).

The extraordinary revolutionary fervour of the time is captured, in particular, by Langdon-Davies in his report of the annual conference of the CNT syndicalist trade union organisation in Zaragoza. 'They discussed everything on the face of the earth – nudism, vegetarianism, esperanto, marriage and sex generally; the need for libertarian soviets, the possibilities of co-operating with socialists and communists, programmes of strikes, sabotage and expropriation' (ibid: 27).

Helped by his command of the language, he paints moving pictures of the poor. In one peasant hut, he meets men who 'had never tasted meat in their whole lives. They greeted us with the courtesy of any Spaniard. They talked and laughed with precisely the same brand of wit as Sancho Panza had. In this room, on sacking, slept night by night three married couples' (ibid: 19).

RADICAL, DEMOCRATIC POLITICS

Like Orwell, Langdon-Davies is clearly inspired by the radical, democratic politics he sees in action. Porta de la Selva, 'a little fishing village in a fold of the Pyrenees', is practically owned by the Fishermen's Co-operative. 'The fishermen own the tools of their trade, not only their nets and their boats, but the curing factory, the stores and storehouse, the refridgeration plant, the shops where daily necessities are bought, the olive oil refinery, the olive groves, the café, the hotel, the theatre and assembly room, everything that they need and use. ... there is something very Spanish about Port de la Selva and its co-operation, the spontaneous local experimenting in the art of living together' (ibid: 39).

In another village, Ansó, the local doctor and schoolmaster show off their library. 'But where are the books?' he asks looking at almost empty shelves. 'They are all out being read,' comes the answer. To which Langdon-Davies responds appropriately: 'I had found the perfect library at last, the library without any dead or sleeping volumes' (ibid: 42).

On his second trip in August 1936, Langdon-Davies travels on a motorbike with his 16-year-old son, Robin, leaving him finally with the 'revolutionary committee' in Puigcerdà for safe keeping. In the Ramblas, Barcelona, he watches the crowds. 'Today there is not a hat, a collar, or a tie to be seen among them; the sartorial symbols of the bourgeoisie are gone, a proletarian freedom has swarmed in along the Calle del L'Hospital and the Calle del Carmen from the Parallelo. ... The *Solidaridad Obrera*, a syndicalist paper has a splendid editorial against hats and ties. So long as there are no hats and ties seen on the Ramblas the workers may know that the victory is on their side. Hats have been a useless symbol of pride and privilege' (ibid: 99).

Similarly, in *Homage*, Orwell highlights the politics of dress, writing: 'In outward appearance it was a town in which the wealthy classes had practically ceased to exist. Except for a small number of women and foreigners there were no "well-dressed" people at all. Practically everyone wore rough working-class clothes, or blue overalls or some variant of the militia uniform' (op cit: 9; see also Chapter 1.). Significantly, at the end of the book, as Orwell and his new wife, Eileen, who has joined him at the frontline, prepare to escape from Spain as the communists ruthlessly suppress the Trotskyists and anarchists, the accompanying dampening of the revolutionary spirit is reflected in clothes. Now the safest thing is to look 'as bourgeois as possible' (op cit: 215).

Langdon-Davies, throughout his assignment, is all eyes. On the last Sunday of August he strolls down the Paseo de Graciá and notices manifestoes from the FAI-CNT trade union groups stuck up on trees. They are headed 'La Organizatión de Indisiplina' and tell how the workers of Spain have succeeded in defeating fascism thanks to the glorious life-giving power of Indiscipline. Langdon-Davies reflects: 'I am not a theologian of the Religions of the Left, and I have no idea at all what the exact difference is between Discipline and Better Organised Indiscipline, but as I read the notice on the tree-trunk I realised once again the strange conflict between order and disorder, between reason and exuberance, that rages over the birth of new things' (op cit: 106).

He visits Barcelona's notorious Fifth District which 'stinks of drains, contains sordid brothels, filthy little cafés, deformed beggars, advertisements for quack cures of venereal disease, nearly every ugly reality that most of us like to forget'. He visits a brothel with his friend, Kim, and they drop into little café bars 'where the most hideous women were serving out anis and rum to habitués who seemed to have grown into the furniture' (ibid: 108). But what strikes him most of all are the residents' dignity and comradeship. 'Because they have almost nothing in the way of possessions, because they have no hope of ever getting out of this squalor, because they live so close together that no individual can wrap himself away from his neighbours in a veil of hypocrisy and pretense, the men and women of the Fifth District understand comradeship. Because they have so little to be proud of outside themselves, they must maintain personal dignity and make of mere existence something to be proud of' (ibid: 109).

PROMOTING WOMEN'S RIGHTS

The revolution has also promoted women's rights. He notices a communist militia march by – with 30 to 40 women (he calls them girls) amongst them. 'These girls were not asking for any special treatment on account of their sex; they had forgotten the he and the she; just as syndicalist, socialist, and republican had scrapped their differences, so maleness and femaleness had gone into obscurity as irrelevant to the moment' (ibid: 125).

One chapter focuses on 'The Burning of the Churches' which, he says, is largely the work of the anarchists and Bakuninites. '…where Marxists are strong, the churches are locked up and the keys deposited in the mayor's office, and where the Bakuninites have the power the churches have been burned' (ibid: 144).

Langdon-Davies's admiration for Largo Cabellero – appointed Prime Minister in September 1936, and whose administration is the first in Europe to include communists – emerges clearly when he interviews him for the *News Chronicle*: '…when you realise that every day he motors out to the Somosierra Front and does his bit of fighting, marches around encouraging his militiamen who worship him – then you see that his physical unimpressiveness is really a positive quality, a useful economy, a machine-like accuracy of mind and body that needs no romantic, theatrical or rhetorical frills' (ibid: 165).

The book ends with a chapter titled 'What it means to us' in which the case for the Spanish revolution is put powerfully – together with a call for the British government to end its policy of non-intervention. 'The simple fact is that Europe is divided into two halves, the Fascist International and the Anti-Fascist International, and our government has done all it can to give comfort to the first and to embarrass the second.' In addition, he damns in no uncertain terms Garvin's *Observer* newspaper for its attacks on what it dubs the 'Red Regime' in Madrid (ibid: 211, 208).

Langdon-Davies duly returns to the UK, bashes out *Behind the Spanish Barricades* in five weeks – and sees it published to acclaim late in 1936. He is back in Barcelona by the following May to witness the street fighting. As Miquel Berga points out, Langdon-Davies begins to make notes sitting in the Rugby Bar at the corner of Pau Claris and Aregó streets at 11pm on 3 May; Orwell ponders the situation from the roof of the Poliorama Theatre on the Ramblas where he has been sent to keep guard on the headquarters of the POUM militia directly opposite (Berga 2016: 286-294).

PUSHING THE OFFICIAL COMMUNIST LINE

In his report for the *News Chronicle*, Langdon-Davies pushes the official communist line – that the street fighting is all down to a frustrated putsch by the Trotskyite POUM. Not surprisingly, Orwell devotes a number of pages in *Homage* to patiently refuting Langdon-Davies's version of events. He writes: 'I am not attacking Mr Langdon-Davies's good faith; but admittedly he left Barcelona as soon as the fighting was over, i.e. at the moment when he could have begun serious inquiries, and throughout his report there are clear signs that he has accepted the official version of a "Trotskyist revolt" without sufficient verification' (op cit: 162).

Langdon-Davies returns to the controversy in his article for the communist *Daily Worker*'s special supplement on Spain, on 21 May 1938, where he takes the opportunity to damn *Homage*: 'The road to Wigan Pier leads on to Barcelona and the POUM. The value of the book is that it gives an honest picture of the sort of mentality that toys with revolutionary romanticism but shies violently at revolutionary discipline. It should be read as a warning' (Berga op cit).

After the terrible events of May 1937, Langdon-Davies's career is quite remarkable. Later that year he and colleagues launch a charity to help children whose lives have been overwhelmed by war, setting up a colony for 200 children in Puigcerdà on the French border. In the UK they raise funds, encouraging hundreds to 'sponsor' a child. Today, that organisation, known as Plan, works with 11 million children in more than 60 countries.

Moreover, after the Soviet/Nazi pact of August 1939, Langdon-Davies becomes a fervent anti-Stalinist and for his services to the British Home Guard during the war he is awarded the MBE. Orwell, one of the greatest writers of the last century, in contrast, wins no award during his lifetime – bar a 1,000 dollar literary prize from the leftist US journal, *Partisan Review*.

REFERENCES

Berga, Miquel (2003) George Orwell in his centenary year: A Catalan perspective, the Anglo-Catalan Society. Available online at https://www.anglo-catalan.org/downloads/joan-gili-memorial-lectures/lecture05.pdf

Berga, Miquel (2016) May Days in Barcelona: Orwell, Langdon-Davies and the cultural memory of war, Rodden, John and Cushman, Thomas (eds) *George Orwell: Into the 21st Century*, London: Routledge

Langdon-Davies, John (2007 [1936]) *Behind the Spanish Barricades: Reports from the Spanish Civil War*, London: Reportage Press

Orwell, George (1962 [1938]) *Homage to Catalonia*, Harmondsworth, Middlesex: Penguin

- **Originally published as 'The forgotten memoir of the Spanish civil war', 22 August 2020. https://orwellsociety.com/the-forgotten-memoir-of-the-spanish-civil-war/**

Appendix

My Seven Lucky Years Immersed in Orwell

> I stepped down as chair of The Orwell Society in 2020. Here, I reflect on the many diverse directions my research into Orwell – the man and his writings – took over those years.

I had always wanted to meet Orwell's son, Richard Blair. While Professor of Journalism at the University of Lincoln in 2012, a colleague told me about the formation of The Orwell Society with Richard Blair its patron. Here was my chance. I contacted the group, was invited to attend committee meetings and, very quickly, was elected chair in 2013. Since then, along with a wide range of other interests – such as media ethics, the media coverage of US/UK imperialism, peace journalism, journalists' ties to the secret state, profile writing, sex and journalism, literary journalism – Orwell's life and writings have been major research topics for me.

Orwell must be one of the most researched writers on the planet yet at the start of the century his novels, essays and works of reportage such as *The Road to Wigan Pier* (1937) and *Homage to Catalonia* (1938) attracted the most academic interest. His 80 'As I Please' columns for *Tribune* between 1943 and 1947 and his war reporting from the Continent in 1945 were largely ignored. So here were just the openings I needed to venture into the crowded world of Orwell Studies. My first foray came, then, in 2001 when my analysis of his war reporting from the Continent in 1945 was carried in *Journalism Studies*. And my study of those *Tribune* columns appeared in a collection of essays on a range of literary journalists I jointly edited titled *The Journalistic Imagination*, published by Routledge in 2007.

Those two pieces provided the base on which I was able to move into other ignored and often controversial areas while OS chair.

Orwell is too often associated with the dull, dystopian world of *Nineteen Eighty-Four* and misrepresented as lacking in humour. For instance, the *Oxford Book of Humorous Prose* (Muir 1990) fails to include any piece by Orwell. I would actually argue that Orwell is one of Britain's greatest humourists. In my role as chair of The Orwell Society I gave public talks. All I had to do was read excerpts from his writings (always so vital and accessible) and people would laugh. In my own studies of Orwell's humour, I explore the lighter side of his personality, the humour amidst the horror of the Spanish trenches in *Homage to Catalonia*, the constant high spirits and droll wit in his 'As I Please' columns in *Tribune* and essays such as 'Some thoughts on the common toad', the many satiric elements in *Nineteen Eighty-Four* – and his polymathic knowledge of (and highly opinionated views on) English humorous writing in his 1,884-word essay 'Funny not vulgar' (first published in the *Leader*, on 28 July 1945).

Much of the debate over Orwell's essay 'Such, such were the joys', about his years at St Cyprian's prep school, concentrates on the extent to which his recollections are truthful or imagined. Little attention has been directed at the literary elements of the essay. Thus in my studies, I examine in detail the literary devices Orwell uses: such as dramatic narratives, verbatim dialogue, the balancing of tones and attitudes, the sexually explicit, the polemical, confessional and intimate voices, historical generalisations, the journalistic style and social/cultural analysis.

Moreover, Orwell's stint as a film reviewer for *Time and Tide* (the vaguely right-of-centre journal edited by Margaret, Lady Rhondda) between October 1940 and August 1941 has been largely ignored by commentators – or his reviews have been dismissed as undistinguished. In my research, I challenge that view arguing – along with my late friend and colleague John Tulloch – that Orwell often came up with original insights in his film reviews and displayed an awareness of its possibilities as both an art form and propaganda tool and its potential for remaking the way we understand the world.

The central place of sexuality in Orwell's writings has too often been ignored by critics and biographers. In contrast, I have explored his daring treatment of homosexuality (at a time when it was illegal in the UK) in *Down and Out in Paris and London*, the homo-eroticism in *Homage to Catalonia*, his almost New Mannish frankness about his own sexual development in 'Such, such were the joys' and his wonderful celebration of the pleasures of sex in his essay on the seaside postcards of Donald McGill in which he combines *faux* shame with a joyful affirmation of the hedonistic, Sancho Panza attitude to life.

Orwell's decision to hand over on his death bed the 'little list' of crypto-communists to the Information Research Department in 1949 remains highly controversial. My research over several essays, however, suggests that the act (which I consider a gross error on his part) is best seen as consistent with those of a man already caught up for a number of years with intelligence – largely through his friendship with David Astor, whose family owned the *Observer*. Indeed, it could be argued that after Orwell's wife, Eileen, died suddenly in 1945, fellow old-Etonian Astor, whose ties to intelligence dated back to 1939, became the most important person in his life. My interests in Orwell, the secret state and sexuality come together in my analysis of *Nineteen Eighteen-Four* in which I focus on the crucial role of Julia, the 'girl from the Fiction Department' with whom Winston Smith conducts a passionate, secret affair. In particular, I examine the many clues, strangely ignored by so many commentators, Orwell provides suggesting that Julia is, in fact, a Party spy, luring Winston into a honeytrap.

The novel's stark warning about a Big Brother surveillance society engaged in constant warfare against manufactured enemies can only be understood in the context of Orwell's complex relationship with the secret state. But Orwell is far too clever to present a definitive picture of Julia since, in a totalitarian world dominated by the myths and lies of intelligence, nothing is certain. In addition, this perspective gives the novel a particularly modern character – making it essentially about the slippery, unstable nature of meaning.

Orwell has drawn, for understandable reasons, particular wrath from feminist critics such as Daphne Patai, Beatrix Campbell and Deirdre Beddoe. Yet, Orwell was a complex man with many sides to his personality – and, as I have stressed, one was distinctly un-misogynistic. His mother was a lively, independent and sports-loving feminist. And many of the women he was to be associated with (Jacintha Buddicom, aunt Nellie, Eleanor Jaques, Stevie Smith, Inez Holden, Mabel Fierz, Celia Kirwan – not to mention his two wives Eileen O'Shaughnessy and Sonia Brownell) were forceful characters who would hardly have tolerated a misogynist. As a father to Richard Horatio, whom he and Eileen adopted in June 1944, Orwell certainly confounded the expectations of his day, displaying considerable affection for the child, taking him for walks in a pram – and even changing his nappies (though with a cigarette in his mouth).

And in a number of his 'As I Please' columns he can surprise with the range of his subject matter. In one, he offers a potted history of women's make-up, of all things. Later, responding to a reader's letter, he uses a serious critique of women's papers – such as *Lucky Star*, the *Golden Star* and *Peg's Paper* (completely ignored by the intellectuals of his day) – to explore the ways in which press proprietors and the ruling class in general promote the notion of the moral superiority of the poor as 'the deadliest form of escapism'. In 1945, Orwell reviews Virginia Woolf's seminal feminist text, *A Room of One's Own*, 'a discussion of the handicaps which have prevented women, as compared with men, from producing literature of the first order'. There is no condemnation. Rather, he suggests that 'almost anyone of the male sex could read it with advantage'.

One of the highlights of this year has been the publication, finally, of Sylvia Topp's superb biography of Eileen. In a number of essays I have sought to highlight the ways in which Topp directs attention to crucial aspects of both her life and Orwell's – totally missed by previous (male) biographers. Topp highlights the probable influence Eileen had on Orwell's writings. Yet she also influenced his politics. For instance, as a paid-up member (like me) of the pacifist organisation, the Peace Pledge Union, she probably encouraged his fervent anti-war stance from 1937 right up until the Russian/German pact just before the outbreak of war in 1939.

I have also given a number of talks on Orwell's impact on higher education – such as in the fields of English Studies, Intelligence Studies, Literary Journalism and Media Ethics. While Orwell is celebrated for having virtually invented the discipline of Cultural Studies with his commentaries on many of the manifestations of popular culture that so fascinated him – crime novels, boys' weeklies, women's magazines, cups of tea, common lodging houses, Woolworth's roses and handwriting – he is less well known for anticipating the emergence of Media/Journalism Studies and Media Sociology with his detailed, critical deconstructions of the press.

In conclusion, it's intriguing to consider that Orwell never went to a university. Yet, in effect, his whole life can be considered an educational project. He had an enormous appetite and curiosity about life – a deep desire to understand himself and the times he was living in. And through his wonderfully original and often witty writings he is seeking to encourage us all to join him on his journey.

- **Originally published as 'My seven lucky years immersed in Orwell', Orwell Society *Journal*, No. 17, Autumn 2020 pp 39-41**

Afterword

Anti-Semitism: Moving Beyond Upbringing and Preconceptions

Tim Crook

George Orwell realised that anti-Semitism was the humanitarian curse of his age, had corrupted his own personal outlook, consciousness and writings – and needed addressing as the ever-present political evil of his time. His own writing on the subject reflects the abiding honesty with which he challenges his own past, culture and prejudices. Although he died so cruelly from tuberculosis in 1950 at the early age of 46, he lived long enough to witness what became known as the Holocaust and the Nazis' 'Final Solution' for world Jewry. This essay examines in detail the debate about whether he fully appreciated their significance.

The experience of concentration camp survival has resulted in some of the most haunting writing of the twentieth century. It challenges the very nature of faith, humanity and literature. Primo Levi's observation: 'Dawn came on us like a betrayer; it seemed as though the new sun rose as an ally of our enemies to assist in our destruction' (Levi 1996: 16) highlights the way in which anti-Semitism threatened all notions of hope and redemption. The Holocaust represented an unprecedented challenge to writers and philosophers who experienced and witnessed it.

THE ORWELL BIOGRAPHERS AND ANTI-SEMITISM

BERNARD CRICK

Bernard Crick highlights the way in which Orwell's reading of Dr Ley's statement that 'inferior races, such as Poles and Jews' do not need so much to eat as Germans (Crick 1992 [1980]: 143) reminds him of his witnessing racism while serving as an Indian Imperial Policeman in Burma (1922-1927). Here, he watched a police sergeant giving a coolie 'a terrific kick on the bottom that sent him staggering across the deck. Several passengers, including women, murmured their approval' (ibid). Crick criticises *Down and Out in Paris and London* (1933) for its 'rather nasty, indeed positively anti-Semitic anecdotes about the swindling Jew who is himself swindled over the face powder that looks like cocaine' (ibid: 201). There is also an account of Orwell's attendance at an Oswald Mosley British Union of Fascists rally in Barnsley – reported in *The Road to Wigan Pier* (1937) – where 'His speech was the usual clap-trap – Empire free trade, down with the Jew and the foreigner' (ibid: 292). Crick references Orwell's encounters with his future publisher Fred Warburg when they both serve in the same Home Guard unit in St John's Wood, London. Orwell is the sergeant; Warburg the corporal and a Jew. Crick describes how Warburg was 'questioned closely and rather sceptically by Orwell about Zionism and the beliefs of British Jews' (ibid: 400).

He reports how Orwell was on the receiving end of racist abuse when 'A dozen or more violently anti-Semitic letters followed an *Observer* review of 30 January 1944 of a book called *The Chosen People*; and his *Tribune* piece of 11 February about these letters touched off another barrage' (ibid: 448). Crick argues that Orwell's public comments and experiences show him 'fully purged of the mild and conventional, but none the less clear, anti-Semitism which appeared early in *Down and Out in Paris and London* and lingered in his *War-Time Diaries*' (ibid). His last reference on the subject is the inclusion of a letter from Orwell to Fred Warburg on 29 October 1948 when he says he has 'just had [Jean-Paul] Sartre's book on anti-Semitism, which you published, to review. I think Sartre is a bag of wind and I am going to give him a good boot …' (ibid: 546).

MICHAEL SHELDEN

Orwell's authorised biographer Michael Shelden does not address the Orwell and anti-Semitism subject at all apart from mentioning Mosley's fascist meeting in Barnsley where 'The blame for everything was put upon mysterious international gangs of Jews who are said to be financing among other things, the British Labour Party' (Shelden 1992 [1991]: 251). There is a brief reference to his views on Ezra Pound's collaboration with the Italian fascist regime and his anti-Semitic broadcasts which Orwell describes as 'evil' when asked about Pound's suitability for the Bollingen poetry prize (ibid: 365).

When Orwell witnesses 'a young Jewish man from Vienna, who was temporarily serving in the American Army' (ibid: 420) kicking a captured SS officer in Germany, Shelden only discusses the event in terms of being 'fascinated by the shabby, wretched appearance of the officer' (ibid: 421) and finding 'he had little desire to see such men pay for their crimes' (ibid) rather than the problematical representation of 'the Jew' in his later published *Tribune* article. 'Revenge is sour' is published on 9 November 1945 and recalls his visit to a prisoner-of-war camp in south Germany earlier in the year. He describes his guide as 'a little Viennese Jew' who has been enlisted in the US army to help with interrogations. Orwell refers to him as 'the little Jew' and 'the Jew' in various ways five times in the article. On the one hand, Orwell says he was 'an alert, fair-haired rather good-looking youth of about twenty-five and politically so much more knowledgeable than the average American officer that it was a pleasure to be with him' (Anderson 2006: 256). He also speculates that the ill-treatment of the SS captives is because 'he was merely – like a man in a brothel, or boy smoking his first cigar, or a tourist traipsing round a picture gallery – telling himself that he was enjoying it…' (ibid: 257).

D. J. TAYLOR

The award-winning biographer devotes an entire four-page chapter on the subject of 'Orwell and the Jews' (2003: 196-199). Later on he reports how Orwell puts forward a rather prejudiced view of Zionism at a *Tribune* editorial meeting after the journal's editor, Aneurin Bevan, 'a notable friend of Israel, launched into a pro-Zionist speech. Orwell remarked that Zionists were merely "a bunch of Wardour Street Jews who had a controlling interest over the British press". Nothing anybody said could shake him from this view' (ibid: 326).

Taylor is critical of Orwell's attitudes to Jews and their representation in his fiction and essay writing. He considers the findings of Orwell's Jewish friend, Tosco Fyvel, who sees three categories of Orwell's thinking regarding Jews: shock at the nature and extent of anti-Jewish feeling; a belief that anti-Semitism was irrational and merely finding a scapegoat for economic grievance and, lastly, that the expressions of popular prejudice had to have a real causal factor. In other words, Jews bore some responsibility for their own persecution (ibid: 196).

Taylor does not spare the evidence of Orwell's prejudice against Jews and later Zionism. He details the complaint that Orwell's first publisher Victor Gollancz has from a reader about *Down and Out in Paris and London*. Mr S. M. Lipsey is appalled that a book 'containing insulting and odious remarks about Jews should be published by a firm bearing the name Gollancz' (ibid: 196). Taylor highlights how Malcolm Muggeridge is intrigued by the large number of Jews present at Orwell's funeral when the man in the coffin has been 'at heart strongly anti-Semitic' (ibid).

Taylor also refers to Orwell's war-time diary when he admits visiting the London Underground in the winter of 1940 after reports of so many Jews occupying the platforms and stations. Orwell detects 'a higher proportion of Jews than one would normally see in a crowd of this size' (ibid), but he thinks it wrong that they should make themselves so conspicuous. Taylor rightly suggests that the description of 'a fearful Jewish woman, a regular comic-paper cartoon of a Jewess', who 'fought her way off the train at Oxford Circus, landing blows on anyone who stood in the way' (ibid: 198) is offensive.

It is not enough that Orwell would later surmise that Jewish people from Whitechapel and the East End were desperately travelling to West End stations for refuge because the bombing in the docklands area had been so intense and the protection of shelters inadequate. That is evidence of penitence, regret and the realisation that he had been culturally and emotionally conditioned by an anti-Semitism embedded and prevalent in the society he had been brought up and educated in. The notion of 'institutional racism' had not been conceptualised when he writes in an essay for *Contemporary Jewish Record*, in 1945:

> And again, the common charge that Jews behave in an exceptionally cowardly way during air raids was given a certain amount of colour by the big raids of 1940. As it happened, the Jewish quarter of Whitechapel was one of the first areas to be heavily blitzed, with the natural result that swarms of Jewish refugees distributed themselves all over London (Orwell 1970 3 [1945]: 381).

Eyebrows can be justifiably raised at the continuing use of denigrating vocabulary such as 'swarms of Jewish refugees'. But in this essay, Orwell is beginning to question himself as much as the wider and deeper psychological roots of racism against Jews. For Orwell says 'there is widespread awareness of the prevalence of anti-Semitic feeling and unwillingness to admit sharing it' (ibid: 381), and that 'People will go to remarkable lengths to demonstrate that they are *not* anti-Semitic' (ibid: 382, italics in the original). He recognises that 'anti-Semitism is an irrational thing' (ibid: 380) and that 'people can remain anti-Semitic, or at least anti-Jewish, while being fully aware that their outlook is indefensible' (ibid). Orwell shifts the analysis from third person to second person: 'If you dislike somebody, you dislike him and there is an end of it: your feelings are not made any better by a recital of his virtues' (ibid).

Then later in the essay he shifts to the first person when he recalls saying to a friend in Burma, 'partly in joke' (ibid: 384), that he had been surprised a young Jewish boy had admitted openly to being 'a *Joo*, sir!' (ibid). He goes on to describe how he believes anti-Semitism is a neurosis 'and will not yield to argument' (ibid: 387) and concludes by saying that everyone, and he includes himself, needs to ask the question: 'Why does anti-Semitism appeal to *me*?' (ibid: 388, italics in the original; and see below).

JEFFREY MEYERS

Jeffrey Meyers, in *Orwell: Wintry Conscience of a Generation*, does not engage with the issue of Orwell and anti-Semitism in any part of the substantial text but does say how Orwell's views about Jewish people change over time in a note for the chapter covering the London Blitz. Meyers references the problematical descriptions in *Down and Out in Paris and London* such as the Jewish owner of the second-hand clothes shop in Paris who tries to swindle his customers and how Orwell thinks 'it would have been a pleasure to flatten the Jew's nose' (Meyers 2000: 354). Meyers argues Orwell's 'attitude changed and hostility to

Jews disappeared from his work' (ibid) once he begins to meet Jewish friends such as Jon Kimche, Rosalind Obermeyer, Michael Sayers, Benjamin Lewinski, Harry Milton, Tosco Fyvel, Arthur Koestler, Victor Gollancz, Fredric Warburg, A. J. Ayer, Julian Symons and Michael Meyer.

GORDON BOWKER

Bowker deals with the issue in the final chapter of his Orwell biography, titled 'Life after death', which considers the author's reputation and legacy. Bowker appears keen to defend Orwell stating: 'Like certain other of his contemporaries, notably Eliot, Orwell has been accused of anti-Semitism, despite his often powerful attacks on it' (Bowker 2003: 430). He argues that Orwell is one of the first English journalists to learn about the Holocaust and speak out against it because he sees it as 'an evil expression of nationalism, which he deplored' (ibid). Bowker emphasises that Orwell is against a separate Jewish state in Palestine, 'believing that the Arab case had simply not been heard, and he objected to British soldiers being murdered by Zionist terrorists. If that constituted anti-Semitism then he was guilty' (ibid). Bowker also presents Orwell's defence of T. S. Eliot in a letter to Julian Symons in 1948 after an attack on him by Tosco Fyvel:

> [In the early twenties], Eliot's anti-Semitic remarks were about on a par with the automatic sneer one casts at Anglo-Indian colonels in boarding houses. On the other hand, if they had been written after the persecutions began they would have meant something quite different. ... Some people go round smelling after anti-Semitism all the time. I have no doubt Fyvel thinks I am anti-Semitic. More rubbish is written about this subject than any other I can think of (*CWGO* XIX: 461).

Bowker's comments connect the issue with the current sensitivity over separating criticisms of Israeli state policy towards Palestinians, the right of Israel to exist as an independent state, Jewish identity and the adoption of official and agreed definitions of anti-Semitism. These are all still controversial today. Significantly, Orwell sends a sympathetic letter to the novelist Roy Fuller over an attack on his depiction of a Jewish character in one of his novels:

> I am sorry that you should have had this annoyance. I must add, however, that by my own experience it is almost impossible to mention Jews in print, either favourably or unfavourably, without getting into trouble (Orwell 1970 3 [1944a]: 128).

Orwell can be rightly criticised for failing to appreciate how the expression 'go round smelling after anti-Semitism all the time' used in his letter to Symons about T. S. Eliot must have been as offensive in 1945 as it is now.

Bowker concedes in these few paragraphs on the subject of Orwell and the Jews that his close and admiring Jewish friend Arthur Koestler did say in a letter written in 1977 to David Walton, then researching for his PhD on *The Expression of George Orwell's Racial and Social Attitudes* (1981), that 'the emotional bias was unmistakably present' (op cit: 430).

REPRESENTING JEWS IN *NINETEEN EIGHTY-FOUR* AND ORWELL'S 'EVOLUTION' ON ANTI-SEMITISM

In 1975, Professor Melvyn New publishes an essay, 'Orwell and anti-Semitism: Toward *1984*' in the journal *Modern Fiction Studies*. The research and writing is ground-breaking because he argues that coming to terms with the implications of the Holocaust between 1945 and 1949 led Orwell to represent the victimisation of Jews in three ways in his last novel *Nineteen Eighty Four*. New believes Orwell 'came to understand intellectually and, in *1984*, artistically the full meaning to the future of what has come to be known as the Holocaust' (New 1975: 81-82). New and other academics are able to survey all aspects of Orwell's essay writings and correspondence about anti-Semitism largely because the editors of *The Collected Essays, Journalism and Letters of George Orwell*, Sonia Orwell and Ian Angus, track, annotate and index the subject in the four volumes, published by Secker & Warburg in 1968 and Penguin in 1970. Peter Davison indexes the issue under 'Jews', 'anti-Semitism' and 'Zionism' for the 20-volume *Complete Works of George Orwell*, published by Secker & Warburg in 1998.

New believes Orwell and Hannah Arendt, both writing for *Partisan Review* in 1948, share similar conclusions about the Holocaust: 'Both perceived that a new and frightening social organization had been conceived and practiced by the Nazis – and that a new kind of victim had been created as well' (ibid: 94). Whereas Arendt, as a philosopher and scientist, analyses the historical and psychological reality of Germany up until the defeat of the Nazi regime, New says Orwell projects this same society into the future warning 'that it could happen again' (ibid).

New identifies 'three Jews in *1984*, though none, significantly, is positively identified. Together they suggest that in the world of *1984*, all men are Jews because all men are potential victims' (ibid: 101): the first Jew is described in Winston's first journal entry when he describes the war film he has viewed the previous night featuring a ship full of refugees being bombed somewhere in the Mediterranean:

> … there was a middle-aged woman might have been a jewess sitting up in the bow with a little boy about three years old in her arms. little boy screaming with fright and hiding his head between her breasts as if he was trying to burrow right into her and the woman putting her arms round him and comforting him although she was blue with fright herself, all the time covering him up as much as possible as if she thought her arms could keep the bullets off him. Then the helicopter planted a 20 kilo bomb in among them terrific flash and the boat went all to matchwood (*CWGO* IX: 10).

New says 'the making of victims, of Jews' is the very essence of war in Oceania and, like the inmates of concentration camps, they 'die solely to indicate to those still surviving that existence – selfhood – is not an individual choice, but a decision of the state' (New 1975: 101).

According to Professor New, the second representation of the persecuted Jew in *Nineteen Eighty-Four* is Emmanuel Goldstein who is portrayed as the 'Enemy of the People', an object of Two Minutes Hate sessions and the putative author of *The Theory and Practice of Oligarchical Collectivism*, the manifesto of the rebel Brotherhood. New says Orwell wants us to think of Goldstein as Jewish because of the description of his long Jewish face and his role as a scapegoat. New also suspects that the name 'Goldstein' may have been plucked from Orwell's memory of the illustration of anti-Semitic poem he had included in his 'As I Please' column from 1944 which begins with the refrain: 'The first American soldier to kill a Jap was Mike Murphy' and ends with 'The first American son-of-a-bitch to get four new tyres from the Ration Board was Abie Goldstein' (Orwell 1970 3 [1944b]: 331).

The third Jew in the novel is identified by New as Winston Smith who is 'condemned to be a victim by the simple act of his existence; condemned, that is, to be a Jew in a totalitarian state' (New 1975: 103). He argues that the novel presents a society which is 'no more and no less than a concentration camp, a society specifically organised to destroy its citizens' (ibid: 105). New explains that Winston Smith can be seen as the third Jew in *Nineteen Eighty-Four* – particularly as he is portrayed towards the end of his tortures. Surely this description has been ignited in the writer's imagination by the media photographs of the survivors of Bergen-Belsen and Buchenwald:

> A bowed, grey-coloured, skeleton-like thing was coming towards him. Its actual appearance was frightening, and not merely the fact he knew it to be himself. He moved closer to the glass. The creature's face seemed to be protruded, because of its bent carriage. A forlorn, jailbird's face with a nobby forehead running back into a bald scalp, a crooked nose and battered-looking cheekbones above which the eyes were fierce and watchful. The cheeks were seamed, the mouth had a drawn-in look. … But the truly frightening thing was the emaciation of his body. The barrel of the ribs was as narrow as that of a skeleton: the legs had shrunk so that the knees were thicker than the thighs. The curvature of the spine was astonishing. The thin shoulders were hunched forward so as to make a cavity of the chest, the scraggy neck seemed to be bending under the weight of the skull (*CWGO* IX: 284).

Forty five years after Melvyn New's article, writer and filmmaker Christopher Angel highlights in The Orwell Society's *Journal* what he sees as the 'significant evolution' in Orwell's expression and experience of anti-Semitism. He has 'confronted and moved beyond his upbringing and preconceptions' (Angel 2020: 28) and in his changing attitude towards the Jewish faith throughout his life is prepared to 'admit fault and move beyond ingrained social lessons, especially publicly to those he may have hurt or insulted' (ibid: 32). Angel agrees with New that by the time Orwell writes *Nineteen Eighty-Four* 'he depicts Jews as empathetic human beings in a way that underpins the horror and darkness of his novel and is an implicit criticism of anti-Semitism itself' (ibid).

ORWELL ON NATIONALISM AND ANTI-SEMITISM

Orwell writes his long essay on anti-Semitism in the same year as 'Notes on nationalism' and in 2018 Penguin publishes them together with 'The sporting spirit' which examines the use of sport for propagandist and nationalistic ends in its special £1 *Penguin Modern* paperback series. In 'Notes on nationalism', Orwell groups anti-Semitism along with Anglophobia and Trotskyism as one of the 'negative nationalisms' (Orwell 1970 3 [1945]: 426). This essay is written in May and published in October 1945. His essay on anti-Semitism in Britain is written in February and published in April 1945.

It could be argued that the insight and contriteness shown about his own problematic social conditioning and negative attitudes towards Jews in the earlier essay is missing in the later one when he categorises Zionism as one of his 'positive nationalisms' and 'the American variant of it seems to be more violent and malignant than the British' (ibid: 423). He is unable to separate Jewish identity, the struggle against anti-Semitism and the aspiration for a Jewish homeland in Zionism. This explains his contradictory argument in the earlier essay:

> It seems to me a safe assumption that the disease loosely called nationalism is now almost universal. Anti-Semitism is only one manifestation of nationalism, and not everyone will have the disease in that particular form. A Jew, for example, would not be anti-Semitic: but then many Zionist Jews seem to me to be merely anti-Semites turned upside-down, just as many Indians and Negroes display the normal colour prejudices in an inverted form (ibid: 387).

Is this not an extension of the earlier anti-Semitism he seemed so sincere and intent on decrying? Tosco Fyvel's interview with Stephen Wadhams and included in *Remembering Orwell* helps answer the question. Fyvel was an ardent Zionist and, indeed, the son of one of the first activists for Zionism. Fyvel believes Orwell never lived long enough to fully assimilate the facts and implications of the Holocaust and the rise of the state of Israel:

> I remember Warburg once telling me that he had a young German Jewish refugee staying with him who was going to agricultural college, and Orwell said: 'Oh, Jews can never go into agriculture. That's a bad joke, isn't it?'

> And after the war he thought that the Jewish refugees could just stay on among the ruins as though nothing had happened. I thought this was fearfully insensitive. I mean he simply didn't know Central Europe or Eastern Europe. He just couldn't understand that at all costs the Jewish survivors in Europe, the wretched survivors, whom the British navy was trying to keep from going to Palestine, should somehow be salvaged. And to him the Zionists were white settlers like the British in India or Burma, and the Arabs were like the native Burmese, which was a crude oversimplification although there was a sliver of truth in it. He was against Jewish nationalism – against all nationalism (Wadhams 1984: 122).

Fyvel had, in fact, analysed his relationship with Orwell and the subject of Jews and anti-Semitism in an article published in 1951 for the US magazine *Commentary*. In 'Wingate, Orwell and the Jewish question', Fyvel compares his friendships with General Orde Wingate and Orwell, two men born in the same year and in colonial India, the former being an avowed Zionist and the latter the exact opposite.

He writes only one year after his death that Orwell was a divided personality who still shared some of the outlook of the English upper-middle class and this included anti-Semitism: 'On the other hand, as a writer, an intellectual, Orwell naturally rejected those prejudices out of hand – and yet this conflict in him was never quite solved' (Fyvel 1951). Fyvel is also a compelling witness to how Orwell's profound concerns about Jewish persecution informed the writing of *Nineteen Eighty-Four*:

> I asked him on one occasion why, in his *Nineteen Eighty-Four*, he had given the name 'Alexander [sic] Goldstein' to the one conceivable rebel left against Big Brother and the Party. Orwell explained that partly his 'Goldstein' was, of course, an obvious skit on Trotsky. But he said he also felt that the likely man to stage a hopeless last revolt against a possible totalitarian regime would be some Jewish intellectual (ibid).

Fyvel recalls they are never able to resolve their disagreement over the Zionist aspiration for refuge and homeland in Palestine:

> And I tried to explain to Orwell: just as he with his strong English tradition felt deeply attached to some odd aspects of English life, so I had many Zionist family connections, I had my own Jewish tradition; all that inevitably shaped my sentiments about Palestine. 'Yes, but ...' said Orwell, looking at me doubtfully (ibid).

David Walton undertakes the most extensive, original and detailed study of Orwell's racial and social attitudes in his 450-page PhD thesis for Brunel University in 1981, and this forms the basis for his 1982 academic journal paper

'George Orwell and anti-Semitism'. Walton agrees with Melvyn New that Orwell's understanding of the Jewish scapegoat role in *Nineteen Eighty-Four* owes much to the Nazi 'Final Solution' for eradicating European Jewry. But Walton goes further in arguing that this was 'the Oceanic version of *The Protocols of the Elders of Zion*'. Walton believes 'Orwell's totalitarian anti-Utopia is in the same tradition as the society of *The Protocols*. It is highly probable that Orwell read them; he certainly referred to them' (Walton 1981: 341-342).

Walton suggests that the prejudice Orwell had been imbued with is 'unable to provide him with the deeper insights which he felt ought and could be attained' (ibid). And he concludes:

> As so often with Orwell, his decency, support for the underdog and appetite for truth, led him along a painful path. Even today, after scores of researchers have produced studies of anti-Semitism, the picture that emerges is enormously complicated – as complicated as the mind of the man itself. The very scope of anti-Semitism should warn us that it fulfils different things for different people (ibid: 342-343).

In 1984, John Rodden reflects on Orwell and Jewish questions in the context also of Catholicism and other religions. He is intrigued with the paradox of Jewish intellectuals claiming Orwell as their own despite his own fierce opposition to organised religions, indications of mild anti-Semitism in *Down and Out in Paris and London* and firm opposition to Zionism. During the 1940s, Orwell was seen as a supporter of Jewish causes and in his essays he could justifiably consider himself a defender and friend of the Jews particularly as so many of his personal friends were Jewish. Rodden argues: 'Sometimes Orwell confused questions of Judaism and anti-Semitism, lumping religious belief, culture, ethnicity and politics together' (Rodden 1984: 45). He continues:

> What would he say about Zionism and the Palestine Liberation Organisation? Of course, these questions are in a sense absurd – for Orwell has been dead thirty-four years and it is impossible to extrapolate from a man's writings what he would say about events after his death and yet most Orwell critics *admit* straight off, while the questions are absurd, they still feel drawn to ask them (ibid: 54, italics in the original).

In 1989, Rodden returns to the theme of Orwell, Zionism and anti-Semitism in his book *George Orwell: The Politics of Literary Reputation* with a sophisticated and revealing analysis of the friendship between Fyvel and Orwell. The former is seen as a home as well as work friend at *Tribune*. Fyvel plays a key role in the canonisation of Orwell as a prophet and Rodden considers how his representation of Orwell's emotional and political standpoint on anti-Semitism and Zionism is more of a process of asking 'through Orwell, those questions of identity begun in their conversations. ... To what degree is an assimilated Jewish intellectual "still different, still a Jew?" ... From his side too, emotionally if not intellectually, the "conflict" over Zionism was never quite resolved' (Rodden 1989: 319).

ORWELL, ANTI-SEMITISM AND PRESENT QUESTIONS

John Newsinger joins the debate through his chapter 'Orwell, anti-Semitism and the Holocaust' in the *Cambridge Companion to George Orwell* published in 2007 and his monograph *Hope Lies in the Proles: George Orwell and the Left*, published by Pluto Press in 2018. Newsinger homes in on the evidential 'lack' and omissions in Orwell's published and private writing. Why is there no mention anywhere of what Fyvel describes as 'Auschwitz, that hell on earth' (Newsinger 2018: 66)? Newsinger argues that Orwell considers anti-Semitism merely a 'casual prejudice' (ibid: 67) and he never fully comes to terms with its historic importance: 'He never successfully engaged with the political anti-Semitism that advocated discrimination, persecution, pogroms, expulsion and even mass murder' (ibid). While Orwell acknowledges the mass murder of Europe's Jewish population, Newsinger complains 'it never became a central concern' (ibid: 69) and this despite there being ample political campaigning, including by his own publisher Victor Gollancz in 1942, to rescue Jewish refugees from mass murder.

Newsinger observes: 'It still seems incredible that such a voracious devourer of pamphlet literature as Orwell never came across one of the most powerful and best-selling pamphlets published in Britain during the war' (ibid: 68). Orwell is not alone in failing to understand the enormous crime of the Holocaust. But he cannot escape the charge that 'more specific, indeed peculiar to him, though was his distaste at the punishment of collaborators and the like' (ibid: 69). As with other critics and biographers, Newsinger cites Orwell's *Tribune* column of 9 November 1945, 'Revenge is sour', and comments: 'One can only sympathise with Tosco Fyvel's outraged response to Orwell's crass insensitivity' (ibid: 70).

Newsinger is very aware of the divided and paradoxical Orwell on the anti-Semitism issue. In the 1940s, he expresses uncompromising hostility to anti-Semitism, yet he is unable to comprehend fully the enormity of the Final Solution. This perhaps explains why in one of his last articles for the American journal, *Partisan Review*, in May 1949, Orwell does not oppose Ezra Pound receiving a poetry prize. This after Pound has broadcast for Mussolini's fascist regime and actually approved the massacre of Eastern European Jews – combining it with a warning to American Jews that their turn was coming. Orwell explains that the attempt to rehabilitate the fascist poet should be tolerated because the murder of the Jews in the gas vans was no longer going on (*CWGO* XX: 100-102).

Newsinger argues that Orwell fails to match his considerable understanding of the evil of Stalin's crimes with those of Hitler's regime. He profoundly disagrees with Melvyn New's theory that *Nineteen Eighty-Four* is an attempt to explain what happened to the Jews under Hitler because there is 'no evidence to show that this was in any way central to his thinking' (Newsinger 2007: 123). However, Orwell's humanitarian conscience is dominated by his understanding, fear and personal experience in Spain of Stalinism:

> This was absolutely central to his thinking. Stalinism was Orwell's most important concern from 1936 onwards and there is a striking contrast between the effort that he devoted to understanding the nature of Stalin's tyranny compared with the effort he devoted to Nazism. ... Disappointing though it might be, the evidence is that Orwell, who was so clear-sighted on so many other issues of the time, never succeeded in comprehending the Holocaust (ibid: 124).

Kristin Bluemel, in 'St George and the Holocaust', is curious to understand why scholars of the Final Solution so frequently invoke George Orwell when they struggle to understand 'the most horrible of modern transformations, grossest of betrayals, the most terrifying meltings of solids into air: the destruction of bodies, identities, homes and communities of six million European Jews' (Bluemel 2003: 119-120). Yet Orwell does not, in fact, write about the Holocaust and is 'ambivalent about the Jews' (ibid: 121).

Bluemel argues that Orwell was unable to write in any detail about the significance of the Holocaust because he was confused by 'his crude analogies between Palestine and India, Arabs and coolies, Jews and the kinds of Anglo-Indian rulers and businessmen that made up his own family' (op cit: 122). On matters of racism, nationalism, empire, Stalinism, Nazism and anti-Semitism, Orwell ties himself into 'logical knots. Analysis of his inconsistencies says as much about his critics' fantasies of Orwell as the man of plain, clear writing as it does about the history or forms of Orwell's ideas themselves' (ibid: 126). Thus, Orwell's most explicit condemnation of English indifference and blindness to the Nazis' Final Solution does not appear in 'Anti-semitism in Britain' but rather in 'Notes on nationalism' where it is lost among paragraphs that testify to Orwell's own version of 'negative nationalism' – his obsession with 'the evil empire of the USSR' (ibid: 128).

Bluemel contends that close examination of Orwellian texts suggests his lingering anti-Semitism stems from his Edwardian upbringing, which explains his mistaken conviction that all nationalisms, including those of Indians and Jews, are totalitarian in nature:

> Orwell's response to the Holocaust should persuade critics to take him down from the sacred pedestal of sainthood so his halo can melt into air with the rest of modernity's holy icons. This is what Orwell himself would have wanted (ibid: 139).

In contrast to Bluemel, the academic Andrea Freud Loewenstein argues that Orwell projects his 'fear and loathing of the female' on to Jewish, and especially male Jewish characters (Loewenstein 1993: 146).

ORWELL ON NAZI IDEOLOGY AND THE PALESTINE QUESTION

As a stark contrast to the critical approaches of Newsinger and Bluemel, Danae Karydaki believes Orwell's interest in and understanding of Nazism have been neglected by intellectual historians of his period and Orwell scholars and biographers. Karydaki considers Bertrand Russell's tribute to Orwell in 1950 when he says he is grateful to men who, 'like Orwell decorate Satan with the horns and hooves without which he remains an abstraction' (Karydaki 2016: 53) and that Orwell is one of those men who has gone through 'either personally or through imaginative sympathy experiences more or less resembling imprisonment in Buchenwald' (ibid).

Orwell's essays and journalism argue 'for introspection, for a comparative approach to Nazi Germany, for fascism as a product of modernity and for a decisive role of emotions in politics' (ibid: 73). Karydaki acknowledges that Orwell's approach is fragmentary, unsophisticated and has numerous weaknesses but, all the same, he detects 'in the self and in Britain some of the psychosocial preconditions that can lead to discrimination and genocide' and to this extent he is 'a remarkably insightful observer of Nazism' (ibid).

Giora Goodman, in 'George Orwell and the Palestine question', suggests that Orwell's views on anti-Semitism and Zionism resound today because they are 'expressed at a time when the Palestine conflict peaked during the last decade of the British Mandate' (Goodman 2015: 321) and because his largely anti-Zionist stance differs from 'the prevailing, passionate beliefs of most left-wing intellectuals of his time, including some of his closest friends and political allies' (ibid).

Goodman agrees with Tosco Fyvel that a significant part of Orwell's dislike for Zionism is the product of his strong anti-colonial emotions: '… to Orwell the Palestine Arabs were Asians and so victims, the Jews were white, technically advanced and so imperialists and oppressors' (ibid: 327). Goodman is unable to explain fully why Orwell writes so little about the Palestine question and is not particularly active on the issue. British soldiers and civilians were being murdered by Zionist terrorists in Palestine at the time and he lives through the war of independence, recognition of Israel by the United Nations and the first Arab-Israeli war of 1948.

Goodman concludes that Orwell's reservations over Zionism are largely based on his socialist rejection of 'narrow nationalist solutions, for his identification of Zionism with European colonialism, and to a certain extent from his own patriotism' (ibid: 329) They reflect his independence of thought and resonate as a 'sharp awareness of facts and problems which many intellectuals on the British Left overlooked at the time, but are very much aware of today' (ibid).

Michael G. Brennan, in his 2017 *George Orwell and Religion*, argues that by the end of the Second World War Orwell is 'recognized as a stern voice against the dangers and barbarism of anti-Semitism and his careful analyses of the reasons for such racial hostilities and genocidal tendencies in supposedly civilised societies remain of importance today' (Brennan 2017: 157). Brennan is also strongly critical of the 'tone of habitual anti-Semitism' (ibid 35) that seeps into *Down and Out in Paris and London* and says it 'remains a problematic and distasteful text for modern readers' (ibid: 36). But he suggests that personal experience brought about a growing realisation of the dangers of anti-Semitism. For instance, his 1939 essay 'Marrakech' explains 'how Moroccan Jewish quarters – prefiguring the Warsaw and other European Jewish ghettoes of the early 1940s – had hardly moved on from the overcrowded, unhygienic living conditions of medieval ghettoes' (ibid: 70). Moreover, the 'most ignominious and genocidal period of religious and racial persecution also provides a key element of the totalitarian repression in the first half of *Nineteen Eighty-Four*' (ibid: 147).

CONCLUSION

Writing the Afterword for Richard Lance Keeble's insightful and inspirational book has been both a privilege and sobering reminder of how George Orwell's writing continually invites honesty, introspection and the questioning of power and injustice. There does not appear to be any subject, idea, or aspect of the human condition during Orwell's lifetime that does not escape his curiosity and attention. On the subject of anti-Semitism, Orwell asks the key questions in the article he writes for *Contemporary Jewish Record* in February 1945 – moving beyond the political to the strikingly personal. The Majdanek and Auschwitz-Birkenau concentration camps have just been liberated:

> … the starting point for any investigation of antisemitism should not be 'Why does this obviously irrational belief appeal to other people?' But 'Why does anti-Semitism appeal to *me*? What is there about it that I feel to be true?' If one asks this question one at least discovers one's own rationalizations, and it may be possible to find out what lies beneath them. Anti-Semitism should be investigated … one might get some clues that would lead to its psychological roots (Orwell 1970 3 [1945]: 388).

It is ironic that somebody who requests in his will that no biography of him should be written has had his attitudes and prejudices, whether publicly or privately expressed, so ruthlessly and relentlessly scrutinised. Yet we can surmise that he would appreciate the irony of the iconoclast being so resolutely attacked, challenged and criticised for his own cherished beliefs and viewpoints. And certainly on the issue of anti-Semitism, this essay argues that Orwell makes a major contribution.

REFERENCES

Anderson, Paul (ed.) (2006) *Orwell in Tribune: 'As I Please' and Other Writings 1943-7*, London: Politico's

Angel, Christopher (2020) An evolution, Orwell Society *Journal*, No. 16 pp 28-32

Bluemel, Kristin (2003) St George and the Holocaust, *LIT: Literature Interpretation Theory*, No. 14, Vol. 2 pp 119-147

Bowker, Gordon (2003) *George Orwell*, London: Little, Brown

Brennan, Michael G. (2017) *George Orwell and Religion*, London: Bloomsbury Academic

Crick, Bernard (1992 [1980]) *George Orwell: A Life*, Harmondsworth, Middlesex: Penguin, second edition

CWGO (1998) *The Complete Works of George Orwell*, XX Vols, Davison, Peter (ed.) London: Secker & Warburg

Fyvel, Tosco (1951) Wingate, Orwell, and the Jewish question: A memoir, *Commentary*, February

Fyvel, Tosco (1982) *George Orwell: A Personal Memoir*, London: Weidenfeld and Nicolson

Goodman, Giora (2015) George Orwell and the Palestine question, *The European Legacy*, No. 20, Vol. 4 pp 321-333

Karydaki, Danae (2016) National Socialism and the English genius: Revisiting George Orwell's political views on Nazi ideology, *Dapim: Studies on the Holocaust*, Vol. 30, No. 1 pp 53-73

Levi, Primo (1996) *Survival in Auschwitz*, New York: Simon and Schuster

Lowenstein, Andrea Freud (1993) The protection of masculinity: Jews as projective pawns in the texts of William Gerhardi and George Orwell, Cheyette, Bryan (ed.) *Constructions of 'the Jew' in English Literature and Society: Racial Representations, 1875-1945*, New York: Cambridge University Press

Meyers, Jeffrey (2000) *Orwell: Wintry Conscience of a Generation*, New York: W. W. Norton & Company

New, Melvyn (1975) Orwell and antisemitism: Toward *1984*, *Modern Fiction Studies*, Vol. 21, No. 1 pp 81-105

Newsinger, John (2007) Orwell, anti-Semitism and the Holocaust, Rodden, John (ed.) *The Cambridge Companion to George Orwell*, Cambridge: Cambridge University Press pp 112-125

Newsinger, John (2018) *Hope Lies in the Proles: George Orwell and the Left*, London: Pluto Press

Orwell, George (1970 3 [1944a]) Letter to Roy Fuller, Orwell, Sonia and Angus, Ian (eds) *The Collected Essays, Journalism and Letters of George Orwell, Vol. 3: As I Please*, Harmondsworth: Middlesex: Penguin

Orwell, George (1970 3 [1944b]) As I Please, Orwell, Sonia and Angus, Ian (eds) *The Collected Essays, Journalism and Letters of George Orwell, Vol. 3: As I Please*, Harmondsworth: Middlesex: Penguin pp 329-333

Orwell, George (1970 3 [1945]) Anti-Semitism in Britain, Orwell, Sonia and Angus, Ian (eds) *The Collected Essays, Journalism and Letters of George Orwell, Vol. 3: As I Please*, Harmondsworth: Middlesex: Penguin pp 378-388; first published in *Contemporary Jewish Record*, April

Palmer, Andrew (1998) Orwell and anti-Semitism, *Jewish Quarterly*, Vol. 45. No.4 pp 41-45

Rodden, John (1984) Orwell on religion: The Catholic and Jewish questions, *College Literature*, Vol. 11, No. 1 pp 44-58

Shelden, Michael (1992 [1991]) *Orwell: The Authorised Biography*, London: Minerva

Taylor, D. J. (2003) *Orwell: The Life*, London: Chatto & Windus

Wadhams, Stephen (1984) *Remembering Orwell*, Harmondsworth, Middlesex, England: Penguin

Walton, John (1981) *The Expression of George Orwell's Racial and Social Attitudes*, PhD Thesis, Brunel University. Available online at https://bura.brunel.ac.uk/handle/2438/5779

Walton, John (1982) George Orwell and anti-Semitism, *Patterns of Prejudice*, No 16, Vol. 1 pp 19-34

- **Tim Crook is a longstanding journalist, academic and writer, Emeritus Professor at Goldsmiths, University of London, President of the Chartered Institute of Journalists and joint editor of *George Orwell Studies*.**

Index

Abrahams, William 31, 70, 81, 209, 212, 213, 215

A Clergyman's Daughter 13, 33-34, 74, 82, 109, 149, 151-153, 159, 164, 229

Adelphi 5, 20, 21, 71, 78, 95, 96, 103, 108, 114, 135, 168, 182, 210, 211, 229

Anarchist/anarchism 3, 4, 16, 17, 18, 40, 82, 93, 94, 98, 100, 101, 104, 105, 106, 108, 114, 139, 159, 162, 163, 164, 197, 199, 212, 215, 235, 236

Animal Farm 5, 61, 69, 132, 136, 149, 157, 160, 162, 164, 176, 198, 199, 201, 215

Astor, David 5, 24, 39, 40, 61, 132, 198, 199, 217-220, 222, 223n, 231, 241

Barbusse, Henri 76, 107, 154, 224n

BBC 11, 12, 17, 18, 19, 31, 45, 69, 70, 78, 79, 96, 97, 107, 131, 132, 149, 157-162, 164, 175, 192, 217, 218, 223, 231

'Benefit of clergy' 61, 80, 155

Bennett, Arnold 79

Biederstadt, Carol 6, 98-99

Blair, Avril 1, 2, 5, 11, 12, 30, 31, 33, 122, 132, 133, 141, 146, 227

Blair, Eileen see O'Shaughnessy, Eileen

Blair, Ida (née Limouzin) 1, 2, 3, 29, 30, 31, 208

Blair, Marjorie 2, 29, 59, 133

Blair, Richard Horatio 3, 5, 6, 12, 29, 39, 40, 41, 98, 132, 141, 192, 197, 214, 222, 227, 231, 239, 241

Blair, Richard Walmesley 1, 2, 3, 7n, 12, 29-33, 41, 208

Blair, Sonia (née Brownell) 5, 181, 192, 211, 214, 216, 219, 220, 241, 248

Bounds, Philip 6, 105, 159, 167-174

Bowker, Gordon 1, 2, 11, 12, 14, 23, 30, 31, 36, 49, 51, 59, 70, 77, 83, 93, 104, 106, 108, 123, 124, 131, 133, 135, 136, 147155, 162, 182, 188, 199, 203, 204, 210, 211, 212, 215, 216, 218, 219-220, 221, 222, 227, 228, 230, 247-248

Brockway, Fenner 107, 198

Buddicom, Jacintha 5, 29, 30, 31, 70, 150, 192, 203, 241

Burmese Days 74, 81, 109, 172, 213, 214, 229

Campbell, Beatrix 191, 241

Catholics/Catholicism 59, 60, 61, 63, 66, 67, 212, 213, 230, 252

Chesterton, G. K. 43, 60, 80, 107, 177

Colls, Robert 20, 22, 30, 93, 150, 153, 167, 182, 188, 227

Comfort, Alex 90, 93-101

Coming Up for Air 1, 3, 11, 33, 34-37, 52, 70, 74, 83, 109, 112, 123, 147, 159, 173, 181, 204, 209, 211, 229

Common, Jack 4, 84, 108, 168, 182, 188, 189

Communist/communism 5, 16, 17, 40, 61, 76, 98, 100, 104, 105, 107, 122, 132, 168, 169, 170, 171, 173-174, 210, 218, 219, 220, 224n, 234, 235, 236, 237, 240

Connolly, Cyril 5, 12, 20, 65, 132, 149, 159, 165n, 198, 212, 213-214, 217, 222, 227-228

Crick, Bernard 1, 2, 12, 30, 31, 39, 90, 93, 130, 132, 134, 153, 162, 182, 188, 192, 199, 209, 212, 214, 215, 216, 217, 220, 223, 227-228, 229, 243-244

Crook, Tim 7, 22, 56, 59, 153, 157, 161, 243-258

Daily Mirror 175-177

Davison, Peter 2, 33, 39, 61, 62, 63, 70, 91, 110, 131, 140, 146, 150, 151, 152, 157, 164, 165, 171, 215, 218, 220, 224n, 248

Dickens, Charles 52, 77, 78, 105, 129, 130, 149, 160, 171, 181, 199, 230

Down and Out in Paris and London 5, 13, 15-16, 21, 104, 111, 112, 117, 118-119, 125, 150, 168, 199, 210, 228, 229, 240, 244, 245, 246, 252, 256

Eliot, T. S. 78, 79, 80, 86, 133, 160, 171, 198, 214, 247

Eton 1, 5, 12, 14, 18, 20, 24, 25n, 30, 31, 60, 61, 69, 70, 73, 106, 108, 111, 132, 135, 150, 159, 193, 197, 198, 203, 204, 207-224, 229, 231, 241

Fascism/anti-fascism 94, 105, 216, 236, 255

Feminism/feminist 3, 33, 85, 107, 183, 184, 191, 192, 193, 194, 241

Fierz, Mabel 5, 12, 102, 241

Gow, Andrew 5, 31, 198, 208-210, 217, 218, 219

Gollancz, Victor 17, 77, 106, 110, 134, 197, 211, 214, 215, 245, 247

Greene, Graham 60, 62, 133

Heppenstall, Rayner 20, 38, 130, 133, 162, 211

Hollis, Christopher 5, 60, 67n, 212-213

Homage to Catalonia 16, 72, 121, 167, 177, 197, 213, 215, 233, 239, 240

Homosexuality 18, 20, 63, 83, 154, 209, 228, 240

Horizon 45, 65, 96, 149, 155, 165n, 213, 214, 227

Hurst, L. J. 1, 2, 7, 30, 209, 210

Huxley, Aldous 25n, 65, 76, 79, 86, 222

Independent Labour Party (ILP) 4, 12, 94, 107, 108, 198, 212

Jackson, Rosie 183-185

Jaques, Eleanor 5, 23, 75, 152, 164, 241

Joyce, James 75, 76, 79, 80, 86, 142, 143, 152, 153, 154, 160

Jura 5, 39, 41, 91, 133, 140, 141, 147, 203, 205, 205n, 211, 216, 220, 227, 230, 231

King-Farlow, Denys 198, 214-214

Kipling, Rudyard 77, 79, 176, 213

Kopp, Georges 4, 217-218

Kopp, Quentin 6

Laursen, Eric 93-101

Lady Chatterley's Lover 23, 69, 75, 76, 77, 85, 200

Langdon-Davies, John 231, 233-238

Lawrence, D. H. 69-86, 108, 160, 164, 171, 183-185, 198, 200, 231

'Lear, Tolstoy and the fool' 162-164

Lehmann, John 210, 216-217

London, Jack 14-15, 105, 228

Mackenzie, Compton 74, 227-232

Manchester Evening News 39, 81, 199, 218, 231

Marx/Marxism/Marxist 76, 104, 105, 108, 135, 156, 158, 167-174, 236

Maughan, Somerset 75, 79

Meyers, Jeffrey 18, 22, 38, 81, 82, 86, 93, 120, 124-125, 131, 132, 133, 152, 153, 160, 162, 183, 188, 211, 227, 246-247

MI5 (British intelligence) 11, 17, 24, 39, 100, 101, 107, 132, 209, 212, 216, 217-218, 224n

Moore, Darcy 3, 6, 156, 212

Muggeridge, Malcolm 4, 61, 62, 132, 133, 216, 219-220, 245

Myers, L. H. 5, 198, 211-212

Myles, Norah 2

Nellie, aunt 3, 5, 107, 122, 188, 192, 228, 241

New Statesman and Nation 79, 80, 93, 114, 213, 214

Nineteen Eighty-Four 5, 13, 21, 23, 29, 37-38, 43, 54-55, 59, 62, 64, 65, 69, 70, 84, 85, 90, 91, 93, 98, 99, 105, 109, 113, 124, 132, 133, 135, 136, 139, 142, 149, 155, 160, 161, 164, 171, 172, 174, 178, 181, 199, 201, 211, 214, 215, 219, 220, 227, 240, 248-250, 251, 252, 253, 256

Observer 3, 24, 39, 40, 61, 132, 159, 199, 208, 217-220, 222, 223n, 231, 237, 241, 244

Old-Etonians see Eton

Orwell, George (Eric Blair) advertisements 43-56; atom bomb 89-92; Cultural Studies 56, 170, 178, 242; diary writing 139-148; dress 11-28; fishing 203-2015; food and cooking 117-136; Journalism/Media/PR Studies 177-178, 242; 'little list' 100, 101, 210, 220, 240; misogyny 184, 191; theatre 149-166

O'Shaughnessy, Eileen 2, 3, 4-5, 16, 24, 38, 39, 40, 46, 52, 84, 117, 122, 131, 133, 139, 140, 146, 147, 181-194, 201, 211, 214, 217, 218, 227, 231, 235, 241, 242

Pacifist/pacifism 61, 72, 90, 93, 94, 95, 96, 97, 98, 100, 108, 134, 162, 163, 164, 197, 210, 212, 242

Partisan Review 18, 43, 44, 45, 63, 90, 95, 96, 98, 176, 238, 248

Patai, Daphne 33, 51, 52, 85, 144, 191, 241

Pleasure principle 129, 136

Polemic 114, 161, 162, 171

Pound, Ezra 79, 171, 244, 253

Powell, Anthony 5, 12, 133, 211, 216

Rees, Richard 5, 22, 51, 95, 108, 135, 167, 198, 210-211, 221, 229

Richards, Vernon 3, 40, 98

Ross, John 4, 12, 13

Royal family 175-177

Salkend, Brenda 5, 32, 75

Secker & Warburg 197, 198, 199, 200, 215, 233, 248

Semitism/anti-Semitism 243-256

Senhouse, Roger 5, 197, 198, 199, 215

Sex 11, 23-24, 33, 35, 37, 38, 47, 56, 61, 63, 65, 69, 70, 71, 78, 81, 82, 83-86, 93, 99, 119, 136, 143, 144, 145, 152, 154, 155, 165, 170, 178, 184, 191, 193, 199, 213, 214, 228, 234, 236, 239, 240, 241

Shakespeare, William 149, 150, 151, 154, 156, 159, 160, 162, 163, 164

Shanghai group 132, 217

Shaw, George Bernard 48, 70, 79, 106, 153, 155, 157, 158-159, 160, 162, 213

Shelden, Michael 1, 12, 32, 77, 93, 157, 162, 182, 183, 187, 193, 200, 208, 211, 214, 215, 227, 244-245

Socialism/socialist 18, 19, 64, 91, 118, 124, 135, 167, 169, 173, 176, 192, 214, 215

Special Branch 17, 98, 218

Stansky, Peter 2, 31, 70, 81, 209, 212, 213, 215

'Such, such were the joys' 69, 83-84, 149, 207, 213, 228, 240

Sutherland, John 2, 4, 13, 25n, 31, 111, 153, 203, 205, 207, 209, 217, 223, 228

Swift, Jonathan 64, 161, 171

Symons, Julian 60, 91, 98, 120, 197, 227, 247

Taylor, D. J. 6, 12, 23, 32, 40, 81, 94, 108, 133, 152, 162, 182, 188, 199, 207, 208, 211, 212, 224n, 227, 245-246

'The art of Donald McGill' 61, 96, 155, 170, 199, 214, 240

The Lion and the Unicorn 44, 124, 156, 169, 176, 198, 222

The Road to Wigan Pier 15, 19, 60, 71, 76, 83, 104, 117, 119, 167, 169, 183, 211, 215, 239

'The spike' 20-21, 103-116, 210

Thomas, Dylan 133, 211

Thoreau, Henry David 100, 146

Tolstoy, Leo 100, 162-165

Topp, Sylvia 4-5, 32, 33, 39, 52, 84, 131, 133, 147, 181-194, 201, 218, 227, 241-242

Tribune 17, 18, 43, 45, 47, 56, 60, 69, 72, 74, 80, 84, 89, 90, 93, 96, 97, 98, 114, 125, 128, 130, 140, 161, 175, 192, 193, 218, 220, 223n, 239, 240, 244, 245, 252, 253

Trotsky/Trotskyism/Trotskyite 4, 16, 61, 199, 215, 235, 237, 250, 251

Tulloch, John 6, 153, 240

Warburg, Fredric 5, 91, 197-201, 215, 222, 244, 247, 250

Waugh, Evelyn 59-67, 86, 165n, 213

Wells, H. G. 52, 73, 74, 76, 79, 86, 132, 133, 157, 169, 197, 198, 208, 215, 227, 229

'Why I write' 30, 141, 144

Wilde, Oscar 106, 149, 159, 160, 164, 170, 172, 173, 229

Wodehouse, P. G. 12, 61, 132, 136, 170, 199, 217, 219

Woloch, Alex 49, 58, 125, 193

Woodcock, George 4, 18, 82, 98, 106, 124, 125, 133, 139, 163, 164

Woolf, Virginia 76, 171, 193, 233, 241

Yeats, W. B. 171, 199

www.ingramcontent.com/pod-product-compliance
Lightning Source LLC
Chambersburg PA
CBHW051041160426
43193CB00010B/1028